THE MAN WHO
INVENTED
THE DALEKS

Michael Heseltine, Turner brings the period alive and offers insights into both sides of a polarised nation'
BBC History Magazine, Pick of the Month

'Turner's account of the 1980s is as wide ranging as that fractured, multi-faceted decade demands ... deft at picking out devilish details and damning quotes from history that is less recent than you think'
Victoria Segal, *MOJO*

'Turner does an excellent job in synthesising the culture and art of the day into the wider political discourse. The result is resolutely entertaining'
Metro

Praise for
Crisis? What Crisis?: Britain in the 1970s

'Alwyn Turner has certainly hit upon a rich and fascinating subject, and his intertwining of political and cultural history is brilliantly done. His book makes me so relieved I wasn't an adult at the time ... This is a masterful work of social history and cultural commentary, told with much wit. It almost makes you feel as if you were there'
Roger Lewis, *Mail on Sunday*

'Turner appears to have spent much of the decade watching television, and his knowledge of old soap operas, sitcoms and TV dramas is deployed to great effect throughout this vivid, brilliantly researched chronicle ... Turner may be an anorak, but he is an acutely intelligent anorak'
Francis Wheen, *New Statesman*

'An ambitious, entertaining alternative history of the 1970s which judges the decade not just by its political turbulence but by the leg-up it gave popular culture'
Time Out

'Entertaining and splendidly researched ... He has delved into episodes of soap operas and half-forgotten novels to produce an account that displays wit, colour and detail'
Brian Groom, *Financial Times*

'Turner combines a fan's sense of populism (weaving in references to a rapidly expanding popular culture) with a keen grasp of the political landscape, which gives his survey of an often overlooked decade its cutting edge'
Metro

'Fascinating ... an affectionate but unflinching portrait of the era'
Nicholas Foulkes, *Independent on Sunday*

THE MAN WHO INVENTED THE DALEKS

THE STRANGE WORLDS OF TERRY NATION

Alwyn W. Turner

First published 2011 by
Aurum Press Limited
7 Greenland Street
London NW1 0ND
www.aurumpress.co.uk

Copyright © 2011 Alwyn W. Turner

A catalogue record for this book is available from the British Library.

ISBN 978 1 84513 609 3

1 3 5 7 9 10 8 6 4 2
2011 2013 2015 2016 2014 2012

Typeset by SX Composing DTP, Rayleigh, Essex

Printed and bound in Great Britain by MPG Books, Bodmin, Cornwall

Contents

Vote Dalek!

The 2005 General Election was not one of the great moments in British political history. There was no doubt from the outset that the result would be a return of the incumbent Labour government, even though its prime minister, Tony Blair, had taken the country into a series of wars, the last two of which at least (the invasions of Afghanistan and Iraq) were proving unpopular. The Conservative opposition was in such disarray that its senior MPs had recently staged a palace coup to remove their leader, Iain Duncan Smith, before he had a chance to lead the party to utter humiliation at the polls, but even his replacement, Michael Howard, was able to do little more than steady the ship, increasing the share of the vote by less than one percentage point. And although the Liberal Democrats did increase their number of MPs, they remained firmly in third place.

In the absence of any discernible interest in the outcome among the general public, the BBC's weekly listings magazine, *Radio Times*, chose to ignore the workings of democracy and instead used its cover to herald a much more interesting event that was also happening that week: the return to television after sixteen and a half years of the Daleks, one of whom was to appear in that week's episode of the newly resuscitated science fiction series *Doctor Who*. There was an acknowledgement of other concerns, with the creatures pictured in front of the Houses of Parliament, echoing a scene from 'The Dalek Invasion of Earth' (broadcast in 1964, a year when Labour's election victory under Harold Wilson really did mark a change in political eras), but there was no doubt what the big story was. Just to be clear, the fold-out cover also promised a free Dalek poster for every reader, and bore the slogan: VOTE DALEK!

It was a striking piece of artwork, good enough that when, in 2008, the Periodical Publishers Association organised a survey to find the best British magazine cover of all time, it came top of the poll, fighting off competition from *Vogue*'s memorial issue for Princess Diana, *Tatler*'s shot of Vivienne Westwood dressed as Margaret Thatcher and *OK!*'s exclusive coverage of the wedding of David and Victoria Beckham. As a tribute to Britain's enduring fascination with the Daleks, it was hard to know which was the greater honour: dominating the *Radio Times* or triumphing over such iconic national figures. In any event it was a handsome compliment to the 42-year-old inventions of a television scriptwriter named Terry Nation, who had died in California eight years before the cover appeared.

It was not, however, the only indication of the durability of his work. Much of his television writing was already enjoying a new lease of life on DVD, while even the few surviving episodes of a neglected comedy series, *Floggit's*, when rediscovered by BBC radio in 2009, were re-broadcast, more than half a century after they first aired. The appeal was not simply one of nostalgia, for his creations continued to inspire new interpretations. The *Doctor Who* episode that the *Radio Times* was promoting, 'Dalek', saw some significant additions to the mythology he had left, and it was followed in 2008 by a remake of his 1970s series *Survivors*. Meanwhile, 2010 saw an American reworking of *And Soon the Darkness*, a film he had co-written forty years earlier, and reports of a continuation − or possibly a revival − of another show from that decade, *Blake's 7*, appeared in the press on a regular basis for many years. Indeed that series remained familiar enough to be lampooned in the cinema short *Blake's Junction 7* (2004), starring Martin Freeman, Mackenzie Crook and Johnny Vegas. Clearly this was a body of work whose resilience transcended its origins in what, at the time of its creation, was thought of as the transient, even disposable, world of the broadcast media.

Beyond his most celebrated work in *Doctor Who*, *Survivors* and *Blake's 7*, Nation's list of credits was equally impressive. He wrote dozens of episodes for action adventure shows such as *The Avengers*, *The Saint*, *The Persuaders!*, *The Baron*, *Department S*, *The Champions*, *The Protectors* and *MacGyver*. He adapted some key science fiction works for television, among them the first ever screen version of a Philip K. Dick story. And he wrote for many of Britain's most celebrated comedians, including Tony Hancock, Peter Sellers, Frankie Howerd, Ronnie Barker and Eric Sykes. There was too a disparate collection of one-off pieces for cinema and television, some of which remain fondly remembered in certain circles, even if they didn't command huge audiences (*The Amazing Robert Baldick*, *The House in Nightmare Park*, even *What a Whopper*), as well as a children's novel, *Rebecca's World*, that retains a devoted following. And on at least one occasion he claimed that a largely forgotten television play, *Uncle Selwyn*, had given him more pleasure than anything else he'd done.

The overwhelming majority of that writing came in the twenty-five years from 1955 to 1980, an era that has come to be regarded as the golden age of British television. Nation was present at the outset, as the dominance exerted over popular culture by the cinema and radio began to fade in the face of the new medium, and his contributions were to help define the period and establish the shape of the entertainment industry. If he is remembered chiefly as a writer of popular science fiction ('I will always be Terry "Daleks" Nation,' he acknowledged towards the end of his life), that does scant justice to the breadth and diversity of his writing.

Nor does it accurately reflect his own taste and interests, for despite his use of alien planets and future societies as settings for much of his best-known work, there is little to indicate any commitment to, or great involvement in, science fiction as it evolved during his adult life. His near-contemporary Gerry Anderson, who made shows like *Thunderbirds* and *Captain Scarlet*, talked of television having a proselytising, pioneering role: 'I have always been a great believer that science fiction entertainment makes a great contribution to the progress that we make in all sorts of spheres.' But Nation never seemed to share that concern. Instead he used the trappings and accoutrements of science fiction simply because they were the conventions expected by the audience, in the same way that when he was writing about a special agent, there would always be a gun, a car and a gimmick. In both instances, the genre requirements were little more than window-dressing, providing a backdrop for his true interest: the telling of a tale of adventure.

Because he was above all else a storyteller, drawing heavily on the literature he had encountered in his childhood, and translating the traditions of adventure-writing from the first half of the twentieth century into a form appropriate for the television age. Certainly that was how he saw the first Daleks story at the time. 'I set out to write a thundering great thriller,' he said in 1964, 'the sort of thing I lapped up when I was a boy.' In a set of notes he submitted for the second season of *Blake's 7*, he spelt out his approach to writing: 'Stories must be strong, well plotted and contain a lot of action and movement. A great deal happens in our stories. Moral points and philosophical discussion must always be well cloaked in our action-adventure.' It is possible to see his work as an extended love letter to the popular thrillers of his youth. 'If he'd been writing novels, you'd have called him a page-turner,' commented Barry Letts, producer of *Doctor Who* in the early 1970s. 'You always wanted to know what would happen next.' Verity Lambert, the founding producer of the series, shared the same opinion: 'I thought he was a terribly good storyteller – that was absolutely his strength.'

Indeed so great was his love of telling tales that it often coloured the accounts he gave of his own life and work. He had a tendency to exaggeration and simplification, reluctant to allow mere facts to get in the way of a good story. When asked in the early days of the Daleks how he'd come up with the name of his creation, he explained that he had taken it 'from the spine of an encyclopaedia. I looked up on the shelf and saw one volume marked "DAL TO LEK".' It was an inspired idea and it continued to circulate, despite his subsequent public retraction. 'It's absolute rubbish, it's a load of lies,' he admitted in 1973. 'Persistent journalists wanted a romantic story about how the name came to be, and I didn't have a romantic story. But then I'm a writer, so I made one up, and that was the story we put around for years.' His instincts were right the first time. The prosaic truth – that the name simply popped into his head – was much less interesting than the version he'd concocted, and the fabricated story of the origin of the Daleks was repeated even in some newspaper notices of his death.

Similar distortions were to be found elsewhere in his interviews. 'I suspect that I've written more TV scripts than anyone else in Britain,' he once declared, going on to enumerate his contributions: 'some thirty episodes of *The Saint*, most of *The Baron*, *The Persuaders!* and forty episodes of *The Avengers*'. Again, this was not strictly true; the real figures were thirteen episodes of *The Saint*, six of *The Avengers*, and seven out of twenty-four episodes of *The Persuaders!*. The claim to have penned most of *The Baron* was more justified, but only just: he had a writing credit on seventeen of the thirty episodes that were filmed, though four of those were co-written. Perhaps it merely felt like he had turned out that many shows; more likely it was a propensity to embroider whether it were necessary or not.

Nation's love of story-telling and the durability of his work are not, of course, unrelated. No one went to his shows expecting to come away with a deeper understanding of the nature of the human condition, or to have looked through a window on to the tortured psyche of the author. There was, it is true, sometimes a commentary on politics and society to be found, though it is not always clear how conscious this was, but it was hardly the chief selling point. That was, and remains, Nation's ability to tell a rattling good tale. He did make some major contributions to the evolution of popular television – he could, for example, claim credit for popularising the ideas of story arcs and season cliff-hangers in television fantasy shows, devices that became taken for granted – but at the heart of everything was pure escapism. 'I believe that what people want on television is entertainment, and action stories are what I want to write,' he explained. 'There are plenty of other people to write sociological dramas.'

It was a lesson he had learnt from the popular writers whose work he so eagerly devoured in his early years. The novelist Edgar Wallace, the most successful of those authors (his dominance of the market was such that in the early 1930s it was estimated that one in every four books read in Britain was written by him), was forthright in his deep dislike of literary fiction, which he saw as being concerned with internal, personal experience; in his own work, he insisted, he sought to remove all elements of subjectivity, concentrating solely on action, on objective events. Such an approach was summed up by the critic Richard Usborne, writing about John Buchan, another of the great adventure writers of the period: 'The stories kept the heroes constantly on the move. But the rolling stones gathered no atmospheric moss of character.' Or, as Britain's most revered film critic, Dilys Powell, pointed out, in a thriller 'too much character clutters up the plot'. The same attitude was easily extended into science fiction, where, Kingsley Amis observed in 1960, there was an 'exaltation of idea or plot over characterisation'.

The novels of Wallace, Buchan and others were part of the staple diet of an imaginative schoolboy like Nation in the 1930s and 1940s, consumed for the same reasons that Dickson McCunn, one of Buchan's heroes, had embraced the work of Sir Walter Scott in his own (fictional) childhood: 'he had read the novels not for their insight into human character or for their historical pageantry, but because they gave him material wherewith to construct fantastic journeys.' And on those fantastic journeys, the reader – and, later, the viewer – was not over-concerned with notions of originality or consistency. H.C. McNeile, who wrote the hugely popular Bulldog Drummond books under the pseudonym of Sapper, borrowed freely from the stories of other writers and never troubled himself with building a coherent narrative across the novels. Even his use of names was inconsistent and he wasn't always sure if a character were alive or dead: Drummond's housekeeper dies in one book, but returns without a scratch, or indeed an explanation, in the next.

The same traits were to be found in Nation's work. The subtleties of characterisation were of little interest, influences were seldom hard to identify, and continuity could always be sacrificed if it got in the way of the tale. He was fortunate to find a sympathetic ally in Huw Wheldon, the controller of BBC1 in the 1960s, who was a big fan of the Daleks; Wheldon was convinced that 'television is overwhelmingly a story-telling medium', and argued that *Doctor Who* was about 'something archetypal: the path into the unknown forest'. That was perhaps further than Nation himself would have gone, but there is in his best writing an element of the myth, or perhaps the fairy tale, that has helped it to endure. And, as in all the best fairy tales, the figures are painted with a very broad brush. Heroes fight seemingly impossible odds and (normally) win, but are frequently eclipsed in the popular imagination by the monstrosity of the villains, whether in the form of the evil scientist Davros in *Doctor Who* or of Servalan, the ruthless dominatrix figure who represented the forces of oppression in *Blake's 7*.

Above all, there are the Daleks, the single most enduring creations to come out of British television in the twentieth century. All the other iconic British screen presences, whether on television or film, were in the first instance literary creations, from Winnie the Pooh and Hercule Poirot through *The Lord of the Rings* and the Narnia stories to James Bond and Harry Potter. The Daleks are the only great popular myth, endlessly reinvented and reinterpreted by other writers, to have been created specifically for television. Their 2005 return came in the midst of a phase of revivals, ranging from the film of *The Avengers* (1998) to the BBC's *Reggie Perrin* (2009), but while the others merely emphasised how frozen in time was the appeal of the originals, the Daleks alone satisfied the demand for nostalgia while also building a huge new constituency. Like any great myth, they have outlived and outgrown their creator, entering the popular consciousness to become instantly recognisable by name alone, even to those who have never knowingly watched *Doctor Who*. Perhaps their only rival is the Doctor himself, and it is arguable that he would scarcely be remembered as anything but a footnote in television history had the Daleks not been such an instantly huge success.

And they were extraordinarily successful. The Dalekmania craze that swept Britain at the end of 1964 saw over a hundred thousand copies of a single toy sold that Christmas; although the fever inevitably abated, a decade later there were still over a hundred Dalek products on the market. The copyright in the creatures was owned jointly by Terry Nation and by the BBC, and it was the royalties from the sales of these products, rather than his writing, that made him a rich man. The scale of the merchandising also inspired the creation of the lucrative BBC Enterprises (now BBC Worldwide), an organisation whose profits rose from a modest £1 million in 1968 to become a major contributor to the corporation's revenues. Beyond that, the Daleks are the most famous aliens and the ultimate baddies in British popular culture, resolutely evil with no pretence whatsoever of redeeming features.

None of which bore much resemblance to the man himself. 'He was the nicest guy you could ever wish to meet,' noted Terrance Dicks, who was for a while his script editor on *Doctor Who*. 'I've never really met anybody who didn't like Terry.' Almost everyone Nation came into contact with had much the same feeling. He made and kept friends, he was a generous host and he was deeply loyal, both to those he knew and to fans of his work. 'He was an intelligent, funny, warm and very friendly man,' commented Roger Moore, who worked with him on *The Persuaders!*. 'He was a joy to have around.' Perhaps the most eloquent testimony was that of a *Doctor Who* director, Richard Martin: 'He had this lovely, rich, pastoral voice. And it sounded good and it sounded wonderful, and it was full of courage and personality. When people say "Terry Nation", I hear his voice.' The identification of the accent was perhaps misplaced – Nation's voice revealed his upbringing in Cardiff, a city that was far from pastoral – but the sentiment is clear.

'Tall, handsome, relaxed,' observed the *Guardian* at the height of his fame in 1966, 'Mr Nation looks like a Welsh James Bond.' Coming from a lower-middle-class background in South Wales, his success enabled him to acquire a taste for good living, and he did so with great gusto, developing a fondness for fine wines, indulging his love of clothes and delighting in his purchase of a mansion in the country. In the early 1970s, remembered Terrance Dicks, he and Nation had come out of a meeting and were walking down Piccadilly when Nation remarked there were a couple of things he needed to talk about further and that there was no time like the present: '"Look, we're just about to pass the Ritz, let's go and have a champagne cocktail and discuss it." And I said, "I like working with you, Terry. You've got style." And he just beamed. He really enjoyed himself. He enjoyed his success, and rightly so.'

'Terry was larger than life,' recalled Deb Boultwood, whose father, Dave

Freeman, had been one of Nation's first co-writers back in 1956. 'He walked into a room and you knew Terry was there.' Again there are traces of the celebrity authors of the 1920s and 1930s. Breathless newspaper reports of the day revelled in the eccentricities of Edgar Wallace, who was so lazy he would always take a taxi rather than walk, no matter how short the journey, and who wrote inside a large glass box, constructed in his study to keep out draughts, while wearing a silk dressing-gown and chain-smoking through an absurdly long cigarette-holder.

Nation's own writing methods were less flamboyant, but shared the same devil-may-care nonchalance, the same casual professionalism, that has always been cherished by lovers of popular fiction. He may not have been able to match Wallace's boast of having once written an 80,000 word novel in a weekend, or thriller writer John Creasey's claim to have written two novels in a week ('and on the Saturday afternoon, I played cricket'), but he prided himself on — and was valued by others for — the rapidity with which he could produce a script. It was a facility that came partly from his reluctance to redraft or rewrite. 'I work directly on to the typewriter,' Nation explained in 1989, 'and because I'm a bad typist I would seldom go back. It really bothered me to have to rewrite things. So if I'd written myself into a corner, I'd write myself out rather than go back and redo it.' For some of those with whom he worked, this was undoubtedly an asset. 'Terry's first drafts often ended up as his final drafts,' noted Philip Hinchcliffe, a *Doctor Who* producer, with approval. 'He was a very professional writer. The construction of his stories and the fast-paced movement of the action — it all added up, and you got a thoroughly professional set of scripts when they landed on your desk.'

It was not, however, an attitude that won universal approval from his fellow writers. 'I've known him to write a script in five days,' remembered Chris Boucher, script editor of *Blake's 7*. 'He simply roared through it, and I have to say when you write that fast, it does from time to time show.' Terrance Dicks agreed: 'He had a habit of falling into patterns. There were a lot of recurrent themes: people planting bombs, and being chased and spraining an ankle. In Terry's scripts, people were always spraining their ankles at moments of crisis.' There were times, he suggested, when Nation didn't seem to put in as much effort as he should: 'Given his successful career, he was obviously a very good writer, but he needed the occasional bit of prodding.' Brian Clemens, who worked with Nation on series like *The Avengers* and *The Persuaders!*, and who co-wrote *And Soon the Darkness* with him, was more forthright: 'Terry had talent, a lot of talent. If he'd concentrated more, he'd have more of a track record. He was a lovely guy and a fine writer, but he was bloody lazy.'

The charge of laziness, of not trying hard enough, was made in reference to Nation's occasional lack of creative engagement with a script, rather than to his work rate, which was undeniably impressive. 'Terry was very ambitious really, but in a nice way,' reflected his long-time agent, Beryl Vertue. 'He really wanted to get on and he liked nice things. He wanted to achieve.' Even at the height of the Daleks' success – when his creations were rivalled only by the Beatles in terms of media coverage and merchandising revenue – he continued to write at an intense pace, driven both by a work ethic that reflected his South Wales upbringing and by a feeling of frustration that he hadn't yet realised his visions. 'I have never ever sat and watched something I've written without a sense of embarrassment and a sense of failed achievements,' he said in 1972. 'It happens to be up there on the screen, but it was never the way I intended it, it was never as successful as I hoped it would be.'

The prodigious scale of the output that resulted was not unique. Nation was part of a tight little group of writers that shaped much British television of the 1960s and 1970s, a group that also included the likes of Brian Clemens, Philip Broadley, Dennis Spooner, Harry W. Junkin, Clive Exton and Donald James. Here too there were echoes of an earlier time, when the thriller-writing boom of the 1930s was dominated by a handful of authors – John Creasey, Sydney Horler, Edwy Searles Brooks and others – all capable of turning out a dozen or more novels a year, often using pseudonyms to cover their tracks for different publishers. 'Between the mid sixties and the early seventies all the episodic film series in this country were being written by about eight writers,' said Clemens. 'We tended to lean on each other.'

It was a reasonable expectation that if a viewer tuned into a popular British drama of the time, one or other of these names would appear in the credits, in the capacity either of writer or of script editor (the latter function also known as story editor, or sometimes story consultant). And the two roles were closely interlinked. As script editors on various series, they would commission each other because, as Nation remembered: 'We all faced the same problem, a daily problem, that there weren't many people who could do scripts. We would tend to rewrite and write for each other. Clemens had done a couple for me, and I had done some things for him.' And, reciprocating the (mostly) friendly rivalry that existed between them, he added: 'Clemens was the fastest writer I had ever come across. He was a little facile, but by God he could turn them out!'

Many of these men came from similar backgrounds. They were not so much a generation, as a tiny slither of a generation. Nation, Exton, Clemens, James and Spooner were born within twenty-eight months of each other; all of them were formed in childhood by the early days of radio and by the glory years of Hollywood; all were slightly too young to have served in the Second World War; and all embarked on their careers just as British television began to take off. Typically they came from unprivileged backgrounds and were not university-educated. 'We all shared the same social experiences and listened to the same radio programmes and so on,' reflected Clemens.

Within a couple of years either side of Nation were also to be found the likes of Leon Griffiths, Tony Barwick, Richard Harris and Troy Kennedy Martin, who worked on the same series that provided him with regular work, whether it were *Out of the Unknown*, *The Saint* or *The Persuaders!*. Between them, these writers were responsible for bringing to the small screen everything from *Z-Cars*, *Captain Scarlet* and *Randall and Hopkirk (Deceased)* to *Poirot*, *Minder*, *The Professionals* and *Shoestring*, as well as Nation's own contributions. Without them, British television would have looked very different indeed. And − in slightly different fields − there were comedy writers including John Junkin and the team of Ray Galton and Alan Simpson, as well as programme-makers like Gerry Anderson and Verity Lambert, all born in the same few years and all of whose paths were to intersect with Nation's career.

For his story is, to some extent, shared by these others, rooted in the same experiences that moulded the country in the decades that followed the war, as it made its uncertain transition from Austerity Britain to Swinging London and beyond into the uncertainties of the 1970s and 1980s.

Chapter One

A Boy's Own Story

Terry Nation moved to London in January 1955 at the age of twenty-four, intending, in his words, 'to be an actor or comedian or something – I wasn't very sure what'. The city that he found was just emerging, somewhat to its own surprise, into the dawn of an extraordinary period in British cultural history. The previous July had seen the celebration of Derationing Day, when bacon and meat finally came off the ration, marking an end to all wartime restrictions on food and other goods. Although the city was still pockmarked with bombsites left over from the Blitz, even in such affluent areas as Oxford Street, there was a sense of having left behind the long, wearying struggle of the Second World War and the ensuing period of Austerity.

In their place came the first stirrings of a new consumer-based society. The year of Nation's arrival was to see key events that would transform the country's identity: the launch of independent television, providing a second channel to break the BBC's previous monopoly; the opening of Mary Quant's Bazaar, the first of the London boutiques that would become world famous over the next decade; and the arrival from America of rock and roll in the shape of the hit single 'Rock Around the Clock' by Bill Haley and his Comets, together with the British response, Lonnie Donegan's 'Rock Island Line', the record that launched the skiffle craze. The following year built on these foundations, with the emergence of Elvis Presley and the coming of the Angry Young Men, the latter announcing themselves in the shape of John Osborne's play *Look Back in Anger* and Colin Wilson's book *The Outsider*. There was also the first sighting of pop art in the exhibition *This Is Tomorrow*, featuring Richard Hamilton's collage 'Just what is it that makes today's homes so different, so appealing?', a celebration of the American dream as revealed through advertising.

Meanwhile the world of comedy, in which Nation hoped to make his mark, was in the grip of the revolutionary radio series *The Goon Show*, though a newly launched radio sitcom, *Hancock's Half Hour*, was fast emerging as an even more influential and popular rival.

But if it were bliss to be alive in those days, no one had told the establishment, which remained largely unaware of this groundswell of innovation, these early manifestations of a youth culture that would soon sweep the country and then much of the rest of the world. The radicalism of the late 1940s had faded from British political life, and when Nation arrived in London, the prime minister was still 80-year-old Winston Churchill, kept in power more by sentiment than sense. Although he was soon to be replaced by the comparatively youthful Anthony Eden (born as recently as 1897), the opposition leaders in the 1955 General Election – Clement Attlee of Labour and Clement Davies of the Liberals – were both in their seventies.

Even these staid circles, however, were soon to be disrupted, first by the humiliation of the Suez Crisis, when it became apparent that British foreign policy could no longer be determined without reference to the USA, and then by the noisy arrival of the Campaign for Nuclear Disarmament, bringing a sense that a younger generation wanted to have a say in building a new country. In the meantime, hopeful young men and women flocked to London from the provinces, determined – like Nation – to make their mark, to embrace the new cultural opportunities that were opening up.

Terence Joseph Nation was born in Llandaff, Cardiff in 1930, the only child of Bert and Sue, as Gilbert Joseph Nation and Susan Nation (née Norris) were generally known. It was not an auspicious time or place. Cardiff was the largest city in Wales, with a population of just over a quarter of a million, but it was already in serious decline, the splendour of its civic buildings looking back to past glories in the late nineteenth century, with little sense of hope for the future. In its heyday it had provided the focal point for the South Wales collieries in the valleys that stretched northwards and westwards from the city; its docks shipped coal to all corners of the world, and attracted labour from similarly far-flung places. Continuing expansion had seemed inevitable and inexorable in the years up to the First World War, but in the 1920s demand for coal began to fall. Shipping turned increasingly to oil for its primary fuel, the international markets struggled to recover from the post-war slump, and production costs rose, the more accessible seams having been worked out. Further losses were sustained as

British industry went into recession at the end of the decade; coal production fell to half its level at the turn of the century and, in the words of one contemporary account, 'unemployment descended on the valleys like a deadly and malignant disease'. More than a third of miners in the South Wales coalfields were out of work by the early 1930s and Cardiff, so dependent on that industry, was registering unemployment levels of over twenty per cent.

In the midst of the decline came the events of 1926, when miners throughout the country went on strike, resisting the mine-owners' attempt to protect profits by cutting wages and increasing working hours. Under the slogan 'not a penny off the pay, not a minute on the day', the conflict dragged on for several months, despite a general strike that was called in solidarity but collapsed after just nine days. It was − in terms of working days lost − the most severe industrial dispute Britain had ever witnessed, and it ended with complete victory for the employers. Memories of the bitterness of the time remained for years to come, exacerbated by the ensuing depression and by the desperation of the miners' hunger march that left Cardiff in 1931, the year that annual coal production in Britain fell below a thousand million tons for the first time in the century. Decades later, when the novelist John Summers, who had known Terry Nation in Cardiff, wrote his classic *Edge of Violence*, a thinly fictionalised retelling of the 1966 Aberfan disaster, he placed that tragedy in the context of a long history of neglect and oppression, looking back to the 1930s when 'foraging parties of starved miners started raiding the farms over the mountain to dig up hardening beets and swedes out of the ground and bring them home to their children small-faced with hunger'. Born in Rhymney in 1928, Summers remembered his childhood 'as a time of soup made from a single slice of bacon and water and salt and an onion'.

Terry Nation, with a self-employed furniture restorer and salesman as a father and with a house-proud mother ('stiff and starchy', as one friend described her), was at one stage removed from those events. The fact that his birth was announced in a paid notice in the *South Wales Echo*, as well as his time in a private school, suggests that this was a family with social aspirations pointing firmly away from the mining villages of the valleys. Similarly the area they lived in was relatively affluent. 'Llandaff,' remembered a resident of the working-class Grangetown district in the early 1940s, 'was a different planet. I could not believe the size of the houses and gardens, but the area did seem dull compared with the clamour and bustle of Lower Grange.'

Nonetheless, it would have been difficult for an imaginative child to live in Cardiff through those times without being affected by the hardship and anger that was everywhere evident, and Nation was to talk in later life of 'the far-left socialism of his youth'.

It was an era that he memorably evoked in 'The Assistant', a 1963 episode of the television series *Hancock*, with a character named Owen Bowen (played by the Welsh actor Kenneth Griffith) recalling the deprivation of the time: 'Unemployment. Men standing brooding on street corners. Sad-eyed women, too proud to beg, laying empty tables.' Despite being ostensibly a comedy, the show also featured a long monologue from Owen recalling the miners' defiance, with not a joke in sight: 'We were striking for a living wage, and they tried to force us into submission through starvation. But we wouldn't bend. So what did they do? They sent in the army. Armed troops against women and children! So what did we do? We formed a solid line, Welshman arm-in-arm with Welshman, a thin line of courage against the might of the English army . . .'

Nothing else in Nation's work came close to this explicit account of the society he was born into, but traces of his hatred of injustice and social oppression run through much of his best writing and surely have their roots here. It's also noticeable that more than once in his comedy-writing days he uses a joke about a character being able to trace their ancestry all the way back to their parents. Mixing in the Oxbridge circles that dominated the BBC in the 1950s and 1960s, he was conscious that he was not from that world.

Meanwhile, popular culture in Cardiff was split between two competing factions. On the one hand, there was the entertainment found in the pubs, clubs and picture-houses through the working week; on the other, religion in church and chapel on Sundays. There were, for example, already fourteen cinemas in the town at the time of his birth, most having made the transition from silent movies to talkies (though some silents were still being shown), but just as significant was the space allocated every week by the *South Wales Echo* for semi-display adverts touting the forthcoming attractions on the Sabbath. It was normal for forty or fifty religious services to be thus promoted, advertising a range of sects that centred on the mainstream world of low church Protestantism – Baptists, Congregationalists, Presbyterians, Wesleyans – while allowing a little room on the fringes for groups such as the Christian Scientists, Spiritualists and Salvation Army.

The divide between the two cultures was such that, on a Sunday, pubs were legally prevented from opening and cinemas were not permitted to show films, regulations that didn't apply twenty-five miles to the east, over the Severn Estuary and into England. It was not until 1952 that it became permissible to screen a movie on the Sabbath, and only in 1961 were local authorities allowed to poll their electorates on whether the bar on pub opening should continue (not all took advantage of the opportunity). But there were, of course, ways around the rules. Private members' clubs – where alcohol could be sold – enjoyed a thriving trade on Sundays, while the cinemas responded to the ban by putting on shows featuring dance bands and comedians, though there were restrictions even on those performances. 'There were all sorts of strange rules and regulations,' remembered Stan Stennett, the city's leading post-war comedian, who lived a couple of streets away from the Nations. 'You could do a show on a Sunday but you weren't allowed to be a double-act or talk to anyone onstage. There was no cross-patter on a Sunday, because of the licence.'

Of these rival claims for his affections, there was little doubt that for Nation the cinema won hands down over church. There was a religious influence on his upbringing – apart from formal church-going, he spent a great deal of time at the house of his father's friend, Bob White, the Anglican verger of Llandaff Cathedral – and the influence of the work ethic fostered by religion was evident throughout his life. 'I'm a prolific writer because I'm always uneasy,' he was to reflect. 'Maybe it's my Welsh guilt that I can't really sit around and not do anything. I feel very guilty if I'm in a room and not actually working at the table.'

But the cinema loomed far larger. He became addicted to the magic of the picture-houses, the dark crowded theatres, thick with clouds of cigarette and pipe smoke through which the imagery of Hollywood could be seen flickering on a screen, briefly transporting a huddled, rain-sodden mass to a far-off land of glamour and wealth. Nation found his escape from everyday reality in that dream of America, as did so much of the country in the years of depression, those slightly older than him fuelling their fantasies with mass-produced clothes bought on hire purchase. 'You may have three halfpence in your pocket and not a prospect in the world,' wrote George Orwell in *The Road to Wigan Pier* (1937), 'but in your new clothes you can stand on the street corner, indulging in a private daydream of yourself as Clark Gable or Greta Garbo, which compensates you for a great deal.'

Nation may have been too young to express his dreams quite so overtly, but he would have understood the sentiment and for him, fantasy was always liable to take precedence over the mundane reality of education. 'He played truant for one whole term,' recounted his wife, Kate. 'He got found out because he'd been given these cheques for his school fees and finally the headmaster rang his mother and asked where the money was. And it was still in his pocket. He'd been to the movies every afternoon.' As he remembered, 'I grew up in the front row of the local Odeon.'

The nature of the films that Nation encountered, however, was not quite as wide-ranging as he perhaps would have wished. Desperately few science fiction movies were available in the late 1930s and 1940s, with the exception of single-reel serials like *Flash Gordon*, nor was the cinema able to satisfy his childhood taste for horror stories. ('I read a lot of horror fiction,' he was to reflect; 'gave myself the scares in the dark'.) There had been a spate of impressive and successful horror movies coming over from America but, in an early panic about the influence of cinema, their popularity had prompted British film censors to introduce in 1937 a new 'H' certificate, restricting the viewing of such material to those aged sixteen or over. A few years later, a decision was made in official circles that fictional horror was not conducive to civilian morale during wartime, and between 1942 and 1945 'H' certificate films were banned altogether; just at the age when an adolescent, particularly one as tall as Nation, should have been trying to sneak in to see a movie for adults, the opportunity was snatched away.

The only home-grown rival to the dominance of the cinema was BBC radio, the first truly national cultural phenomenon that the country had known. The British Broadcasting Company had begun transmissions in 1922, at which stage there were just 35,000 licences in the country, permitting the bearers to receive the early broadcasts. By the time of Nation's birth, that figure had risen to three million and it was to treble in the following decade, while the BBC had been transformed into the British Broadcasting Corporation, established under a royal charter as the monopoly provider of services: the first nationalised industry. It was not, though, without rivals, particularly at the weekend, when the entertainment on offer left a great deal to be desired. For John Reith, the first director general of the corporation, shared with the Welsh establishment a determination that Sundays should be 'quiet islands on the tossing sea of life', and that the programmes broadcast on that day should therefore ensure that 'the lamps are lit before the Lord and the message and music of eternity move through the infinities of the ether'.

As the social clubs and cinemas of Wales had demonstrated, however, a resourceful people could always find an alternative to the sober fare that resulted from such attitudes, and a number of foreign-based stations soon emerged, aiming their transmitters at Britain and broadcasting in English in the expectation of picking up advertising revenue (the BBC was, of course, a non-profit making enterprise that didn't air commercials). Among these foreign rivals were Radio Lyons, Radio Normandy, Radio Toulouse and, most famously, Radio Luxembourg, which started in 1933 and was within a few months broadcasting from noon to midnight. With the most powerful transmitter in Europe and the most expensive advertising space in the world, Luxembourg was seen as a threat by both the BBC and Fleet Street and was met with a complete news blackout in Britain: its schedules weren't included in the radio listings, and its existence was simply ignored. Nonetheless it soon attracted some five million listeners, proving particularly popular on the Sabbath; the BBC lost half its Sunday audience, and a survey showed that sixty per cent of listeners had acquired the habit of tuning into the continental stations.

The departure of Reith in 1938 allowed some relaxation of his rigorous standards – 'I do not pretend to give the public what it wants,' he had once proclaimed – but it was not until the outbreak of war in September 1939 that there was a genuine move to respond to the wishes and demands of the new mass audience. A second national channel was launched, aimed at those in uniform and known as the Forces Programme, with the existing channel being renamed the Home Service. Considerably lighter in tone than the BBC had previously allowed itself to be (the first show, on Sunday 7 January 1940, was a half-hour broadcast by Gracie Fields), the Forces Programme heralded a new era, with the radio becoming ever more influential.

The structure of the audience also changed. In the early days, listening to the radio had been primarily a communal, friends-and-family affair, so that the broadcast of George V's speech opening the British Empire Exhibition at Wembley in 1924 had been heard by six million people, many times more than the number of receivers in the country; it was the first time in British history that a substantial section of the population had been able to hear their monarch's voice and, apart from anything else, there was considerable interest in what he actually sounded like. But conditions were different now: most households boasted their own radio set, millions of men were away from home in the forces, and the continental competition had been snuffed out. (Luxembourg ceased broadcasting immediately after war was declared, making a return only when its facilities were taken over by the Germans and used to broadcast the propaganda of William 'Lord Haw Haw' Joyce.) In this world, the BBC acquired a new role, linking atomised households and individuals, making them feel part of a whole, and bringing them together under a common national banner; even the new king, George VI, and his family were reported to be fans of the country's biggest comedy shows, *Band Waggon* and *ITMA*. This was still a shared experience – particularly in those factories where radio was ever-present – but domestically its nature was evolving. The old image of a family congregated around a wireless set had, to some extent, been replaced by the solitary listener at home, conscious of the fact that he or she was a member of an audience comprising anonymous millions of others.

This was especially true of Nation and his contemporaries, the first generation to grow up with radio as a soundtrack to their lives. And of particular significance for this generation were two drama series, *Saturday Night Theatre* and *Appointment with Fear* (the latter memorably hosted by Valentine Dyall, the Man in Black), that started in 1943 and brought tales of mystery, detection and suspense to a cult audience. Together with occasional shows like *The Saint* (1940), adapted from the stories by Leslie Charteris, these were the first examples of broadcast drama to make a major impact. 'They were very influential,' reflected Brian Clemens. 'I used to listen to them in the Blitz, because I lived in Croydon, which was heavily bombed, and I spent most of my sleeping time in an Anderson shelter or a Morrison shelter.'

Nation too lived in the shadow of the Blitz, with the first big air raid on Cardiff coming in January 1941, at the cost of more than 150 lives. 'For over five hours German planes, sweeping over the city, dropped thousands of incendiaries and numerous high explosive bombs,' reported the local paper, while the account in *The Times* said the intensity of the firebombing was such 'that it was possible to read a newspaper in the street'. Although the Luftwaffe saw the docks as its primary target, areas further inland were also hit: Llandaff Cathedral, a few hundred yards from the Nations' home, was damaged so badly it was obliged to close its doors for fifteen months. The imagery of the Second World War and of the Nazis was to recur through much of Nation's adult work, to such an extent that it was sometimes mocked by critics ('a common Nation trait', notes one guide to *The Avengers*), though it would perhaps have been more surprising if it hadn't been present. 'I was a wartime child,' he reflected. 'My dad went off to the army and my mother was an ARP, an air-raid warden. I was an only child and I used to spend nights alone in an air-raid shelter. And I would make up stories for myself – I was entertaining *me* in those days. There was no television, of course, but I used to listen to the radio, and I also read a great deal.'

It was that reading, intensified by the experience of the bombing, that did most to shape Nation's future writing. The range was diverse: there was some science fiction, primarily H.G. Wells and Jules Verne; there were detective stories, still dominated by Arthur Conan Doyle's tales of Sherlock Holmes, though augmented in the early 1940s by the sensational arrival of Raymond Chandler; there was horror literature, particularly the great myths of the late Victorians, *Dracula* and *Doctor Jekyll and Mr Hyde*, as well as the Edwardian ghost stories of M.R. James and W.W. Jacobs; and above all there was a rich vein of adventure stories that reached back to the likes of H. Rider Haggard and G.A. Henty and continued forward to John Buchan and C.S. Forester, as well as a host of their imitators.

This latter was a deep and exciting tradition for a boy in the 1930s and 1940s, celebrating quests to distant, exotic lands, and telling tales of tunnels and treasure maps, jungles and journeys, war and discovery. It had no interest in the bureaucratic administrators of later colonial fiction, looking rather to the glory days of frontier imperialism, when the world still lay spread out for the taking, if one only had the good fortune to be born British, with a streak of derring-do and a taste for pushing oneself to one's limits. Set in a world populated almost exclusively by men, though often with a boy at the centre of the narrative, these novels made it clear that true romance lay in loyalty and honour, rather than in love and women. The spirit of the knight errant was reborn on the African veldt, in the jungles and remote mountains of Asia, and on the high seas.

This was the heritage, the mythology that still loomed large, even though by the time of Nation's own childhood it seemed as though there was precious little left of such pioneering aspirations, particularly in the aftermath of the war that was supposed to end all wars, and that certainly – for a while at least – had ended the fictional romance of war. It was a long way from the heroic death of General Gordon, standing proud in the face of the Mahdi masses in faraway Khartoum, to the anonymous slaughter at Passchendaele, and as society struggled to adjust to that change, it seemed far less amenable to the old breed of hero. John Buchan's novel, *The Island of*

Sheep (1936), the last to feature his secret agent Richard Hannay, begins with our hero on a suburban train in southern England, reminiscing about the great days at the turn of the century when 'the afterglow of Cecil Rhodes's spell still lay on Africa, and men could dream dreams'. As he looks 'round the compartment at the flabby eupeptic faces' of commuters returning home from the City, he reflects melancholically on the realities of modern Britain: 'Brains and high ambition had perished, and the world was for the comfortable folk like the man opposite me.'

In due course, a new generation of hero emerged from the pens of Sapper and others. Wealthy young men of action, they mostly operated in the high society of London in the inter-war years, though they were happy enough to step outside society's conventions of behaviour when justice demanded it. Stories featuring some of this new breed – Leslie Charteris's Simon Templar, aka the Saint, and John Creasey's Baron – were later to be adapted for television by Nation, but there always seemed to be a place in his heart for the previous generation, whose attitudes survived in the stories found in the boys' weekly magazines of the 1930s, the likes of *Wizard*, *Champion* and *Hotspur*. Here the Wild West still loomed larger than the Western Front, and the only acknowledgement of the recent war came in tales not of the trenches, but of the much more glamorous exploits of the Royal Flying Corps (Nation was a big fan of W.E. Johns's books about the air ace Biggles). The core of such magazines were detective stories, tales of exploration, and colourful adventures that featured variants on stock characters such as Tarzan and Robin Hood; there was little that couldn't have been found in the Edwardian era, save for the emergence, towards the end of the 1930s, of some science fiction, primarily concerned with space travel, Martians and death rays.

This adventure tradition, both in novels and magazines, dominated the reading of boys in the 1930s, and Nation's love of it runs through his own writing. Its celebration of the spirit of adventure, of improvised resourcefulness, of the qualities of leadership, were to form the backbone to much of his own work, finding their happiest incarnation in the character of Jimmy Garland in *Survivors*, a joyously triumphant throwback to the world of Buchan. 'He's acting like a character from a boy's own adventure story,' snorts one of Garland's enemies. Indeed he was, and no one was more aware of it than Nation, whose writing resonated with echoes of this world.

Given his voracious reading ('I read everything that was available to me'), it wasn't long before Nation was making up his own stories, 'mostly with me as the hero'. Such a quality was not always appreciated in a society dominated by the very literal values of the church. 'I was always believed to be a terrible liar,' he said in later life. 'Nowadays they would say, "He's got a wonderful imagination," but in those days I was just "that liar".' On one occasion in school, the class was set the standard writing assignment of 'What I did on my holidays'. Having done nothing much, he wrote instead a fictional tale of a holiday on a barge. 'The teacher looked at me and said, "Were you on a barge, Nation?" I said, "No," and he said, "This is all bloody rubbish then, isn't it?"' The lack of encouragement seems to have done little to dissuade him. A friend, Harry Greene, who met him in 1945, recalls him telling stories that were 'often stretched beyond what was credible', as when he deliberately set out to scare Elsie White, wife of the verger Bob, with a tale about seeing a ghost through the window of Llandaff Cathedral.

His view of the schooling he received was to be seen in a passage from his original script for 'The Daleks' (though it was cut from the final version), in which the Doctor berates his companion, Ian Chesterton, for failing to understand the significance of the metal floors in the Dalek city: 'Chesterton, your total lack of imagination appals me. When I remember that you were a schoolmaster, it makes me glad that you are now here, and can no longer influence the minds of those poor unsuspecting children who were once your pupils.'

Nation's childhood absorption of influences was to change markedly following the 1941 bombing of Pearl Harbor and America's subsequent entry into the war. However remote those events may have appeared, it wasn't long before GIs were arriving in Britain, and with them came a new note in the cultural life of the country. Signs of an interest in American culture had already been apparent when the BBC Forces Programme began to air bought-in comedy shows such as *The Jack Benny Half Hour*, *The Bob Hope Programme* and *The Charlie McCarthy Show*, but the real breakthrough was the appearance of the American Forces Network (AFN), which started broadcasting from London on 4 July 1943 and was relayed around the country. 'They did transmissions of all the American shows,' remembered Nation, 'and I'd hear Bob Hope, Jack Benny and all the big stars of that time. I loved the American sound, the jokes, the *feel*.'

He wasn't the only one to fall under the spell, for a whole generation of future writers was to find its tastes affected. 'We listened closely to American comedy shows transmitted on the American Forces Network in Europe,' remembered Frank Muir, one of the first new comedy writers to emerge after the war. 'We had a lot to learn from American radio comedy in those days.' Another of the coming men, Bob Monkhouse, would later talk about 'our personal pantheon of comedy gods like Bob Hope, Bing Crosby, Jack Benny and Phil Silvers', and the Welsh comedian Wyn Calvin similarly recognised the impact made by AFN: 'Youngsters with an ambition to be amusing were glued to those programmes. It gave them a new comedy, away from the variety programmes.'

The memory of those shows was to remain with Nation all his life, long after their direct influence had evaporated. Well into the late 1980s he was still jokingly claiming to be thirty-nine years old, a running gag in Jack Benny's routines that he had first encountered in his childhood. But even more important was the stationing of large numbers of American troops in Cardiff. 'Suddenly there they were,' he recalled, 'with their ice cream, their chocolate and their comic books. Those wonderful American comic books became an influence, too. *Superman*, maybe *Batman* too. They were a great breath of fresh air after the *Dandy* and the *Beano*.' For the first time, the transient images of America that had illuminated the cinemas for the last decade and more were acquiring a tangible, physical presence; now there were holy relics of the promised land that could be handled and taken home, cherished and consumed.

The luxury of those items, the lavish size and quality of the comics in particular, was almost unimaginable to a child living in a country that had by now survived the worst of the Blitz, but was still struggling through on ration books and the occasional foray into the black economy. The publisher D.C. Thomson had begun something of a revolution in British comics in 1937 with the launch of the *Dandy*, followed swiftly by the *Beano* and by *Magic*, all of them cheerier and cheekier than their predecessors, but they faced a major setback with the outbreak of war. Paper in Britain was made primarily from wood pulp shipped from Scandinavia and, with the growing threat of U-boat attacks, such supplies were hard to come by. Newspapers voluntarily reduced their size by around fifty per cent in an attempt to preserve paper stocks, and children's comics were similarly hard hit; *Magic* disappeared entirely, and the *Beano* and *Dandy* switched from weekly to fortnightly publication, alternating with each other, while they too shrank in size. Other titles, popular with boys as well as adults, also went out of existence, including *Detective Weekly*, home of Sexton Blake, and *The Thriller*, which had nurtured gentlemen outlaws of the 1930s like the Saint, the Toff and Norman Conquest. In March 1940, just before the fall of

Norway made the position even more precarious, the formal rationing of paper was introduced by the government.

By 1944 book production was at less than half its pre-war level, and educationalists were warning of a serious crisis as textbooks became ever more difficult to obtain. The situation had been exacerbated by the actions of the Luftwaffe, with an estimated 20 million volumes destroyed as a result of the bombing of Britain. Demand for books remained high, partly – it was argued – because of the need for escapism, and partly because the absence of so many goods from the shops meant that people had a higher disposable income than before the war, but there was a desperate shortage of supply. In this context, an American *Superman* comic would fall into the hands of a 13-year-old boy like Terry Nation as though it were manna from heaven. The child psychologist P.M. Pickard campaigned in the 1950s against the influence of the American comics, but even she recognised their appeal: 'The glossy paper, the brilliant colours and the clear type far outshone anything the war-surrounded children remembered ever seeing.' The contrast between the real experience of Britain and the fantasy imagery of America instilled a fascination with that country that was to dominate the post-war era, for Nation as for so many others.

Paper shortages continued after the end of the war. It wasn't until 1949 that Harold Wilson, then president of the Board of Trade, was able to announce that the rationing of paper was to end, by which time the damage had, for many, already been done. *Strand* magazine, where the likes of Sherlock Holmes and A.J. Raffles had made their first appearances, announced that year that it could no longer afford to continue, though the *Beano* and the *Dandy* had survived and were able to return to weekly publication. In the interim, the departure of the GIs had left a generation bereft, and the publishers of American comics, having discovered that there was a voracious appetite in Britain, responded by flooding the country with imported material, to the immense annoyance of their rationed competitors; in the immediate post-war years, the entire British publishing trade was restricted to around 2,000 tons of paper per month, the same quantity that was being shipped in every year in the form of comics. For Nation, who remained an avid reader of the imports, the gulf between the American and British productions was now even more marked, with a clear age divide having opened up; it was not until 1950 and the launch of the *Eagle* that comic publishers at home recognised that there was a demand to be met not simply among children but among adolescents as well. And by then, although he was fond of the *Eagle*, it was really too late for him.

Nation celebrated his fifteenth birthday on the day that the Soviet Union declared war on Japan, the event that precipitated that country's surrender and finally brought the Second World War to a close. The previous month a General Election had swept out of power the Conservative administration of Winston Churchill and replaced it with a Labour government headed by Clement Attlee. Among its reforms were the creation of the National Health Service, under the guidance of South Wales's most famous politician, Aneurin Bevan, and the nationalisation of the mining industry; on New Year's Day 1947 notices appeared right across the country's coalfields proclaiming: 'This colliery is now managed by the National Coal Board on behalf of the people.' If that was to prove a little optimistic, it did at least reflect a desire that the hardship of the depression should never be allowed to happen again, and a similar feeling on the part of the five million men and women who had served in the armed forces that their sacrifices should lead to a more just society. When Spike Milligan, serving in the Italian campaign in 1943, believed that his death was imminent, he wrote himself an epitaph: 'I died for the England I dreamed of, not for the England I know.' Now was the time to build that new country.

The political mood for change was mirrored, though it was not as immediately apparent, by a determination on the part of the returning servicemen that culturally their voices should be heard, and it was on the radio, and particularly in comedy, that the resulting loose-knit movement was first to make its mark. In Wales it produced the revival of *Welsh Rarebit*, a radio series that had proved more popular in the principality even than Tommy Handley's *ITMA* during the war, and which was reborn in 1949 as an hour-long variety show. With its theme song of 'We'll Keep a Welcome in the Hillsides' – written by the show's producer, Mai Jones – *Welsh Rarebit* went out on the Light Programme (as the Forces Programme had now been renamed) and became principally known as a showcase for new Welsh comedians including Harry Secombe, Stan Stennett and Wyn Calvin. 'Up until the advent of radio,' noted the latter, 'Wales had no reputation for comedy.' That was slightly overstating the case, but certainly the success of *Welsh Rarebit* – it even enjoyed a brief transfer to television in the 1950s – helped fuel the ambitions of those in South Wales with aspirations towards becoming entertainers, among them Terry Nation: 'I wanted to be a comedian. I wanted to be a stand-up.'

On leaving school Nation had joined his father's furniture business, working – not very well, he was later to admit – as a salesman. One of the few benefits of this position was that he had a justification for fussing over his wardrobe, in which pride of place went to a leather-buttoned, Harris tweed jacket. 'He was always dressed beautifully,' remembered his friend Harry Greene (who worked as an unpaid assistant on *Welsh Rarebit*). 'I don't know if it was hand-me-downs from his dad, because Bert was a good dresser as well. I think that was part of his front for selling.' The work meant that he had money in his pocket, but Nation was already preoccupied with dreams of performance. He remained passionate about film, becoming a member of the Cardiff Amateur Cine Society, while engaging in amateur dramatics with the left-wing Unity Theatre, based at the local YMCA, and other groups. He was also a regular visitor to the New Theatre, where Greene sometimes worked backstage and could get him free tickets to shows featuring the cream of British comedy at the time, including Arthur Askey, Nat Jackley and Norman Evans.

Through Greene too, he was to meet the future novelist John Summers, who had similar experiences of the limited horizons offered by a South Wales education. In schools whose 'job was to turn out more cogs for the industrial machine', wrote Summers in his semi-autobiographical book *The Raging Summer*, a child who showed too much imagination 'was to be quickly hammered and stamped back into regular shape before he could get out and become dangerously loose in the world'. There was 'an instant recognition of brotherhood', remembered Greene; the two men 'had similar interests, were about the same age and got on very well, often walking off into the castle grounds to talk, where we'd lose them for hours'.

Nation became part of the student-dominated social scene that congregated upstairs at the Khardomah café on Saturday mornings, and the fact that he was happily mixing with such a group, many of whom were a significant couple of years older than him and had served in uniform, was an indication both of his affable nature and of the fact that 'he was the epitome of self-confidence'. Although not a student himself, he participated in many social events, helping to organise the first Cardiff Arts Ball (inspired by the Chelsea Arts Balls) in 1949, and forming part of the team that created a sketch called 'The Poor Man's Picasso' for the 1948 rag week. The idea for the sketch was that the performers would draw objects on a white flat screen and that the drawings would then become functional, so that a hatstand would be drawn and a coat then hung upon it, a picture of cupboard doors would be opened, and so on. The main practical difficulty was to find a drawing implement big enough to be seen from the back of the theatre, a problem to which Nation, displaying an inventive resourcefulness that would become characteristic of his fictional heroes, found the solution: a condom with a rolled-up piece of carpet stuffed inside and filled with purple ink, the whole thing being bound with elastic bands to form a prototype marker pen. The performance at the Capital Cinema was filmed by members of the Cine Society and eventually reached the attention of a television producer; consequently, in 1955, Harry Greene and another student, Ivor Olsen, appeared on the BBC show *Quite Contrary* under the names Pedro and Pinky with a revived version of the routine, almost certainly the first time that a condom had been seen on British television.

By the end of the 1940s, Nation was also beginning to develop his solo comedy act, which he was to take around the circuit of pubs and social clubs in the area, already home to Stan Stennett and Wyn Calvin and soon to be illuminated by a teenage singing prodigy from Cardiff named Shirley Bassey. The highlight of his routine was a series of funny walks, mostly exploiting his gangly physique, though one variation saw him walking on his knees, with his trousers rolled up and shoes acting as knee-pads, in the manner perfected by José Ferrer when playing Henri de Toulouse-Lautrec in the 1952 film *Moulin Rouge*. Again it was an aspect of his early life to which he would return when writing scripts for the 1963 *Hancock* series. In the episode 'The Writer', Tony Hancock tries to convince a professional comedian named Jerry Spring that every comic needs a funny walk, and proceeds to do an impression of Groucho Marx's stooping prowl and Stan Laurel's loose-limbed lollop, before giving his own suggestion that Spring should imitate a penguin. Similarly, one of the jokes that Hancock tries to foist upon Spring has all the hallmarks of coming from the repertoire of an inexperienced stand-up in South Wales. A man walks into a cottage in the Rhondda Valley, covered head to foot in coal dust, and when his wife exclaims at the state of him, he asks why, after twenty years of him coming home from work every day in this condition, she's still surprised. 'Well, after all, Dai,' she replies, 'you *are* a milkman!'

'I thought myself a rather good comedian at the time, and used to get laughs around the pub,' reflected Nation in later life. 'But if you're paying for the drinks, people will laugh.' More significant, in terms of his later career, was his discovery that other comedians, particularly those who were starting to find broadcast work, would pay for jokes. 'I used to be a member of the Overseas Club, in Park Place, right next to the BBC, in those days. I actually sold my very first scripts to an up-and-coming young comic I met there – Stan Stennett.' Stennett, who was beginning to make his name on radio shows including *Variety Bandbox* and *Workers' Playtime* as well as *Welsh Rarebit*, needed a supply of fresh material; although such work was entirely uncredited and none is known to have survived, it was at least a suggestion of an alternative future. It also gave Nation a chance to work with his first partner, another Cardiff-born writer, Dick Barry, and to try to put into practice the American style of gag-telling that he had heard on AFN. 'Terry was doing the more upbeat, up-to-date, quick-fire sort of comedy,' remembered Stennett.

By the early 1950s, however, the Khardomah set that Nation had been part of was starting to break up. In recent years, South Wales had been able to boast a number of famous sons, pursuing a wide range of cultural occupations, from the novelist Howard Spring and the poet Dylan Thomas, through Ray Milland, winner of the 1946 Best Actor Oscar for his role in *The Lost Weekend*, to the boxer Tommy Farr, who came desperately close to taking the world heavyweight title off Joe Louis in 1937. But all had had to leave home to achieve their success. The truth was that South Wales was still a place of origin rather than a land of opportunity. For those who were troubled by ambition, curiosity or simple impatience, it was primarily somewhere to look back upon from what was then called the refreshment car of the London train.

So it was to prove again. Among Nation's friends and acquaintances, Harry Greene joined Joan Littlewood's travelling theatre company as an actor, set designer and general handyman, ending up at the Theatre Royal, Stratford East before embarking on a television career, while John Summers worked his passage around the world, with spells in Canada and Australia, before making his way to Fleet Street. Nation himself was a little way behind them, but in January 1955 he bought a one-way ticket to London, and he too took his leave of Cardiff.

Chapter Two

Goings On

In later life, Terry Nation was often to tell the tale of his early months in London, the doomed struggle to make it as either a comedian or an actor. 'I auditioned as a stand-up comic, and I failed time and time again. Somebody told me, "The jokes are very good; it's you who's not funny." That was hurtful, but then I figured I had to make a living.' So he concentrated on writing, and was still getting nowhere when his fairy godmother appeared in the improbable guise of a Goon, as detailed by the *Guardian* in a 1966 interview: 'His first break was an interview with Spike Milligan. He arrived so worn and woebegone that Milligan said, "You look terrible!" wrote out a cheque for £10, and told him to go away and try to write a script for *The Goon Show*. He did. Some of it, at least, was used on the air, and Milligan took him on as a writer.'

Although there is no evidence of Nation's work ever being used in a broadcast edition of *The Goon Show*, much of the rest of this was true, insofar as it went. Harry Greene remembered him turning up backstage at the Theatre Royal, Stratford East, in January 1955 during a famous production of *Richard II* with Harry H. Corbett in the title role (Greene was playing Bushey): 'He told me he was writing comedy scripts and trying to work as an actor and comedian, but wasn't having much luck.' But Greene also remembered earlier forays to London, reconnaissance trips that Nation made in 1954, but which didn't form part of his personal mythology. Also missing from most of Nation's versions of those early days was the fact that it was the BBC who sent him to see Spike Milligan in the first place.

Milligan and Eric Sykes, both established comedy writers but neither with full-time representation, had decided to form their own agency in the summer of 1954, bringing in the younger team of Ray Galton and Alan Simpson to create Associated London Scripts (ALS). Sykes and Milligan already shared an office above a greengrocer's shop in Shepherd's Bush, West London, and this was to become the home of ALS, one of the most influential institutions in the cultural life of post-war Britain. 'The intention was to encourage new writers,' explained Beryl Vertue, then the secretary at ALS, though later to become a successful television producer in her own right. 'And this was a bit of a godsend for the BBC, because when they found comedy writers, they'd often say: Why don't you go down and see those people in Shepherd's Bush. And so Terry would have arrived as part of that.'

Nation had indeed already been to the BBC, having had a meeting with the script editor and producer Gale Pedrick in March 1955, and it was from there that he was sent to see Milligan at ALS. But an even more significant oversight in Nation's later accounts was the failure to mention his partner, Dick Barry, who accompanied him to that meeting. The earliest press coverage Nation ever received came in a *South Wales Echo* article in May 1955, which saluted the 'tenacity, initiative and guts' of 'two young men from Cardiff', and made it clear that those early months of struggle were not endured alone: 'Terry Nation was a furniture salesman and Dick Barry an accounts clerk until early this year. They had started to write scripts for their own amusement some months before, but in January they threw up their steady jobs. Off they went to London like Dick Whittington to seek some fortune.' The two men went together to see Pedrick, and the meeting appears to have been cordial enough, for Nation wrote to thank him for his 'encouragement and advice' and promised to 'submit some [scripts] to you as soon as possible'. In the event, however, they had no further dealings with him, seemingly finding no need once they had been referred to Shepherd's Bush and found themselves taken under Milligan's wing.

Their timing was impeccable. They were not the first recruits to the agency, for a handful of others (notably Johnny Speight, later to create Alf Garnett) had already become part of ALS, but these were still early days in a venture that was to transform the role of writers on radio and television. Indeed they were still relatively early days for the concept of comedy scriptwriters at all.

In the days when comedians had been solely concerned with live performance, it had always been assumed by audiences that they wrote their own material. 'Obviously there had always been many a humorist scripting patter and sketches for comedians,' remarked Eric Sykes, 'but the names of these backroom stalwarts were a closely guarded secret. They were in a backroom under a forty-watt bulb.' As *The Times* later put it, with a wistful touch of nostalgia: 'We never heard the names of scriptwriters when Little Tich or Harry Tate were around.' When comedians did start being broadcast by the radio, they were still able to rely on their existing material, since their appearances were for the most part short, sporadic and unheralded items in the midst of a variety show (often with a voice-over to cover the more visual gags).

It was not until 1938, with the arrival of *Band Waggon*, starring 'Big Hearted' Arthur Askey and Richard 'Stinker' Murdoch, that a regular comedy series made its debut on the BBC and things began to change. 'An idea, novel in every respect to broadcasting in this country was approved by the BBC Programme Board today,' the *Daily Mail* informed its readers, and the fact that it had to explain how this was going to work indicated just how new it all was: 'The programmes will be in serial form to the extent that the same artists and characters will be retained, but each episode will be complete in itself.' *Band Waggon* was also one of the first entertainment shows to be broadcast each week at a fixed time on the same day; the idea of regular schedules did not become standard until the paper shortages of the Second World War meant that listeners could not be guaranteed to receive their copy of the listing magazine *Radio Times* and therefore needed some certainty of what to expect.

The sheer quantity of material required for a weekly show was of a different order to anything anyone had experienced while touring the music hall circuit. Ted Kavanagh, who wrote the wartime hit series *ITMA*, calculated that every half-hour show contained eighteen and a half minutes of dialogue, in which there were 'supposed to be one hundred gags – or one every eleven seconds'. Such a discipline meant an abandonment of the established practice whereby a comedian could retain the same act for years on end, perhaps for an entire career. Even Tommy Handley, who, as the linchpin of *ITMA*, was probably the biggest radio star Britain has ever known, came out of this tradition; he played his sketch 'The Disorderly Room' around the music halls for twenty years, right up until 1941, when he finally switched his entire attention to broadcasting. Now, it seemed, the voracious demand for new material meant that a policy of hiring writers specifically for radio work would have to be adopted. But there was no rush to publicise this development. Vernon Harris was responsible for much of *Band Waggon*, but his contribution was unacknowledged: 'I never got a credit – it was the policy of the BBC that they wanted the public to believe that

Arthur and Dickie made it up on the spot! It was as ingenuous as that, so they would *not* give me a credit.'

It was Kavanagh who was most responsible for remedying this lack of public recognition. The unprecedented success of *ITMA* during the war years eventually pushed his name forward and, when Tommy Handley died suddenly in 1949, thus forcing a premature end to the series, he was big enough that Radio Luxembourg (back on the air after the war) signed him up for *The Ted Kavanagh Show*, the first time on British radio that a writer had stepped into the spotlight. He had by then formed his own agency to promote the role of writers, and had struck gold when he signed up a new team in the shape of Frank Muir and Denis Norden, who were always keen to pay tribute to their mentor. 'Pre-Ted Kavanagh and *ITMA*,' wrote Muir, 'scriptwriters simply did not exist in the public mind.'

Muir and Norden were the first to benefit from the new acceptance of celebrity writers. In 1948 their most influential show, *Take It From Here*, was shown in the *Guardian*'s radio listings with their names but with no indication at all that it starred Jimmy Edwards and Dick Bentley. By the early 1950s they were famous enough to be appearing on the panel games that proliferated in the early days of television, shows like *What's Your Story* and *The Name's the Same*. They became the yardstick of success, so that the *South Wales Echo* article in 1955 said of Nation and Barry that 'their ambition is to follow in the steps of Frank Muir and Denis Norden as top script writers for BBC variety shows'.

It was into this new world that Associated London Scripts was launched by Milligan, Sykes, Galton and Simpson. Their timing was fortuitous, for the imminent launch of ITV meant that opportunities were about to increase dramatically. 'When Ray and I started,' said Alan Simpson, 'there were just enough writers to service the BBC. But when ITV started, immediately you had double the requirement, so more writers came in to supply the demand. Which coincided with when the agency started.' As Sykes put it: 'With the advent of television comedy, writers were emerging like weeds through a crack in the pavement.'

The material that flowed from the founders of the agency, let alone from their subsequent recruits, represented an impressive diversity, from the anarchic alternative world of Spike Milligan, through the extended comic stories of Eric Sykes, to the pinpoint observations of human nature and behaviour perfected by Galton and Simpson. To some extent, this was the result of their very different lives thus far — their ages at the start of ALS ranged from twenty-four (Galton) to thirty-six (Milligan), and there was a division between those who had served in the war and those who had not – but they also had key characteristics in common.

None, for example, had a university education; unlike the satire boom that was to occupy so many column inches in a few years' time, the comedy revolutions that came from ALS were not shaped by student revue. It was a trait characteristic of the era, for the leading writers among the Angry Young Men – John Osborne, Colin Wilson, Alan Sillitoe, John Braine – were similarly from working-class and lower-middle-class backgrounds and had received no formal education after leaving school. Those authors, however, were trying to break into established and reputable fields of work, whereas the members of ALS were embarked on a career path that had yet to be fully explored; they were writing comedy at a time when such a profession was practised by very few people indeed, which forged a certain sense of unity. Perhaps, too, there was the fact that they were all working in a very British tradition, largely unaffected by the American comedians on the American Forces Network. This was particularly true of Milligan, the one of the four for whom Nation had the greatest respect and admiration; his work showed no point of contact with American comedy, and his countervailing Englishness had a strong influence on the young writer.

ALS was described by Alan Simpson as 'a mutual protection society'. Though this perhaps glossed over the business side of the company – it was still an agency that charged its clients 'the usual agency commission of ten per cent' and rented them office space – there was an enormous benefit to be derived from working in an office adjacent to those occupied by some of the country's leading writers. 'If you got stuck with an idea, you could walk down and knock on Eric's door,' recalled John Junkin, who joined the agency in 1955. 'And he'd help. They were all like that. Eric, Galton and Simpson, Spike – they were always very, very helpful, and not in the least bit condescending to the new chaps.' Beryl Vertue too noted the assistance offered by the founding partners: 'In an altruistic manner, they were very helpful to the boys and when they had series, they would often encourage them to come and work on them. It was a tremendous opportunity for the new ones.' The other significant advantage to being on the books of ALS was the access it gave to the BBC, as Junkin explained: 'This was obviously the great value of the agency: they had the contacts.'

This was to be of considerable benefit to Terry Nation and Dick Barry. Just two months after that meeting with Gale Pedrick at the BBC, they were commissioned to write a 13-week radio series for Kitty Bluett, an Australian comedienne who was already a familiar voice on the highly popular show *Ray's a Laugh*, playing the assertive wife of comedian Ted Ray. On the strength of that performance, which had been running since 1949, the decision was made in 1955 to spin off a new series based on her, to be called *All My Eye and Kitty Bluett*. Even with a strong supporting cast that included Stanley Baxter, Terry Scott and Patricia Hayes, however, and with musical interludes provided by the cabaret star Leslie 'Hutch' Hutchinson, the show was not a success; it failed to receive a recommission, and Bluett rejoined *Ray's a Laugh* for the following series in 1956 after her year's absence. Nation was later to describe it as 'a rotten show, a terrible show'. He also admitted that it was a huge step to have taken, from writing the occasional short sketch to being jointly responsible for thirteen half-hour shows, and he talked about coming 'through a real ordeal by fire, getting something out there every week, getting it prepared, whether it was funny or not'.

Despite the challenges of writing *All My Eye*, and despite its failure to win the affection of the audience, Nation and Barry hadn't blotted their copybook entirely with the show's producer Alastair Scott Johnston, for he was to employ them later in 1955 as contributors to *The Frankie Howerd Show*. ('Everybody wrote for Frankie Howerd,' noted Alan Simpson.) In fact the amenable Johnston was to emerge as one of Nation's chief supporters at the BBC in the early days, seeing something in the young writer that was worth nurturing. 'He was supportive of people,' remembered Beryl Vertue of Johnston. 'He was very double-barrelled all the way down the line. He always wore a blazer. Very BBC, very nice, not pushy. He was good at his job, but he was not what you would imagine a typical producer to be.' Ray Galton had similarly fond memories, though shaded with a significant qualification: 'He was a lovely man, a man you could trust, a man you'd go into the jungle with. But not a man you'd want to produce your programmes.' Others evidently came to the same conclusion, for although Johnston went on the BBC course to become a television producer, he never did make that leap, as so many of his colleagues did; instead he had to content himself with bringing to the radio its longest-running comedy series, *The Navy Lark*, which debuted in 1959 and lasted for over eighteen years, helping to establish the reputation of its stars Leslie Phillips and Jon Pertwee.

The partnership of Nation and Barry was not destined to last long. They were, by all accounts, an oddly assorted team. Ray Galton remembered them arriving at ALS 'all hairy tweeds and walking sticks', but the image appears to have been determined more by Nation than by Barry. 'Terry tried to be extremely well dressed,' recalled Alan Simpson, and the same memory struck Beryl Vertue: 'He was always well dressed, liked nice things.' A slightly more sardonic take was offered by Ray Galton: 'He came down here with a cane. He was looking like an upper-class guy with a stately home somewhere, and he was acting a part of being amongst the peasants. He did try to look like a country gentleman. We all used to take the piss out of him.' Though, as Simpson pointed out: 'He must have got away with it with people who didn't know him.' Dick Barry, on the other hand, was remembered primarily for being self-effacing, in stark contrast to his more extrovert colleague. 'He was a nice bloke, you knew straight away he was a nice guy,' commented Galton, while Vertue added: 'He was a very quiet person in the place, very quietly spoken.' Simpson concluded: 'Dick was much more diffident. He was very quiet. They were as different as chalk and cheese, apart from their accent.'

Perhaps the differences proved too much, or perhaps it was the need to break from their background and reinvent themselves, but by the end of 1955 the partnership had split. Barry teamed up instead with Johnny Speight, and made immediate progress. Over the next eighteen months or so, they wrote BBC television shows for both Frankie Howerd and Norman Evans, as well as providing the independent channel with *That's Life, Says Max Wall* and *The Dickie Valentine Show*, in which Britain's first true pop star was joined somewhat incongruously by Peter Sellers. Their biggest hit was the ATV variety show *Get Happy*, which made a household name of the comedian Arthur Haynes, though when he got his own long-running series, *The Arthur Haynes Show*, it was written by Speight alone, fast emerging as the most plausible rival in ALS to the four founding fathers. Soon afterwards, Barry was to emigrate to Australia, where he continued to find work writing for television.

Meanwhile Nation, rather than striking out on his own, had formed a new partnership. ('None of them were fully fledged writers, so they gravitated towards each other,' noted Beryl Vertue.) This time it was with two of the newer arrivals at ALS: John Junkin and Dave Freeman. Of the trio, Freeman was significantly the senior. Born in London in 1922, he worked as an electrician before enlisting in the Royal Naval Fleet Air Arm on the outbreak of war. On being demobbed, he had joined the Metropolitan Police, spending some time in the Special Branch, before becoming a security officer at the American Officers' Club in Regent's Park. Throughout this period, he had harboured ambitions of writing, submitting stories to *Lilliput* magazine as early as 1941, while still serving in the Pacific. But it was at the Officers' Club that he found his true calling, involving himself in the booking of entertainment acts and striking up friendships with new comedians, most significantly with Benny Hill. By 1953 he was selling gags to Frank Muir, who provided him with the encouragement to continue, and in September 1955, having contributed material to Hill's television series and to the Terry Scott and Bill Maynard vehicle *Great Scott − It's Maynard*, he abandoned his existing career path and joined ALS as a full-time writer. 'He was quite gentle,' recalled Ray Galton, 'a tall fellow, big bloke.'

So too was Junkin, who like Nation and Freeman was well over six foot tall. Born in 1930, the son of a London policeman, Junkin had spent three years as a teacher in an East End primary school, though his career in education ended with an incident when he saw a boy in the back row chewing gum. Calling the child to the front, he issued the familiar instruction, 'In the bin!', and was horrified at the extent of his own power when the boy misunderstood and climbed into the bin, looking humiliated, resentful and hurt. Concluding that he 'was not cut out for the teaching profession', Junkin took up dead-end jobs to allow him time to try writing. Following the same path claimed by Nation, he wrote a script for *The Goon Show* and submitted it to Spike Milligan. Milligan's response was sufficiently favourable − 'I think you can write and I think you should' − that Junkin too ended up on the agency's books.

In January 1956 the new team of Nation, Junkin and Freeman had a meeting with Alastair Scott Johnston at the BBC to pitch an idea for a radio comedy they had devised, to be titled *The Fixers*. The stories would centre on a trio of characters: Colonel Harry Lashington, his cockney manservant Herbert Cooper (or perhaps Collins, the proposal gives both names) and a fiercely patriotic Welshman named David Owen Glendower, who 'is intensely proud of his family tree, which he can trace back as far as his parents'. Together, they seek to right wrongs, motivated by 'a strong sense of moral justice', though 'unfortunately they have more enthusiasm than good judgement' and are liable to 'insist on helping their fellow men whether their help is wanted or not'. The suggested storylines included the rebuilding of a house for an old lady who can't get her landlord to do any repairs (though they get the wrong house), and the rescuing of a Victorian music hall comedian who was lost in the Amazonian jungle in 1901 (and doesn't want rescuing); they return him to civilisation, 'well, not quite civilisation, but show business'.

The fact that each of the three central characters sounds as if he could be played by one of the writers might suggest that they were keen to be behind the microphones themselves, but Nation's covering letter to Johnston made clear that this was not the case, as well as outlining the 'cinematic technique' they wanted to use: 'We feel that it is essential that a show of this sort should be performed without an audience. The construction of the show will depend not upon gags but situations. Using actors rather than comedians, we feel it would be dangerous to hope to influence the audience who are notoriously "idea killers". We hope to experiment to some degree with recorded background music, and with your assistance, microphone techniques which emphasise voice.' And they provided a wish-list for the cast they would have liked to see, all the names being up-and-coming actors with some experience behind them: Dennis Price as Lashington, Bill Owen or Dick Emery as Herbert, and – a star of *Welsh Rarebit* – Anthony Oliver as Glendower, with either Kenneth Kendall or Robin Boyle as the announcer.

It was an intriguing proposal, and some way ahead of its time. Though writers were beginning to acquire star status, comedy shows were still at this stage built around comedians. It was to be six years before the practice of using actors in sitcoms became fashionable, with the television series *The Rag Trade* (written by Ronald Chesney and Ronald Wolfe) and with Galton and Simpson's pilot for what turned out to be *Steptoe and Son*. For three virtually unknown writers to be making such a suggestion revealed considerable self-assurance. So too did the idea of doing away with a studio audience altogether; there had been a few radio comedy series without an audience, such as the Marx Brothers-inspired *Danger – Men At Work*, first broadcast in 1939, but they were very much the exception rather than the rule. In an attempt to head off any doubts arising from these innovations, Nation was quick to add that 'we have devised this as a low budget show, which we trust will be a point in its favour'. Even so, the confidence was impressive, and perhaps reflected the support they found at ALS, as well as a sense that anything was possible. These were young men, seeking to make their mark on the world with the encouragement of older-brother figures. 'We were beginning to sense our own importance,' noted John Antrobus, another of the ALS new boys. 'We were going to kick the rest of the Fifties up the arse and start a New Decade.' As Beryl Vertue pointed out: 'They were unafraid because they didn't know what to be afraid of.'

If in retrospect the basic set-up of *The Fixers* sounds like an early try-out for the 1970s television comedy *The Goodies*, the initial concern at the time was that it smacked rather too much of *The Goon Show*. Nation, however, reassured Johnston that Spike Milligan had seen the revised synopsis and 'sees no similarity to his show at all'. Suitably impressed, Johnston passed the proposal on up the BBC hierarchy, explaining that it came from 'Terry Nation, one of the Frankie Howerd writers, plus two new assistants, Dave Freeman, who has some experience of TV writing, and John Junken [*sic*], who is more or less new,' and suggesting that 'the idea is worthy of serious consideration'.

How much consideration it actually received is unknown, but the proposal was rejected, and *The Fixers* never came into being. In its place the three writers were put on a completely different project, though in the meantime they had received their first commission in a more direct manner: in February 1956 ALS engaged them 'to script material for two shows for the Peter Sellers series *Idiot Weekly*' at a fee of £150 per script 'to cover all interests'. (The commissioning letter carefully pointed out that the writers were still liable for the ten per cent agency fees from this sum.) The sketch show involved was more properly titled *The Idiot Weekly, Price 2d* and ran in the London region for just five episodes in the spring of 1956. Made by Associated-Rediffusion, which held the ITV weekday franchise for London at the time, it was directed by Richard Lester, starred Spike Milligan and Eric Sykes as well as Sellers, and was the first time that the Goons' humour was explored on screen. The writing was credited simply to Spike Milligan and Associated London Scripts, giving no indication of who was responsible for what, but the fact that Nation, Junkin and Freeman were invited to contribute at all was an indication of their acceptance within ALS. Junkin even appeared in one episode, deputising for an ill Sykes.

The BBC offer that emerged from the failure of *The Fixers* was to write a new series titled *Floggit's*, starring Elsie and Doris Waters in their long-running Cockney characters of Gert and Daisy. The Waters sisters (their brother was Jack Warner, best known as the police officer George Dixon in the television series *Dixon of Dock Green*) had been working as a double-act since the 1920s, and for twenty-five years they had been big stars, appearing regularly in films, on records and on stage, but particularly on the radio: they were regulars on *Workers' Playtime* and headlined series including *Gert and*

Daisy's Wedding Party and *Petticoat Lane*. The sisters had even received OBEs in 1946 in recognition of their contributions to the war effort. Much of their work has survived better than that of their contemporaries, for their rapid crosstalk sketches were mostly written by themselves, as were their songs, and their focus on finding humour in the everyday lives of women, together with the quiet, detailed observation of their character studies, was among the most advanced comedy to be heard.

By the mid 1950s there was a feeling that the homeliness of the act was perhaps turning into blandness, but there was life left in Gert and Daisy yet, and it was proposed that taking them away from their familiar setting in Knockhall Street, London, might help find new comedic possibilities. Nation, Junkin and Freeman were asked in May 1956 to produce a trial script, and when that proved satisfactory, a further fifteen episodes were commissioned. Committed to four months' employment, the trio rented an office in the ramshackle Shepherd's Bush home of ALS and set to work. 'They cleared the potato sacks out of the spare room and put in a table and three chairs, and Terry, David and I moved in there,' remembered Junkin.

They were now firmly part of the ALS world, a convivial society in which the pressures of meeting deadlines didn't interfere with having fun. 'You'd go to lunch when you wanted, you'd go home when you wanted. You knew what you had to do, but how you did it was up to you,' said Junkin. 'There were days when some of us never got much work done before lunchtime,' remembered another writer, Brad Ashton. 'So in Terry Nation's office – which was quite a long office with a long strip of green carpet down the middle – we might play golf for about an hour or so, then we'd go into Lew Schwartz's office – he had a big dartboard on his wall – where we'd play darts for another hour, and then we'd go to lunch.' Lunch itself could stretch out until, fuelled by cigarettes and alcohol, the writers would resume a work programme that might last well into the evening; Milligan in particular was known to work so late that he ended up sleeping in his office.

Floggit's, the series created by Nation, Junkin and Freeman during those late nights and between those long lunches, was based on the premise of Gert and Daisy inheriting from their Uncle Alf a general store – after which the show was named – set in the fictional village of Russet Green. There was, however, a snake in this rural paradise: 'We expected life to be a bed of roses, and what turns up but deadly nightshade in person, Old Mother Butler.' The gossipy, small-minded Ma Butler, played then as now by Iris

Vandeleur, had been a regular antagonist of the pair and she was to remain their chief foe in the village, the butt of many of Daisy's jokes. (Gert would have joined in but she was always a little slower on the uptake.) Beyond her, the series was crammed full of incidental characters played by an impressive cast that included Hugh Paddick, Kenneth Connor, Ron Moody, Anthony Newley and Ronnie Barker, the latter appearing for the first time as Ronnie, rather than Ronald.

Best of all was Joan Sims, fresh from her role as a nurse nicknamed Rigor Mortis in the 1954 Dirk Bogarde film *Doctor in the House*. In *Floggit's* she played a variety of parts from Ma Butler's sidekick, Emma Smeed, through to a sickly sweet little girl – in the same lineage as Monica in *Educating Archie* and Jennifer in *Ray's a Laugh* – who lisped her way through soppy stories about her life ('I've been down in the meadows talking to the squirrels and bunny rabbits'), but still managed to con Gert and Daisy out of money at every opportunity. Somewhere in between was an outrageously flirtatious barmaid, Greta, whose banter hinted at an impressive level of sexual promiscuity, and who got many of the best lines. 'What do men talk about when they're together?' she asks a regular customer. When he replies, 'I don't know, the same as women, I suppose,' she is deeply shocked: 'Well, you should be ashamed of yourselves!'

Like *Hancock's Half Hour*, now the most popular comedy on air, *Floggit's* was a continuous thirty-minute programme without benefit of musical interludes (previously the bane of radio comedy shows), and was broadly a situation comedy, though there were some breaks from the storyline: Greta, for example, never meets Gert and Daisy, and plays no part in the plots, her contributions being simply stand-alone sketches. The stories themselves were vanishingly simple – a tree outside the shop becomes unstable and needs to be chopped down, they take in a stray dog who they nickname 'Orrible (played by Peter Hawkins) – but there was a gentleness and charm to the proceedings which has lasted well, even if it was considerably more mainstream than the material that Nation, Junkin and Freeman had wanted to write for *The Fixers*. And there were some good jokes, often referencing contemporary popular culture (the sisters have a couple of chickens named Marilyn and Sabrina, with the latter jealous of the former), while Daisy is always capable of coming up with epigrams that are slightly more acerbic than they appear at first sight: 'Bonfire night's no good without fireworks,' she observes. 'It's like television without Richard Dimbleby.' There was also – surely one of Nation's contributions – the story of a Welsh perfumer trying to sell a new range of scents, including Evening in Caerphilly, Moon over Tonypandy and Ashes of Anthracite.

The series was produced initially by Alastair Scott Johnston and then by Bill Gates, and although it didn't win any critical plaudits ('All they have to say is "Nice cupper tea," or "On your way, Stirling Moss" to a bus driver, and the audience roars like a giant being tickled,' wrote Paul Ferris disparagingly in the *Observer*), it proved a popular success. The first run was followed by a Christmas special and, in 1957, by a second series of eighteen shows, for which Ronnie Barker and Anthony Newley were dropped from the cast, allegedly because the stars felt they were getting too many laughs.

In between those two series, Dave Freeman had found more lucrative work. The first series of *The Benny Hill Show* on BBC television in 1955 had been a major hit – Hill was named Personality of the Year in the National Television Awards – and for the second series of six hour-long shows, starting in January 1957, he called in Freeman to act as his official co-writer, a partnership that was to last into the 1960s and produce some of the most inventive visual gags of the early television era. Freeman did return to the fold for the second series of *Floggit's*, but thereafter his path diverged from that of Nation and Junkin, and he went on to specialise in writing television shows for comedians including Sid James, Jimmy Edwards, Charlie Drake and Arthur Askey, as well as scripting *Carry On Behind*, one of the later entries in the long-running film series.

In Freeman's absence, Nation and Junkin formed a more stable pairing, though their first step together was more of a stumble. In 1956 Alastair Scott Johnston had produced a Sunday night variety show titled *Calling the Stars*, and when new writers were required for the second series, he had recommended Nation and Junkin. By the time the first scripts were submitted, however, a new producer had taken over. John Simmonds (later to produce *Round the Horne*) was far from impressed by the material he received in January 1957, and rejected it as being simply unfunny. He also implied that he felt a little cheated by the absence of Freeman, who he had expected to be part of the team. At this point Spike Milligan, whose deep distrust of the BBC was by now approaching paranoia, involved himself in the issue, and it took Beryl Vertue's conciliatory intervention to find a way forward. Nation and Junkin were given twenty-four hours to produce a rewrite of the first episode, with a guarantee from ALS that Milligan, Galton and Simpson would all look at the script before it was resubmitted. This having been done, the writers withdrew from the show at their own request, and Ronald Wolfe was appointed in their place.

But Milligan couldn't quite let the matter drop, writing to Simmonds after the broadcast: 'I should like you to know that the material which Peter Sellers did so uproariously well on your *Calling the Stars* programme, was written by the writers (John Junkin and Terry Nation) who were elbowed out of your programme as not quite up to it. Somebody's wrong.' Simmonds's response was a masterly piece of barbed criticism: 'May I say how wonderful I think Peter Sellers is, to be able to get a laugh by making a funny noise, having only said "Good evening, ladies and gentlemen". I am sure you understand what this remark means.'

This hiccup did nothing to dissuade Alastair Scott Johnston from promoting his protégés, and later in 1957 he commissioned Nation and Junkin to write the new series of the popular *Variety Playhouse*, providing continuity material for the show's host, the comedian Ted Ray, as well as a weekly sketch. And despite Ray's reputation as an easy-going, family-orientated comedian, there was a slightly darker side to some of the material than might have been expected, a hint of bleakness behind the gags. 'Then came the great day,' reminisced Ray in a routine about his wartime exploits. 'They were going to drop me into France. We waited by the plane. It was a beautiful British summer's night – you could hear the owls coughing with bronchitis.'

As a further sign of his confidence, Johnston recommended that the two writers should, on the basis of their work thus far, be given a long-term contract by the BBC. It took nine months for the suggestion to be fully considered, but in June 1958 they were signed up to a year's contract, with an option to renew, guaranteeing them a minimum payment of 2,000 guineas, their actual fee being calculated at 85 guineas for each half-hour show. (This put them marginally above the average annual salary of non-manual male workers.) In the meantime, Nation and Junkin had scripted a new series of *Fine Goings On*, the show that had given Frankie Howerd his first headlining role when broadcast back in 1951. Then it had been written by Eric Sykes, Howerd's first and finest collaborator, but the 1958 series was less impressive (a typical gag ran: 'We can't go to the Costa Brava.' 'Why not?' 'Because of the costa living!') and certainly less well received, with the *Observer*'s Paul Ferris – the only radio critic on a national newspaper who paid any attention to such shows – again unimpressed by the writing: 'His script would disgrace a small pier on a wet Monday.'

Nation and Junkin's BBC contracts were not renewed when they lapsed at the end of May 1959, and – although they contributed some material for a new young comic, Harry Worth – there had been a sense during that twelve-month period that there was a shortage of projects for the two writers to work on; among other attempts, Beryl Vertue tried to get them a job on the Terry-Thomas radio series *London Lights*, but made no progress.

In fact there was to be just one more radio show to come from Nation and Junkin. The 1961 series *It's a Fair Cop* starred Eric Sykes as a police constable at the rural Blossom Hill station, with Hattie Jacques playing his sister – the same combination that had just completed the fourth series of the highly acclaimed television sitcom *Sykes and a . . .* They were joined by Deryck Guyler as the sergeant and by Dick Emery as an habitual prisoner who, like Harry Grout in the 1970s series *Porridge*, has made himself fully at home. 'He has been in and out for a long time,' noted the *Radio Times*'s preview of the show, 'and so has learnt to make himself comfortable with the armchair and television set provided by his solicitous gaolers.' The same article did the series no favours by claiming that it would appeal to fans of *Dixon of Dock Green*: 'It may be pure coincidence, but the setting for Eric's radio series bears a striking resemblance to Dock Green.'

Yet again, Paul Ferris was less than enthusiastic: 'There is funny Ealing-film-type music going oompah-oompah, and the script says things like "You're late." – "That's no reason for putting my sausages in the cornflakes." In desperation the writers use an astonishing number of tiny scenes, each barely supported by the basic competence of actors, certainly not by the jokes.' He was a little harsh in not recognising the acting talent of Jacques at least, who provided a splendidly inhospitable landlady: 'I want you to treat it like it was your own 'ome. No cooking in the room, no pets, no musical instruments, no visitors after six in the evening.' She exits with a parting shot at her new guests: 'I'll leave you to settle in. If there's anything you want – get it yourself!'

The fact that Nation and Junkin were producing material for Sykes, who was not only a founder of ALS but one of the very best writers in the business, was clearly occasioned by him being overstretched with his commitments to the television series. 'Because of the voracious appetite of radio and television,' he later noted, 'once accepted as a reliable writer you were forever swimming, with no time to tread water.' The invitation to work for him was nonetheless to be seen as a compliment, and Junkin's memory of the series was a positive one: 'It did okay. It got a nice, warm reaction and pretty decent ratings, and I think we would probably have done more than one series had Eric's TV series not been such a big hit so quickly.'

By this stage, the pair had effectively turned their backs on radio and – a little way behind Nation's former co-writers, Dick Barry and Dave Freeman – were focused now on television work, where the prospects were greater and the money was better. The shift in power in the broadcast media was already clear, but in case anyone was in any doubt about who now called the shots, there had been a symbolic changing of the guard in February 1957 when the *Radio Times* was redesigned so that instead of the radio schedule preceding that of the television, the order was reversed. Four years later a further, more subtle change made the same point. The magazine had previously run from Sunday to Monday, giving primacy to the Sabbath, the observance of which had been so important to John Reith; now it capitulated to television's love of the weekend, and started its listings on Saturday. The effect of the rise of television on the other dominant form in popular culture was still more devastating. In 1950 there were 1,400 million cinema admissions in Britain; ten years later that total had collapsed to just 500 million. During the same period, the number of television licences increased by ten million, while those for radio (the radio licence was not abandoned until 1970) fell dramatically. Television, clearly, was the medium of the future.

The first breakthrough for Nation and Junkin – excluding their contributions to *The Idiot's Weekly, Price 2d* – came in December 1957 with the one-off show *Friday the 13th*, starring Ted Ray, with whom they had just worked on *Variety Playhouse*. When he returned with his regular television series, *The Ted Ray Show*, the following year, they were retained as writers, and were primarily responsible for seven hour-long editions, though three sketches were contributed separately by Dave Freeman. Another involved in the series was a BBC staffer named David Whitaker; then a light entertainment script editor, he would later emerge as a significant figure in Nation's story. As well as script editing, Whitaker contributed lyrics to some of the songs used in the show. Audience research carried out by the BBC on 22 November 1958 indicated that the series was proving popular. The reaction index gave it a score of 74, some way above the average of 67 that was expected of a Saturday night light entertainment show, and the report noted: 'The script, too, was commended as being witty and topical.'

The series was produced by George Inns, who was also responsible for a couple of one-off programmes by the Scottish comedian Jimmy Logan, then the biggest live draw in Glasgow. When the comic was given his own twelve-part series by the BBC in 1959, Inns brought in Nation and Junkin to write the shows, since Logan had already exhausted his existing stock of material. As with *Calling the Stars*, however, a change in producer was to cause problems. Inns became fully occupied with *The Black and White Minstrel Show*, which he had brought to the screen and which had become an unlikely success story (Stan Stennett was one of the resident comedians), and he passed over production duties on Logan's series to Bryan Sears, the man behind Morecambe and Wise's notoriously disastrous show *Running Wild* five years earlier.

The Jimmy Logan Show was to fare little better, at least if its star was to be believed. Logan was deeply unhappy with the change in personnel, and came to see the producer as an enemy and saboteur: 'He didn't like me, so he had decided to do his best to make my show as bad as possible.' Nor was he overly impressed with the material he was offered. 'They made me sick because every single one was terrible, and obviously terrible,' he commented of the first batch of scripts. 'A good comedian can make good comedy out of a bad situation, but these scripts were way beyond salvage.' For the last four editions, new writers were brought in, though with the benefit of hindsight, Logan's biggest regret over the whole affair was that he didn't walk out halfway through filming the series, as his misery deepened. The consequence was, he claimed, that 'it took me at least two years to re-establish my credibility outside Scotland.' Nonetheless, he returned to BBC television in October 1961 with a one-off 45-minute special. Although there was a new producer, the script was again by Nation and Junkin.

These ventures into television had been a moderate success and had provided an income, but they had hardly set the country alight. Nor had they provided much creative satisfaction for their writers. As an alternative, in the summer of 1960, Nation, Junkin and Johnny Speight approached the BBC with a new proposal for a series to be titled *Comedy Playhouse*, an anthology strand which would feature one-off sitcoms from a variety of writers and starring actors rather than comedians. The suggestion did eventually materialise, some eighteen months later, but in a modified form that dispensed with the multiple authors – instead the sixteen episodes that comprised the first two seasons of *Comedy Playhouse* were all written by Ray Galton and Alan Simpson (and included 'The Offer', which became *Steptoe and Son*). Like *The Fixers*, it was an idea ahead of its time, and clearly one that the BBC felt couldn't be entrusted to unknown writers.

Meanwhile, in the absence of more substantial sustenance, Nation's partnership with John Junkin was withering away. Junkin had already made some appearances as an actor at the Theatre Royal, Stratford East, and in the autumn of 1960 he opened there in a new play, *Sparrers Can't Sing*, opposite Barbara Windsor; he was still in the production when it transferred to the West End. There were a couple of collaborations with Nation yet to come (*It's a Fair Cop*, the special of *The Jimmy Logan Show*), but from now on Junkin was to see his career as being centred on performance and acting as much as it was on writing. He became a regular fixture on British television over the next forty years, playing in both comedy and drama and appearing as himself on game shows.

Meanwhile Nation too was becoming disillusioned with the way his career was failing to make significant advances. On a personal level, he was now happily married to Kathleen Grant, more commonly known as Kate, a classical pianist and the daughter of a Yorkshire miner, whom he had wed in March 1958; their marriage was to last for the remainder of his life. But professionally there was no comparable progress. As the new decade dawned, he could reasonably claim to have paid his dues since coming to London, with over a hundred episodes of radio series and more than a dozen television shows to his name (albeit in partnership with others). And yet he had failed to find an individual voice of his own or a stable vehicle for his talent. The positions of Spike Milligan, Eric Sykes, Ray Galton and Alan Simpson at the top of the ALS tree might have seemed too remote to challenge, but others who had joined the agency around the same time as him were making much greater strides: Johnny Speight with *The Arthur Haynes Show*, Eric Merriman and Barry Took with the hit radio series *Beyond Our Ken*, which would later evolve into *Round the Horne*, and Dave Freeman with television series for Benny Hill and Charlie Drake. Meanwhile Maurice Wiltshire, Lew Schwarz and (until his untimely death in 1959) Larry Stephens were all busily supplying scripts for *The Army Game*, the most popular comedy on ITV.

The failed proposal for *The Fixers* had suggested that Nation was keen to create an original and distinctive show. Instead he was writing for Ted Ray, a man who shared his fondness for Jack Benny and American patter, and who was an engaging and amiable comedian, but one who had no great need for material that would set him apart from his rivals. Ray was essentially a teller of gags, and there was nothing much to separate his jokes from those of other comedians. The BBC contract had not been renewed, and Nation's partners had moved on to other projects. Things weren't going the way he had hoped.

'I was getting into a very depressed state with the feeling that comedy wasn't going the right way – not progressing,' he remembered some years later. 'I felt I'd like to go into drama, and after a heart-searching evening with my wife, I decided to write a television play. I'd finished it in two weeks – a comedy set in Wales called *Uncle Selwyn*.'

Chapter Three

The Lads Themselves

While Terry Nation and John Junkin had been toiling in what was still essentially the variety tradition of light entertainment, there had been a substantial shift in the relative status of the founding members of Associated London Scripts. At the time that Nation joined the agency, there was no doubt that Spike Milligan was the biggest name, writing and starring in Britain's most celebrated comedy, *The Goon Show*. But as the decade wore on, Milligan became increasingly frustrated with the format and with the limitations imposed on him by the BBC: 'I'm the most progressive comedy writer in the country,' he told the press in 1958, 'but they don't want ideas.' And, he added, 'I resent being called a Goon.' Rumours of the demise of *The Goon Show* were already circulating and, although they were a little premature, the programme did finally end in January 1960, with the tenth, rather perfunctory, series. Milligan had until now failed to hit upon a format that would allow him to translate his surreal fantasies into visual expression – despite the brief flourishes of *The Idiot Weekly, Price 2d* and its television sequels, *A Show Called Fred* and *Son of Fred* – and it was unclear where his future path lay.

In the same period, however, the stock of Ray Galton and Alan Simpson had enjoyed a spectacular rise, thanks to their work with Tony Hancock, a comedian who came with a reputation for being extremely demanding of his writers. Back in 1952, when he was still trying to make his mark, Hancock was co-hosting the radio series *Calling All Forces* when he decided that the script, by Bob Monkhouse and Denis Goodwin, was below par. Monkhouse remembered him breaking up the read-through as he stormed out shouting: 'This is shit! And it's written on shit paper so I'll take it away and have a shit and wipe my arse with it!' Shortly afterwards, Monkhouse and Goodwin were replaced by Galton and Simpson, beginning an association with Hancock that would transform the careers of all three men, and in the process change the face of British comedy.

The show they created, *Hancock's Half Hour*, ran on radio from 1954 to 1959, and on television from 1956 to 1960. On both media it was, after a slow start, a huge hit and it elevated Hancock to the position of Britain's most successful comedian. As the show evolved, the attention to detail became ever more profound, and the portrayal of the central character acquired depths that broke new ground for broadcast comedy; the constrained, claustrophobic setting of 23 Railway Cuttings, with its taut relationship between the intellectual and social aspirations of Hancock and the know-your-place attitude of Sid James, set the standard for future British sitcoms. Long before George Costanza tried to pitch the idea of a 'show about nothing' to television executives in the 1990s series *Seinfeld*, Hancock, Galton and Simpson had already mastered the concept on radio with the tedium of 'Sunday Afternoon at Home', and on television with 'The Bedsitter', the latter comprising a full twenty-five minutes of Hancock alone in a single room, trying and failing to keep himself amused. That show came from the final BBC series in 1961, simply titled *Hancock*, which dispensed with Sid James and achieved still greater heights of critical and popular success.

If, for many fans, the radio shows remain the pinnacle of Hancock's career, there is no doubt that the television version made the more influential contribution to the evolution of comedy. The novelty of the format was such that the term 'situation comedy' itself was a recent coinage (its common abbreviation to 'sitcom' was a 1970s development), and there were many who didn't entirely approve of this new concept, among them a correspondent of *The Times*: 'comedians, inclined by stage experience to pack everything they have into a ten-minute act, are driven by television into situation comedy, so that a single idea, which might have burnt out in one incandescent flash, can smoulder on for several weeks.' *Hancock's Half Hour* was the most prominent exception, the show that proved the potential of television as a vehicle for comedy to break finally with the music hall tradition. For now at least, it seemed as though the future lay in the character-based style of Galton and Simpson.

Something of the sort seems to have been in Terry Nation's mind, for when he submitted his play *Uncle Selwyn* to the BBC in 1960, it was as a possible pilot for a six-part series, based around a group of recurrent characters in a very definite historical setting.

The timing was right, for the corporation was, for the first time, in need of new scripts. Television drama on the BBC was, in its early days, firmly rooted in the stage, so that, for example, regulations insisted on a break of five minutes between the acts of a broadcast play, mimicking the conventions of the theatre. These gaps were filled with the much-loved 'interlude' films: restful shots of a windmill, a kitten playing with a ball or, most famously, a potter's wheel. The material was similarly dependent on remaking the classics and, particularly, on bringing in existing theatrical productions; new work tended to mean plays that had only recently debuted in the West End. The same policy had applied for three decades on radio,' but while the arrangement worked for both sides – the box-office success of John Osborne's *Look Back in Anger* was the result of an extract being broadcast to five million viewers – it was now starting to look a little unadventurous in contrast with ITV's *Armchair Theatre*, busily blazing a trail for new commissions. In response the corporation was changing its emphasis and in 1959, for the first time, more than half its drama output was written specifically for television.

But even in this propitious climate, *Uncle Selwyn* failed to make the right impression; it was rejected by both the light entertainment department in 1960 and, the following year, by the script department. Meanwhile the head of programmes in Wales concluded that it was 'too crudely farcical and derivative'. In slightly modified form, however, the piece did eventually appear in the *Play of the Week* strand on ITV in February 1964, coincidentally just after the first Daleks serial had finally made Nation's name.

Set in the aftermath of the First World War, the play told the story of the eponymous Selwyn's return from a German prisoner-of-war camp to his home village of Pontynarvon in the Rhondda Valley, where he discovers that he's inherited his father's oil-lamp shop. (His father, we learn, has been killed by a runaway beer barrel – it rolled into his shop, he drank the contents and died in a drunken stupor.) Unfortunately he also discovers that, in his absence, 'the colliery owners put the electric in all the houses', and that the demand for oil lamps is now virtually non-existent. In an attempt to make some money, he rents out his back room to a group of old men who, he learns by accident, are actually a secret society of anarchists plotting a bomb attack on London. Seeing his chance, he joins the group and steals their bomb so that he can blow up the local power station, in order to revitalise the market for oil lamps.

The cast included Mervyn Jones, John Glyn-Jones and Talfryn Thomas, while Selwyn himself was played by Tony Tanner, a stage actor who had taken over the starring role in Anthony Newley's West End musical *Stop the World – I Want to Get Off* on Newley's departure for the Broadway production, but who thus far had little television experience. His performance was praised by the critics and, according to the preview publicity, he relished the part: 'At first Selwyn seems to be all sweetness and naivety with a determination to please. But when it comes to it and Selwyn conceives his devious plan, far from being conscience-stricken, he carries it through without a qualm. In fact, with a good deal of enthusiasm.' His real feelings were considerably less positive: 'The play sucked, I almost fell asleep in rehearsal and the director was no fucking good.'

Nation was later to claim that the piece 'proved very successful' and was 'incredibly well received', but his memory was playing him slightly false. The *Guardian*'s television critic, Mary Crozier, couldn't work out whether it was supposed to be a comedy or a farce. 'It was a queer jumble, and its lack of form and drive made it often just a farrago of rather boring dialogue,' she wrote. 'Like so many plays on television this never got a grip, because it was impossible to believe in the plot or the people, and not all the Welsh accents or the character acting could pick it up and put it on its feet.' Disillusioned by the increasing trend towards new works for television, she yearned to turn back the clock: 'Why don't the companies and BBC do more of the many good plays that have been written already, that is from the established repertory of drama for the stage?' The *Daily Mirror*, on the other hand, was more taken with *Uncle Selwyn*: 'Some of the humour was well in period, smelling of old chestnuts, but the comedy and farce were as continuous as the soft rain on a chapel roof. The fault lay in the many characters who swallowed each other up: no one stood out as a peg on which to hang the main theme of the action.' The reviewer concluded: 'I look forward to more of Mr Nation's humour – but less confused, please, next time by too many actors trying to get a word in edgeways.'

All of this, however, was for the future. In 1961, with the play having been rejected by the BBC, with John Junkin increasingly committed to his acting career, and with only the brief run of *It's a Fair Cop* to sustain him, Nation needed work. He found it in the unlikely shape of a film screenplay for Adam Faith.

Faith was by this stage perhaps the biggest pop star in the country (or at least, according to the *New Musical Express*, he ranked alongside Cliff Richard and Lonnie Donegan as one of 'the big three') and, despite his rather lightweight hit singles, he was emerging as something genuinely new in

British rock and roll: an intelligent, articulate, sharply dressed performer who was taken seriously by the artistic establishment. The director Lindsay Anderson wanted him to appear in a production at the Royal Court Theatre in London, he won over his critics with an interview on the prestigious John Freeman show *Face to Face*, where he enthused about J.D. Salinger and Jean Sibelius, and he received the ultimate cultural accolade of a reference in 'The Blood Donor', the best-known episode of Tony Hancock's career. 'There's Adam Faith earning ten times as much as the prime minister. Is that right?' reflected Hancock. 'Mind you, I suppose it depends on whether you like Adam Faith and what your politics are.'

Faith also harboured ambitions of being a serious actor and sidestepped the standard movie format offered to pop singers – star mimes a handful of hits while trying to save the local youth club from greedy property developer – in favour of more intriguing film choices: the Soho exploitation classic *Beat Girl* (1960, US title: *Wild for Kicks*) and the Peter Sellers vehicle *Never Let Go* (1960), in which he played a petty thief. His third film was perhaps less impressive, but it did have its moments.

What a Whopper was credited as having a screenplay by Terry Nation, 'based on an idea by Trevor Peacock and Jeremy Lloyd', though in truth the idea is wafer thin. Faith plays a struggling writer whose latest attempt at a novel has just been returned by yet another publisher. Figuring that his story of the Loch Ness Monster will stand a better chance if there's a new sighting of the creature, he fakes a photograph and sets off to Scotland with a few friends, taking with him a tape of an electronically generated roar which he intends to play at full volume in the vicinity of the loch. Into this is woven, none too subtly, a sub-plot about the landlord of a guesthouse trying to keep the fruits of his salmon poaching from the local police, while further complications come from the aristocratic and alcoholic father of one of the women accompanying Faith, who mistakenly believes that she's eloped (though Loch Ness is a considerable overshoot by anyone aiming at Gretna Green). Much comedy confusion, many mistaken identities and some simple knockabout humour ensue.

The film's producer, Teddy Joseph, was later to declare that *What a Whopper* was 'a marvellous family comedy', though that was a little over-generous. More accurate was *Variety*'s comment that 'the British appetite for this type of unpretentious, slapstick comedy appears to be insatiable.' Faith himself, who celebrated his twenty-first birthday during filming, was apparently not too taken with the end result, for he managed to avoid any mention of it in his autobiography; his 2003 obituary in the *Independent* was more forthcoming, dismissing the movie as 'dire'. That was unkind and not entirely accurate, for there is much that followers of British comedy can celebrate, as one would expect from a cast that included Sid James, Wilfred Brambell, Terry Scott and Clive Dunn, accompanied by Freddie Frinton giving his customary portrayal of a drunk. There is also a cameo by Spike Milligan, as a tramp fishing for trout in the Serpentine in Hyde Park, and best of all a brief but fabulous appearance by Charles Hawtrey as an artist who is developing a technique of flinging paint off his palette-knives at a canvas, titled 'Daphne in the Nude'. When he's described as a painter, he bristles at the suggestion: 'Not just a painter,' he insists haughtily. 'A flicking painter.' The opening sequences meanwhile foreshadow what would soon become clichés of Swinging London, with a depiction of artistic types sharing a house in Chelsea; virtually the first words uttered by Faith are: 'I saw a couple of fabulous birds on the King's Road.'

It was not quite Nation's first foray into the cinema, for he and John Junkin had provided what was described as 'additional material' for the 1959 film *And the Same to You*, a similarly patchy movie that is saved by its cast: Sid James, Tommy Cooper, Brian Rix and – a man who would soon loom large in Nation's story – William Hartnell. Nor was it quite his first solo venture, for in 1956 he had written a fifteen-minute sketch for his old Cardiff friend Harry Greene and his wife, Marjie Lawrence, who were fresh from staking their claim to television history as the stars of the soap *Round at the Redways*, the first show made by ITV. Booked to appear in a revue titled *Off the Cuff* at the Irving Theatre in London's West End, they had approached Spike Milligan for a sketch; when his contribution was turned down by the show's producer, the job was passed on to Nation, who delivered within twenty-four hours a routine parodying the movies, drawing on his love of Hollywood. 'Howard and Marjorie Greene performed with as much carefree zing as though the small, cool audience had been huge and enthusiastic,' commented *The Stage*, 'and after their delicious demonstration of the growth of the film industry, it had at least become enthusiastic.'

But *What a Whopper* was Nation's first big solo project and his first full film screenplay. And it revealed some of his strengths as well as some of the flaws that would become familiar to television viewers. On the positive side, there was his Welsh fondness for ornate verbosity, as Wilfred Brambell describes his sighting of the Loch Ness Monster: 'A terrible sight it was. A yellow mist hung over the waters, and a great brooding silence filled the loch. No breath of wind stirred the air, and as I looked towards the black waters, I saw it! Its terrible head rising slowly and turning towards me, its jaws open . . .' There was, too, his refusal to develop a simple situation in a straight line, instead adding new complications at every opportunity, heaping up the material in a way that would find better expression in his thrillers than it did in his comedy. On the negative side, there was a certain loss of concentration, so that later parts of the script start to flounder a little and some loose ends never get tied up (the book that Faith's character was supposed to be promoting, for example, disappears from the story, once it has done its job of taking the cast to Loch Ness). And then there's the inescapable, overt borrowing from others: it would be hard not to see in the early scenes, with Hawtrey's flicking and with parodies of modern sculpture and *musique concrète*, the influence of Tony Hancock's film *The Rebel*, scripted by Galton and Simpson, which had great fun mocking the follies of contemporary art, and which was released just three months before filming started on *What a Whopper*.

The Rebel was in fact the last collaboration between Hancock and the scriptwriters who had worked with him for nearly a decade. Having conquered Britain so completely, Hancock was becoming restless for inter-national acclaim and, particularly, for acceptance in America. The failure of *The Rebel* (unwisely and hubristically retitled *Call Me Genius* for the US market) to achieve that elusive goal led him to believe that he needed to break from his existing persona, to find what he thought of as a more universal comedy, even though – as plenty were prepared to warn him – he ran the extreme risk of losing his own identity in the process. In October 1961, seemingly on the brink of even greater achievements, he bluntly informed Galton and Simpson that the partnership was over: 'I have decided that I don't want to do any more programmes with you.' With all parties recognising that it would be difficult for Hancock to continue to be represented by his existing agent Beryl Vertue, since she also represented the two writers, he became at the same time the client of his younger brother, Roger Hancock, who was an agent and also part of ALS. The break came after six months of trying to develop a film project and was a complete shock. 'We were staggered,' remembered Vertue. 'It was the first time I personally had seen his ruthless quality. He had given no warning and made no apology.' (A decade later, after the sense of betrayal and hurt had diminished, Galton was to reflect that perhaps it wasn't personal: 'all comics loathe their writers'.)

The first project after the split with Galton and Simpson was a movie, *The Punch and Judy Man*, which Hancock co-wrote with Philip Oakes, and which was an artistic, if not a box-office, triumph. When he was then offered a television series by ATV, one of the ITV franchise-holders, he asked Oakes to be the script consultant. But that relationship, like so many others around this time, collapsed under the weight of Hancock's increasingly erratic and autocratic behaviour; he was alcoholic by this stage and his marriage was coming to a difficult and sometimes violent end. 'Without any discussion,' wrote Oakes, 'he commissioned writers and scripts which I thought were below par.' Oakes walked out and, seeking a new writer with whom to work, Hancock alighted on Terry Nation, whom he had encountered in the ALS offices. (These had now moved to 'a more salubrious address in Cumberland House, Kensington High Street', and were soon to move again, even further upmarket, to Orme Court in Bayswater, though Nation did not have an office at this final location.)

The interview process for the new position, conducted at Hancock's house in Surrey, was far from conventional. 'To my amazement all he wanted to do was talk about the universe and what part we played in the cosmic scheme of things,' Nation remembered. 'I had always been interested in science fiction, but Tony's thinking was far more involved, far more philosophical.' Evidently, however, Nation made the grade and, the issue of intellectual compatibility having been established, the two men set to work on a Friday night. They were still going the following Monday morning, when Nation had to return home for a change of clothing, having not slept and having combated the soporific effects of alcohol with uppers taken from Hancock's copious supply of pills. The relationship seemed to work on both sides. 'He was a wonderful audience,' Nation said. 'I would try a joke on him and he would fall off his chair, he thought it was so funny.' The only problem came with trying to pin Hancock down to anything definite: 'When Tony first acted out an idea, we would collapse in giggles. When it was on the page in black and white, he went cold. It was as if the act of writing anything down sparked a huge and lingering doubt, first in the material and then in himself to deliver it.'

In October 1962 Nation accompanied the comedian on a series of week-long theatrical engagements in Southsea, Liverpool and Brighton. Officially his role was that of writer, but Hancock's extreme nervousness about using new material, exacerbated by his dislike of live performances (he woke on the first morning 'visibly shaking and covered in sweat', according to

Nation), meant that very little of the work actually appeared in the show. Instead Hancock reverted to the music hall tradition of repeating the old favourites from his repertoire, and Nation ended up in an unexpected role as companion and nursemaid: 'I had finished the writing and he could have got rid of me at any time. But he was paying me £100 a week virtually to baby-sit with him.'

Nation described his job as properly starting when they got back to the hotel. 'They would leave cold food for us, and some booze, and we'd sit up until about two in the morning. Then we'd go to bed, and he insisted we share a room, so we could go on talking. And we would talk about the meaning of it all, what was it all about, all these things. And I would finally fall asleep, and the next thing it's eight in the morning and he's called for hard-boiled eggs and champagne. That's how the day started and we were off again.' Those all-night discussions would range from ideas for sketches that never materialised right through to the current international situation, at a time when the Cuban missile crisis was causing many, including Hancock, to believe that the third world war was about to break out; like Nation's other comedy mentor, Spike Milligan, he was much troubled by the spectre of nuclear conflict.

On a more personal level, there was the unfortunate incident after the final performance in Liverpool. The party were returning to London on the overnight sleeper train, somewhat the worse for drink, when Nation was awoken by a disturbance in the adjoining compartment occupied by the singer Matt Monro, who had been opening the shows. 'When I got to Matt's compartment, Hancock was naked and cowering in the corner,' recalled Nation, describing the episode as 'more shocking than surprising'. Monro was threatening not only to quit the tour but also to prosecute for sexual assault, and Nation was obliged to calm the situation down. 'I had to work very hard to get him to change his mind. In the end we agreed never to mention the incident again.' Hancock appeared to have no memory of what had transpired, though he was full of his usual apologetic concern the next morning: 'I didn't offend anyone last night, did I?' Nonetheless the story evidently did the rounds of showbiz gossip, for a decade later Kenneth Williams was to record in his diary a conversation with Sid James in which the latter related the anecdote: 'Matt Monro told him he'd woken up one night to find Hancock going down on him for the fellatio, and that Matt had "given him a right-hander".'

The live appearances were supposed to be part of Hancock's preparation for his return to television, some eighteen months after the screening of *Hancock*, his final, triumphant series for the BBC, which had contained such classic episodes as 'The Bowmans', 'The Radio Ham' and 'The Blood Donor'. Nation ended up writing four scripts for the new ITV show, also confusingly titled *Hancock*, and acting in an unofficial script-editing capacity. It was an irresistible opportunity for an ambitious writer – a huge step forward from providing scripts for Ted Ray and Jimmy Logan – but, as everyone recognised, taking on the country's best and best-loved comic was a poisoned chalice.

Quite apart from dealing with Hancock's insatiable pursuit of perfection and his consumption of alcohol and drugs, there was the weight of expectation that came with the job. Even Philip Oakes, who could justifiably point to *The Punch and Judy Man* as one of Hancock's most impressive pieces of work, referred to Galton and Simpson as 'his best-ever scriptwriters', and Nation could only agree: 'I was never, ever as good as Galton and Simpson. They *were* Tony Hancock. He was wrong, in a way, to abandon them.' They cast a very long shadow, out of which no one was ever truly to emerge. As Ray Galton said of those who followed: 'They were on a hiding to nothing. The greatest writer in the world would have a job coming in and assuming someone else's character that had taken nine years to develop.' Nation, of course, was not the greatest comedy writer in the world, but he did rise to the challenge and there were moments on *Hancock* that were of a higher standard than anything he had previously produced.

The series opened on 3 January 1963, and Hancock was in confident mood in that morning's papers. 'I don't want to be quite so common as in East Cheam,' he explained, distancing himself from his earlier incarnation. 'In this series I'm a little more posh. I live on a small allowance from my aunt. But I'm still the same, mate.' The newspapers were also able to report the unfortunate coincidence whereby the second series of Galton and Simpson's new show, *Steptoe and Son*, started on the same night. IT'S HANCOCK V. STEPTOE IN THE BIG FIGHT FOR LAUGHS, read the headline in the *Daily Mail*, though it was not actually a direct clash: *Steptoe* finished at 8.25 p.m., allowing viewers just enough time to make a cup of tea before *Hancock* started at half past eight.

The first episode was 'The Assistant', credited as having a script by Terry Nation with 'original story by Ray Whyberd' (this pseudonym concealing the identity of Ray Alan, better known as the ventriloquist who worked with Lord Charles). Perhaps it was the mixed parentage, but the plot didn't make a great deal of sense. Hancock complains about the rudeness of a shop assistant in a department store and the manager, trying to explain how hard it is for staff to maintain their manners, challenges him to work there for a week without losing his temper; if he is successful, then the long-standing arrears on his account with the store will be cleared. It's a transparent device to put Hancock into a new situation – or rather a sequence of situations, for he goes on to work in three different departments – and even allowing for his desire to change his style, the implausibility of the premise sat ill with everything an audience expected of him. Galton and Simpson had taken great care to ensure that their plots, at least in the latter years, were rigorously logical, rooted in reality; here the business of the wager is so weak that, having kick-started the plot, it isn't referred to again, and the episode ends without reference to who has won the bet. In short, it's a story with a beginning, several middles and no end. Being more charitable, one might view it as a series of sketches rather than a sitcom, though nothing in the rest of the series suggests that this was intentional.

There is also the problem that it is never entirely clear what Hancock's character is. As in the BBC series, he is by turn pompous, boastful, childish, grudging and naïve, but rather disturbingly he's also deliberately and unpleasantly rude to the shop assistant in a way that he never used to be. Insulting Hattie Jacques's character Griselda Pugh in the radio shows never came across as particularly cruel humour, since she was more than prepared to fight back and there was always an implied element if not of friendship, then at least of shared misery. The note struck here, however, is less of banter than of bullying. When the assistant delivers a long litany of sufferings and misfortunes (admittedly in an appalling whine of a voice), he responds not with a joke, or even a putdown, but rather with a blunt and unfunny 'Ah, shut up.' It was an element that made Alan Simpson wince: 'Tony was being unnecessarily nasty. You can't be nasty without a reason and be funny,' he insisted.

Despite the flaws, the show is not a disaster, and there are some decent jokes that work well, capturing the characteristic Hancock phrasing. 'A gentleman never loses his temper. It's a question of good breeding, and you cannot whack good breeding,' he declares, before going on to boast of his pedigree: 'I can go back to Hancock the Red.' 'Who was he?' asks the manager, and Hancock is deflated in the customary manner: 'Well, he was my father actually.' But he swiftly recovers: 'An early communist, you know. Yes, the pater was a great friend of Lenin . . .' And he's off again into fantasy reminiscences.

There's also some fine use of language; Hancock clearly relishes using words like 'deshabille' and 'hoyden' and making reference to a bloater-paste sandwich. Then there's Kenneth Griffith's magnetic appearance as Owen Bowen. 'I'm from the Rhondda Valley, boyo, where the best coal in the world comes from,' he tells Hancock. 'But you wouldn't know where that is, would you? You English, you never know nothing. Sitting in comfort and never a thought for those noble lads sweating away in the bowels of the earth, clawing the coal from the naked rock, risking their lives, working in filth and dirt. Thousands of brave Welsh boys digging coal just to keep you warm.' 'Thousands of them?' retorts Hancock. 'I only use a shovelful a night!'

Later shows by Nation were structurally simpler, with a conventionally circular sitcom narrative, and also contained some nice lines. 'How do you know when a woman is married?' Hancock ponders to himself, answering with perfect logic: 'Her husband comes around and punches you.' (He had not yet embarked on his affair with Joan Le Mesurier, wife of John Le Mesurier, his co-star in *The Punch and Judy Man*.) Indeed some of it could have been vintage Hancock, as when he's browsing through the wine list in a pub: 'Ah, you've got some! Chateau Latour, what a magnificent wine! Some of us bibbers consider it to be the finest claret in the world. Yes, you've got to hand it to these Italians – they do know how to turn out a little bit of plonk. It's something to do with the feet, I suppose.' He asks to see the bottle, lavishes praise on it, and then orders a small brown ale.

That routine had a personal edge to it, drawing on Hancock's own character, for as Philip Oakes pointed out: 'Hancock fancied himself as a wine expert, a role in which he could, at times, become wearisome.' Nation, on the other hand, was an eager student, and was later to admit that in due course he too became 'a wine snob'. Even more personal was the episode 'The Night Out', which opens in a hotel's penthouse suite strewn with the debris of what was clearly a hard-drinking party, as Hancock wakes up with an enormous hangover to deliver lines that Nation had often heard him utter, particularly on the morning after that train journey from Liverpool. 'I didn't insult anybody?' he repeats again and again, seeking reassurance from the entourage he has accumulated in his pub crawl the night before. 'I didn't offend anybody, did I? I mean, I was all right?' The best variation on the theme is a lovely piece of nervous jocularity: 'I do know I can be a bit of a wag when I'm on the milk stout.' Hancock's response on first reading the script, remembered Nation, was a grinning acknowledgement of the truth of the piece: 'You bastard.'

In 'The Writer' Hancock talks his way into becoming the writer for 'Britain's leading funny-man' Jerry Spring (played by John Junkin), who specialises in the American-style patter that Nation grew up with. 'Bob Hope, 1945, word for word!' he exclaims on first seeing Spring's existing act. But he soon discovers that writing comic material, actually putting the words down on paper, is more difficult than he imagined, so much so that he finds himself resorting to stealing gags from an old box of Christmas crackers. It's hard not to see this as being a *cri de coeur* on the part of Nation, an implied rebuke to a comedian who would talk about concepts for sketches all night, so long as the drink was flowing, but who panicked when asked to approve a script.

The first show was widely covered, receiving more first-night notices than anything else that Nation would ever do. The *Guardian*'s Mary Crozier, who would later give *Uncle Selwyn* a pasting, revealed that she was one of the few people, let alone critics, who hadn't appreciated the mundane perfection of Hancock's last few series: 'I have sometimes in the past got tired quickly of Hancock, finding amusement grow less as his predicaments seemed too self-centred,' she admitted. 'In the series on ATV there is more going on than I seem to remember in the last BBC series. If this is "situation comedy" there is a lot of changing situation which is all to the good.' *The Times* was even more enthusiastic: 'It is all very funny, because Mr Hancock is funny, and the material suits him to perfection. If Messrs Simpson and Galton do not need him, he does not need them.' Maurice Richardson in the *Observer* also started with a little, albeit fainter, praise: 'If we had never seen him before, we should probably have hailed his debut in "The Assistant", in which he clowned about a bit behind the scenes of a big store, as distinctly promising. We should have complained of the scrappy hackneyed script and might have suggested that here was perfect material for the more intelligent BBC scriptwriters such as Galton and Simpson.'

But Richardson's conclusion was ominous: 'Perhaps he will recover, and it will be wonderful if he does, but the first of this new series will have to go down in clowning history as a remarkable act of self-sabotage.' And Michael Gowers in the *Daily Mail* went further still: 'The sad, unpalatable truth is that his ATV debut must have left strangers to his enormous talent, if there are any, wondering what all the past stuff has been about.' He ended on a similarly bleak note to that of Richardson: 'My devoutest wish is that he could find himself again, but it is probably already too late.'

Hancock was bullish about the negative critical reception. 'I expected it,' he shrugged. 'The critics seem to resent the fact that I want to progress and try something new. No matter how good the programme might be, they would have attacked me. That is something I have grown to live with and it doesn't bother me. That is because I am satisfied with the series. It is well produced and just as funny as anything I have done on the BBC.' But the public didn't see it that way and the audience declined rapidly. 'The Assistant' was the third most watched programme of the week, but by episode four the show had dropped out of the top twenty and was not to return. To rub salt in the wounds, *Steptoe and Son* continued to ride high, peaking at number two in the ratings.

Having started out with confidence, and having turned in the best performances of which he was capable (his facial reactions to Owen Bowen's tales are as mobile and expressive as ever), Hancock was by now actively contributing to the decline. 'The series was doomed,' remembered Nation. 'Tony wouldn't rehearse and for the first time he was boozing while he was working.' Unable to learn his lines because of the drink, Hancock became ever more dependent on teleprompters, to the extent that by the end of the filming there were said to be more such machines on set than there were cameras. Given the mix of writers – in addition to Nation, Godfrey Harrison contributed six scripts, while Richard Harris and Dennis Spooner co-wrote another three – and considering how poor some of those scripts were, it required a consistently strong central performance by the show's star to keep any semblance of unity and coherence; regrettably he was in no condition to provide it.

There was one more encouraging review to come, from Richard Sear in the *Daily Mirror* following 'The Night Out'. 'My second look at *Hancock* was easier to take than the first,' he wrote. 'The script, by Terry Nation, was not hilarious, nor the situation original, but it let Hancock spread as he woke in an hotel room, wondering where he was, wondering if he was trapped into marriage. Lost, trapped, even haunted, Hancock pressed on, raising a chuckle at regular intervals – and always interesting.' It sounded as though he were describing life rather than art, but in any event his was a lone voice, and Roger Hancock's memories of the series were more typical and more pertinent. 'There were no happy moments,' he said. 'And also it wasn't very good. The public are not idiots. They were right.'

Though the series was a flop, little blame could be attached to Nation. Faced with the prospect of writing for Hancock, he had raised his game and, if his scripts weren't as good as those of Galton and Simpson, then at least they were as good as he could make them in the circumstances. But the whole episode did nothing to help his career in the immediate future. Indeed the taint of being associated with such a public failure may have been detrimental: no further offers of work developed and, although Hancock was paying well, there was still no financial stability. On a creative level, however, it had been an invaluable experience; writing two hours of material for such a painstaking and obsessive comedian had given him a renewed self-confidence, evident in those scripts where he was prepared to laugh at Hancock's foibles. The long hours of drinking and talking in hotel rooms had moreover allowed him extraordinary access to the mind of a man who had so recently been Britain's most adept television performer. In the longer term, the benefits were clear, both in the growth of his writing and in the status he acquired. 'I was very proud to have worked with him,' Nation commented in later years. Had he done nothing of note afterwards, the association with Hancock would still have accorded him a place in British entertainment history.

And, testament to his easy-going nature, he had managed to remain on good terms with Hancock, which would have been something of an achievement at this stage even if they hadn't been surrounded by the wreckage of a failed television series. The professional and personal relationship continued beyond the end of the show and in the spring of 1963 the two men, accompanied by their respective wives, Cicely and Kate, departed for a holiday in the south of France, where Hancock kept a yacht.

It was, recalled Nation, 'a strange three weeks'. Cicely was by this stage drinking as frequently and excessively as Tony, and both were using tranquillisers in an attempt to numb the pain of their collapsing marriage. The two couples shared a cabin, and the Nations were kept awake much of the night by the sounds of the Hancocks arguing and fighting. Among Nation's most vivid memories of the holiday was a pathetic scene on the yacht as a collective attempt was made to teach a parrot the Stanley Holloway refrain 'Brown Boots': 'Hancock in rags crouched with a bottle of booze and a glass, and me crouched beside him looking just as bad, and the girls looking pretty terrible crouched nearby, and all of us singing "Brown Boots" to the parrot.'

Chapter Four

Into the Unknown

Just four months separated the broadcasting of the final episode of *Hancock* from Terry Nation's creation of the Daleks. But the change of direction was not quite as abrupt as it might appear, for there had been precedents, both direct and indirect, and there was a reservoir of work on which he could draw.

There had been, even during his years of writing comedy, the influence of Spike Milligan, whose scripts for *The Goon Show* took up the nonsense tradition in British humour and extended it to the point of pure fantasy. The fourth series of the show, for example, broadcast during Nation's last year in Cardiff, included episodes such as 'Through the Sound Barrier in an Airing Cupboard', 'The First Albert Memorial to the Moon' and 'Ten Thousand Fathoms Down in a Wardrobe', titles that indicated a blend of absurdism and what would – in other circumstances – be considered science fiction. When interviewed at the time, Milligan was keen to expound his theory of Dimensionalism, arguing that the listener 'is in a dream world, where the rigid dimensions of time-space unity need not confine him'. The free rein he thus gave to his imagination was not far removed from Nation's own comment: 'The wonderful thing about science fiction is that if the author says a thing is so, then nobody can deny it.' Writing patter for Ted Ray might not have given Nation much scope for such adventures, but the proposal for *The Fixers* made it clear that Milligan's work had helped shape his ideas of what was possible in comedy.

More immediately obvious, there had been, as Nation tried to find work as a solo writer, a transition period of scripting science fiction and non-genre drama that predated his involvement with Tony Hancock and that was to extend beyond it. Though not a phase of his career on which he tended to dwell in later life, it contributed markedly to the range of his writing, and it gave him a grounding in contemporary science fiction. None of the programmes have survived (in common with so much from the era, copies were not kept), but they were significant both in their own right and in terms of their influence on Nation's later work. And it's notable that, following his disappointment with the BBC over the rejection of *Uncle Selwyn*, this opportunity to find a new direction came not from the corporation that had nurtured him, but from ITV.

The launch of independent television in Britain in September 1955, though widely reported in the national press, was not actually a national phenomenon. London was the only region capable of receiving the service at that stage, and it took several years before the availability of programmes spread through the entire country. Even at the start of the 1960s some outlying regions, including the north of Scotland and south-west England, weren't covered, and only in 1962 were the Channel Islands and north Wales finally included in the exciting new world of two-channel television. After a hesitant few months, however, the experience everywhere was the same; in each new region that it reached, ITV had an enormous and virtually instantaneous impact. By 1957 the new channel was attracting a seventy-nine per cent share of the viewing audience in those areas where it could be seen, and was claiming that in London, of the 542 programmes that made the top ten that year, the BBC was responsible for just three. The experience was strongly reminiscent of Radio Luxembourg's success in the 1930s, when the BBC had been similarly eclipsed by an upstart rival.

The public's enthusiastic embrace of the alternative offered to them was evidently a response to ITV's populist stance, its deliberate departure from the paternalism that still pervaded the BBC twenty years on from John Reith's 'I do not pretend to give the public what it wants'. The commercial channel, receiving no money from the sale of radio and television licences, could afford no such lofty disdain for its viewers' taste; its task was to deliver the largest possible audience so that advertisers would wish to invest their money, thus ensuring the survival of the service. 'This is free television in a free country,' insisted Sir Robert Fraser, director general of the Independent Television Authority (ITA), 'and people will get the television they want, as they get the press and government they want.'

Inevitably there was, in the circles of the great and the good, much criticism of allegedly low standards, particularly when the report of the Pilkington Committee on broadcasting was published in 1962; too heavy a reliance, it was said, on game shows, variety entertainment, American westerns and cheap and cheerful swashbuckling dramas. In pursuit of an audience, however, ITV also demonstrated in its early days a willingness to take risks that the BBC conspicuously shunned. It had the best rock and roll shows in Jack Good's *Oh Boy!* and later in *Ready Steady Go*, it commissioned avant-garde comedy such as *The Idiot's Weekly, Price 2d*, and it took a chance on oddities like Gerry Anderson's puppet science fiction shows. It also ended the BBC's deferential – sometimes even craven – handling of politicians, setting new standards for political coverage. Even when it came to highbrow programming, it had a record to be proud of, giving Sir Kenneth Clark, the founding chairman of the ITA, free rein to produce arts documentaries long before he made the celebrated series *Civilisation* for the BBC, and introducing the brilliant history lectures of A.J.P. Taylor (again subsequently to be poached by the BBC). Perhaps most significant of all, the independent franchise company ABC recruited to head its drama department Sydney Newman, a man who – among all his other achievements – was to play a crucial role in Terry Nation's career.

Newman was one of the most charismatic and divisive figures in British television over the span of a decade to the end of the 1960s, a big enough character both to hold his own in the frontier years of ITV and to ruffle establishment feathers at the BBC. Peter Luke, a script editor who worked with him, described him as 'a cross between Genghis Khan and a pussy cat', while another colleague, Leonard White, saw him as 'the non-conformist outsider', adding: 'Sydney was noisy. And unsubtle.' Moustachioed and bow-tied, he was more impresario than tycoon, 'a suave character,' according to the *Observer*, 'with a strong line in gently outrageous conversation, whose appearance and purring voice suggest a Tennessee Williams gone right'. The value of his work was even more hotly disputed; according to the *Daily Mail* in 1962, 'to some he was the great impresario of commercial television, to others the purveyor of pretentious pigswill.' There was no question, though, that he changed completely the nature of television drama in Britain, and that he brought to the screen two of the most iconic series of the 1960s: *The Avengers* and *Doctor Who*.

Newman had formerly been responsible for drama at the Canadian Broadcasting Corporation, where he had promoted the work of young writers including the future novelist Arthur Hailey and Bernard Slade (later to give us *The Partridge Family*), and had been part of the great era of television plays in North America in the mid 1950s. Arriving in 1958 to take over the existing ABC series *Armchair Theatre*, he began by exploring the London stage having, on an earlier visit, been to the Royal Court to see John Osborne's *Look Back in Anger*, a play whose claustrophobic domesticity and dissatisfaction with modern Britain was not dissimilar to that of *Hancock's Half Hour*, though without the jokes. (Ray Galton and Alan Simpson paid tribute in a radio parody with Hancock entitled 'Look Back in Hunger'.) Enthused by the possibilities that such an intimate and direct style of drama offered for television, Newman began to commission new work by the likes of Alun Owen, Harold Pinter and Angus Wilson. 'The policy I adopted for *Armchair Theatre* was to do plays about contemporary Britain,' he was later to explain. 'No adaptations from theatre or literary sources were wanted. The plays had to be fast and exciting and concerned with the turning points in contemporary society.' He cherished his reputation as the man who helped British drama make its move from the drawing room to the kitchen sink: 'I am proud that I played some part in the recognition that the working man was a fit subject for drama, and not just a comic foil in a play on middle-class manners.'

Armchair Theatre was accorded a highly desirable programming slot, following on from one of ITV's guaranteed ratings winners, the variety show *Sunday Night at the London Palladium* (so popular that some churches rescheduled their services to allow the flocks to watch), and the strand achieved impressive audiences. Harold Pinter's first play for television, *A Night Out* (1960), was the most viewed programme in the week that it was broadcast, an achievement repeated later that year by Ray Rigby's *The Cupboard*. Actual viewing figures, as opposed to relative chart positions, are difficult to determine for the era, but at the time the *Daily Mail* claimed that the audience for the series exceeded 16 million, while the *Daily Mirror* put it at 21 million.

Despite its embrace of social realism, *Armchair Theatre* had a wider remit than was sometimes acknowledged, and included some original works of science fiction. ('I've always been a sucker for science,' admitted Newman.) Donald Giltinan's *The Man Out There* (1961) was a grim tale of an astronaut, played by Patrick McGoohan, on a doomed mission, while Jimmy Sangster's *I Can Destroy the Sun* (1958) and James Forsyth's *Underground* (1958) both dealt with the threat of nuclear weapons. The latter, set on the London Underground in the aftermath of a nuclear explosion, was one of the last plays in the strand to go out live, its broadcast being overshadowed by the heart attack and death during the performance of one of the actors, Gareth Jones. The show continued, largely under the direction of a production assistant named Verity Lambert, with Jones's role being hurriedly written out. The success of these and other plays helped persuade Newman to accept a programme proposal from Irene Shubik, a script editor on *Armchair Theatre*, and in 1962 the company launched *Out of this World*, an anthology series of one-off science fiction dramas. It was a significant moment in British television, partly because it opened up new avenues for young dramatists, including Clive Exton and Leon Griffiths as well as Terry Nation, and partly because it arguably did more to popularise contemporary science fiction in Britain than anything since the heyday of H.G. Wells.

There had, of course, been broadcast science fiction in Britain before, and much of it had been highly popular. In 1954 the BBC had shown Nigel Kneale's adaptation of George Orwell's *Nineteen Eighty-Four*, turning a novel with respectable sales into a paperback best-seller and a modern classic: the second broadcast (not strictly speaking a repeat, since it was another live performance) attracted what was then the largest audience for a British television broadcast. Kneale's own *The Quatermass Experiment* the previous year had launched the eponymous character, and two more serials featuring Professor Quatermass were to follow later in the decade, again finding large audiences of over eight million; all three were subsequently made into movies by Hammer Films. Even on the wireless, Radio Luxembourg had in 1951 catapulted into space Dan Dare ('pilot of the future') from the *Eagle* comic, and for five years he had been central to the station's post-war rebuilding of its audience, despite the incongruity of his daily serial being sponsored by Horlicks. The popularity of *Dan Dare* was sufficient to prompt the BBC into launching *Journey Into Space* (1953–9), created by Charles Chilton, which regularly achieved audiences of two and a half million.

But these were isolated pieces and appeared to have little impact in terms of promoting science fiction among the general public. Even as late as 1962, the year after the celebrated television series *A for Andromeda*, the BBC felt that the opportunities were limited, that science fiction was, in the words of an internal report, 'too remote, projected too far away from common humanity in the here-and-now, to evoke interest in the common audience'. The report's summary was not encouraging: 'Our conclusion therefore is that we cannot recommend any existing SF stories for TV adaptation.'

While the genre was building a substantial following in other countries – particularly the United States and the Soviet Union – it languished in Britain, seemingly unable to break through either to a mass market or to intellectual respectability in the way that, say, detective fiction had. 'In the late 1950s,' J.G. Ballard was later to write, 'science fiction was generally regarded as not much better than the comic strips.' There was a small hardcore of support, its numbers perhaps suggested by the 5,000 members of the Science Fiction Book Club, though the American magazine *Astounding Science Fiction* claimed a British circulation in 1959 of 35,000, and there were a handful of home-grown magazines, one of which – *New Worlds*, edited by John Carnell – conducted a survey of its readers in the middle of the decade. 'Ninety-five per cent are male, their average age 31,' it was reported. 'More than a third were technicians of some kind and six per cent were in the RAF. Nine per cent had been to university.' There was also anecdotal evidence to suggest that readers had a marked political inclination to the left, reflected in the fact that, among the national newspapers, it was the *Observer* and the *Guardian* who were most supportive, the former running a competition in 1954 for new short stories set in the year 2500.

There were, however, signs of change by the end of the decade. In 1959 Kingsley Amis demonstrated that he was a better critic than he was a novelist, with a celebrated series of lectures at Princeton University on the current standing of the tradition, subsequently published as *New Maps of Hell*. In the same year the British Science Fiction Association was launched in an attempt to combat the negative image; the scale of their task was such that even the name was contentious and some argued against the use of the term 'science fiction' at all. The support of established writers including Amis, Angus Wilson, Robert Conquest and Edmund Crispin began to attract more mainstream coverage, though there was still some confusion over what was seen as the divided nature of the writing and its followers. 'The most baffling characteristic of this vastly uninhibited conference,' noted the *Guardian* correspondent who attended the Association's 1961 gathering, 'was the peculiar mixture of juvenile delight in gimmicks and facetious humour with a great deal of serious discussion.' The imagery of the 1930s pulp magazines, dealing with what Amis referred to as 'man-eating, death-ray-dealing aliens' and commonly referred to by the shorthand phrase 'bug-eyed monsters', was proving hard to shake off, even if the genre was now attracting those with a proselytising belief that, in Ballard's words, 'science fiction was the true literature of the twentieth century'. It offered, argued Wilson, 'more vitality, a more expanding prospect, than any other branch of fiction today', despite the fact that, at its worst, it was 'the most pulpy product of a pulp-producing age'. The problem was convincing the rest of society that there was intelligent life beyond the pulp.

The chief exception in 1950s Britain, the one writer capable of breaking out from the limited fan base into widespread popularity, was John Wyndham, whose work harked back to the tradition of H.G. Wells and was sometimes disparaged by the more self-consciously literary practitioners of the genre. His 1951 novel *The Day of the Triffids* was reported to have sold over 100,000 copies by the end of the decade, and had been broadcast on BBC radio both as a reading, in 1953, and as a six-part drama in 1957, before being filmed in 1962. That book had been followed by a series of other best-sellers, including *The Kraken Wakes* (1953), *The Chrysalids* (1955) and *The Midwich Cuckoos* (1957), the latter of which was also filmed, in 1960, under the more sensationalist title of *Village of the Damned*. Unsurprisingly, therefore, it was one of his stories, 'Dumb Martian' (published in 1952), that was selected by Irene Shubik to launch *Out of this World*; though in the event the play was screened within the *Armchair Theatre* strand on Sunday 24 June 1962 as a trail for the new series, which started officially the following Saturday.

Out of this World took its title from a series of anthologies edited by Amabel Williams-Ellis and Mably Owen, and published by Blackie from 1960 onwards. The first volume had included work by the likes of Arthur C. Clarke, Arthur Porges and Fredric Brown, as well as the obligatory Wyndham, and the thirteen-week television series that bore the same name was to feature a similarly diverse collection of writers, among them the Americans Philip K. Dick, Isaac Asimov and Clifford D. Simak. In all three cases, it was the first time that any of their work had been adapted for the screen, whether cinema or television, and thus the first time that it was encountered by a sizeable audience in Britain. Shubik later commented that 'science fiction of the "adult", as opposed to the "bug-eyed monster", kind had always been a pet subject of mine', and her selection of material, assisted by John Carnell of *New Worlds*, was to set new standards for the treatment of the genre. Her intentions were strictly serious, and hinted at the campaigning spirit of Ballard and Wilson. 'I think everyone is interested in the idea of life on another planet and what the future holds,' she remarked, as she promoted the show. 'I'm fed-up with kitchen sink drama and plays about who goes to bed with whom. Science fiction at least has a philosophical speculation behind it which I find fascinating.'

Terry Nation's involvement in the series – he adapted two existing short stories and contributed an original tale – came as something of a surprise to his colleagues at Associated London Scripts. 'I can't really remember him being interested in science fiction,' commented Ray Galton, and Beryl Vertue was similarly unaware of his interest: 'I don't remember him talking about it hugely.' Fortunately Nation's friend, Clive Exton, thought he knew better. A stalwart of *Armchair Theatre* – six of his plays were screened in the strand in 1960 alone – Exton was already being hailed by *The Times* as 'one of the most subtle and individual among the new generation of dramatists produced by television', and he had earlier encouraged Nation to write *Uncle Selwyn*. Somewhat more helpfully, when he was commissioned in 1962 to write 'Dumb Martian' for *Out of this World*, he suggested to Shubik that Nation was a science fiction aficionado and would be ideal for the series. Nation was later to admit that this was overstating the case ('I had nothing to back this up with at all'), for he was out of touch with modern science fiction and had never adapted anyone else's work, but he made a suitable impression when he met Shubik and he was sent away with a story to adapt.

Only one episode of *Out of this World* – Leo Lehman's dramatisation of Asimov's 'Little Lost Robot' – has survived, but from contemporary reviews and the memories of those involved, it is evident that Nation largely stayed faithful to his source material. The first of his adaptations was Philip K. Dick's story 'Imposter' (1953), set on a future Earth that is engaged in a deadly and protracted war with unknown forces from the Alpha Centauri star system, known as Outspacers. One of Earth's most important research scientists, Roger Carter (called Spence Olham in the original), is on the verge of a major breakthrough in the development of a new weapon, when he is suddenly arrested on suspicion of being a robotic replica who has killed the human Carter, and who is concealing in his chest cavity a bomb that will destroy the project he is working on. Unable to prove that he is who he knows himself to be, Carter escapes custody and hunts down the imposter, eventually finding a dead body in a crashed Outspacer ship. At which point he realises that the dead man is the real Carter and that therefore he must indeed be the robot. That realisation is the trigger for the detonation of the bomb he is carrying inside himself.

The second adaptation was of Clifford D. Simak's 'Immigrant' (1954), a story that lent itself less readily to television, being a slower-paced, more deliberately didactic piece that lacks the dramatic drive of 'Imposter'. For nearly a hundred years the best and brightest humans from Earth have been emigrating to the planet Kimon, but still virtually nothing is known about their destination, save that it seems blessed with fabulous mineral wealth.

The Kimonians are an advanced species, further down the evolutionary road than humans, adept at telepathy and telekinesis, but they have no desire to establish diplomatic relations with any other planet, and are extremely choosy about who they allow to visit their planet: only those with the highest IQ scores are considered and even then, following years of study, only one in a thousand taking the final tests is accepted. None of those who have emigrated have ever returned; they confine themselves to sending money home in letters that tell of the extraordinary wages paid, but reveal nothing of their life on Kimon.

The story follows Seldon Bishop, one of the few who are accepted, as he endeavours to make a new life in this 'galactic El Dorado'. The material rewards are all that he expected, and the standard of living is luxurious in the extreme, but it doesn't take long to discover why previous immigrants have been so reticent in their accounts of the place. For the Kimonians regard humans as being on a level somewhere between household pets and playmates for their children: 'You might have a doctorate on Earth, but still be no more than a kindergarten youngster when you got to Kimon.' Rather than admit this fact, the humans on Kimon privately nurse their wounded pride, and engage in the traditional expatriate activities of sport and drinking. Yet, as Bishop discovers, for those prepared to adopt the correct attitude, there is hope: 'There is only one thing that will crack this planet and that is humility.' And finally the Kimonian project becomes clear to him. They want to provide the opportunity for future human evolution, to teach those who wish to be taught, those who are prepared to accept that as yet they know nothing and that their schooldays are only just beginning. The theme of a wiser, older civilisation taking humanity under its nurturing wing was not unusual in Simak's work.

Of the two stories, there is little doubt where Nation's sympathies lay. The simple narrative of 'Imposter', driven by action rather than philosophy, was much more to his taste than the ruminative fantasy of Simak, as was Dick's pessimism; elements of the tale – the perpetual state of war and the concept of a robotic double – were to return in his subsequent writing. His own contribution to the series, 'Botany Bay', was certainly more in the mould of Dick. Set in a psychiatric institution, it depicted evil aliens taking over the bodies of the inmates with, as *The Times*'s reviewer reported, 'an ingenious twist' in which 'we were made to realize that we ourselves, the inhabitants of Earth, were the sinister intruders on some simpler future world: that not only were the wrong 'uns winning, but they were us after some further centuries of decadence.'

The series was a success in terms both of ratings and critical acceptance. It attracted larger audiences than the BBC's science fiction offering for the summer — *The Andromeda Breakthrough*, a sequel to Fred Hoyle's *A for Andromeda* the previous year — and there was widespread praise. 'The level of writing and direction has been encouragingly high,' said *The Times*; 'certainly the most intelligent and best written of its genre since *Quatermass*', approved *Kinematograph Weekly*; while the *Yorkshire Evening Post* went one better: 'the most accomplished thing of its kind TV has yet produced'. The *Daily Mail* was quick to praise its ultimate creator: 'the series as a whole has been surprisingly good. Much of the triumph belongs to ABC's story editor Irene Shubik — one of the few women to get real satisfaction out of science fantasy. Miss Shubik is an enthusiast, the venture was a labour of love for her, and it showed.' For Nation himself, it had the added benefit of allowing him to work with one of his great Hollywood heroes, since each episode was introduced by the legendary horror actor Boris Karloff. 'That was a great moment,' remembered Kate Nation, 'when he met Boris Karloff.'

The other beneficiary from the success of the show was Sydney Newman, who had shown that he could spin off hit series from *Armchair Theatre*, first with *Armchair Mystery Thriller* (1960) and now with *Out of this World*. His standing within the industry was so high that the BBC, desperately trying to catch up with its independent rival, recruited him to become its own head of drama in early 1963. BBC SIGNS ITV 'DUSTBIN' MAN, read the headline in the *Daily Mail* and, keen to cement his reputation as the nation's chief purveyor of social realism, Newman created for the corporation *The Wednesday Play*, which was to prove even more controversial than his work on ITV. In his new role, he was also responsible for the drama output on the new channel, BBC2, that was due to launch in 1964, following the recommendations of the Pilkington Report. And one of those he recruited to staff this expansion was Irene Shubik, who became the script editor on *Story Parade*, a series of single dramas adapted from contemporary novels, 'a sort of anthology of new fictional writing'.

It was a lucky break for Terry Nation, who now had, for the first time, a supporter within the drama department of BBC television. He had been trying since *Out of this World* to find an opening within the corporation, but without success. He submitted a proposal, titled 'The Thousand and Several Doors', for the series *Suspense*, but it was rejected as being 'too derivative' (the same conclusion that had been reached with *Uncle Selwyn*), and although he was commissioned to write a script for *Z-Cars*, it was never made. His one non-genre piece to be broadcast had come in October 1962 with an episode of the long-running police series *No Hiding Place*, which was again an ITV production. *Story Parade* was to change his run of poor luck at the BBC, and he was commissioned in 1964 to write three plays for the series.

Of these the most significant was an adaptation of Isaac Asimov's novel *The Caves of Steel*, first published in *Galaxy* magazine in 1953. Shubik was an admirer of Asimov's work, and indeed of the man himself; 'one of the most interesting and amusing men I have ever met', she was later to comment of the writer whose stories, particularly those dealing with robotics (a word he coined), had made him one of the leading figures in science fiction. *The Caves of Steel* was among his best work, and the resulting BBC production was immediately acclaimed as a triumph.

Set three thousand years in the future, the novel depicts a society in which Earth has colonised fifty other planets, the Outer Worlds. A division has arisen between the overcrowded, primitive Earth and these Outer Worlds, on which the descendants of the settlers, known as Spacers, are technologically more advanced, and where human and robot societies are closely integrated. In the Great Rebellion, the Outer Worlds achieved independence from Earth, and the Spacers and Terrestrials now live in uneasy harmony. The Spacers are still human, but have been genetically selected over many generations and have therefore evolved differently – among other things, they have a life expectancy in excess of three hundred years, largely thanks to the abolition of disease.

The story is set in New York, which, like other major population centres on Earth, is now a massive conurbation, enclosed in a vast steel dome (hence the title of the novel) so that it has become like a super-sized mall, with no view of the outside to disturb its air-conditioned security. Inside the dome, society is run as a strict hierarchical bureaucracy, with no room for 'individualism and initiative' (despite an underground movement of dissidents known as the Medievalists). This artificial community is entirely dependent on technology and therefore highly vulnerable; as one character explains, water has to be brought into the City, air requires constant circulation inside the dome, and the whole thing is powered by nuclear plants that need uranium supplies: 'The balance is a very delicate one in a hundred directions, and growing more delicate each year.' Any interruption to this ecosystem would have terrible consequences. 'When New York first became a city, it could have lived on itself for a day. Now it cannot do so for an hour. A disaster that would have been uncomfortable ten thousand years ago, merely serious a thousand years ago, and acute a hundred years ago would now surely be fatal.' This was to become one of Nation's favourite themes, though in the Asimov story the more immediate threat to social stability comes from the robots that are gradually being introduced into everyday life. 'Do you fear robots for the sake of your job?' a character is asked, and he replies, 'And my kids' jobs. And everyone's kids.'

Within this setting, the plot is essentially that of a detective novel. A scientist, living in the Spacer community just outside the City, has been murdered and a New York detective named Elijah Baley is assigned a humanoid robot partner for the investigation. The deliberate, and mostly successful, mixing of science fiction and mystery conventions inspired many other writers, including Nation himself, who – particularly in Blake's 7 – was to use science fiction as a base from which to explore other genres; the episode 'Mission to Destiny' was similarly a straight murder mystery, even if it were set on a spaceship. Other elements of The Caves of Steel were also to be evident in his later work, especially that idea of the fragility of modern life.

The one major change made by Nation is the imposition by the Spacers of a 48-hour deadline for solving the case; unless the murderer is caught within that time, New York City will be occupied or destroyed. The introduction of a time limit makes perfect dramatic sense until, with just half an hour left, the threat of violence is withdrawn; instead there's a new deadline, this one taken directly from the book. Nation's fondness for countdowns, which was to become a feature of his writing, is here an awkward and unnecessary intrusion.

Elsewhere, however, there is some fine writing, particularly in the opening shot of the domed city, with a voice-over by Baley (played by Peter Cushing): 'New York City. The culmination of man's mastery over environment. Fourteen million people crowd beneath its protective dome. And out there in the open country: Spacetown. Unwelcome and unwanted. With its handful of Outer World scientists seeking to change us, interfering, trying to impose new cultures.' The terse phrasing drew on the style of contemporary American police shows, reapplied to paint a compelling vision of the future in a beautifully succinct piece of scene-setting.

Broadcast in June 1964 and repeated the following August, the play was a popular hit for the new BBC2, which was seen as something of a minority channel from the outset. The repeat attracted a respectable audience share of 13 per cent and got a reaction index from the BBC's sample panel of viewers of 61, slightly above the average rating of 60 for television drama of the era (even a play as celebrated as Nell Dunn's *Up the Junction* only rated 58). It also won over the critics. 'A fascinating mixture of science fiction and whodunit which worked remarkably well,' judged John Russell Taylor in *The Listener*, 'despite a slightly specious, dragged-in attempt to suggest a parallel between the characters' attitude to robots and ours to racial minorities.' *The Times*'s reviewer was likewise impressed, calling it 'highly successful', though he too wondered about the subtext: 'the story hinges on a fanatical hatred of robots by most humans in a remote future. Why do they hate them? We are supposed, apparently, to link up immediately with race hatred in the modern world, but that, though it may work in a novel or short story, just will not do in a play. In a play we want to know more of the whys and hows.' Unequivocally enthusiastic was Dr Anthony Michaelis, the *Daily Telegraph*'s science correspondent: 'I could find no fault whatsoever with the scientific extrapolation to the future. Every small item was remarkably well thought out and beautifully achieved.' His praise was spoilt only by a sideways dig at another series with which Nation was already involved: 'The first science fiction programme on BBC2 last night was an outstanding success and certainly surpassed most similar works on BBC1, such as Fred Hoyle's *A for Andromeda* and *Doctor Who*.'

Nation was also responsible for an adaptation of Ira Levin's 1953 novel *A Kiss Before Dying*, a less significant contribution to the series, partly because it had already been filmed – with Robert Wagner and Joanne Woodward in 1956 – and partly because it was a straightforward thriller, a genre much more familiar on British television than futuristic science fiction. Its status has been further eroded by the success of subsequent films of Levin's work, including *Rosemary's Baby*, *The Stepford Wives* and *The Boys from Brazil*. Even so, the story of an amoral social climber who seduces three sisters in turn, killing each before moving on to the next, was well received at the time: 'a highly polished, holding piece of light entertainment', noted *The Times*. Nation, too, was happy with the result: 'I actually sat back and forgot I'd written it and watched it and enjoyed it.' The piece was, like 'The Caves of Steel', directed by Peter Sasdy, a Hungarian who had fled to Britain after the crushing of the 1956 uprising. Sasdy was also in line to make the third of Nation's commissions for *Story Parade*, an adaptation of Ray Bradbury's short story 'The Fox and the Forest', though in the event it was left to the less experienced Robin Midgley to direct.

Indeed the whole production history of 'The Fox and the Forest' was plagued by problems. Nation himself was not the first choice of writer; the project had already been to two others, Ken Taylor and Ilona Ference, and the latter had produced a full script, which Shubik rejected. She instead offered the job to Nation, noting: 'I am confident he will do an excellent job on it, as both his other adaptations have been first class.' When he delivered the script, however, three months behind schedule, she was less impressed, considering it too violent and too rooted in contemporary gangster slang. Even after he did a rewrite and received his fee of £500, it was passed on to yet another writer, Meade Roberts, who was paid a further £200 to rework it further. Since Bradbury was receiving $1,000 for the rights with, unusually, an additional $1,000 for each repeat (the standard arrangement saw a 50 per cent reduction for repeats), it was already proving to be an expensive production.

The story concerned two fugitives from a future dystopia – Earth in 2155 – who have been granted the highest possible privilege of being allowed a holiday in time. Arriving in Mexico in 1938, they decide to try to lose themselves in the crowd and remain in a happier age, but are hunted down by an agent from their own time, who explains that they cannot so easily evade their responsibilities. 'The rabbits may hide in the forest,' he tells them, 'but a fox can always find them.' It's a tense but very brief tale that, unlike Nation's two other commissions for *Story Parade*, required some expansion, and his response was a device that was to become characteristic of his work: the raising of hopes only to dash them. One of the renegades is caught and about to be deported back to the future, when the other appears and shoots dead their pursuer. But it's a false salvation and eventually they are recaptured. Nation also tried to change the period to 1963, just before the assassination of John F. Kennedy – playing on contemporary anxieties as he would on *Doctor Who* – though he was overruled by the director and Bradbury's original pre-war setting was restored.

The delays in the writing process meant that 'The Fox and the Forest' didn't appear in *Story Parade*, as originally intended. Instead it formed part of the first series in 1965 of *Out of the Unknown*, a new BBC2 project, again helmed by Irene Shubik, which was explicitly based in science fiction and was essentially an extension of *Out of this World*. The play was finally broadcast in November 1965, appropriately enough on the second anniversary of Kennedy's assassination, and it received some critical praise; it was 'one of the most convincing produced plays in the series', according to *Television Today*, and Mary Crozier in the *Guardian* wrote that the 'feeling of remorseless pursuit was steadily instilled with a nightmarish intensity'. But Shubik herself was unhappy with the final product, and the audience too was unimpressed: the piece received a reaction index of just 52, the lowest for any of the twelve episodes in the season. It never received a repeat screening.

By this stage, however, its success or failure made little difference to Nation. For by now he was one of the most successful television writers in the country, fully occupied on a variety of projects, many of which were concerned with the creatures that had finally catapulted him out of the ranks of the unknown.

Chapter Five

Life on a Dead Planet

In July 1963 Tony Hancock again ventured out on a string of stage performances, this time one-week engagements in Nottingham and in Manchester in preparation for a six-week residency at the Talk of the Town in London, and again he was accompanied by Terry Nation. In the event, however, Hancock's confidence, already fragile following the failure of the television series, was further dented by poor ticket sales, and he cancelled the London booking. His state of mind was not improved when, during the first week, he finally split with Nation; having previously parted from Ray Galton and Alan Simpson, and then from Philip Oakes, he was clearly struggling to keep hold of his writers.

It was while they were in Nottingham that Nation was contacted by his agent with an offer of work: 'The BBC are planning a new children's science fiction show, would you like to do it?' His immediate response, as someone who had never written for children, was entirely negative: 'How dare they? I don't do things like that.' Hancock demonstrated supportive outrage, resorting to a catchphrase from his early days on the radio show *Educating Archie*: 'A writer of your calibre, writing for flippin' kids!' Then came the falling out: yet another argument about Hancock's reluctance to use new material, a feeling on Nation's part that he was being underused and undervalued, a blazing row and a storming out. Only on the train back to London did Nation calm down enough to realise that he was now out of work, with no income to speak of and with considerable domestic expenditure looming (he had committed himself to the installation of central heating in the three-roomed Hampstead flat where he and Kate lived). There was only one offer on the table. Fortunately it was still available and, having retracted his refusal, he was duly sent the writer's guide for the new series, which he learned was to be entitled *Doctor Who*.

There was, however, one further contribution from Hancock, at least in his own mind. During those all-night conversations with Nation, the two men had ranged freely over a large number of subjects, including an idea for a film about Earth after the final death of humanity, a planet populated entirely by robots. Hancock's concept of how these androids might look was said to be 'an inverted cone, covered in ping pong balls and with a sink plunger sticking out of its head'.

The concept of the new series came, as did so much at this time, from Sydney Newman. There was an awkward gap in the BBC television schedules around teatime on Saturdays, falling between two firmly established presences: the four-hour sports show *Grandstand*, which ended at five o'clock once the football results had been broadcast, and the BBC's token pop show, which had occupied the slot just after six o'clock ever since Jack Good's ground-breaking *Six-Five Special* had been launched in 1957 (it was now the home of *Juke Box Jury*). Thereafter the evening programmes for adult audiences began in earnest, with the likes of *Dixon of Dock Green* and *The Rag Trade*. Some of that difficult hour was filled with the news, but there was, felt Newman, a need for a regular drama show that would primarily appeal to children, but wouldn't alienate the adult audience left over from *Grandstand*, a transition programme suitable for family viewing. 'It was never intended to be simply a children's programme,' he insisted in later years, 'but something that would appeal to people who were in a rather child-like frame of mind.' And he concluded that what was needed was a science fiction series.

It was not an entirely novel concept. Apart from encouraging Irene Shubik's ventures into science fiction, Newman had, while he was at ABC, brought to the screen *Target Luna* and its spin-off *Pathfinders in Space*, which itself spawned other *Pathfinders* series. Written by Malcolm Hulke and Eric Paice – who had earlier written for a television series of Gert and Daisy – these were straightforward children's shows, but there were elements that would reappear in the broader-based *Doctor Who*, particularly the use of cliff-hanger endings to episodes, with the protagonists left in a situation of danger.

Newman shared Shubik's distaste for the bug-eyed monster tradition of science fiction, and the new concept was intended to avoid this, revolving around a 'senile old man' in a machine that was capable of travelling through space and time. Since he couldn't quite control the ship (later named the TARDIS, standing for Time and Relative Dimension in Space), it repeatedly plunged him and his companions into adventures that would be both entertaining and educational. Sketchy as it necessarily was at this stage, the idea already had the one key element that was to make it so distinctive. The central figure was not a blue-eyed, square-jawed space ace, as a generation used to the likes of Dan Dare might expect; rather he was to be an eccentric scientist, the kind of man you would normally expect to see shuffling around his laboratory, mumbling to himself, but now let loose in the universe. As an outsider, Newman appeared to have a slightly disparaging view of Britain's potential for space exploration: bumbling rather than barnstorming, hesitant rather than heroic.

The format that emerged was largely shaped by Verity Lambert, who had worked as Newman's assistant on *Armchair Theatre* and was now promoted to be producer of the new series, and by David Whitaker, the script editor. The central character, known at this stage as Doctor Who, was to be accompanied by his granddaughter, to allow the young audience a figure with whom to identify, and by two of her teachers; since they taught science and history, these latter would be able to expound upon the futuristic and historical situations in which they found themselves. They were to carry no weaponry and were to be reliant only on their ingenuity and initiative to escape any dangers they might encounter. (The addition of the teachers indicated the would-be educational element of the show, augmenting the traditional combination of scientist and young woman common in science fiction since it was first borrowed from Prospero and Miranda in Shakespeare's *The Tempest*.) A first script was commissioned from Anthony Coburn, and Whitaker then approached a number of writers who he thought might be able to provide stories in four to six episodes for a series that was scheduled to run for fifty-two unbroken weeks. 'They were all friends or friends of friends,' he later explained. 'People I knew I could trust not only to produce a good story within the restrictions we had, but also to work to a tight deadline.'

Among them was Terry Nation, whose work on *Out of this World* qualified him for embarking on a science fiction project, and who knew Whitaker from the days when they had worked together on *The Ted Ray Show*. He was not, however, impressed by the writer's guide he received. 'When I first read the brochure the BBC had prepared for writers and producers,' he would say in later years, 'I was absolutely convinced it couldn't last but four weeks. I thought it was dreadful.' Deb Boultwood remembered him visiting her father, Nation's old writing partner Dave Freeman, at the time and being no more enthusiastic: 'Terry came round and Dad asked, "What are you doing?" And he said: "I've got a series; it's children's TV but it brings in the money." And that was the Daleks.'

For the remainder of his life, Nation was to be asked about the act of creation that brought the Daleks into being, and he was never able to provide an answer that satisfied his inquisitors. 'I suppose they were born in a flash of inspiration,' he commented once, 'except that makes it sound altogether too poetic. I was sitting at a typewriter, doing a job of work for money, and I needed a monster. And that's when they were born.' Similarly the name, notwithstanding his story about the encyclopaedias, had no obvious spur: 'Basically I wanted a two-syllable word that had a mechanical sound about it,' he recalled, though its rhythm clearly echoes that of 'robot', a term introduced in Karel Capek's 1920 play *R.U.R.* – *Rossum's Universal Robots* and derived from the Czech word for 'serf labour'. Dalek too proved to be a real word, meaning 'remote' or even 'alien' in Croatian, though this was no more than a happy accident, and came as a surprise to Nation when he subsequently learned of it; as he pointed out: 'I don't have many friends who speak Serbo-Croat.' He was, despite his misgivings, sufficiently excited by his inspiration that he enthusiastically broke the news to his wife, Kate. 'I've had this brilliant idea for some baddies. I'm going to call them Daleks,' he enthused. To which she replied, 'Drink your tea while it's hot.'

He submitted a storyline, titled 'The Survivors'. A fully developed and impressive piece of work, it was considerably more detailed than expected (twenty-two pages rather than the recommended three or four), and contained virtually all the elements that would turn up in the final version. By the time it was accepted, however, and he was commissioned to produce a full script on 31 July 1963, he had received a far more attractive offer to write material for Eric Sykes, who was signed up to host a variety show, *Wish You Were Here*, in a joint production by the BBC and a Swedish television channel. Although the *Doctor Who* script was not due for delivery until 30 September, the Sykes programme was scheduled for 7 September and required Nation's earlier presence for rehearsals. Short of time, and seeing the *Doctor Who* story as the lesser of the two commitments, he finished the script within a week (writing an episode a day, for each of which he was paid £262), delivered it to Lambert and Whitaker and left for Sweden.

The serial went through various titles, including 'Beyond the Sun', before ending up as 'The Mutants', though in retrospect it has come to be known simply as 'The Daleks', in tribute to its central villains. Set on the fictional planet Skaro, the story features two races, the Daleks and the Thals, who long ago fought a devastating centuries-long war, ending with the detonation of a neutron bomb that has left the planet scarred by radiation. The surviving Daleks have retreated into an underground network beneath their chief city and taken refuge inside individual protective shells, while a handful of Thals keep themselves alive on the surface of Skaro with anti-radiation drugs. There has been no contact since between the two races, who are each unaware of the other's continued existence, but this is to change with the arrival of the TARDIS, bringing the Doctor (as Doctor Who had now become known) and his companions: his granddaughter, Susan, and her teachers, Ian and Barbara. Landing in the midst of a petrified forest, the travellers discover in the distance the Dalek city, and the Doctor tricks the others into exploring the place by pretending that he's in search of mercury to refill the fluid link (a vital component in the workings of the TARDIS). They are captured by the Daleks, from whom they learn something of Skaro's past, but manage to escape and join up with the Thals. Together they stage an attack on the city to regain possession of the fluid link, and the story ends with the defeat and death of the Daleks and the departure of the TARDIS crew, leaving the planet in the hands of the Thals.

It was a simple story that drew rather more deeply on Nation's childhood reading than on the modern science fiction he had adapted for *Out of this World*. In particular there is a clear debt to H.G. Wells, whose 1895 novel *The Time Machine* had foreseen an Earth inhabited by the subterranean Morlocks and the surface-dwelling Eloi, twin races not far removed from the hideous, violent Daleks living underground and the beautiful, peaceful Thals. Wells's later book *The War of the Worlds* (1898) had centred on a race of aliens who could only operate on Earth if they were inside machines of their own construction, and this combination of an organic life-form within a robotic casing is evoked in the nature of the Dalek: a 'frog-like animal', according to Nation's original storyline, who lives inside a metallic travelling machine. 'They are invulnerable, they are pitiless,' a character remarks of the Martians in Wells's novel. Then there are traces of Jules Verne's *Journey to the Centre of the Earth* (1864) as Ian, Barbara and a group of Thals travel through swamps full of mutated creatures and caves fraught with danger to attack the city from the rear. One might even see, in the depiction of the Doctor and Ian as the man of science and the adventure hero (for it is Ian who tends to lead the action elements of the story), something resembling the relationship between Professor Challenger and Lord John Roxton in Arthur Conan Doyle's *The Lost World* and its sequels.

None of this, it should be noted, was out of kilter with the original conception of the series. Sydney Newman had talked about the concept of the TARDIS being based 'on the style of an H.G. Wells time-space machine', while the first adventure, Anthony Coburn's '100,000 BC', had carried echoes of another Wells tale, 'A Story of the Stone Age', published in 1897.

But if the literary references were more than half a century old, they were heavily reworked to address entirely contemporary themes. Whereas Wells had seen the Morlocks and Eloi evolving from current humanity, the extreme products of a split between the proletariat and the bourgeoisie, Nation was interested less in class war than in nuclear war. The development of the neutron bomb, which was to cause such contamination on Skaro, had been widely covered in the media of the early 1960s (a fact noted by Ian in the original script, though his comments were deleted from the final version), and a bomb had in fact been constructed and tested by America in 1963, though that was not publicised at the time. What was very much in the news, as Nation sat down to write, was the signing on 5 August 1963 of the Test Ban Treaty by America, the Soviet Union and the United Kingdom, the three countries that then possessed nuclear weapons; for the first time an international agreement had been negotiated that attempted to regulate the development of such armaments. In retrospect it became clear that this triggered a collapse of support in Britain for the Campaign for Nuclear Disarmament (it was to return in the 1980s), but for the moment CND remained the great cause of the left, included in whose ranks were many of those with whom Nation mixed socially and professionally.

A large part of the central section of 'The Daleks' deals explicitly with a debate over pacifism, as represented by the Thals, who have abandoned their past incarnation as warriors and instead become farmers. 'Fear breeds hatred and war,' declares Temmosus (Alan Wheatley), the leader of the Thals, as he prepares to encounter the Daleks. 'I shall speak to them peacefully. They'll see that I'm unarmed. There's no better argument against war than that.' He is promptly killed by the Daleks with their death rays. 'Can pacifism become a human instinct?' wonders Barbara, and Ian dismisses such beliefs as pure idealism: 'Pacifism only works when everybody feels the same.' He later proves his point by seizing a Thal woman named Dyoni (Virginia Wetherell) and threatening to hand her over to the

Daleks, thereby provoking Alydon (John Lee), the new Thal leader, into hitting him. Meanwhile the Doctor, ethically a more complex figure than he was later to become, is proving even more bellicose. 'We have a ready-made army here,' he declares, and when it's pointed out that the Thals don't believe in violence, he waves away such petty objections: 'This is no time for morals.' After further agonising – in which a key role is played by Dyoni, telling Alydon that she's glad he stood up for her ('If you hadn't fought him, I think I would have hated you') – the Thals decide to abandon centuries of non-violence and join the TARDIS crew in attacking the Dalek city.

The provocation of Alydon is a little glib, derived perhaps from the question so often put to conscientious objectors in the First World War: What would you do if you saw a German trying to rape your sister? (To which the homosexual writer Lytton Strachey famously replied: 'I would try to interpose my body.') But in the context of a children's television drama, the simplicity is effective enough, and it was certainly an issue that caused Nation some soul-searching. 'I had a bad time with the first episodes of *Doctor Who*,' he commented in 1966. 'The Doctor had to say to the Thals: "If you are worth keeping, if you have anything to contribute, it is worth fighting for, it is worth laying down your life for." It was against all my beliefs, but I made him say it.' He added, with the tone of a man more preoccupied with the Second World War than with a possible third: 'It is a problem we all have to face. I don't have the answer.'

There had been in Nation's first storyline, 'The Survivors', one further echo of the times. The original concept had been that both the Thals and the Daleks blamed the other side for having started the war on Skaro. It is only at the end – when the Thals have beaten but not (in this version) killed the Daleks – that the Doctor pieces together the historical records of the two races and deduces that 'both hemispheres were destroyed simultaneously, and there is evidence that before the attack the radar had recorded something in space'. The idea of two power blocs being provoked into war, and thus destroyed, by a third party chimed with contemporary fears about the rise of China, which was then widely seen as a potentially destabilising influence on the fine balance between the USA and the Soviet Union, particularly after the Sino-Soviet split became public in 1960. (An early script for the subsequent story, 'The Dalek Invasion of Earth', included a reference to China being at war with both the USA and the USSR.) Unusually for Nation, however, the storyline ends on an entirely upbeat note: rockets arrive on Skaro carrying representatives of this third power, who explain that 'they have realised the enormity of the crime committed by their forefathers. They have waited for the radiation level to fall, and now they come to make reparations and assist in rebuilding the planet.'

Fortunately this entire plot development was jettisoned, to be replaced by the destruction of the Daleks, thus avoiding the terrible possibility of viewers being left with an image of Thals and Daleks living together happily ever after. Such a denouement would have sat uncomfortably with the imagery of the preceding episodes, dominated as they were by overt Nazi references to the extermination of opponents. The very word 'exterminate' was firmly associated in the public mind with the Holocaust, a connection reinforced recently by its repeated use during the 1961 trial of Adolf Eichmann for his part in the Final Solution. And a happy ending would have gone utterly against the grain of the scene in which the Daleks rank up alongside each other, raise their right arms in a stiff salute and announce: 'Tomorrow we will be the masters of the planet.'

Despite these allusions to serious and current issues, however, there remained the unavoidable fact that the Daleks were dangerously close to the 'cheap-jack bug-eyed monsters' that Sydney Newman insisted should play no part in *Doctor Who*. 'David Whitaker and I both thought it was a terrific story and very exciting,' remembered Verity Lambert, but Donald Wilson, the head of serials, to whom they were directly answerable, was less impressed. 'This is absolutely terrible,' he told them. 'I don't want you to make it. What else have you got?' The answer was that they had nothing else. 'The Daleks' had originally been intended as the fifth story in the series, but the scripts for the projected second story had been rejected, and with production due to start shortly, there was an urgent need for a replacement. The speed with which Nation had delivered his scripts meant that his piece was the only option available. 'Had we had anything else,' said Lambert, 'I don't think the Daleks would ever have hit the screen. We had to make it.'

Nation's description of the Daleks captured their essence, without going into great detail about their appearance: 'Hideous machine-like creatures, they are legless, moving on a round base. They have no human features. A lens on a flexible shaft acts as an eye. Arms with mechanical grips for hands.' The responsibility for turning this description into usable props fell to the nascent visual effects department at the BBC, the design being the responsibility of Raymond P. Cusick, with the realisation of that design falling to his colleagues Jack Kine and Bernard Wilkie. The first decision was that the machines would have to be operated by humans inside the props. 'If you had anything mechanical, ten-to-one it would go wrong on the take,' explained Cusick. Having further established that the initial idea of having the operators standing up would be far too tiring, 'I drew a seat, ergonomic height, eighteen inches, got the operator down, and then drew round him; that's how the basic shape appeared.' Other limitations came from the budget. Cusick wanted the lower half to be a curved skirt made from fibreglass, but was told the material was too expensive. Instead he designed it using plywood panels, only to find out that Shawcraft Models – the firm who manufactured the props – had used fibreglass anyway.

The final version stood four foot six inches off the ground, ran on castors (concealed by a thick rubber skirt at the base) and had just enough room for an operator, whose task it was to move the object with his feet, while controlling the two arms, the eye-stalk and the lights on the top that flashed to indicate which Dalek was speaking. This latter requirement also meant that the operator had to learn the script, even though he did not himself provide the voice. It was a set of skills not dissimilar to those demanded of a one-man band, with the added problem of restricted vision through the mesh section at the top.

The finished props were not, as objects, immediately inspiring to the crew. 'The first time I saw them, I laughed,' reflected William Russell, one of the original stars. 'It seemed ridiculous.' And he was not alone. 'I remember looking at it and thinking, "This'll never take off",' commented Jack Kine. 'But once the actors got inside, the things took on a life of their own.'

The one point that Nation had made from the outset was that the Daleks were to be as non-human as possible. 'I had been a cinema-goer all my life and loved going to what were rated in those days as horror movies. But whatever the creature was, somewhere in your heart of hearts, you knew it was a man dressed up. So my first requirement was to take the legs off. Take away the humanoid form and we were off and running.' He was insistent that there should be no visible means of propulsion, citing as his inspiration the Georgian State Dance Company, who had recently been seen on British television performing a dance in which the women wore floor-length skirts, concealing the movement of their feet, so that they appeared to glide across the stage. They were not, however, the only act exploring this concept. Earlier in 1963 the comedian Hattie Jacques, whom

Nation knew from her work with Eric Sykes and Tony Hancock, had appeared at the Players' Theatre in London in a routine described by Joan Le Mesurier: 'I saw Hattie, dressed as a little girl, sing "I Don't Want to Play in Your Yard". She moved as if she had wheels concealed under her dress.'

This non-human appearance was a significant departure from established images of robots. The Daleks are actually cyborgs, rather than robots, combining the organic with the mechanical ('inside each of these shells is a living, bubbling lump of hate', as the Doctor explains in a later story), but the outer casings are clearly in the robotic tradition; Nation described them as being 'simply the vehicles', a similar formulation to Kingsley Amis's definition of a robot as 'a mere peripatetic machine'. And the tendency of robots within the science fiction of the time was very clearly humanoid, as seen in films such as *The Day the Earth Stood Still* (1951) and *Forbidden Planet* (1956), and as elucidated by Isaac Asimov. 'The human form is the most successful generalised form in all nature,' argues a character in *The Caves of Steel*. 'If you want a design capable of doing a great many widely various things, all fairly well, you could do no better than to imitate the human form.' In that novel, and in Philip K. Dick's 'Imposter', the ultimate aim of creating robots was to make them as indistinguishable from humanity as possible. The Daleks, both in intention and in final design, swam firmly against that current. As Terrance Dicks, who was to bring them back to the screen in the 1970s, said: 'They were original in their time; there hadn't been anything even remotely like them.'

Cusick's work in bringing the concept to life met with Nation's approval. 'He made a tremendous contribution,' he was to acknowledge. 'He took rough notes of my ideas for the Dalek's behaviour, the electronic eye, mechanical hands and so on, and although I didn't have a clear visual image in my mind, when I saw his finished Dalek design it seemed very familiar.' Perhaps Cusick's only mistake was that, while having lunch with Bill Roberts of Shawcraft Models, he demonstrated the gliding movement he was trying to realise by picking up a pepper pot and moving it around the table, and then told the story to the press, thereby providing the media with a ready-made cliché: 'Ever since then, people say I was inspired by a pepper pot. But it could have been the salt pot I picked up . . .'

The other major addition to the creatures was the Dalek voice designed by Brian Hodgson of the BBC Radiophonic Workshop, feeding a human voice through a ring modulator, set at a frequency that turned the signal on and off thirty times a second, and then passing it through a graphic equaliser. The voices themselves were provided, in a flat monotone that at times of stress rose to an hysterical scream, by David Graham and Peter Hawkins, the latter having last been heard in a Nation-scripted broadcast playing a stray dog in *Floggit's*.

In identifying the main contributors to the development of the Daleks, recognition must also be given to David Whitaker, the script editor. It is unclear who was responsible for the revisions that were made to the script, but certainly the final version had evolved from the original storyline, not least because of the deletion of the argument over who had started the war on Skaro. As a consequence the Daleks became harsher, more extreme creations. When one of them says 'The only interest we have in the Thals is their total extermination', the screened version dispensed with the original clarification that this was because they feared the Thals might launch another war; stripped of justification for their actions, the motivation was now genocidal megalomania: 'Only one race can survive'. Their language and speech patterns had also developed. In the original scripts, the staccato phrasing was less consistent: 'I can understand your reluctance to tell us anything,' one of them says, almost chattily, to the Doctor. 'But you'll have to tell us.' The incarnation that reached the screen was a sharply focused portrait of ruthless, amoral survivalism, with no suggestion of any saving grace. One must assume that these changes were primarily the work of Whitaker, and that he too could claim to have helped bring the Daleks into being.

There were, then, plenty of other hands involved in shaping the Daleks – even Hancock, if he was to be believed. 'That bloody Nation!' was his response to seeing the Daleks on television for the first time. 'He's stolen my robots.' But while Nation was always happy to recognise the work of these 'enormous contributors', he remained clear on the centrality of his own role. 'I was the one who got the credit for it, and I was perfectly willing to take it,' he said. 'Because although a lot of other people contributed and made them work, I did invent the Daleks.' The issue of who was ultimately responsible for the Daleks never quite went away, however, and towards the end of his life Nation returned to it repeatedly in interviews. 'I've been reading a lot of magazines over the years, and it seems that, over the past two or three years I'm finding an article by a director or a producer or somebody at the BBC all in some way claiming to have been really responsible for the success of the Daleks,' he said. Referring to his (much less celebrated) second story for *Doctor Who*, he added sardonically: 'I've noticed that nobody is taking any credit for "The Keys of Marinus".'

The first episode of *Doctor Who* was broadcast on 23 November 1963, the day after John F. Kennedy was shot dead in Dallas (the cast and crew heard the news of the assassination just as they were about to start filming the second episode of 'The Daleks'). The regular cast comprised Carole Ann Ford as Susan, and William Russell and Jacqueline Hill as her teachers, with William Hartnell – star of the film *And the Same to You*, partially written by Terry Nation and John Junkin – as the Doctor. The fact that the lead character was an alien from another time, and perhaps another planet, was a major departure for televised science fiction, and the first episode, 'An Unearthly Child', went out of its way to locate the show in a recognisable portrayal of Britain, to counterpoint the strangeness encountered later. It opens with a bobby on the beat wandering by as though he had strayed out of *Dixon of Dock Green*, while the TARDIS takes the (then) familiar shape of a police telephone box, and is initially located in a scrapyard in Totters Lane – 'totting' being a slang reference to the rag-and-bone trade that could hardly fail to evoke images of *Steptoe and Son*, whose own yard was in Oil Drum Lane. Susan may have been an alien adolescent, but she is presented as sharing the concerns of human teenagers; when we first see her, she is dancing, transistor radio in hand, to the sounds of a fictional band named John Smith and the Common Men. This gentle introduction ends when the TARDIS, carrying the Doctor, Susan and their two unwilling companions, is plunged back for the first proper adventure to the Stone Age at a time when the art of making fire is being discovered.

Viewing figures for that first four-part story were respectable but hardly startling; they reached a peak of seven million, but tailed off for the final episode and averaged just six million over the course of the serial. Many at the BBC were unimpressed with the show, and even at this early stage there were suggestions that the 52-week run might be truncated to just thirteen weeks. The arrival of 'The Daleks', which started on 21 December, ended all such talk. By the end of the story, the audience was well over ten million, and the average across the seven episodes was nine million, a success that ensured the survival of the series. As Verity Lambert was later to acknowledge of Nation's monsters: 'They put *Doctor Who* on the map.'

What made the difference was simply the appearance of the Daleks themselves. The first episode of the story ends with Barbara flattening herself against a wall and screaming as she looks straight into the camera at something that we cannot see; all that is visible to us in the foreground of the shot is an out-of-focus stick, with a black blob at its end, as though it's a weapon. We subsequently discover that this is the arm of a Dalek, but at this point it is impossible to identify what it is that's terrorising Barbara. The cliff-hanger is simply her fear and our uncertainty as to what is causing it. The effect was reminiscent of the already classic shower sequence in Alfred Hitchcock's film *Psycho* (1960), with Janet Leigh attacked by a foregrounded knife, stabbing downwards at her.

The second episode reprised that ending, but then cut to the Doctor and Ian squabbling over the radiation levels on the planet, over the Doctor's deceit in pretending that he needed mercury to repair the TARDIS's fluid link, and over their next step – whether to look for Barbara or simply to get out. When they finally decide to go searching for Barbara, they step out of the room and immediately find themselves surrounded by a swarm of Daleks. It's our first sighting of the creatures, and it comes as something of a shock. The arguments between the Doctor and Ian have largely driven from our minds the horror that Barbara has witnessed, and their sudden appearance is the more effective for having had no forewarning and no fanfare.

The impact of the Daleks was immediate, as Nation himself remembered: 'After that first episode, my phone started to ring, with friends calling to say, "What the fuck was that?" Then the following week the Dalek appeared and it was an instant hit. I had had a few small successes by then, and maybe once in a while, a fan letter. But then I started getting mail addressed to "the Dalek Man, London" and the Post Office was bringing it! First they came with a bag full, and then there were vans coming – truly, vans full.'

The BBC too was inundated with letters from viewers, most requesting photographs and autographs, though others were more hopeful. 'I would be very grateful if you would send me a Dalek,' wrote one boy from Manchester. 'I thought you might have just one that you don't want and could send it to me please.' Another fan from High Wycombe invited the human cast to a birthday party, adding a note that the Daleks would also be welcome, and that there would be 'nuts and bolts stewed oil drink' for them. Typical was a letter from a young viewer in Welwyn Garden City after the story had ended: 'In the series Dr Who the Darleks have been destroyed and evrybody will forget about them. I think Dr Who is the best seriel ever put on BBC television and I don't want to forget them so could you send me a photo of one of the Darleks so I can remember them for a long time after the seriel is finished.' A little surprising was the range of ages evidenced by the letters. At one extreme a woman from St Helens wrote to say that her four-year-old son 'loves those Daleks which have been appearing on the BBC serial Dr Who. He talks about them all the time and he can hardly wait for Saturdays to come so that he can watch them again. He was heartbroken last Saturday when they were all killed off.' Then there were three teenage girls from Worthing who displayed scant interest in the Daleks, but were much taken by their blond, muscular rivals on Skaro; Sydney Newman had dismissed the Thals as 'blond faeries', but the girls knew better and wanted the *Radio Times* to print a picture of 'those fabulous handsome Thals Alydon and Ganatus. I am sure that any picture will be joyfully received by many girls.'

There were also some observant viewers who, while appreciating the Daleks, were concerned at inconsistencies in the programme: 'The neutron bombs which the darleks explode are supposed to petrify everything,' noted a ten-year-old from Oxford. 'Why do they petrify the forest and not the grass and trees by the swamp? I would appreciate an explanation.' And even at this early stage an eight-year-old from Sheffield had spotted a crucial design flaw: 'I have watched your programme Dr Who, and would like to know how the Daleks get up and down the steps please.' A note on the letter, written by someone at the BBC, wondered: 'Do we know?'

The instant popularity of the Daleks took everyone by surprise, not least Nation himself who, having returned in September 1963 from his Swedish engagement with Eric Sykes, had managed to join the roster of writers on the ITV adventure series *The Saint*. He was asked to provide another set of scripts for *Doctor Who* – an historical tale set during the Indian Mutiny of 1857 – but, as the year neared its end, he still saw the show as being some way down his list of priorities. The public response to the Daleks changed his life, but he was as baffled as everyone else by their appeal. 'They're amoral – there's no goodness about them,' he said in 1964. 'I can't understand why children like them.' Suggestions were offered by others, ranging from the Freudian interpretation that the Doctor represented a father figure and that children therefore identified with the creatures who wished to destroy him, to that of television critic Nancy Banks-Smith, a keen cyclist, who saw them as symbols of motor cars: 'those metal bodies, that determination to exterminate'. She even put the idea to Nation: 'But he couldn't see it. I was very sad really, so I didn't explain to him that the TARDIS was, in fact, a television set.'

The remorseless, unrelieved viciousness was clearly part of the attraction, both for children – used to seeing the world in stark black-and-white terms – and for their parents, who could pick up on the Nazi references. As Nation put it: 'Adults can see the Daleks as absolute mindless bureaucracy and children can see them as nice, frightening, anti-teddy bear figures.' Perhaps, too, the imagery tapped into a deeper resonance, a long-standing human fascination with the collective consciousness of hive communities. This was to become more apparent in later storylines, as a Dalek hierarchy emerged, but the sensation was there from the outset that these creatures resembled nothing so much as hive insects.

In the heyday of the British Empire, when the virtues of order and discipline were seen as desirable attributes, the idea of the hive had been much celebrated, the insect of choice normally being the bee. Rudyard Kipling's parable 'The Mother Hive' (1909) told the cautionary tale of a wax-moth stirring up discontent among the worker bees and destroying the stability of the social order, while Robert Baden-Powell's endorsement of the insects in Scouting for Boys (1908) was even more forthright: 'They are quite a model community, for they respect their queen and kill those who won't work.' With the rise of totalitarian regimes across Europe, however, such notions were rapidly replaced by a much more negative portrayal. In 'The Man Who Liked Ants' (1933), one of Leslie Charteris's stranger stories about the Saint, a scientist named Dr Sardon concludes that the ant 'is the destined ruler of the earth. Can you imagine a state of society in which there was no idleness, no poverty, no unemployment, no unrest? We humans would say that it was an unattainable Utopia; and yet it was in existence among the ants when man was a hairy savage scarcely distin-guishable from an ape.' All that's holding the ants back, argues Sardon, is their physical size, so he works to speed up evolution, using selective breeding and radiation to create monstrously huge creatures, 'to give them their rightful place a million years before Time would have opened the door to them'.

More recent work continued the same theme. The insect image was to occur in John Wyndham's The Day of the Triffids, a novel that also borrowed from Wells's The Time Machine and which influenced some of Nation's other work, including his second Daleks story. 'It seems to me that the triffids have something in common with some kinds of insects,' reflects one character of the carnivorous, mobile plants that are stalking Britain. 'They sort of work together for a purpose the way ants or bees do.' Nigel Kneale's

Quatermass and the Pit (1958) suggested that the ancestors of humanity had been taken to Mars by a species that the professor compares to 'termites and wasps', and Robert A. Heinlein's novel *Starship Troopers* (1959) – written as a riposte to the anti-nuclear movement – had taken the next logical step when envisaging an Earth under attack from insectoid aliens: humanity itself creates a proto-fascist society resembling a hive in order to fight the menace. Nation doesn't go this far, though his reluctant acceptance that the Daleks must be fought could be seen as a step towards the philosophy of Heinlein's world, that violence 'has settled more issues in history than any other factor'. The depiction of a peaceful people stirred into action to defeat a hive culture would have been immediately recognisable to an adult viewing public: anyone now old enough to be the parent of a seven-year-old child would have personal memories of the Second World War. More immediately, there were also associations with the rise of China, commonly seen in similar terms, as in Bernard Newman's novel of the near-future, *The Blue Ants* (1963), which concerns the Sino-Soviet war of 1970.

But the central appeal was to children, as evidenced in the rapid spread of Dalek imitations across the playgrounds of the country. Here the key factor was surely that they were so easy to mimic: it was simply a question of tucking one's elbows into the sides of one's ribcage, sticking the forearms forward and moving in a jerky way, while uttering the catchphrase 'exterminate' again and again in an approximation of the Dalek voice. 'Things come together fortuitously, and they work,' reflected *Doctor Who* writer Terrance Dicks. 'The design, the story, the voices, everything just happened to work at that time for those monsters and they became a craze.' He also suspected that there was an empowering element for children: 'Inside the Dalek is a small, vulnerable, helpless creature, and I think for a kid the idea of getting inside a Dalek and then going down to school and blasting all the teachers, or blowing up the school bully, is immensely appealing.'

Nation himself was to try to replicate the formula with further creations for *Doctor Who*, including the Voords and the Mechanoids, and others were also keen to emulate his success. 'Every writer had that ambition,' said Dicks; 'to do it again with his monster.' None ever impacted on the culture of the nation in the same way. Cybermen, Ice Warriors and Sea Devils all had their fans, and all made repeated visits to *Doctor Who* over the years, but they failed to establish an existence beyond the limits of the series. The Daleks, on the other hand, like Dracula or Frankenstein or Jekyll and Hyde, became recognisable to those who had never encountered them in their original habitat, transformed by the public imagination into something that approached mythical status. 'They were slightly magical, because you didn't know what the elements were that made them work,' admitted Nation. 'I wish I could tell you what quality they have, because I've tried to analyse it myself many times; obviously if I knew, I'd do it again.'

The closest he came was to attribute them to his subconscious. 'The one recurring dream I have,' he explained in 1979, 'is that I'm driving a car very quickly and the windscreen is a bit murky. The sun comes onto it and it becomes totally opaque. I'm still hurtling forward at incredible speed and there's nothing I can see or do and I can't stop the car.' The inability to escape, he argued, was the motivating force for the Daleks: 'However much you plead with someone to save you from this situation, everybody you turn to turns out to be one of "Them". The Daleks are all of "Them", and they represent for so many people so many different things, but they all see them as government, as officialdom, as that unhearing, unthinking, blanked-out face of authority that will destroy you because it *wants* to destroy you.'

The attempt to identify the secret of the success was, of course, ultimately doomed to failure. That first story worked largely because Nation had intended to do nothing more than spin a yarn – and it is a great piece of story-telling – for a television show that he didn't think would last more than a couple of months; his task was simply to produce an adventure tale that would entertain an audience for seven 25-minute episodes, and to do it as quickly as possible so that he could get back to writing jokes for a variety show. Had he consciously set out to create an enduring myth for the age of the mass media, it simply wouldn't have worked.

By the beginning of February 1964, when the final episode aired, his fortunes had been utterly transformed. At the age of thirty-three, his big moment had clearly arrived and he was keen to embrace every opportunity. 'I was now a hit,' as he was later to put it. 'I had a hit show!' His only real problem was that he had killed off his unexpectedly popular creatures at the end of the serial. 'And I had to think: in God's name, we've got to get them back.'

Chapter Six

Dalek Invasion

When Sydney Newman first saw the Daleks on screen, he was furious. 'I told you, goddammit, no bug-eyed monsters!' he shouted at Verity Lambert. But that was before the viewing figures came in and the sacks full of letters began arriving. When they did, he had little option but to concede gracefully. 'Ironically the series became famous,' he admitted, 'because of the Daleks, the BEMs I never wanted.' Just a few weeks after the final episode of 'The Daleks' had seen the monsters wiped out ('the travellers, in alliance with the Thals, have destroyed the Daleks for good,' spelt out the *Radio Times* unequivocally), Verity Lambert was having to announce to the press that they would be brought back: 'We had no intention of doing so originally, but in view of this large demand we have changed our minds.' A second Daleks story was pencilled in to close the season, so that if the show didn't get recommissioned, it would at least end on a high note.

Meanwhile, the success of the serial had changed the nature of the programme itself, shifting the balance from educational evocations of the past to futuristic tales set on alien planets. In January 1964 the idea of 'The Red Fort', Nation's story set during the Indian Mutiny, was abandoned, and he was asked instead to produce – at very short notice – a new science fiction piece, to be screened in April. It took just four weeks from commission to approval of the six scripts.

In consultation with David Whitaker, Nation developed 'The Keys of Marinus' as an episodic serial, effectively an anthology of four tales, loosely linked through a framing story. It was a format that Nation was to perfect later in his career, particularly in *Blake's 7* (and there are elements of 'Marinus' that he explored more fully in that series), but the tight writing schedule perhaps militated against him on this occasion; although 'The Daleks' had also been written quickly, that had been his choice, not a deadline forced upon him. In any event, the resulting story is seldom cited as one of the classic *Doctor Who* serials. Indeed even he was to struggle to recall it in any detail later in life. 'Were the Keys of Marinus four pieces that come together?' he wondered. 'Just that, I think. We did one in the jungle, we did one on ice, and I can't remember the others.' Nonetheless, there were plenty of good ideas in 'The Keys of Marinus', and some strong indications that, when he wished to, Nation could turn his hand to more subtle science fiction concepts, including the illusory pleasures of consumption, the acceleration of plant metabolism and the depiction of an alternative judicial system.

The story is set on the planet Marinus, where a machine, known as the Conscience of Marinus, was long ago set up to act as a 'judge and jury that was never wrong'. Subsequent improvements enabled it to control the minds of the planet's inhabitants, instilling virtues of justice and non-violence, until a race called the Voords found a way around its influence, to the detriment of everyone else. 'Our people could not resist because violence is alien to them,' explains a priest of the machine. Thus far, the whole thing looked like a poor man's version of 'The Daleks', and the Voords were even talked up in the press as potential rivals to their predecessors. 'They are a willowy six feet tall,' shuddered the *Daily Express*. 'Their torso resembles a man's. But they have the heads of enormous beetles and on top of their noses antennae sprout. All in all pretty horrible. Now it remains to be seen whether they will be as popular with children as the Daleks.' They were nowhere near as popular, partly because they hardly appear in the story, but mostly because they look precisely like the men in monster suits that Nation so disparaged.

Thereafter, the serial improved markedly. The inset stories see the TARDIS crew transported about the planet, using travel bracelets, on a quest to locate the four microcircuit keys that will modify the Conscience of Marinus, and thereby bring the Voords back in line. As Nation correctly remembered, one tale was set in a jungle, featuring a scientist who has discovered a way of speeding up the tempo of nature; he is under threat from rampant vegetation, as the encroachment of the undergrowth, which should take years, happens before our eyes; a second was set in the frozen wastes of the planet, with a key sealed in a block of ice and surrounded by four warriors, who are themselves set in ice – any attempt to defrost the key also brings the guards to life. There is also a courtroom drama, with Ian accused of murder under a system where the defendant is presumed guilty until proven innocent; the Doctor acts as his defence counsel and doubles up as a detective uncovering the real killer. 'Oh, elementary, elementary,' he exclaims in approved Sherlockian manner, as he solves a locked room mystery. The episode allowed William Hartnell to deliver one of his most entertaining performances as the Doctor, though its lack of action seems to have lost the attention of some of the younger viewers, causing a drop in audience figures. It also pitched him against 'a vicious, dangerous woman' named Kala (Fiona Walker), who dresses entirely in white and whose heartless scheming surely makes her a precursor of Servalan in *Blake's 7*.

Most interesting is 'The Velvet Web', the first story of the serial, in which the travellers find themselves in a 'decadent and sensuous' city named Morphoton, a sequence reminiscent of the Lotus-Eaters in Homer's *Odyssey*. They fall prey to the apparently lavish lifestyle they find there, with the exception of Barbara who has escaped the power of suggestion and can see that the luxury is an illusion. Through her agency, the truth is uncovered, that the whole city is a fantasy created by four beings whose 'brains outgrew our bodies'. These creatures live on in glass jars, enormous brains with eyes growing out on stalks, controlling the actions of their human accomplices through hypnosis. They need external agents, they explain, because 'the human body is the most flexible instrument in the world. No single mechanical device could reproduce its mobility and dexterity.' The Daleks had come to different conclusions, but since creating them, Nation had read Isaac Asimov's *The Caves of Steel* with its similar endorsement of human adaptability. The image of the brains in jars might also suggest that he had read the cheerfully misanthropic story 'William and Mary', written in 1954 by Roald Dahl (another writer who grew up in Llandaff) but only published in 1960; there were other versions of disembodied brains, including those in Curt Siodmak's 1942 novel *Donovan's Brain* and 'Hypnotic Sphere', a 1963 episode of the puppet science fiction series *Fireball XL5*, but Dahl's had the added detail of the attached eyeball.

All this, however, was little more than a holding operation, keeping the pot bubbling until the return of the Daleks. In March 1964, Nation was commissioned to write 'The Return of the Daleks', which became 'The Dalek Invasion of Earth', and in May that year he signed a contract, through a writer and editor named Jack Fishman, with Souvenir Press for a book to be titled *The Daleks Book*, for which he received a £300 advance.

The fact that he was able to do such a deal, without the involvement of the BBC, reflected an anomalous arrangement that was to prove highly beneficial. The corporation had for many years relied on an internal script department which employed writers directly, so that, for example, Nigel Kneale was a salaried employee of the BBC at the time he wrote the original *Quatermass* stories; consequently he didn't benefit as he might have done when they were remade by Hammer Films, since the copyright didn't reside with him. But part of Sydney Newman's reforms included the closing down of the script department in June 1963, with writers henceforth contracted on a self-employed basis. The early script commissions for *Doctor Who* were among the first under this new system, and the rules were not yet set in stone, as Beryl Vertue at Associated London Scripts was to discover. 'I was a new agent,' she remembered, 'I was learning. All these contracts had a copyright clause, and I used to think, well, they'll never sell this, so it was a clause I used to run a pen through. And I must have done it on Terry's contract as well.' The consequence, unintended by the BBC and unexpected by ALS, was that the copyright position of the Daleks was left entirely unresolved.

At the time of the first serial, this seemed of little relevance to anyone; during the run, the BBC even turned down an approach for licensing from an entrepreneur named Walter Tuckwell, on the grounds that the creatures were due to be killed off at the end of the story. But as the Dalek craze took off, and as more and more companies began to turn up on the corporation's doorstep looking for merchandising rights, it rapidly became clear that some agreement had to be reached. In March 1965 R.J. Marshall, assistant solicitor at the BBC, wrote to Beryl Vertue stating: 'My instructions are that the Corporation recognises ALS Management Limited (on behalf of Mr Terry Nation) as having interest in the merchandising proceeds on the grounds not of joint copyright but of goodwill.' His draft for this letter had specifically referred to ALS having 'a fifty per cent share in all mer-chandising proceeds' and, although this didn't appear in the version that was sent, it became the basis on which all future deals were made; the Daleks became the *de facto* joint property of the BBC and of Nation. As Nation was later to point out: 'we were breaking new ground in many ways.'

The Dalek Book was the first indication of what was to come. Co-credited to David Whitaker and Terry Nation, it was compiled under the guidance of Jack Fishman, with suggestions from the latter's young son, Paul, who was paid ten shillings for each idea. It comprised prose stories and comic strips, mostly illustrated by Richard Jennings, familiar to many potential purchasers from his work on the *Eagle* comic, together with the kind of factual, educational material common to annuals of the era, though notably with no humorous items or jokes. There were also the first stirrings of the desire to create a Dalek mythology, including an anatomy of one of the monsters, and a Dalek Dictionary. It was an unexpectedly huge success. The screening of the second Dalek story had been postponed when it was learned that *Doctor Who* had secured a recommission, and instead of appearing at the end of the first season, it was held over to the second, running for six episodes in November and December 1964. Even before it was aired, however, the book was being reported in the trade press as 'one of the fastest selling children's titles of 1964', with the prediction that 'sales are likely to reach stratospheric figures'.

When the series was finally broadcast, it signalled the outbreak of what was swiftly dubbed Dalekmania, in tribute to the Beatlemania that had gripped the nation since the middle of 1963. Indeed so big an event was the start of a new Dalek story that the Beatles themselves were pressed into service by ITV as part of the resistance; they starred in a special edition of the music show *Thank Your Lucky Stars*, screened against *Doctor Who* in an attempt to steal the BBC's thunder, though the result of the clash only proved how big Nation's creatures had become. 'I remember with great pride,' he said, 'that the commercial channel was running the Beatles when they were really at their peak, at the same time as a *Doctor Who* episode with the Daleks, and *Doctor Who* got the ratings. I was pretty pleased with that.'

For a few months, the Daleks were the biggest consumer story in the country, and that Christmas the creatures were to be seen everywhere. They appeared on *Blue Peter* and other supportive BBC shows, and were the hit of the Schoolboys and Girls Exhibition at Olympia in London, but they also turned up in a bewildering variety of unexpected guises all over the country: in a Christmas grotto in Belfast, in an amateur pantomime at Springfield Lane Junior School in Ipswich (a production of *Snow White*), at the circus (Bertram Mills's Christmas show in London), as part of a road safety campaign in Cwmbran, and in a specially staged Dalek race at a charity fund-raising event in Croydon, with authentic props borrowed from Dr Barnardo's Homes (to whom a couple of Daleks had been donated by the BBC after the filming of the first story). They could even be seen in church, as the Reverend G. Mountain, rector of St Paul's Church, York, took a toy Dalek into the pulpit with him for his Christmas Day sermon, in order, he explained, to highlight the contrast between fiction and 'the real invasion from outer space when Jesus came not to destroy the world, but to save mankind'.

There were a handful of unaccountable exceptions to the craze. The *Aberdeen Evening Express* reported that no toy shops in the city were stocking any Dalek products, apparently due to lack of interest: 'We would stock them if there was any demand,' shrugged a spokesperson for one shop. Even here though, a Dalek was appearing in pantomime, and the fact that the newspaper was prepared to report customer indifference was itself a tribute to how big the story had become.

Every report, every sighting, merely stoked the fires of the craze further, and helped boost what became the toy phenomenon of the season. The range of products available that first Christmas was fairly limited by later standards, but it was already possible to buy jigsaws, badges, birthday cards and sweets, as well as a single, 'I'm Gonna Spend My Christmas with a Dalek', by the Go-Go's (written by Johnny Worth, who had earlier contributed the theme song to *What a Whopper*), which seemed to miss some of the menace of the monsters:

> I'm gonna spend my Christmas with a Dalek,
> And hang him under the mistletoe,
> And if he's very nice,
> I'll feed him sugar spice
> And hang a Christmas stocking from his big left toe.

The record quite rightly failed to trouble the charts, but the toys attracted massive attention. Most desirable were the five-foot-high Dalek suits, retailing at £8 15s 6d. 'Within days of the start of a new Dalek story in the *Doctor Who* serial three weeks ago, our whole stock was sold,' commented the head buyer at Hamleys, the biggest toy store in London. 'Some parents were buying two at a time, and if I had hundreds more they would still sell.' It was reported that frustrated parents, desperate to keep their children happy at Christmas, were trying to buy them off customers lucky enough to have secured one, offering up to twice the retail price. Meanwhile six-inch-high mini-Dalek toys, costing 15s 11d, were also doing extraordinary business. 'Sales have been fantastic,' said the spokesman for Cowan, de Groot Ltd, the company manufacturing them. 'By only showing a photograph we sold out our first batch of Daleks before they had even arrived in this country. A new shipload has just arrived and we are working flat out to distribute them. People have gone Dalek mad.' A hundred thousand units were sold.

The press threw its weight behind the craze. The *Daily Express* obtained fifty of the full-size suits, and used its front page to offer them as prizes in a 'Name the Dalek' competition (winning entries included Bleatnik, Bleatle, King Klonk, Frankintin and – appropriately for what was ultimately a Welsh creation – Dai Leek). Celebrities too saw an opportunity for some easy publicity. The comedian Norman Vaughan, then the host of *Sunday Night at the London Palladium*, managed to get two separate articles in the *Daily Mail* with the same story of buying a Dalek suit and ostentatiously donating it to Oxfam. 'I was going to give this Dalek to my son for Christmas, but other children obviously need the money that this Dalek will raise,' he pontificated. 'I think we should all give to save.'

Cartoonists also joined in, with contributions from Franklin in the *Daily Mirror* and Giles in the *Daily Express* among dozens of others. Leslie Illingworth of the *Daily Mail* depicted a meeting of NATO leaders, busily discussing a proposal for an Atlantic nuclear force and being interrupted by the Degaullek, a monster topped with the familiar nose of French president Charles de Gaulle. Politicians themselves, who were then less keen to jump on passing bandwagons than they later became, took slightly longer to get off the mark, but at the 1966 Conservative Party conference, the future MP Hugh Dykes made up for lost ground by calling the defence secretary, Denis Healey, 'the Dalek of defence, pointing a metal finger at the armed forces and saying "We will eliminate you".' He got the catchphrase wrong, but it was nonetheless an indication of how readily the creatures had passed into the language. A survey earlier that year of slang terms used in the mining industry found that the term Dalek was being used in that context to refer to 'Rescue men wearing oxygen apparatus.' In the new high-security wing of Durham prison, meanwhile, it was the warders operating the modern electronic security system who were nicknamed Daleks by the inmates.

The story even reached America, where *Doctor Who* had not yet been seen. Under the headline HECK WITH THE BEATLES – HERE COME THE DALEKS!, the press reported on the British sales frenzy of Christmas 1964, and quoted one sales director as promising that 'Next year it's inflatable, floating Daleks for the beach'. In fact 1965 – with the copyright question now resolved – saw a tidal wave of products, from soap to slippers, candles to kites, Easter eggs to wallpaper, crockery to sweet cigarettes. Licences were issued for almost anything that could be branded with the logo of a Dalek, and the Harrogate toy fair that year saw some twenty-five companies exhibiting products, including – for those who wished to resist the onslaught – anti-

Dalek guns. The craze ('the startling "I-am-a-Dalek" boom', as the *Guardian* called it in October 1965) continued until the following Christmas; though it tailed off a little thereafter, new products still continued to appear, with a full-sized Dalek for amusement arcades making its debut in 1967.

The concept of marketing on this scale was entirely new to the BBC, and there was initially no structure in place to deal with the situation. 'We started the merchandising,' remembered Beryl Vertue. 'There wasn't a department at the BBC or anything.' Terry Nation's own memory was similarly of the corporation's unpreparedness: 'The BBC, not being the great commercial operator, wasn't ready. It had taken us all by surprise, so there was no merchandising, there were no plastic Daleks, there were no buttons, there were no anythings. My God, was that to change! Within the year, there were Dalek everythings.' Previously some of the corporation's more successful radio and television shows had spawned the occasional book or record, and some even turned up in comic-strip form in the magazine *Radio Fun*, but there had been nothing to hint at this level and diversity of sales, and it opened the BBC's eyes to the possibilities of subsidiary income from popular programmes. By the autumn of 1966 the press were reporting the successes of BBC Enterprises, 'formed lately to deal with broadcasting's commercially viable byproducts, in film, print and on records'; the new body was inspired directly by Dalekmania.

The phenomenon made Terry Nation a wealthy man, collecting half of the licensing fees; since these averaged ten per cent, he was thus entitled to five per cent of the sales, less his agency fees. He was still being paid for writing the show, though only at the standard BBC rates of 275 guineas per episode of *Doctor Who*, and by now additional work was coming in. But when the *Daily Mirror* estimated in March 1965 that he had earned £300,000 from the Daleks, it was clear that – even if that figure (almost £4.4 million at 2010 prices) was almost certainly overstating the case – his primary source of income was no longer the scripts he turned out. 'It was the first outbreak of merchandising,' noted Terrance Dicks, 'and Terry got rich off it. I always used to say that he was the only man to get rich off *Doctor Who*.' More than that, in one bound he leapt past his colleagues at Associated London Scripts, including the founding members. 'He was the first one of the group to get a manor house,' said Vertue, 'which was lovely.'

The house was Lynsted Park, a mansion dating back to Elizabethan times, complete with the crypt of what had been a family chapel, standing in 35 acres of ground near Sittingbourne, Kent, and it was purchased in the summer of 1964, just in time for Nation to celebrate his thirty-fourth birthday with a party. 'He threw good parties,' remembered *Doctor Who* actress Carole Ann Ford, who went on that occasion, though her chief memory was of his excitement at having a swimming pool in the garden, and then discovering that 'it was full of rubbish'. Deb Boultwood went to a later party with her father, Dave Freeman, and reflected the general impression that Nation was enjoying his new-found wealth: 'They had loads of champagne and food, and there was Roger Moore in a blue jumpsuit with Luisa Mattioli. And Linda Thorson and Patrick Macnee and all these people. It's one of my happiest memories. I think we stayed till dawn before we drove back; Terry and Kate were very good hosts.'

It was a time when a new, supposedly meritocratic, showbiz aristocracy was emerging from popular culture in Britain, an era when pop stars and photographers, designers and hairdressers were being courted and celebrated by the media. Nation was, if not a member of this aristocracy, at least a peripheral part of their world, embodying the rewards that talent and (in his case) enduring dedication could bring. After nearly a decade of trying to make ends meet in London as a writer, he was determined to enjoy his moment in the sun. 'He sort of invented a life for himself,' was Brian Clemens's perception of Nation in the 1960s. 'He wore wonderful Liberty-print shirts. He looked American. He was a bit flamboyant and he drove a big American car for a while. And when he swapped that, he had an open E-Type. He was a bit of a poseur.' As the *Guardian* put it in January 1966: 'He is proud of his material success, of his country house and the nearby cottages he has bought for his parents and his wife's mother and father.' In fact, Nation was spending less time at Lynsted Park than he might have wished; pressure of work meant that he mostly lived in a flat in Swiss Cottage in North London, not far from the Hampstead flat that he had recently vacated, supposedly to move to the country. His own memory of the period was the way that the Daleks seemed to be taking over his career: 'They became such a large business concern in their own right that I had very little opportunity to do much else.'

In all the noise and excitement of Dalekmania, it was sometimes possible to forget that the Daleks were not officially supposed to be the stars of the show. The BBC as an organisation was, of course, earning as much as Nation from the merchandising, but he was the only individual from *Doctor Who* to benefit directly from the bonanza. As the extent of the marketing enterprise became clear, Raymond P. Cusick asked his boss: 'Is any of this money coming my way? I got an answer the following week, and that was: No!' As a BBC employee, Cusick was entitled to nothing more than his salary for having produced the original Dalek design, though he was later given 'an ex-gratia payment of £100, which after tax came to £80 10s 6d'. He left the show in 1966, partly because he felt he was not being given the recognition he deserved: 'I worked on the programme for three years but quite honestly I got fed up with it. Nobody, apart from my bosses, was actually saying thanks to me.'

Terrance Dicks insisted that there was no resentment among the other *Doctor Who* writers then or later about Nation's wealth: 'Envy, I think, not resentment. You thought: good luck to him.' But there was a very real danger that the series itself might get swallowed up by the burgeoning Dalek empire, a fact of which the production team were well aware. Their concern was presumably the reason why the press were able to report that the creatures would definitely be killed off in 'The Dalek Invasion of Earth', and that this time it would be for good: 'this, according to Television Centre, is positively their last appearance.' When the *Daily Mail* journalist John Sandilands interviewed Verity Lambert during the run of the serial, he found the message being spelt out very clearly: 'Tall, dark and shapely, she became positively forbidding when I suggested that the Daleks might one day take over *Doctor Who*. "I feel in no way obligated to bring them back for a third time even if this present story is a tremendous success," she said with a noticeable chill.'

In fact a third story had already been commissioned, though Nation's own comments suggested that there might be some disagreement between the BBC hierarchy and the programme-makers. 'I don't want to bring them back,' he told the press in December 1964, as the new serial ended. 'They've hit such a level of popularity that nothing they do can be quite as popular again. The Beatles and pop groups have dropped a bit in popularity, and the Daleks seem to have filled the gap. I can't see them hitting this level for much longer. But what can one do? I don't want the Daleks back, the BBC does. They've insisted on it.'

If this had indeed been the swansong for the Daleks, they would at least have gone out on a high, for 'The Dalek Invasion of Earth' was one of the best scripts Nation was to contribute to the series. It was written at weekends, he later explained, because he was busy at his day job, writing episodes of *The Saint*, during the week, and consequently there was a two-month gap between the delivery of the proposed storyline and the finished scripts; he still insisted, however, that it took him only eight hours to write each episode.

The first problem to be solved was bringing the creatures back from the extinction to which he had consigned them. There had been precedents for such resuscitations, of course, most notably in the case of Sherlock Holmes, who was killed off by Arthur Conan Doyle in the 1893 story 'The Final Problem' before making a return in 'The Empty House' a decade later. Then too it had been public demand that forced the change of heart, and Doyle dealt with the issue by revealing that Holmes had not actually died in his struggle with Professor Moriarty at the Reichenbach Falls, but had gone into hiding for a couple of years. In between those two stories, however, Doyle had published the novel *The Hound of the Baskervilles* (1901), set retrospectively before Holmes's disappearance, and this was the model that Nation chose to follow. 'I remembered Conan Doyle's problem with Sherlock Holmes,' he later explained, and he wrote in a simple lesson in time travel, delivered by the Doctor: 'What happened on Skaro was a million years ahead of us in the future. What we're seeing now is about the middle history of the Daleks.' It was the first time that one *Doctor Who* storyline had deliberately referenced another, a toe in the water of continuity, even if for Nation at this stage it was simply a neat solution to an immediate problem. Having wrapped that up nicely, he got on with making the creatures even more scary than before by bringing them into our own world.

The story opens under a semi-derelict bridge, on which there is a poster bearing the enigmatic and sinister message: EMERGENCY REGULATIONS: IT IS FORBIDDEN TO DUMP BODIES INTO THE RIVER. A man appears, tearing away in anguish at the helmet encasing his head. He walks down some steps and plunges into the river, apparently committing suicide. It's an instantly arresting image, topped only by the closing shot of the first episode: we're back at the same point on the river – which we now know is the Thames – and, as we watch, a Dalek emerges slowly and menacingly from beneath the waters, its weapons pointing directly at the camera.

Having delayed the appearance of a Dalek until the final shot of the opening episode in the previous storyline, Nation repeated the trick here to what should have been startling effect. Except, of course, that the massive blaze of pre-publicity was such that the revelation of a Dalek was never going to be a shock; apart from anything else, the front cover of the *Radio Times* that week had been given over to the show, heralding the return of the monsters. As a result the late arrival was distressing for all the wrong reasons. 'A howl of anguish went up all over Britain,' reported the press. 'Angry viewers protested that the Dalek's appearance was far too brief; that children who had waited months for another sign of the monsters were weeping and refusing to go to bed.' A BBC spokesperson admitted: 'Our switchboard was flooded with calls from viewers who thought the Daleks would be on for the major part of the programme.' Undeterred, Nation was to make the shock reveal in the final scene something of a signature for his Dalek tales.

It transpires that we are in London in the year 2164, exactly two hundred years into the future, and that Earth has been taken over by the Daleks. Some humans have been brainwashed to act as the occupying force's henchmen – these are the Robomen, one of whom we saw in the opening scene – while others have formed a determined, if largely ineffective, resistance. It would be difficult to see this as being anything other than a development of the Nazi associations of the Daleks, an extension of that theme into an invasion of Britain (for, despite the title, we don't leave south-east England). The serial's director, Richard Martin, was more than aware of the connections: 'Terry and all of us who were making it were very influenced by the Second World War, because those images and those wrecks were still abundant. There were still bits of London where you could find the weeds growing, that they hadn't rebuilt. So when I was looking for locations, and when he was describing locations, he was describing the stuff that we had intimately known during the Second World War.'

It was an impression reinforced by key scenes over the course of the six episodes. Daleks swagger – inasmuch as Daleks can swagger – around London landmarks like Trafalgar Square and the Albert Memorial; human beings are used as slave labour in a mine, under the direction of uniformed Robomen; and there is a genuinely shocking scene when Barbara and Jenny, a member of the resistance, having escaped from London into the country and found refuge in a cottage, are betrayed to the Daleks by the two elderly women who live there. 'We're old, child,' one of the women tells Barbara in a deleted passage from the original script. 'Times are difficult. There's only one law now – survive.' And just in case there might be any mistake, in the last episode the commander of the Daleks issues the ultimate orders: 'Arrange for the extermination of all human beings – the final solution.'

Nation was not the only person pursuing such imagery. A coincidence of timing had seen the release a month earlier of Kevin Brownlow and Andrew Mollo's film *It Happened Here*, which had been eight years in the making. The movie's portrayal of what Britain would have looked like in the aftermath of a Nazi invasion in 1940 bore some striking, if accidental, parallels with 'Invasion', not only in broad terms – both are set some years after the invasion has actually taken place – but in particular scenes: the shots, for example, of German troops around key London landmarks, including the same two sites of Trafalgar Square and the Albert Memorial. (Nation had also suggested, but didn't get, Daleks at the statue of Peter Pan in Kensington Gardens, in symbolic destruction of existing children's fiction, and – a fine piece of self-aggrandisement – Daleks invading the BBC Television Centre.) The central figure in *It Happened Here* is a nurse named Pauline Murray, who a doctor friend tries to recruit into the resistance, using arguments not dissimilar to those employed in 'The Daleks': 'The appalling thing about fascism is that you've got to use fascist methods to get rid of it.' But Pauline is worn out by standing up for her principles, and has no appetite for a prolonged struggle: 'My point is we've fought a war and lost it. There's been a terrible lot of suffering on both sides, so why prolong that suffering?' Many of the same issues had also turned up in Robert Muller's novel, *The Lost Diaries of Albert Smith*, published earlier in the summer of 1964, which told the story of contemporary Britain sliding into fascism, while Gillian Freeman's *The Leader*, on a similar theme but a smaller canvas, was to come the following year.

This was not the image of the country that was being propagated for international consumption. London was fast approaching its anointment as the swinging capital of the modern world, but that development could hardly be deduced from these works, or from 'Invasion' – the scene of Daleks in Trafalgar Square could only have been less swinging if they'd actually blown up a red double-decker bus. And reality was no more encouraging than fiction; when the production crew arrived at 6 a.m. one Sunday morning to film the Daleks, they had to move out of shot not the dedicated followers of fashion stumbling homewards after a night on the town, but several vagrants who were sleeping rough in the West End. The General Election in October 1964 had seen the removal of an ageing, tired Conservative government, to be replaced by a Labour Party under Harold Wilson, who made great play of his meritocratic credentials, his comparative youth (he was the right side of fifty) and, therefore, his alleged solidarity with the thrusting new generation that was threatening to transform the popular culture of the western world. But already doubts were being raised within that same cultural movement about Britain's self-image; there was a stark discrepancy between, on the one hand, Wilson's vision of a country reforged in the white heat of the technological revolution and, on the other, Nation's grim portrayal of the English countryside overrun by Daleks.

And some of it was very grim indeed, especially in the context of a teatime children's show. Some viewers found even the opening scene, with the Roboman committing suicide, too much to take. A woman from Uxbridge wrote to the BBC to complain: 'My two children aged 5 and 7 were quite looking forward to seeing more adventures with these weirdly amusing robots. Unfortunately I found the beginning of the series so horrifying as to compare with the *Quatermass* series of some years ago where at least it was for adults.' She spared the children further horrors by switching off, but still, 'the little they did see caused them considerable distress at bedtime'. For those who stayed with the serial, there was more horror to come. The fratricidal reality of a society under military occupation achieves literal expression when a resistance fighter named Larry discovers that his brother has become a Roboman; in an ensuing fight between the two, they slay each other. As David, another member of the resistance, warns Susan: 'Not all human beings are automatically allies. There are people who will kill for a few scraps of food.'

Meanwhile the debate about pacifism in the first serial has a successor in the shape of an argument, spread over two episodes, about how best to respond to the Dalek occupation. 'What's the point in running away all the time?' asks the history teacher Barbara, and Jenny replies: 'I'm not running. I'm surviving, that's all.' She later spells out what she sees as Barbara's illusions: 'You've got this romantic idea about resistance. There is nothing heroic about dying. There's no point in throwing lives away just to prove a principle.'

The idea of surviving, of simply living in the face of overwhelming odds, was a concept to which Nation was repeatedly to return, and in his original script for 'Invasion' there was a more explicit statement of the theme than finally appeared. 'The world you have come into is one where friendships mean very little,' David was to have told Susan. 'There's been no place for sentiment in society. Just staying alive is the most anybody has time for.' Susan reflects on her own experience of extreme situations, the positive element of how they can build stronger ties between people: 'The four of us faced dangers together and it seemed to give us a greater understanding of one another.' So it was to prove here, for the story ends, after the defeat of the Daleks, with Susan staying behind on the future Earth to help David in the reconstruction of society, a prospect they have already contemplated. 'One day this will be all over,' says David. 'It'll mean a new start.' Susan is enthused by the challenge: 'A new start? Rebuilding a planet from the very beginning. It's a wonderful idea.' One might see here the germ of the idea that would become *Survivors*.

There were other elements that would recur in Nation's work, including the central conflict between a totalitarian state and a scattered resistance movement. And the resistance is painted in the same, extravagantly idealist colours that would become a feature of Nation's writing. The group we meet are led by a wheelchair-bound scientist named Dortmun, who – having developed a hand-held bomb that he believes will be effective against Daleks –organises a raid on a ship at their launching pad. As it turns out, the bombs are completely ineffective against the Daleks' casings, but it is in any case a deeply flawed plan; this is intended as a symbolic strike that will galvanise other resistance groups, but how anyone would hear about it when the Daleks control all the communication systems is far from clear. Here, as elsewhere, one gets the impression that while Nation's enthusiasm might be of use to the leaders of an underground movement, they would be loath to turn to him for practical advice. Like Barbara, he often seems seduced by 'this romantic idea about resistance'.

None of these themes, of course, is allowed to get in the way of what is at its heart a thundering good tale about terrifying aliens invading our world and being seen off. As a piece of television, it also benefited hugely from a move to a more spacious studio and from the extensive location shoots used for the first time in a *Doctor Who* story; consequently it looks much bigger than 'The Daleks' or 'The Keys of Marinus'. Much more than the first story, this felt like a major piece of work, a modern myth in the making. In particular, the scenes of Dortmun being hurriedly pushed in his wheelchair through deserted London streets, with the knowledge that Daleks might be lurking around any and every corner, were disturbing in a way not previously seen on British television, though it had been fore-shadowed in literature with the chapter 'Dead London' in *The War of the Worlds*. (Nation suggested getting footage of a depopulated London from the 1950 film *Seven Days to Noon*, a thriller about a scientist trying to force the country to abandon nuclear weapons, which suggests another source of his vision.)

Much of the plot is gleeful nonsense – the Daleks are trying to extract the molten core of Earth so that they can use the planet as an intergalactic spaceship – and the denouement that sees their evil plan thwarted is confused at best, but Nation is clearly enjoying himself, and the absurdities are less intrusive than might be expected. The one exception is perhaps the Slyther, an alien creature kept as a pet by the Black Dalek, who is heading the mining operation. (The idea of a hierarchy within Dalek society was beginning to emerge.) As it appears on screen, the Slyther is patently a man in a monster suit, looking like a homemade approximation of a deep sea sloth; though it's supposed to be a terrifying beast that eats humans, it gets killed without adding anything of any value to the story. It was, however, meant to be more impressive than that. Drawing on his radio experience, Nation was keen to convey the creature essentially by sound – 'this awful panting, gasping sound' – and his original conception of 'a huge, black jellyfish' that we never quite see, just 'the hint of a shapeless, pulsating mass', had a hint of Lovecraftian menace that was never realised. Even so, the creature prompted a number of complaints to the BBC about it being too horrific for children's television.

As was already characteristic of Nation's writing, there are echoes of other stories. There is, for example, a hint of John Wyndham's *The Day of the Triffids* in the account of how the Dalek invasion was preceded by a cosmic storm of meteorites, and by a plague that killed off a large part of the population: 'The Daleks were up in the sky, just waiting for Earth to get weaker. Whole continents of people were wiped out: Asia, Africa, South America. They used to say the Earth had a smell of death about it.' Likewise the Daleks' plan to burrow to the Earth's core is reminiscent of Arthur Conan Doyle's *When the World Screamed* (1928), in which Professor Challenger drills through the Earth's crust to prove his theory that the planet is actually a living organism in its own right. The result of his experiment is a series of explosions and volcanic eruptions all over the world, just as at the end of 'Invasion', and the Doctor's comment could well have come from the mouth of Challenger himself: 'The Earth rebelled and destroyed the invaders.'

The story ends with the departure of Susan, Carole Ann Ford having become bored with the role. 'I just felt my part wasn't really going anywhere,' she explained. 'It seemed to me that the people coming in – our visitors – were always getting much more interesting things to do than I was.' Behind the scenes, David Whitaker also left the production team, though his work with Nation on the Daleks was to continue. His replacement was Dennis Spooner, another client of Associated London Scripts, who had earlier been introduced to Whitaker by Nation as a possible writer for *Doctor Who*. Spooner specialised in historical tales, including 'The Reign of Terror' and 'The Romans', pointing out, as he took over the job of script editor: 'Writers have to be divided into those who can cope with trips back into the past and those who can write adventures set in the future. Very few can do both.' He too was to contribute to the emerging mythology of the Daleks.

Meantime 'The Dalek Invasion of Earth', fuelled by the Dalekmania of Christmas 1964, was a major triumph, bigger even than 'The Daleks' had been. For the first time *Doctor Who* broke into the weekly top ten of the most watched programmes, and its position as the country's favourite science fiction show was assured. That second story broke new ground for the series: the first monsters to return, the first invasion of Earth, the first attempt to establish continuity between two different serials. There was no guarantee that it would work, for much of this was without precedent in science fiction on British television. *Quatermass* may have enjoyed periodic revivals, but it was the humans not the aliens who were the common factor. Nor was there a parallel in the movies, with the possible exception of the alien children in *Village of the Damned* and *Children of the Damned* (1964), adapted from John Wyndham's *The Midwich Cuckoos*, though the second film is a straightforward sequel.

But the extraordinary wave of Dalekmania made the triumph seem like a foregone conclusion, and it was clear at the end of 'Invasion' that this was not the end of the story; the Doctor had encountered them twice now in their history and we knew that he would do so again. Nation was on a roll, but then he never admitted to harbouring any doubts. Even before the serial was broadcast, he was positive and confident of its success. 'I met Terry after we'd shot about three of them,' Richard Martin remembered. 'We had a showing, and he was over the moon. He was a lovely, ebullient, rounded sort of Welshman, and he clasped his hand around my back and said: "Well, boy, we had to come back big, and by golly we did!"'

Chapter Seven

Action Men

When the first ITV franchises were handed out in the mid 1950s, while Terry Nation was still struggling to establish himself as a writer of radio comedy, one of the big winners was ATV, which won the right to broadcast to London at weekends and the Midlands during the week. Fronted by Lew Grade, the theatre impresario and – as he never failed to remind people – the former Charleston Champion of the World, ATV became over the next decade the most powerful and profitable of the independent companies, pioneering practices that would become standard in the British industry. It was also to provide gainful employment for Nation through much of the 1960s and into the 1970s.

At this stage a requirement was placed on the new channel that fourteen per cent of its broadcasting should be home-grown programmes, and Grade responded by commissioning – via his company ITC (Incorporated Television Company) – material from independent production companies to fill the quota. He struck gold immediately with *The Adventures of Robin Hood*, made by Sapphire Films and first broadcast in 1955, which proved so successful that it was rapidly followed by a slew of other swashbuckling series set in a fictionalised family-friendly history, including *The Adventures of the Scarlet Pimpernel* (1956), *The Count of Monte Cristo* (1956) and *Ivanhoe* (1958). Even more influential than its subject matter, however, were the commercial opportunities that *Robin Hood* opened up. Grade sold the show to the CBS network in America, thereby providing a blueprint that ATV was to spend much of the next two decades striving to emulate with other productions. So fixated on American sales were these shows that *Sir Lancelot* was even made in colour, a full ten years before the first experiments in colour broadcasting were made in Britain.

Much of this enterprise was dominated by the charismatic figure of

Grade himself. Born in the southern Ukraine in 1906 as Lev Winogradsky, he was just five years old when his family fled the anti-Jewish pogroms and arrived in Stepney in London's East End. He and his younger brothers, Boris and Laszlo (later known as Bernard Delfont and Leslie Grade respectively), found an escape from the poverty of their childhood in the world of show business. 'If you didn't want to starve, you earned money,' remembered Bernard. 'It all bred a desire to achieve something better. That feeling came as naturally as breathing.' All three brothers were to become hugely powerful players in British entertainment, but it was Lew who really captured the popular imagination. A natural showman who never displayed less than absolute faith in whatever he did, he revelled in the public role that came with his reincarnation as a television mogul, even though he faced considerable hostility from the outset. 'Is this the man you want to choose the programmes for your children?' asked the *Daily Express*, with just a whiff of anti-semitism, over a picture of Grade looking the very embodiment of the Jewish plutocrat, complete with his trademark eight-inch cigar.

Grade displayed a personal, paternal concern for his shows, though he had little interest in the mechanics of making programmes; Roger Moore remembered him paying just one visit to the set of *The Saint* throughout its seven-year run. His preference was rather for the wheeling and dealing involved in selling the work to other companies in the ITV network and, preferably, abroad, priding himself on his buccaneering salesmanship. He boasted in 1966, for example, that all three American networks were interested in a new series, to be titled *The Champions*, which had not even been cast, let alone filmed: 'We have two scripts so far,' he explained to the press, revelling in his ability to make bricks without straw. His other great boast was that he never broke his word, so that – in a reversal of Samuel Goldwyn's famous formulation – a verbal contract was worth more than the paper it was written on. He was in many ways the perfect television executive: impulsive in his commissions, intensely loyal and supportive, and with no great appetite for interference. Consequently he received the same loyalty and support from those in his employ. 'Lew was a wonderful human being,' said Moore simply.

After five years of heroic histories, ITC moved into new territory in 1959 with an adaptation of Edgar Wallace's thriller characters, *The Four Just Men*, followed by *Danger Man*, a secret agent series starring Patrick McGoohan, and by the television debut of *The Saint.* The latter was something of a coup, for the character of Simon Templar, the gentleman vigilante known internationally as the Saint, was already one of the most successful British cultural exports, having appeared in more than thirty books, in several movies, in cartoon strips and in radio series in both Britain and America (where he was most famously played by Vincent Price). Indeed his creator, Leslie Charteris, had moved to America in the 1930s, as the Saint's fame began to spread across the Atlantic, and subsequently became a US citizen. Templar had never, however, appeared on television, though it was not for want of trying. Most recently, Roger Moore, the star of *Ivanhoe*, had been advised by his father when that series ended that, in the interests of controlling his future career, he should buy the television rights to one of the old action heroes, either John Creasey's Toff, or the Saint, and he 'made a half-hearted attempt at acquiring the rights' but without success. Charteris, it appeared, had one overriding concern: 'Money — I have had negotiations with many people at various times but I held out for more money.'

The men who came up with the right offer turned out to be the British production team of Robert S. Baker and Monty Berman, whose previous cinematic work included *Blood of the Vampire* (1958), *The Flesh and the Fiends* (1960) and *The Hellfire Club* (1961). 'After many years of noble and lofty-minded resistance,' explained Charteris, 'I finally broke down and sold the Saint to the Philistines of television.' Having failed to sell the idea of a series to Associated Rediffusion, Baker and Berman approached Lew Grade at ATV. The character of the fantasy hero had an instant appeal for Grade, who defined his approach to television in distinctly un-Reithian terms. ('I am not here to educate the public,' he insisted, 'I am here to entertain them.') With his blessing, Simon Templar made his television debut in October 1962, in the same week that *Dr No*, the first James Bond movie, was released. Despite the prior claims of *Danger Man* and *The Avengers*, the latter already into its second season, this was the true start of the action hero genre that would dominate 1960s popular culture, much of it harking back to the style of the 1920s and 1930s.

The Saint, indeed, was of precisely that vintage, having first appeared in *Meet the Tiger* in 1929. Simon Templar was a wealthy daredevil about town, cosmopolitan enough to explain to a French-Canadian waiter — in his own language — how to mix a perfect Rumhattan cocktail, while roguish enough to steal the man's wallet on the way out of the bar. Conceived as a latter-day Robin Hood, he was a freelance campaigner for justice in a society riddled with corruption and career criminals, a man who didn't baulk at breaking the law if it was in a worthy cause. He was 'a terror to the underworld and a thorn in the side of Scotland Yard, a gay crusader in modern dress', and his enemies tended to be upper-class domestic tyrants, confidence tricksters, crooked businessmen and anyone else who might be tempted to place a damsel in a position of distress. He sided with the oppressed, but remained aristocratically arrogant and anti-democratic, with a particular distaste for nouveau riche types who don't know their place in society. At times he would admit to a contempt not only for modern society but for most of humanity, and despite his leaden attempt at humour, the message was clear: 'The human race is a repulsive, dull, bloated, ill-conditioned and ill-favoured mass of dimly conscious meat, the chief justification for whose existence is that it provides a contrasting background against which my beauty and spiritual perfection can shine.'

He was thus a step further on from his near-contemporary, Sapper's creation Bulldog Drummond, whose exploits filled books from 1920 to 1954. Like Templar a wealthy crime-fighter, independent of the police or other agency of the state, Drummond was above all a simple man of action with little discernible intellect, who leapt from one implausible scenario to another, including – to take random examples from just the first book in the series – an acid bath, a deadly tarantula, even a gorilla loose in an English country garden (the latter Drummond slays with his bare hands). Templar, on the other hand, while retaining much of this spirit of exotic adventure, had ostentatious trappings of sophistication and style, an ability to concoct complicated plans of action on the spur of the moment, and – after the carefree nonchalance of his earlier years – an air of slightly pained world-weariness that could only be stirred into action by the sight of injustice or of a woman in need of assistance. He was part of society, even of high society, but somehow remained aloof from it, an outsider rather than an outlaw. He was, in short, the prototype of Ian Fleming's James Bond.

Much of this survived into the screen incarnation of the Saint presented by Robert S. Baker and Monty Berman. Three decades on from his creation, he was still an international playboy who revelled in conspicuous consumption, still a deadly foe of wrong-doers, even though he himself enjoyed an ambivalent relationship with the law. Charteris wanted David Niven as the star of the series (Niven was also Ian Fleming's preferred choice to play James Bond), while Grade was keen to use Patrick McGoohan, but Baker and Berman chose instead to give the role to Roger Moore, a younger, more casual, less overtly English presence. Among his other credentials, Moore had, following *Ivanhoe*, just starred in *The Alaskans* and *Maverick* on American television, gaining valuable exposure in the target export market; he was also a client of the management agency run by Lew Grade with his brother Leslie.

It was an inspired piece of casting. Moore looked superb in the role, boasting a highly lacquered, swept-back hairdo and an enviable ability to wear beautifully cut clothes, while his deceptively easy acting style allowed him to inhabit the character of Templar and yet maintain a slightly amused distance from him. The result was the definitive portrayal of the character, providing all the thrills and excitement a viewer could ask for, without demanding that any of it be taken too seriously; he was always a raised eyebrow away from commitment. 'We wanted to do the show slightly tongue in cheek,' noted Baker, and Simon Templar started every programme with a direct address to camera, welcoming us into his world while establishing a light ironic tone which ran as an undercurrent through the ensuing episode. The show's American script editor, Harry W. Junkin, once claimed that there were three reasons why *The Saint* was such a successful series: Roger Moore, Roger Moore and Roger Moore.

Changes were made, of course, a slight smoothing of the darker side of the original. In the old days, for example, Templar used to carry a knife strapped to his forearm; as the novelist Colin Watson noted, this was uncharacteristic in an action hero of the pre-war years, when the convention was clear: 'only foreigners and very low-grade criminals used knives for fighting purposes.' The practice was dropped for the television series. 'I made a decision that knives were definitely out,' remembered Baker; 'he had to fight by the Marquis of Queensberry rules.' Such weapons were to be again restricted to those with no sense of honour and fair play, though the change didn't go unremarked even within the show itself. In one of Terry Nation's scripts, a French villain (we can tell that he's a villain because he puts his cigarette out in Templar's drink) pulls a knife from his jacket sleeve with a dramatic flourish. 'I used to carry one like that,' shrugs Templar. 'Found it frayed my cuffs.'

Also played down was the implicit xenophobia that permeated much of the adventure literature of the 1930s. Charteris, born Leslie Yin, the son of a Chinese father and English mother, was much less inclined than many of his contemporaries to break out into explicit racism, but there was still an occasional tendency to refer to 'the birds with the fat cigars and names ending in -heim and -stein who juggle the finances of this cock-eyed world', or to 'foreign-looking birds with ugly mugs'. The latent anti-semitism, which attracted little or no attention at the time, looked horribly inappropriate in a world coloured by the Holocaust, whilst a fine line had to be trodden, in a series aimed at overseas sales, between a celebration of traditional British culture and anything that smacked of superiority It was possible, however, to detect an implied nostalgia for imperial dominance, a sense of using the past as a stick with which to beat the present. Templar ends a 1967 episode, Michael Pertwee's 'When Spring Is Sprung', by telling his Russian enemies: 'For some years now the rest of the world has been systematically underestimating the British. To them – you – we are a second-rate power. Which means that everything about us is second rate.'

This belief in Britain's post-war decline, in the enfeeblement of the national character, and in the need for heroes who might keep the flame of freedom alive, was a common theme in the popular fiction of the time, but it was not a theme to which Terry Nation found himself attracted; in his scripts for the series, the Saint simply didn't express such opinions. More broadly, although his heroes were almost exclusively British, either overtly or – as with *Doctor Who* and *Blake's 7* – by depiction, and although he drew heavily on the pre-war tradition, there was never a trace of jingoism in his work. There is even a suggestion that nostalgia for the bold days of exploits and exploration is misplaced. 'We're the last of the adventurers,' a character named Miles Hallin boasts to Templar, trying to ingratiate himself. 'Living for excitement is a lost art.' The Saint is decidedly unimpressed, reviving the argument that Richard Hannay had made forty years earlier in *The Island of Sheep*. 'I wouldn't go that far,' he replies dismissively, but Hallin won't let it go: 'Why, sure it is. Today, kids get their kicks by taking pills. They don't hunt big game or climb mountains. How can they know what life is about unless they've looked at death?' We're not much surprised when Hallin turns out to be a bad sort.

For Nation, whose love of adventure tales had been honed on the noble heroism of Biggles in childhood, a figure like the Saint was something of a gift. He had been an impressionable ten-year-old when Terence de Marney began appearing as Simon Templar on Friday evenings on the Forces Programme, around the same time that George Sanders was creating the first great screen incarnation of the character in a series of movies for RKO. He knew this material, and the genre whence it came, intimately, and he displayed considerably more enthusiasm for the idea of writing *The Saint* than he had shown for *Doctor Who*. Here, he knew, he would be in his element; even though he was working with characters – and sometimes plots – that were not his own, there was a sense of him coming home with his ITC work. 'I think he felt more comfortable in this niche,' commented Beryl Vertue. 'It was something really new, more his own.'

Nation's entry into the world of *The Saint* came via Harry W. Junkin. 'I was given a terrible story by Leslie Charteris,' he recalled. 'There wasn't much to it, and very little you could do with it, but I was supposed to adapt it. All those original *Saint* episodes were supposed to be adapted from Charteris's stories.' Evidently his adaptation was successful enough, for he was then commissioned to write more, and turned out nine scripts for the show in 1964–5. The stories ranged across the globe, from South America to London, from Haiti to the grouse moors of Scotland, and covered a similarly diverse range of subjects: there were revolutionary groups, voodoo priests, blackmailers, murderers and jewel thieves. And, despite his complaints about the source material, most of his adaptations stayed close to the originals.

The 1964 episode 'Jeannine', for example, relocated the action from New Orleans to Paris and added a minor sub-plot about 'a couple of rather unsavoury French hoods', but the essential story – of Templar and others trying to steal a pearl necklace – remained intact. He did, however, make a change to the denouement.

Early on in Charteris' story, Templar tells a police officer the tale of Cleopatra giving Caesar a goblet of wine into which she drops a pearl; it promptly dissolves and is lost for ever, thus demonstrating the extent of her wealth and power. Having subsequently acquired the necklace, he then confounds the police by reminding them of the tale and directing them towards the oxtail casserole he has spent all day preparing. In the casserole, heavy with red wine, the police find just a two-foot-long loop of thread, and they troop out despondently, having lost any desire to pursue what they know will be a fruitless search. The Saint, of course, is bluffing; he has the pearls in his pocket and he's merely slipped an empty string into the stew. In a final twist, it's revealed that 'the story of pearls being dissolved in wine was strictly a fable, without a grain of scientific truth'. Nation's version garbles the sequence of events, missing the point of the casserole bluff, but it also omits that last detail about it all being 'strictly a fable', conveniently leaving the idea in the public domain, available for future use. And he did reuse it in 'Legacy of Death', a 1968 episode of *The Avengers*, in which a pearl is successfully dissolved in a glass of wine, again with reference to Cleopatra. 'I thought everyone knew,' says Steed. 'Pearls dissolve in wine.' (On a purely factual note, a pearl will actually dissolve in wine, but only if it has first been ground into a fine powder – this was not how it happened in *The Avengers*.)

Nation also added a political edge, updating the story from the aftermath of Indian independence to the present, so that the owner of the necklace is now Madame Chen (Jacqui Chan), the representative of a dictatorial oriental nation, and one of those chasing the pearls is Lo Yung (Eric Young), a hotel waiter from Chen's own country, intent on striking a blow for freedom: 'My people starve. They are taxed beyond endurance. Any voice that is raised in complaint is instantly silenced by force of arms.' He plans to steal the necklace so that he might sell it to raise funds for the revolutionary cause. 'In the history of all oppressed people, a leader emerges from the crowd and takes his people into freedom,' he explains, after a failed attempt to lift the pearls. 'Until that man appears, the suffering goes on. The pearls would have brought some relief – food, medical supplies.' It is he who ultimately benefits, when Templar gives him the stolen necklace, having concluded that Lo's need is greater than anyone else's.

Elsewhere in Nation's scripts, lest he be misunderstood, the Saint makes clear that his is not a dewy-eyed celebration of revolution for its own sake. 'Whenever people get killed, I'm bothered,' he explains. 'That's what revolution means: death and misery on a large scale.' But he's always keen to take sides in a political dispute, particularly in the context of decolonisation. In 'The Sign of the Claw' (1965), his opening address to camera abandons the usual tone of dry detachment, striking instead a much more serious note: 'The jungles of South-East Asia are amongst the hottest spots in the world right now. There is a full-scale war going on, except nobody calls it a war. Officially, it's an anti-terrorist campaign. But no matter what the politicians call it, it's a battleground. Probably the most savage on the face of the earth.' The references are seemingly rooted in the long-running Malayan Emergency, which had seen British and Common-wealth troops battling communist guerrillas throughout the 1950s, though the resonance with the recently escalated conflict in Vietnam could hardly be avoided.

The story itself is set in an unnamed post-colonial country and features Max Valmon (Godfrey Quigley), who's lived here all his life and is now in cahoots with a mercenary, Dr Julias (Leo Leyden), to destabilise the new government, for reasons that he explains to Templar: 'Six months ago when this country became independent, the government was taken over by a bunch of wogs. They started ordering us about, telling us what we could do and what we couldn't do.' Templar replies laconically: 'Seems reasonable. It's their country.' Valmon is outraged: 'Their country! Without us, they'd still be in their straw huts.' But the Saint has no time for such arguments, and no inclination to stand in solidarity with white colonialists: 'I'd say whatever you've put into this country, you've taken out again, with considerable interest.' He succeeds in scuppering their plans and, by repositioning the lights on a jungle landing-strip, he causes a plane, full of supplies for the counter-revolutionaries, to crash. When he's congratulated on the success of his brilliant plan, he shrugs off the compliment: 'I'm afraid the brilliance is not mine really. I read about it in an adventure story years ago.'

That last little joke was characteristic of Nation's scripts for *The Saint*, which frequently included such knowing comments. 'If you're smart, you'll pull the trigger on me right now,' a crook tells Templar in one episode. 'Because if I stay alive, I swear they're going to be picking up little pieces of you all over this crummy town.' The Saint is amused by his turn of phrase: 'Haven't changed much, have you, Jack? You still talk like a hoodlum in a second-rate gangster movie.' This trick of letting the audience know that they were in on the joke of fiction, making them aware that they were suspending their disbelief, derived from Charteris himself. In a 1931 collection of short stories, as the Saint falls into the hands of yet another villain determined to put an end to his career, Templar points out that he is immune to all danger: 'I've got such a lot to do before the end of the volume, and it would wreck the whole show if I went and got bumped off in the first story.' As he puts it in a Nation-scripted episode from 1968: 'I know the rules. I've been to the movies.'

Indeed there were, if not rules exactly, then certainly conventions to which a writer was expected to adhere in the action adventure series of the 1960s, many of them derived – as with that stricture on the carrying of knives – from the literary heritage, and many passed on to future generations. It was axiomatic, for example, that a hero can take any number of blows to his face and still get up to fight back, but will be rendered instantly unconscious by a single strike to the back of the head, and that, even after a night or two of informal imprisonment, he will still look crisp and clean-shaven in a suit and tie. Similarly a man who is shot will suffer either a minor flesh wound or death; there is no other possibility between these extremes, though death will sometimes be sufficiently delayed for one last message to be gasped out, or for the victim to fire one final shot from his own gun. Heroines, on the other hand, tend to be kidnapped rather than shot, though curiously – given that much of the show promotes their sexual attractiveness – they are never raped or sexually molested. (There is an exception in the *Doctor Who* story 'The Keys of Marinus', in which Barbara is clearly being threatened with sexual assault, but mostly Nation's scripts for that series obey much the same conventions.)

Even the physical accoutrements were reasonably predictable. This is a tradition awash with miniature cameras and radio transmitters, with Swiss bank accounts and wall-safes, with knockout gas and secret weapons. It's a world in which hotel bedrooms can invariably be accessed from the room next door via a narrow, high ledge, and in which any room entered at night will probably contain uninvited guests, to be revealed when the light is switched on. Equally dangerous are big houses in the country, the rooms of which can usually be locked from the outside. Brainwashing is a constant danger, and plastic surgery can give a man an entirely new face (the same is presumably true of women, but no one has ever tried). Perhaps, given the restrictions, it is not entirely surprising that there was some repetition of plot.

To these conventions, ITC added a few of its own, most significantly the insistence that language should be made appropriate for export sales to America: cars ran on gas, pedestrians were to be found on sidewalks and references to money tended to be in dollars. This was not a practice shared by *The Avengers*, produced by the rival television company ABC. 'We always called a lift a lift, and not an elevator,' noted associate producer Brian Clemens. 'What we did was give them a picture of England that they all imagine it's like. England is all people in bowler hats, or it's all covered in fog. We never bent down to make it easier for them to understand.' He did, though, point out a number of other limitations in the series: 'There are a number of things we can't do. We don't kill women, though we may brutalise them. We do kill men, but we don't have any blood effects, so that it must be quite apparent that when the scene is over the actor just gets up and walks away.'

Despite making such concessions, however, the early series of *Danger Man* and *The Saint* initially proved less successful with the American market than had the 1950s swashbucklers. In the pre-Beatles era, Britain was still expected to provide historical rather than contemporary television. *Danger Man* ran for a season on CBS to little effect and Lew Grade failed to sell *The Saint* to a US network, instead having to rely on syndicating the show, piecing together a patchwork of deals with local stations. That was to change, but first there was a split in the creative team behind the series.

In 1965, remembered Roger Moore, Lew Grade approached him about the possibility of a fifth season of *The Saint*, this time to be made in colour so that it would be more acceptable to American television. Moore replied, 'I'd happily work with Bob, but not Monty.' Grade went along with the idea, suggesting that *The Saint* be left in the hands of the emollient Robert S. Baker while the more abrasive Monty Berman was given his own show. *The Baron*, featuring an adaptation of John Creasey's character, was also to be filmed in colour. Of the two partners, Berman was generally perceived to be the hard man of the partnership. 'I remember Monty Berman being the one that everybody feared a little bit,' remembered Sue Lloyd, who starred in *The Baron*, while some of the production crew were known to refer to him as Martin Bormann, in reference to the missing Nazi leader whose remains had not then been discovered. It was, however, Berman who provided Nation with a step up the career ladder, from freelance writer to salaried script editor on *The Baron*.

Nation in turn brought in Dennis Spooner to assist him. His new partner was just a couple of years his junior, and the two men had pursued similar careers: like Nation stage-struck since childhood, Spooner had spent some years struggling to make it as a stand-up comedian before drifting into writing (though he was also briefly a professional footballer with Leyton Orient), and the two had credits on several shows in common, including *Hancock* and *No Hiding Place* as well as, more recently, *Doctor Who*. It was the first time since the break with John Junkin that Nation had worked so closely with a co-writer and, after several years of working from home, he was now writing again in an office (in the Elstree studios where *The Baron* was filmed). In these changed circumstances, the need to form a new partnership — albeit more loosely than before — evidently reflected the transition from writer to script editor.

The role of script editor had emerged on ITV and been taken to the BBC by Sydney Newman. It was intended to form a bridge between producer and writer, though not all directors approved of the arrangement. 'I wasn't allowed near the authors,' complained Richard Martin of his experiences on *Doctor Who*. 'There was always a script editor in the way. You were never encouraged to talk to an author. By and large, that was a bad barrier between two creative people.' From the point of view of the script editor himself, however, it was still a creative process and one that gave him considerable influence over the direction and nature of a series. 'I'd have the writer in and sometimes I'd have the germ of an idea, or they would come in with an idea,' explained Brian Clemens. 'I'd sit at the typewriter, and we'd kick it backwards and forwards and we'd block it A to Z, like little telegrams to ourselves. And sometimes if a line of dialogue suggested itself, I would type that in too. And then at the end of that session, which might take all day, I'd give the writer four or five typewritten pages with every step of the story there and send him on his way. And the idea was that if he stepped outside the studios and got run over by a bus, I could write it.'

Having established the concept of the piece, the script editor's function was to make such changes, or recommendations for changes, as were deemed necessary to ensure continuity within the series and to allow the translation to film. 'It's an odd sort of balance,' reflected Terrance Dicks, the most influential of the *Doctor Who* script editors in the 1970s. 'You want a writer with clear ideas, who defends them, but you don't want a writer who says this is holy writ and you mustn't change a word. There's a middle ground in between, in which the writer accepts that in the end it's going to be done the way the script editor and the producer want it.' From his perspective, he concluded, 'Terry was, perhaps, if anything, a little too easy-going.' Beyond this link with the writer, there were further responsibilities. 'As story editor,' noted Spooner, 'you've got to liaise with make-up, costume and all the other departments. You've got to look after your producer. You've got to take the director in hand.'

The role of the script editor at ITC was less central than at *Doctor Who* but it was still a new experience for Nation. As a writer, he had been almost entirely removed from the production process and was seldom seen on set. He did go to one rehearsal of 'The Daleks', but as far as the director, Christopher Barry, was concerned, that was all: 'I only met Nation once. He seemed to have as little time for me – or the programme – as I came to have for him.' John Gorrie, who directed 'The Keys of Marinus', had even less contact: 'He was never around. I never saw him.' Actors had the same tale of absence to tell; whether it were Tony Tanner, star of *Uncle Selwyn*, Peter Purves, who appeared in two of his Daleks stories, or David Gooderson, who portrayed Davros, they never met Nation. He admitted himself that this was his reputation: 'They say: Nation never appeared. Nobody ever saw him, and he didn't do anything.' In this context, the value to him of Spooner, who had just spent a year as the script editor of *Doctor Who* and who had considerably more experience of television production, was obvious.

Even so, when filming began in July 1965, it became clear that this was a different world to that of the Doctor. To start with, an increased scale of resources was available at ITC: an episode of *The Saint* had a budget of £30,000, ten times larger than an episode of *Doctor Who* (though, of course, they were twice as long, running at around fifty minutes). But there was also a different philosophy of programme-making, rooted in the social differences between the two channels – the Oxbridge BBC and the working-class ITV – and manifest in a division between the stage and the movies. The BBC, despite the changes made by Sydney Newman, still essentially saw television drama as an offshoot of the theatre, and recruited accordingly, so that many of the key figures in the early Daleks stories came from a theatrical background: director Richard Martin, designer Raymond P. Cusick, costume designer Daphne Dare among others. So too did most of the actors, and there was some nervousness about whether appearing on television was a wise career move. 'As a theatre actor,' reflected William Russell, 'you thought: I wonder if I should?'

Over on ITV, on the other hand, the perception was that television drama was most closely related not to theatre but to cinema. Baker and Berman had both come from the movies, as had many of the other senior production crew. Charles Crichton had directed Ealing classics like *The Lavender Hill Mob* (1951) and *The Titfield Thunderbolt* (1953) before moving on to episodes of *Danger Man* and *The Avengers*; Jeremy Summers directed Tony Hancock's *The Punch and Judy Man* and then *The Saint*; while Roy Ward Baker – who worked on *The Avengers* and *The Baron* – had learnt his trade as Alfred Hitchcock's assistant in the 1930s. Gil Taylor was the cinematographer on *Ice Cold in Alex* (1958), and received a BAFTA nomination for his work on Roman Polanski's *Repulsion* (1965) during the course of filming *The Baron*. And Brian Clemens's colleague Albert Fennell, who produced *The Avengers*, had earlier been associate producer on Michael Powell's *Peeping Tom* (1960). As Clemens said: 'All the credits are great filmmakers.'

This divergence of approach was reflected in the end products. Although *Doctor Who* was not broadcast live, it was recorded almost as though it were, on a multiple-camera setup, with as few breaks in filming as possible and with retakes strictly discouraged. Just as in live theatre, things sometimes went a little wrong, actors occasionally bumped into the scenery or fluffed their lines – most frequently William Hartnell, who on one memorable occasion referred to 'anti-radiation drugs' as 'anti-radiation gloves' before correcting himself. The BBC considered such mistakes to be perfectly acceptable in a performance that was only expected to be viewed once; these were not works intended to be preserved for posterity, and indeed many of them haven't survived at all, wiped from the record in order that the expensive videotape might be reused and not incur the cost of storage.

Lew Grade, on the other hand, with his eyes fixed firmly on selling his shows around the world, insisted that they be shot on 35mm film and approached as though they were movies, using a single-camera mode of production. 'Our shows were, in fact, seen and treated as mini-films,' pointed out Roger Moore. And although a great deal of stock footage was used – establishing shots of Paris or London or Monte Carlo – as well as a single street set at Elstree that was re-dressed and reused in episode after episode, these elements were blended in well with the indoor scenes to give the impression of a much larger production. Other elements were borrowed from movies being made elsewhere in the studios. 'You'd walk onto a Hammer set, for instance,' remembered Nation, 'and they'd been doing some big mountain-climbing thing, and I'd say, "Can we save this set for another two weeks?" And I'd write an episode to fit it.' Consequently, the ITC shows, even without a great deal of location shooting, look almost epic in comparison with their contemporary equivalents on *Doctor Who*. Viewed in the light of later television, the limitations are a little obvious, but that wasn't the impression of either viewers or critics at the time: 'if Associated Television doesn't take *The Saint* on location,' wrote *Variety*, 'it sure seems that way.'

The key, as ever with Grade, was America, and in 1965 he proudly announced that he had sold a new extended version of *Danger Man* (US title: *Secret Agent*), together with *The Saint* and *The Baron*, to the American networks CBS, NBC and ABC respectively. The first two of these turned out to be the company's big hits of the decade, notching up 86 and 118 episodes respectively and winning big US audiences. They also sold everywhere else – *The Saint*, boasted Grade in 1965, was 'number one in Finland' – with Moore and McGoohan purveying an international image of the English gentleman (even though Moore was the son of a South London policeman and McGoohan was an Irishman born in New York). Moore's Templar, in particular, was one of the symbols of the age in the same way that James

Bond was proving to be. Driving an exotic car – albeit a Volvo P1800, as opposed to the fictional Furillac or Hirondel of the Charteris tales – and flitting between his London mews house and his New York apartment, he was the ultimate swinging bachelor, hanging out in clubs, bars and restaurants with a succession of young women, upholding standards of justice and decency while having a thoroughly good time. He epitomised a decade that seemed enthralled by the emergence of an international jet set. If consumerism was the new faith of the post-war western world, then Simon Templar was one of its high priests. (Though this metaphor probably wasn't what Lew Grade had in mind when he responded to a criticism that ATV didn't produce enough religious programming: 'We put out *The Saint*. What more do they want?')

The Baron was much less successful than those two series, losing its American network slot during its thirty-episode run and failing to get a recommission, but it sold well around the world, from Poland to Nigeria, and it still made a contribution to ITC's $10 million of foreign earnings in 1965, a figure that grew to $15 million the following year. In 1967 and again in 1969, ITC's parent company ATV won the Queen's Award to Industry for exports, while Grade himself was knighted at the end of the decade. ('I have sold everything we produce, except the weather forecast and the Epilogue,' he boasted in 1967.) As Dennis Spooner was to point out: 'ITC was basically an exporting company. We were earning foreign currency.' He added, in answer to the charge from Howard Thomas at the rival ABC franchise, that Grade seemed to be straying from his Midlands audience, focusing more on Birmingham, Alabama than Birmingham, England: 'It's no good trying to sell a locomotive in America if you insist on building it for the gauge of track that's relevant in Britain. I don't see why people get upset when you do the same thing in television.' But perhaps it was by making too many concessions to transatlantic taste that *The Baron* fell down; perhaps it simply wasn't English enough, failing to play to the American perception of Britain, however distorted that might be.

As originally conceived by John Creasey, the character of John Mannering was firmly in the mould of E.W. Hornung's late-Victorian hero, Raffles, who had spent his days as a gentleman cricketer and his nights as a jewel thief. A 'Mayfair bachelor and man-about-town', Mannering's easy passage through elevated social circles conceals a less respectable alter ego, for he is also a celebrated burglar and jewel thief, known to the police and to a mostly admiring public only as the Baron. Mannering was never as fully rounded a figure as Raffles, nor so subversive – the Wildean subtext of Hornung's stories, for example, is absent – but he was exciting enough, displaying a physical prowess of which even that amateur boxer Sherlock Holmes would have approved: cornered by a pair of savage Alsatian guard dogs, he's capable of rendering them unconscious with his fists. So although he was neither Creasey's best-known hero (that was the Toff), nor his most critically acclaimed (Gideon of Scotland Yard), he was certainly popular, appearing in nearly fifty books, and he had loyal fans, among them the French poet Jean Cocteau, who was heard to murmur that the Baron was his favourite character in all crime fiction.

Mannering's first appearance came in *Meet the Baron* (1935, US title: *The Man in the Blue Mask*), a 75,000-word novel written in just six days to meet the deadline for a competition being run by the publisher George G. Harrap. It took the £1,000 first prize, a huge sum at a time when publishers paid an average of just £50 for a thriller novel, and, published under the pseudonym Andrew Morton, it set the struggling Creasey off on a most extraordinary literary career. Over the next four decades, he produced more than six hundred books, using a couple of dozen different pen names, and at the time of his death in 1973, some four hundred titles were estimated still to be in print. The exploits of the Baron ran right through that career (indeed the last two books in the series were published posthumously), though the character calmed down a little as the years went by. He got married and strayed from the path of crime, setting himself up as an antique dealer with a shop in Mayfair, from where he assisted the police and even his own customers, when they found themselves caught up in jewel robberies and the like. Still charismatic, he was now seen in more conventional terms as 'Ronald Colman, Rex Harrison and Greg Peck rolled into one'. In truth, it was not such a big step for Mannering, for he had never really been criminally minded. Even when robbing country houses, he had been primarily motivated by concern for the downtrodden, particularly if they were attractive young women or distressed members of the gentry; like the Saint, he saw himself as something of a Robin Hood for the modern age and 'he used the profit more for other people than himself'.

By the time ITC turned to the Baron as a vehicle for a new show, Creasey's work had already been raided for the series *Gideon's Way* (1964, US title: *Gideon CID*), produced by Baker and Berman. It came with one huge attraction for a producer: where Leslie Charteris had insisted on retaining storyline approval for *The Saint*, no such restrictions were imposed by Creasey. The results were immediately apparent when the first episode of *The Baron* was broadcast in September 1966. To begin with, the entire history of the character, his disreputable early career as a jewel thief, had been dropped, while the name of his antique dealership (now an international chain of shops) had changed from Quinns to the more literal John Mannering. More startlingly, he was now American, a former cattle-rancher from Texas – hence, apparently, his nickname – who had served in the war, tracking down artworks stolen by the Nazis. (Old comrades tend to refer to him as Captain Mannering, which sounded less incongruous in the days before *Dad's Army*.)

As portrayed by the American actor Steve Forrest, this Baron was courteous, good-natured and likeable; tall, broad, handsome and well-dressed. Unfortunately he was also utterly lacking in sex appeal, and despite being furnished with a decorative sidekick in the form of Cordelia Winfield (Sue Lloyd), whom he first meets while she's taking a bath in his hotel room, he managed to avoid any hint of flirtation whatsoever. Even the 1930s original was more explicit in its acceptance that Mannering might have a sex life; after all, he had first taken up crime when his marriage proposal was spurned, and much of his early law breaking was an attempt to protect the woman he loved from the blackmailing demands of her estranged husband. Also lacking in the 1960s incarnation was the division that had once existed between the character's two guises. When engaged in an escapade as the Baron, we were told, he used to undergo 'a psychological change', effectively ceasing to be John Mannering as he put on his trademark blue mask, almost as though he were one of the emerging host of superheroes. Not only the alter ego, but also the mask, were absent from the television version, who remained resolutely Mannering throughout, with only the occasional passing mention of his nickname to remind us of the show's title.

These changes aside, and even allowing for the fact that the stories were all new, the television Baron was still in the mould of the 1930s heroes. He is absurdly well-connected, 'one of only three men in this country who have immediate and unquestioned access to the security vaults of the Bank of England', and he acts on occasion as an informal agent for a government organisation known as Diplomatic Intelligence, answering to a crusty English gentleman, Templeton-Green (Colin Gordon). He also retains an instinctive sympathy for the underdog, however much he protests that his only interest is financial reward. In 'Red Horse, Red Rider' he finds himself trying to wrestle a statuette of the Four Horsemen of the Apocalypse from the clutches of a military dictatorship in the Balkans, in order to sell it to provide funds for the resistance. As he rides the railroads, pursued by the secret police, his companion, a beautiful young rebel named Savannah (Jane Merrow), wonders why Mannering is here at all: 'I don't understand you. What are you doing riding in this box-car across this godforsaken country of mine? You own three of the most exclusive antique shops in the world, you are a charter member of the jet set, you have beautiful women. Why are you doing this?' 'Money,' he replies unconvincingly. 'I'll make a hundred thousand dollars from the sale of the Horsemen. If I have to dodge a few bullets along the way, it's all part of the game.' 'Is there no other reason?' she insists, and his reply comes as much from the twinkling of his eyes as it does from his shrugged 'Maybe.'

Solidarity with the oppressed is a running theme. Several of the episodes written or co-written by Nation for *The Baron* are relatively straightforward jewel heists, ranging from standard tales of released prisoners going back to dig up their treasure hoards, all the way up to an attempt on the Crown Jewels in the double episode 'Masquerade'/'The Killing'. But there is elsewhere a strong vein of broad-brush politics. In 'A Memory of Evil' the Baron battles an Austrian neo-Nazi group called the New Front, while in 'Night of the Hunter' he is back in the Balkans confronting another military dictatorship, this one presided over by a general so evil that he wears sunglasses after dark and a uniform that includes matching brown leather boots and gloves. His manners are little better than those of the French thieves in 'Jeannine', for he puts his cigar out in the milk jug, and when Mannering suggests that it's not a good thing to destroy a democratic regime in a military coup, he behaves as a thriller villain should, laughing at such foolishness: 'Democracy! Hah! It's merely an archaic word, not a political creed.' Again Mannering is bringing in money for the anti-government rebels.

'And Suddenly You're Dead' featured another familiar figure from the thriller library, with the mad scientist Ingar Sorenson (Kay Walsh). In a nod towards Nation's later series, *Survivors*, she has developed an extremely contagious virus that kills anyone exposed to it, which she is offering to anyone in search of a biological weapon and who can meet the asking price. Voicing one of Nation's recurrent themes, she explains her abandonment of the high principles of science. 'A long time ago, I decided to market my work, and leave morality to the buyer,' she says, arguing that this is the way of the modern world. 'The defence budget of any world power could finance enough research to rid us of all our ills. But ask any government to believe that drugs are more important than rockets . . .' Inevitably she kills herself accidentally with the last of her deadly bacteria, and the final portentous word is left for Mannering: 'It's all over. Until somebody comes up with the same thing again. Or something worse.'

In the best plotline of the series, the double episode 'Storm Warning'/ 'The Island' sees the Chinese government funding a plan to bring down America's latest space rocket. By hacking into the rocket's com-munication system, it is intended to change its re-entry into Earth's atmosphere so that it splashes down 1,500 miles off course, where a ship is waiting to fish it out of the ocean, hauling in the most advanced technology in the world. It's a fiendish plan worthy of feature-film treatment (though perhaps a little too reminiscent of the James Bond movie *Dr No*) and the production mostly does it justice. Much of the action is set on board the waiting ship, on to which Mannering has smuggled himself in yet another attempt to rescue Cordelia. For she was not one of the more resourceful heroines of the ITC stable; captured by villains on an almost weekly basis and never allowed to do any fighting, she did display a cool, slightly ironic tone in counterpoint to Mannering's rugged openness, but Sue Lloyd struggled to make a great deal of the role. 'I had to make her more Lucille Ball,' she commented later, 'because of being ridiculously weak at the last moment.' Mannering suffered from no such shortcomings; as adept with a sub-machine gun as with his fists, he was the action hero as all-American jock.

Unlike *The Saint*, the atmosphere of *The Baron* was a little to one side of the carefree, wisecracking, bachelor romp through Swinging Britain. The jaunty theme tune was there, as was the jet-set lifestyle, but this was a hero who didn't go in for womanising and who lacked the jovial repartee that had been de rigueur in British thrillers ever since Bulldog Drummond. In the absence of the self-mocking humour that Moore brought to *The Saint*, *The Baron* was a much more serious proposition. The shows had no straight-to-camera introduction and tended to end abruptly at the denouement, without an epilogue or additional explanation; there was no easing in and out of the tale, just an action-packed adventure.

And on occasion those adventures could be very dark. The last episode of the series, 'Countdown', featured a fine array of evocative settings – a scrap yard, railway sidings, a film set, a crypt and a windmill – as the backdrops to five unpleasant deaths, including a man kicked out of a railway compartment in front of an oncoming train, another impaled on an antique sword, and a third being tortured with a lit cigarette before being crushed under a concrete block. If this had been *The Avengers*, the killings would have been depicted as witty self-parodies of the action genre; here they are treated seriously, looking forward to the violent British gangster films (*Performance*, *Get Carter*, *Villain*) that were to come. The same episode also included a guest appearance by Edward Woodward as a rival antique dealer, Arkin Morley, who walks on the shady side of the street and has a nice line in arrogance; asked how good his Latin is, he replies, 'I speak it and read it with a fluency which can only come from a very superior English education.' (Leslie Charteris, who went to Rossall School, was also fond of sideways attacks on the public school system.)

Much of this undercurrent of unease was attributable to the influence of Nation, who was creatively – though not personally – inclined to pessimism. It is notable that one of the few times that *The Baron* broke the ITC convention on using American currency is in the episode 'The Man Outside', in which an Italian-American gangster named Bruno Orsini (David Bauer) attempts to bring six million pounds in forged notes into the country. Orsini explains to Mannering that he's motivated not merely by greed but by a desire for revenge, having previously been deported from Britain. 'You know what this much fake money could do to a country's economy, Mannering? Smash it! It could make the pound worthless,' he rants. 'I'm going to see this whole stinking country go bankrupt. I'm going to push in millions more notes, give them away if I have to. By the time I'm finished, the pound'll be just so much coloured paper.' The episode was, in a quiet way, Nation's comment on the vulnerability of the British economy to international speculation, and was broadcast in April 1967, in the midst of a continuing currency crisis that would, later in the year, force the Labour government to devalue sterling.

Nation's influence can also be seen in the resourcefulness of the Baron, his ability to improvise his way out of tricky situations. It was a trait common to many of Nation's heroes, and he evidently stockpiled any ideas he came across for later use in his scripts. Ted Ray, with whom he worked so closely at the end of the 1950s, used to tell an anecdote about an alcoholic music hall comedian of his acquaintance who sometimes ran out of people from whom to scrounge a drink. 'If nothing else, he was resourceful. Once he went into the Gents, removed the light bulb from its socket, inserted a halfpenny, and replaced the bulb. The first person to switch on the light produced a short circuit and plunged the whole house into darkness. It was the easiest thing for Cyril to grope a bit and gobble up someone else's pint.' When, in 'Storm Warning', Steve Mannering finds himself locked in the cold room used for storing meat on the ship, he employs precisely the same trick, enabling him to slip quietly out when a crewman comes to investigate the power cut.

With the pressure of writing so many original stories himself while at the same time fulfilling his duties as script editor, Nation also dipped into his previous work for inspiration. Ingar Sorenson in 'And Suddenly You're Dead' is not exactly the first fictional scientist to discover the ultimate secret weapon, but it was perhaps careless of Nation to give her a name quite so redolent of Professor Soren in 'The Inescapable Word' (one of his scripts for *The Saint*), who has developed an equally deadly weapon: 'It destroys all life, but leaves no trace of radiation. The classic death ray.' Soren too is killed by his own invention. Similarly, both 'The Crime of the Century' in *The Saint* and 'Epitaph for a Hero' in *The Baron* feature robberies that require the pumping of poison gas through a ventilation system to put armed guards out of action.

But such minor borrowings were as nothing compared to the pure self-plagiarism of 'Portrait of Louisa' in *The Baron*, which not only lifted wholesale the plot of 'Lida' in *The Saint*, but also recycled large chunks of dialogue. Nation wrote both scripts, adapting 'Lida' from a Charteris story, and, although he added several layers of complication to the tale (and took the trouble to relocate it from the Miami of Charteris's original to the Bahamas and then, in 'Portrait of Louisa', to England), he was perhaps fortunate that he didn't run into trouble with the Saint's creator. As so often in Nation's career, there were precedents for this practice to be found among the writers of his youth. Edwy Searles Brooks, for example, one of the most prolific of those writers – he produced an estimated 36 million words in his career – was, like Nation, not averse to turning his hand to self-plagiarism: many of his 1940s novels about the character Norman Conquest were literal rewrites of his own earlier work, when the central figure had been Waldo the Wonder Man.

On this occasion, however, Nation's sleight of hand did not go unnoticed. In an ill-timed piece of scheduling, both 'Lida' and 'Portrait of

Louisa' were shown on the same weekend in America, and the comparisons were hard to avoid. 'It was an embarrassment for Terry,' shrugged Johnny Goodman, the production supervisor on both shows, 'but I suppose there are a limited number of stories in the world.'

Chapter Eight

Dalek Empire

'I was, for that short time, the most famous writer on television.' Terry Nation's assessment of his position as 1965 dawned was perfectly accurate. He was being invited to appear on the prestigious BBC2 discussion show, *Late Night Line-Up*, he was the subject of admiring profiles in serious newspapers, his stories were appearing on an almost fortnightly basis on *The Saint* and he was still the 'Dalek-man', recipient of sacks full of fan mail. Dalekmania showed no sign of abating, and he formed a company, Dalek Productions (the other directors were Kate Nation and Beryl Vertue), to deal with the continuing expansion: this year the monsters were to be seen again on television and in books, and were to make their debut in comics, on record, on stage and in the movies. The conquest of Britain was virtually complete, but for someone of Nation's generation, raised on fantasies of Hollywood and on comic books from GIs, there remained the ultimate allure of America.

The image of America dominated British culture in the post-war years. That it was possible for British creativity to make it big in the States had been demonstrated by a handful of success stories, including those of Leslie Charteris, Alfred Hitchcock, David Niven and Dylan Thomas, but these had been isolated cases, and Tony Hancock was just one of many who had tried and failed. Meanwhile Britain's evolving relationship with its former colony was captured by artists like Richard Hamilton, Peter Blake and Eduardo Paolozzi, the early practitioners of pop art: a fascination with the movies, magazines and mass culture that came across the Atlantic, a craving for jazz, both ancient and modern, an infatuation with the cult of stardom that worshipped ready-made icons in Marilyn Monroe, Elvis Presley and Popeye. There was sometimes a note of detached irony in pop art, but that was mostly overridden by an unmistakable sense of celebration, a revelling in the industrial production of entertainment. At a time when much of the left was loftily dismissing American imports as 'culture poured out over a defenceless people by the millionaires', pop artists as well as early British rock and roll stars were embracing precisely the same material. And crucial to all of it was that this was culture consumed at one remove from the real thing, for few had ever experienced America at first hand.

At the turn of the 1960s this began to change, as the isolated successes began to mount up into something resembling a trend. A number of photographers (David Bailey, Terence Donovan, Brian Duffy) began to make names for themselves in the fashion industry. The new wave of British cinema was exporting successfully, with Oscar nominations for Laurence Harvey in *Room at the Top* (1959) and Laurence Olivier in *The Entertainer* (1960), while Peter Sellers made a successful move to Hollywood. In New York satirists from *Beyond the Fringe* and from Peter Cook's Establishment Club both enjoyed successful theatre runs in 1962, as did Harold Pinter's play *The Caretaker* and Anthony Newley's musical *Stop the World – I Want to Get Off*, swiftly followed by Lionel Bart's *Oliver!*. All were unmistakably British works, and critics began to talk about the 'British domination of Broadway'. There was also James Bond; already a hit in America via the novels of Ian Fleming (Bond was said to be John F. Kennedy's 'favourite fictional hero'), he broke through to a mass audience when the film of *Dr No* was released in 1963, a year later than in Britain.

And then came the Beatles. Having dominated the British music industry in 1963, the group released 'I Want to Hold Your Hand' in America in January 1964, visited the country the following month and, by the end of March, held all top five places in the US singles charts, accounting for 60 per cent of all record sales. In a society still reeling from the shock of President Kennedy's assassination, their cheerful simplicity swept all before them. In their wake came a host of other bands, from Herman's Hermits to the Rolling Stones, and where the previous year just one British record ('Telstar' by the Tornados) had made the American top ten, the figure rose to thirty-four in 1964. So big were the Beatles that when they made their record-breaking appearance on *The Ed Sullivan Show*, attracting 74 million viewers, their slipstream was powerful enough to launch the Cardiff-born music hall star 'Two Ton' Tessie O'Shea on a successful American career, simply because she also appeared on the programme. And into the breach opened up by the Beatles came British television, both programmes – *The Avengers, The Saint, The Baron* – and individuals in the shape of David Frost and

Jack Good. As John Mortimer was to put it in *Paradise Postponed*, his 1985 novel of post-war Britain, for a brief moment 'life in England was thought to be interesting to the American public'. Ironically, one of the few failures of the era was a 1963 exhibition in New York of British pop art.

Terry Nation experienced some of this excitement as a writer on the ITC series, but those were other people's shows. What he really dreamt of was making it in his own right, and in August 1965 the *Sun* confidently reported that he was 'negotiating with American TV companies for the rights of what they want to call *The Dalek Show*'.

By now the Daleks were acquiring a life of their own, far beyond the confines of *Doctor Who*. The success of *The Dalek Book*, and particularly the comic strips illustrated by Richard Jennings, was extended in January 1965 when the same artist provided a strip for the first issue of the magazine *TV Century 21*, launched by Gerry Anderson to promote his Supermarionation puppet shows, *Stingray* and *Fireball XL5*. 'I suppose the thing that attracted me to the Daleks,' reflected Anderson, in explanation of why he included a rival show in his magazine, 'was jealousy.' The series ran for 104 instalments over two years, with Jennings's *Eagle*-derived artwork replaced by the more contemporary style of Ron Turner halfway through. It focused entirely on the Daleks, with no sign at all of the Doctor, gradually building an entire alternative mythology, expanding substantially on the television stories. Officially credited to Nation, the writing was actually the responsibility of David Whitaker, who had already written a novelisation of 'The Daleks' (as *Doctor Who in an Exciting Adventure with the Daleks*, published in 1964), and who was fast becoming Nation's understudy in all things related to the planet Skaro. The *TV Century 21* strip attracted its own loyal following, but for Nation it was primarily of significance in establishing that stories about the Daleks could potentially work even when removed from their original context: it could be seen as something between a storyboard and a calling card.

The same was not quite true of the 1965 film *Dr Who and the Daleks*, since it was based on the scripts for the first television serial, but it was notable that the monsters got equal billing in the title and completely dominated the posters. Directed by Gordon Flemyng, the movie featured Peter Cushing in the lead role, in the hope of attracting attention in America, where he was already well known as an actor. For the benefit of an American audience who were new to the concept, the nature of the central figure was also fundamentally changed; the Doctor was here known as Dr

Who and, no longer an alien time traveller, was an amiably eccentric human inventor of apparently Edwardian vintage. Ian too was unrecognisable; played by Roy Castle, his function was to provide comic relief rather than to lead the action.

As a consequence, the film has not always been warmly embraced by many followers of *Doctor Who*, but viewed in its own right, it works perfectly well as a quirky little fantasy movie for kids. With a reported budget of £180,000 – a long way removed from the average of around £2,500 per episode for the first season of the television version – and with the benefit of being in colour rather than black-and-white, it has a sense of scale that was lacking in 'The Daleks'. It may still look tied to its sets, but those sets are much more impressive and, on occasion, it displays a grandeur that television simply couldn't match, particularly in the advance on the Dalek city. As Barbara, Ian and the Thals make their way across a deadly swamp, over mountains and through rocky tunnels, accompanied by an heroic orchestral score from Malcolm Lockyer, the sequence acquires something of the majesty of an H. Rider Haggard adventure. And there are some nice details, starting with the opening shot, a slow pan around a living room that reveals first Susan reading Eric M. Rogers's *Physics for the Inquiring Mind*, then Barbara reading a book titled *The Science of Science*, and finally Dr Who himself, absorbed in a copy of *The Eagle* with Dan Dare on the cover. There was also a telling addition to the script, with the Thal leader Alydon (here played by Barrie Ingham) explaining that 'There were many mutations after the final war. Most of them perished. But this form – two hands, two eyes – has always been best for survival.'

In terms of the Daleks themselves, the biggest change came simply from them being in colour, which enabled distinctions to be made between those with different functions and ranks. 'I was trying to make them into a full-grown culture with levels,' reflected Nation. His own involvement in the film, however, was minimal. The screenplay adaptation of his scripts was the work of Milton Subotsky, the creative talent behind Amicus, the film company responsible. Subotsky once claimed that his love of horror movies stemmed from the fact that 'it was the only kind of cinema where you could avoid sex and violence', and the reviews of *Dr Who and the Daleks* largely agreed that he'd lived up to his ambitions. 'One of the few modern films to have a nubile heroine who never so much as touches her boy friend,' noted the *Guardian*, concluding that it was 'not likely to do more harm to childish minds than many other modern weapons of the communications industry'. 'Shoddy,' was the verdict of the *Observer*, 'but the children might like it.'

Despite the criticisms, the film was as successful as everything featuring the Daleks that year and it reached the box office top ten. 'The money came in so fast,' claimed Nation, 'they were in profit within the year, and they actually had to pay me, which was wonderful.' Even before its release, a sequel was planned, which emerged in 1966 as *Daleks – Invasion Earth 2150 A.D.*, an adaptation of the second television story that removed the Doctor entirely from the title. The central characters were much the same – though Bernard Cribbins replaced Roy Castle as the comic relief and Barbara was dropped in favour of Dr Who's niece, Louise – and there were again some improvements on the original version, thanks to the shorter running time; the Slyther, thankfully, was absent altogether, though an even more risible scene was added of Cribbins and the Robomen engaging in a choreographed comedy routine. By now, however, Dalekmania was on the wane, and the film not only got the expected poor reviews ('Grown-ups may enjoy it,' sniffed *The Times*, 'but most children have more sense'), but also failed to emulate the takings of the first venture. Plans for a third movie, based on the third Dalek serial, 'The Chase' (screened on television in 1965), were quietly shelved, and some of the Daleks used in the films were given to Nation, who kept them in the house at Lynsted Park.

The absence of a film of 'The Chase' was something of a missed opportunity, since the television scripts – the last that Nation would write alone for seven years – were full of excellent ideas that were either rejected or toned down, while those that did make it to the screen suffered heavily from the show's low budget. The director was again Richard Martin, who was unconvinced by the idea of returning to the monsters, but was talked into it by Verity Lambert: 'We're in a stick, the rest of the scripts for the next series aren't ready. I've talked with Terry Nation and he thinks we can do one more thing with the Daleks.' Returning to the anthology format of 'The Keys of Marinus', Nation had the Daleks in their own time machine, pursuing the TARDIS through space and time, and he crammed into the six episodes a total of five alien life-forms, three planets, three separate stories set on Earth in the past, present and future, two Doctors and two time machines, as well as finding room for appearances by Dracula, Frankenstein's monster, the Beatles, William Shakespeare and Abraham Lincoln. As one of contributors to the BBC's audience research report pointed out, 'All we need now is Yogi Bear and we've had the lot.'

It also provided a solution to the mystery of the ghost ship the *Mary Celeste*, discovered in 1872 floating in the Atlantic, its crew having vanished with no indication of what had happened to them. Eighty years after Arthur Conan Doyle had written a fictionalised explanation of the crew's disappearance (renaming the vessel the *Marie Celeste*), Nation finally revealed the truth: the Daleks materialised on the ship and the crew threw themselves overboard in fear.

A sense of playful imagination runs through much of the serial, but not as much as there was in the original script. In the first episode, the crew of the TARDIS enjoy themselves with a Time-Space Visualiser, 'a sort of time television' that enables them to view moments from history. Barbara chooses to see William Shakespeare, Francis Bacon and Queen Elizabeth I, though the encounter is a not very inspired account of a royal command to write *The Merry Wives of Windsor*. As originally intended, however, the scene ended with the two writers bemoaning the dwindling numbers attending the theatre, and saw Bacon giving Shakespeare a manuscript for a new play titled *Hamlet*. Back on the TARDIS, the Doctor was then to have revealed that Shakespeare had told him this was simply a publicity stunt: expecting to be overheard, the two men hoped to whip up controversy about the authorship of the play with the aim of boosting the box office. In what remained of this idea, Bacon merely suggests to Shakespeare that the story of Hamlet would make a fine subject for a play; if anything, this played into the hands of those who subscribed to the Baconian authorship of the works, rather than mocking the claim.

It was not simply the wit that got lost. The first tale in the serial was set on the planet Aridius, once covered by a vast ocean beneath which lay the city of the Aridians. (There were shades here of H.G. Wells's 1896 story 'In the Abyss', which also told of humanoid life-forms at the bottom of the ocean.) But then the seas dried up, killing all life save two species, the Aridians and the Mire Beasts, each of which – as is clear from the original script – sees the other as its primary food source, so that both are simultaneously predator and prey. It's a lovely, teasing detail, but it disappeared from the final version, while Nation's visualisation of the Aridians was also jettisoned. 'These are tiny men with vast humped backs,' he had written. 'They are incredibly ugly facially, their mouths distorted and a secondary set of eyes on their foreheads. Thick black hair hangs lankly, framing their faces. Their hands have only four fingers each. They are perhaps twice as long as human fingers. Arms appear to trail the ground, whilst the legs seem foreshortened.' To which Verity Lambert objected strongly: 'I think Terry has gone too far in making the Aridians unpleasant looking,' she wrote to Richard Martin. 'It seems to me that this is just presenting unpleasantness for the sake of it.' The resulting creatures looked instead like a cross between the Tin Man in *The Wizard of Oz* and a merman with cauliflower ears, and not even an early appearance by the actor Hywel Bennett could save them from ridicule.

Most severely affected was the brief sequence set in a haunted house, familiar from the Universal horror films of the 1930s and their imitators, complete with bats, skeletons, ghosts and suits of armour. According to Nation's original conception, it represented a manifestation of the fears of millions, preconditioned by horror stories to imagine that this was what nightmares looked like. (The Doctor was to cite the work of Mary Shelley, Bram Stoker, Edgar Allan Poe and W.W. Jacobs as examples.) The house exists, argues the Doctor, 'in the dark recesses of the human mind. Millions of minds secretly believing that this place really exists. The immense power of those minds, combined together, have *made* this place a reality. It's a classic house of horrors.' The Doctor challenges Ian to predict what will happen next, and event follows description, as Ian says a door will creak open and a man will appear saying . . . And Baron Frankenstein, who has indeed appeared, duly speaks. This playing with narrative was not far removed from some of the ideas in the fourth series of *The Avengers*, broadcast later in the same year, and prefigured the strand of post-modernist horror films that started with *Wes Craven's New Nightmare* (1994) and *Scream* (1996). It also, somewhat cheekily, elevated the Daleks, busily charging round the haunted house, to the level of classic horror figures like Dracula and Frankenstein's monster.

The whole sequence, the blurring of the lines of reality, was an intriguing concept, and was possibly suggested by Nation's recent reading. The first two of his Leslie Charteris *Saint* adaptations to be broadcast ('Lida' and 'Jeannine') came from the 1949 book *Saint Errant*, which ends with a tale even stranger than 'The Man Who Liked Ants'. In 'Dawn' Simon Templar finds himself, as a real person, apparently caught up in the dream of a bank clerk whom he has never met, but who is addicted to thrillers. A cast of other characters turn up, all of them clichéd figures from the thriller repertoire, leaving Templar to wonder whether this is reality or whether he truly is trapped in a second-hand dream world, and he reflects that the whole thing 'sounds like one of those stories that fellow Charteris might write'. The climax is reached when a fat man – clearly based on Sydney Greenstreet in *The Maltese Falcon*, and identified by Templar as such – shoots the Saint and kills him. When Templar wakes up alone twelve hours later, still alive and with no sign of any of the characters he has encountered, he concludes that it has all been his own dream. Until he checks out the address of the bank clerk and finds that, having been in a coma for three days, the man died last night, recovering consciousness just long enough to shout something 'about a saint'.

Nation's tale similarly played with notions of fiction becoming fact – 'We're in a world of dreams,' exclaims the Doctor – and represented a major break with the programme's founding concept. 'While the premise,' noted *Kinematograph Weekly* of *Doctor Who* in 1963, 'is fantastic, the treatment of various places and periods will be treated realistically.' It was a formulation that restated the founding document of the horror and fantasy tradition, Horace Walpole's 1764 novel *The Castle of Otranto*; in the preface to that book, Walpole had explained his rationale for dealing with the supernatural: 'Allow the possibility of the facts, and all the actors comport themselves as persons would do in their situation.' The haunted house sequence in 'The Chase', however, turned its back on such an approach, instead allowing every possibility, and, coincidentally, came much closer to what would shortly become known as the new wave of science fiction. Then in its infancy – Michael Moorcock had only taken over the editorship of *New Worlds* magazine in 1964 – the new wave was to refocus attention from outer to inner space and much of it looked to the experimental work of William S. Burroughs for inspiration; Nation, by drawing on the far less celebrated experimentalism of Charteris, ended up in a not dissimilar place.

It was all too much for Lambert. 'I think that if we go into these realms of fiction we are opening a door on the *Doctor Who* series which may run us into considerable trouble in the future,' she noted. 'I do not feel that the Daleks should arrive in a place which is an Earth fictional place, and if they do not, it really means that the place does not exist at all, except in the minds of our four characters.' Much of the more ambiguous dialogue was dropped and an ending added that showed, after the travellers had left the house, a ticket booth identifying the place as 'Frankenstein's House of Horrors', an exhibit at the 1996 Festival of Ghana. All the monsters, we were now informed, were mechanical toys intended to divert tourists. 'I think there's a much simpler explanation,' Ian had responded when the Doctor explained his theory of the 'collective human mind'. Indeed there was, but it was nowhere near as interesting.

Other elements in the serial included a clip of the Beatles on the Time-Space Visualiser performing 'Ticket to Ride' (it was hoped the group would film a special sequence showing them as old men playing a fiftieth anniversary show, but their manager, Brian Epstein, scotched that suggestion); the creation by the Daleks of a robot replica of the Doctor (an idea surely deriving from Philip K. Dick's 'Imposter'), who then duels with the real Doctor, using walking-sticks as swords; and carnivorous vegetation in the form of the thoroughly unconvincing Fungoids. There were also the Mechanoids, large, globe-shaped robots sent from Earth to prepare the planet Mechanus for colonisation – the anticipated ships full of human immigrants, however, never arrived and the robots had since created their own society. The climactic battle between the Daleks and the Mechanoids is one of the better realised elements of the serial, and clearly used up a substantial proportion of the budget.

The Mechanoids, again designed by Raymond P. Cusick, also turned up in the *TV Century 21* comic strips, and on an EP featuring this element of the story, which was released on Gerry Anderson's Century 21 Records. They were designed by Nation to be a potential rival to his more famous creations. 'You had your eye on the chance that anything could possibly catch on,' he reflected. 'The Mechanoids were manufactured as toys, but of course they didn't take off.' Part of the problem was that, being large and spherical with spindly little arms, they were both difficult and unattractive to imitate in the playgrounds, while for the production crew on *Doctor Who*, they were simply too big for the restricted studio sets that were then available. 'The Mechanoids would have caught on if they'd been pushed a bit more,' believed the serial's script editor, Dennis Spooner. 'But they weren't pushed because no one could have stood the problems it would have caused if they had caught on. They were just physically impossible to get in and out of the studio. They were just designed wrong. Terry was very unhappy about it.'

Although 'The Chase' had lost some of the imagination and ingenuity of Nation's script through production decisions and shortage of funds ('in TV inspiration costs money,' as Spooner observed), it did still demonstrate that there were new angles to be taken with the Daleks, as long as the background kept changing to compensate for their lack of variety. Having been seen first at home on Skaro, and then visiting Earth, they were now rampant throughout the universe, with no apparent limit to their possibilities. Except, of course, for their inbuilt limitations. The protective shells were designed for use in the underground city on Skaro, a Dalek-friendly environment with no known enemies, to which they were perfectly adapted. Now that the creatures were seen aggressively venturing forth, it became clear that their lack of speed and mobility, as well as their inability to engage in hand-to-hand combat, made them slightly less terrifying than they were painted. They ran the risk of becoming victims of their own success: the design flaws were only revealed when they began to expand and talk about universal domination, but by then the public appetite demanded that the creatures remain essentially the same, while posing ever greater threats to all other life-forms. For the most part, however, the audience went happily along with this, even when attention was drawn to their drawbacks (in a line probably added by Dennis Spooner to 'The Chase', Ian suggests that the travellers hide upstairs, because 'Daleks don't like stairs').

The willing suspension of disbelief was shared by their fans in high places. Chief among these was Huw Wheldon, who had recently become controller of programmes for BBC1 and whose mother-in-law was much taken with the Daleks. Wheldon expressed his disappointment at the brevity of their appearance in the first episode of 'The Chase' (the final shot had been of a Dalek emerging from beneath the sands of the Aridian desert), and although he was assured that they would appear more substantially in the subsequent episodes, and that they were pencilled in for a fourth story later in the year, he was keen that there should be still more of the creatures, asking if the forthcoming series couldn't perhaps be extended. Others in the BBC hierarchy agreed and, against the wishes of the production team, 'The Daleks' Master Plan', intended as a six-part serial, was extended to twelve episodes.

Now fully engaged in his work on *The Baron*, Nation simply didn't have time to complete such a major project. David Whitaker was already handling much of the expansion of the Daleks mythology in *TV Century 21*, so Nation turned to his other colleague, Dennis Spooner, to share the burden of 'Master Plan'. Nation was responsible for the basic storyline but wrote only six of the episodes; the remainder were contributed by Spooner, who had in the meantime handed over the duties of script editor on *Doctor Who* to Donald Tosh in order that he too could work on *The Baron*. Other changes in the programme's personnel had seen the departure of the characters Ian and Barbara at the end of 'The Chase', and shortly thereafter that of producer Verity Lambert, to be replaced by John Wiles, who inherited 'Master Plan' despite his distaste for its unwieldy length. Even Nation was far from convinced by the scale of the undertaking: 'If I was a producer on a show like that,' he reflected later, 'I don't think I would ever commit myself to a three-month Dalek story without a lot of other stuff in it as well.'

To add to the burden, another single-episode Dalek story, 'Mission to the Unknown', had also been commissioned, intended to serve as a prelude to 'The Daleks' Master Plan' and to feature none of the regular cast, since they were due to be on leave at the time of filming. In their place, Nation created a new organisation named the Space Security Service (SSS), an official agency tasked with defending the Earth and its colonies, whose agents – in overt tribute to James Bond – are 'licensed to kill'. One of those agents is Marc Cory (Edward de Souza), who finds himself, in 'Mission to the Unknown', on the planet Kembel on the track of the Daleks. He knows they're here because there are Varga plants on Kembel, and the Varga is 'a thing part-animal, part-vegetable' that was invented by the Daleks on Skaro; they 'use their roots to drag themselves along' and they attack people with their spikes, turning the victim into a Varga. In short, they are a cross between a triffid and a vampire.

If Nation was not at his most original in concocting this blend of familiar elements, he was clearly preparing the ground for an attempt to extricate the Daleks from *Doctor Who* by giving them a new set of foes to combat. And he was breaking away from the English eccentricities of William Hartnell's Doctor to create a character template that was intended to have far greater international appeal, even if it was less intriguing than anything yet seen in the TARDIS. For the SSS agents in 'Master Plan', Bret Vyon (Nicholas Courtney) and Sara Kingdom (Jean Marsh), were as derivative as Marc Cory had been; the former is described as 'the 007 of space' in Nation's storyline, and the latter is not very far removed from Honor Blackman's character, Cathy Gale, in *The Avengers*: glamorous but good with a gun and always up for some unarmed combat.

Nonetheless, there's a great deal of fun to be had in Nation's first five episodes of the story. The Doctor and his companions travel rapidly around the universe, starting on Kembel before moving on to a penal colony planet, Desperus, then to Earth and thereafter to a distant planet named Mira, inhabited by invisible beings called Visians. But there is also some rather downbeat material. Marc Cory was killed at the end of 'Mission to the Unknown', and in 'Master Plan' his fellow agent, Bret Vyon, is killed by Sara Kingdom, who believes him to be a traitor; he wasn't but it does turn out that he was her brother (returning to the fratricide seen in 'The Dalek Invasion of Earth'). Sara too fails to survive the serial, while Katarina, a woman from ancient Troy brought along on the TARDIS from the previous story, 'The Myth Makers', dies in an act of heroic self-sacrifice.

Counterpointing the Doctor's adventures is the story of Mavic Chen (Kevin Stoney), the most powerful man on Earth and holder of the office Guardian of the Solar System. Despite his initially dignified bearing, he turns out to be a power-crazed despot who is secretly in alliance with the Daleks, providing them with the vital component, Taranium, needed to complete the Time Destructor, with which they intend to conquer the universe. In characteristically excessive fashion, Taranium is said to be 'the rarest mineral in the universe', and the Time Destructor 'the most dangerous weapon ever devised'. If the Daleks are, as ever, derived from the Nazis, then Mavic Chen is clearly modelled on Stalin, his first appearance including a reference to a Non-Aggression Pact, which can hardly fail to bring to mind the Molotov–Ribbentrop Pact of 1939 (it was even signed in the year 3975).

After these five episodes, Nation handed over to Spooner to complete the story, returning only for the seventh episode, 'The Feast of Steven', which was broadcast on Christmas Day 1965 and which therefore, in accordance with BBC practice at the time, abandoned the storyline for some fun. The TARDIS materialises in 1960s Liverpool, where the crew run into trouble with the local police (originally it was hoped to tie in with the cast of Z Cars, though this didn't work out), then finds itself in Hollywood during the silent movie era, complete with a Keystone Kops-style slapstick chase sequence and a desert melodrama, the latter dominated by a glamorous hero who, Nation noted, should be 'very superior and good looking in the tradition of Valentino'. It ended with the crew safely back on board and celebrating the festive season. 'A happy Christmas to all of us,' toasts the Doctor, before turning to the camera: 'Incidentally a happy Christmas to all of you at home.'

The Daleks, however, make no appearance in that interlude, and rather more chilling was Nation's sign-off to episode five, the last of his Dalek tales to be screened for more than seven years. As the Doctor and his companions are discovered by the monsters, he goes further than ever before in admitting defeat: 'I'm afraid, my friends, the Daleks have won.'

They hadn't, of course, and nor had we seen the last of Sara Kingdom, although she crumbled to dust in the final episode, victim of the Time Destructor as it accelerated her ageing. She was back later in the year as the star of her own comic strip in the final spin-off book that Nation authorised for publication by Souvenir Press, *The Dalek Outer Space Book* (written by an ALS colleague, Brad Ashton), as well as featuring heavily in his plans for his next enterprise.

Meanwhile, Spooner's six scripts kept the story moving along at the same pace and with the same balance of fun and terror (the materialisation of the TARDIS on a cricket pitch during a Test match is especially pleasing in its incongruity). As script editor, Donald Tosh felt – as others were later to find – that Nation's scripts for the Daleks needed some reworking, but it was a process with which Nation pronounced himself perfectly happy. 'I've already told Donald that any changes he wants to make in the script will meet with my approval,' he wrote to John Wiles in September 1965. 'I'm sure we're all aiming at the same thing.' In the same letter he ruminated on the nature of names for fictional characters: 'Our Victorian dramatists had a splendid system of immediate identification. For instance, a Roger could not be anything but a clean limbed, bright eyed, decent chap, whereas a Jasper had to be a moustache twirling, whip cracking hound.' In this context, he approved of the name Bors being given to one of the characters on the penal planet: 'Obviously any man called Bors started his day with a murder and by lunch time had worked up to really serious crimes. Splendid name.'

That Christmas saw the production at Wyndham's Theatre in London of *The Curse of the Daleks*, a play credited to Terry Nation and David Whitaker, though again it appears that the primary responsibility for the writing actually fell to Whitaker. Aimed squarely at a young audience, it concerned a spaceship with a human crew and passengers, including two prisoners, that lands on Skaro and encounters the Thals and the Daleks. 'It's all good clean fun,' thought the *Daily Express*, while *The Times* complained that for a story set in the twenty-first century the dialogue was 'strangely reminiscent of British war films, with upper lips being kept resolutely stiff', but concluded that it was 'an ultimately exciting adventure'. Significantly, in terms of the Daleks, it was another outing in the absence of the Doctor, while Whitaker's programme notes introduced for the first time the concept of the Dalek Chronicles. These were supposedly a set of microfilms that Nation had found in his garden containing the history of the race, whence all the stories had come. The tag of the Dalek Chronicles was to be used in *TV Century 21* and ensuing books.

Nation's relationship with Whitaker ended with that play and the two men did not work together again. Paul Fishman, who as a child had witnessed some of the writing sessions that produced the Souvenir books under the direction of his father, Jack, was only surprised that the partnership had lasted so long. He recalled Nation struggling to deal with the starchier end of the BBC and, perhaps under the pressures of feeding the fire of Dalekmania, actually coming to blows with Whitaker: 'There was a terrible fight. Terry took out David Whitaker. It was because he couldn't handle this Oxbridge attitude. It was the first time I'd ever seen anybody hit somebody.' It should be remembered, however, that Whitaker had been, alongside Verity Lambert, the first champion of the Daleks at a time when the BBC hierarchy was distinctly unimpressed. 'The Daleks were a smashing invention,' he said later. 'I would say they're worthy of Jules Verne.' And he was adamant that, even if it might appear to focus on forbidden bug-eyed monsters, the first serial had fitted perfectly within the remit given to *Doctor Who* by Sydney Newman: 'Actually, that Dalek story was educational in a subtle way – it showed the dangers of war, pacifism and racial hatred. It contained many admirable and idealistic truths in it, and it was also a jolly good adventure story.' It was the encouragement, rather than the altercation, that Nation tended to remember: 'I got along well with David,' he reflected in 1995. 'He supported me very thoroughly.'

Notwithstanding the outbreak of Dalekmania the previous Christmas, 1965 was the great year of the Daleks: they appeared in a record fourteen episodes of *Doctor Who* that year, as well as in the cinema, on stage, in comics and in two books. And emerging from all that work was a pattern that was clearly related to Nation's comments in August about the possibility of an American television series of the Daleks. The intention to break away from *Doctor Who* was self-evident.

It was not, however, until the late spring of 1966 that any firm steps were taken to make this a reality. Beryl Vertue had attempted to persuade American television that a stand-alone series could be viable. 'I had a go at that,' she remembered. 'I tried to talk about science fiction, and how well *Doctor Who* had gone in the UK.' But the initiative only really got off the ground through her contact with a toy manufacturer, Fred Alper, who was intrigued by the merchandising opportunities if the creatures could be launched in the States. Nation formed a new company, Lynsted Film

Productions Ltd, and he and Alper met with BBC Enterprises to pitch the idea of producing a pilot for American television, with the hope that the corporation would come in as joint partners. There was sufficient interest for Nation to develop a storyline, which he then worked up into a full script for a half-hour pilot episode, 'The Destroyers', featuring an SSS team that centred on Sara Kingdom, Captain Jason Corey (evidently drawn from the same source as Marc Cory in 'Mission to the Unknown') and an android named Mark Seven.

The concept for *The Daleks*, as the series was to be called, was fairly novel, pitching a team of security agents against a single race of alien monsters, with a female lead character, but it was not immediately clear how this could be sustained over an entire series. Certainly the pilot gave little indication of breaking new ground, relying instead on characteristic Nation elements: jungles, caves, killer vegetation. Considerably more problematic, from the point of view of the BBC, was that when Nation submitted his script in October 1966, it came with an estimated budget of £42,000, appropriate for an American production but wildly excessive by the corporation's standards. Even then there were doubts that it could be brought in on budget. There was concern too that the peak of the craze had already passed ('I have very serious reservations as to the audience pull of the Daleks in the UK at this late stage,' noted a senior figure in BBC Enterprises), leaving the financial success of the project entirely dependent on the unknown American market.

Aware of the pressures of time – it was proposed to film the pilot in December, ready for the buying season in American television the following March – Fred Alper had a contract drawn up that would split the investment costs for the pilot and a subsequent series between the BBC on the one side and himself and Lynsted Park on the other. But the BBC, panicked by how fast the commitment was escalating into a series, got cold feet and backed out of the project altogether. By the end of 1966 it was clear that they no longer had an interest, save in the merchandising rights that might result, and over the first few months of 1967 discussions took place about what the level of these would be. Still talking about raising the finance elsewhere, Nation visited America in search of potential partners. 'I went to the United States,' he remembered. 'I went there to hustle and got very close to doing it.' But by now the impetus had been lost, and the entire proposal slowly withered away during the course of the year. It had, however, come remarkably close to realisation. There had been talk of interest from the American network ABC and, in a mistaken belief that the BBC were more committed than they actually were, Nation had even booked time for the shoot in Twickenham Studios, where construction work had begun on the sets.

Meanwhile, there were new Dalek serials on *Doctor Who*: 'The Power of the Daleks' (1966) and 'The Evil of the Daleks' (1967). Nation had been given the first option of writing the stories, in line with his agreement with the BBC, but was unable to commit himself to the project and agreed instead that they should be written by David Whitaker. Nation was later to express his disapproval of the serials ('I didn't like them and I responded very badly to them'), and his attitude was not much ameliorated by the fact that he received little more than a nominal sum for the use of his creation: he was paid £15 for each broadcast that featured the creatures in a script written by someone else, which even the Head of Business at Television Enterprises was later to acknowledge was 'a ludicrously small fee'.

These were intended to be the last ever Dalek stories in *Doctor Who*, leaving the field clear for Nation's proposed series, but the continuing importance of the monsters to the show was demonstrated when William Hartnell left the programme in 1966 and the concept of regeneration was hurriedly invented to allow for a transition to another actor. Just as the Daleks had been used to smooth the departures of Susan, and then of Ian and Barbara, so they were employed in 'The Power of the Daleks' to make the transformation from Hartnell to Patrick Troughton easier for viewers to absorb. Even so, viewing figures, which had been falling in the later Hartnell stories, did not regain the peaks to which they had been pushed a couple of years earlier by 'The Dalek Invasion of Earth'.

With their apparent farewell from *Doctor Who* and the abandonment of the solo series, it seemed by the end of 1967 that the era of the Daleks had drawn to its close. There were no more annuals forthcoming from Souvenir Press, the idea of a third movie had fallen through, and the comic strip had also come to an end – having moved from *TV Century 21* to *TV Comic* at the beginning of 1967, with a different writer and artist, it had lasted only a few months. In December that year, Nation did agree in principle to the idea of a new story for the 1968 season, but refused the BBC's suggestion of pitching his creations against the new monsters on the block, the Cybermen, and nothing came of the proposal. At their height, the Daleks had ensured the survival and then the success of *Doctor Who*, and had at times completely eclipsed the programme itself, but now they were finished, and the series was continuing.

They had had a good run, and it's unarguable that Nation had reaped enormous rewards from their glory years, but the failure to secure an American series was a bitter personal blow. 'Terry was really ambitious,' said Beryl Vertue. 'He wanted to be international.' By that he meant, as did all his British contemporaries, that he wanted to make it in America, where the real money and prestige was to be found. From 1966 onwards, as BBC Enterprises began serious efforts to sell *Doctor Who* around the world, he received a steady stream of income from sales to dozens of countries, from Australia to Zambia, but that wasn't the same thing as breaking the States. And it wasn't his show. He was also receiving only the standard BBC royalties due to a writer, an arrangement that made no allowance for the significance or merit of the work; 'The Daleks' earned a little more when it was sold to Jamaica than did 'The Keys of Marinus' in the same territory, but only because it comprised seven episodes rather than six.

None of this was a substitute for the real thing. In a career as long as Nation's there were bound to be any number of missed opportunities, projects that never materialised, but the failure of *The Daleks* was perhaps the biggest and most significant of all. Yet it's not easy to imagine it being much of a hit, even if the series had been commissioned by a US network. The verdict of the BBC hierarchy on the pilot script was encouraging enough but was hardly a ringing acclamation of a major new piece of work: 'representative children's science fiction', thought Shaun Sutton, the head of drama serials; 'a typical – and therefore excellent – *Doctor Who*-type story', was the verdict of David Attenborough, then the controller of BBC2, as he turned down the idea of taking the proposed series for his channel. These were experienced broadcasters who knew how big the Daleks had become, and still their enthusiasm was strictly limited.

Even if the show had made it on to American television, it seems unlikely that it would have lasted for more than one series, if only because the variations that could be wrung out of the situation were so limited. The formats of British shows that had translated successfully to America, such as *The Avengers* and *The Saint*, had a flexibility that made them capable of almost endless permutations; the Daleks, a purely evil creation with no shades of grey, were a much more restricted proposition. To take a slightly unfair example from a different field, the Daleks had for a moment at Christmas 1964 rivalled the popularity even of the Beatles, but in terms of creativity they had been left a long way behind. The Beatles had then been singing 'I Feel Fine'; by the time Nation was looking for investors in *The*

Daleks, they had moved on to 'Strawberry Fields Forever'. The Daleks were capable of no such development.

For they were ultimately handicapped by their voices and their lack of visual response. There was a very definite limit to how long a viewer could take a conversation between Daleks, as Nation seemed to have recognised in his scripts for *Doctor Who*. Unusually for that series, the Daleks were seldom the sole alien life-form on display, their lack of variety being compensated for by the presence of the Thals, or the Aridians and the Mechanoids, or the Vargas and the Visians, while in 'The Dalek Invasion of Earth' the Robomen had fulfilled the same function. In purely technical terms, there were related problems; as Richard Martin pointed out, the director had to work hard at camera angles just 'to give them a sort of dynamic that they themselves did not possess'. Had the special effects available at the time been capable of reproducing the full Dalek empire depicted in *TV Century 21*, it might have been different, but they weren't, and however big the budget seemed from a British perspective, it was always going to look a bit cheap compared to American shows.

And a failure in America would surely have finished the Daleks off for good. It would have been extremely difficult for the BBC to countenance them traipsing back, metaphorical tail between metaphorical legs, to *Doctor Who*. Paradoxically, the collapse of *The Daleks* probably ensured the ultimate survival of the monsters. Untainted by their likely malfunction elsewhere, they remained in the storage lockers of the TARDIS, ready for exhumation at a later date. The truth was that, without their original and greatest foe, they were never going to be as much fun on their own. 'The Daleks have no value outside *Doctor Who*,' was Terrance Dicks's conclusion. 'Terry made several attempts to launch the Daleks by themselves, and none of them were really successful. They're *Doctor Who*'s main monster, and they're inviolable in that position, but that's the only position they've got.'

Chapter Nine

Avenging and Persuading

Although *The Daleks* was never to materialise, the amount of time and energy that Terry Nation put into the project can be gauged by the fact that between April 1967 and October 1968 – the best part of eighteen months – not a single new script for any series on British television bore his name. It was his longest absence from the broadcast media since *It's a Fair Cop* had aired back in 1961, though he did appear in person at the beginning of 1968 on the documentary programme *Whicker's World*, in which he was interviewed by Alan Whicker at Lynsted Park; surrounded by Dalek props from the Amicus movies, he looked as though he were reaffirming his status as a major television writer, even if there was presently no new material on screen.

Those eighteen months, as he put aside the dashed hopes of an American show and returned to the world of British television, saw a major shift in the cultural mood. The rise of liberal and radical politics had been one of the defining features of the decade thus far, reaching a peak in the spring of 1968 as the movement against the Vietnam War hit critical levels in America amid a spate of riots, as a general strike paralysed France and as the reformist government of Alexander Dubček in Czechoslovakia seemed to offer state socialism a way forward from totalitarianism. Immediately thereafter, however, came a powerful reaction. Richard M. Nixon was elected US President, the party of Charles de Gaulle won a landslide election victory in France, and Soviet tanks rolled into Prague to crush dissent, while the Conservative MP Enoch Powell made race relations the most controversial issue in British politics with his 'rivers of blood' speech. As if to emphasise the victory of conservatism, two great liberal heroes, Martin Luther King Jr and Robert F. Kennedy, were assassinated.

The same year also saw the suicide of Tony Hancock. The comedian had never recovered his position after that ATV series and, alone in Australia, with his second marriage having ended as catastrophically as his first, he took an overdose of pills, washed down with vodka.

The days of Swinging London were receding fast and Nation, who had benefited from that era but whose work had never sat entirely comfortably in it, was ultimately to find fertile ground for his darker visions. For now, however, the only opportunities that presented themselves were essentially more of the same, returning him to the position he had been in before the *Daleks* project: successful, wealthy and writing scripts for ITC.

A new season of *The Saint* was in preparation – the second to be filmed in colour and the last of the Roger Moore incarnation – and Nation contributed four episodes. This time they were original stories, since the back catalogue of Leslie Charteris's tales had by now been heavily depleted. 'Television is a monster, like a great big garbage disposal,' noted Charteris, 'and it can eat up a lifetime's output in a matter of seasons.' It was a lesson that the music hall comedians had learned a long time back, but the stockpile was not entirely used up, and there is a suspicion that the switch to newly commissioned stories was also made in the hope of ending Charteris's complaints about the liberties he saw being taken with his work. He was supposed to have a degree of script approval, but it didn't always work out in the way he wished, and he tended to make his displeasure known. 'I always saw the scripts and made my comments and criticisms, but they were not always necessarily followed,' he recalled later. 'I had no veto and I can't say I was always pleased with what I saw on the screen.'

Unfortunately he was to be no happier with the new material. And perhaps he was right not to be, for there was little discernible change between the adaptations and the new stories; after more than seventy episodes, the production line was running with such efficiency that the format and the style continued smoothly through the transition. Nation's scripts were not among his best work, though there were some good moments. In the episode 'The Desperate Diplomat' a British representative, Jason Douglas (John Robinson), is stationed in a newly independent country and keen to expose the abuse of international aid to Africa: 'When independence came, I went to work for the new regime. The new leader started with good intentions. Then corruption set in. Aid from America, from Britain was used to furnish palaces, buy cars, jewels. Government officials lived in luxury while the people starved.'

Even before this, Nation had already written a couple of episodes for a

Left: Llandaff Cathedral following the bombing raid on Cardiff in January 1941
Mirrorpix

Right: Mr Herbert's class at Radnor Road Boys' School in 1938, with Terry Nation (middle row, far right)
From Stewart Williams' Cardiff Yesterday Vol. 21

Below: Rehearsal of the 'Poor Man's Picasso' sketch onstage at the Capital Cinema, Cardiff in 1948 with Terry Nation (third from right) and Harry Greene (far right)
Courtesy of Harry Greene

Above: Beryl Vertue with the founding members of Associated London Scripts: Eric Sykes, Alan Simpson, Spike Milligan and Ray Galton *Popperfoto/Getty Images*

Above and below: John Junkin, Dave Freeman and Terry Nation in their office at ALS in Shepherd's Bush *Courtesy of Deb Boultwood*

Left: Tony Hancock in 'The Assistant', *Hancock* (1963) *Topfoto*

Above: Peter Cushing as Elijah Baley in 'The Caves of Steel', *Story Parade* (1964) *BBC Photo Library*

Overleaf: The Dalek city in 'The Daleks', *Doctor Who* (1963) *Courtesy of Raymond P. Cusick*

Above: The Doctor (William Hartnell) in 'The Daleks', *Doctor Who* (1963) *BBC Photo Library*

Below: Publicity still from 'The Keys of Marinus', *Doctor Who* (1964), showing the creatures from 'The Velvet Web' *Courtesy of Raymond P. Cusick*

Opposite: Terry Nation and Raymond Cusick *Alamy*

The Daleks take over London in 1964's 'The Dalek Invasion of Earth' (above) and Cannes for the 1965 Film Festival (left)
BBC Photo Library and Getty Images

Below: William Hartnell with toy Daleks *Getty Images*

NATO

Above: Leslie Illingworth's cartoon of Charles de Gaulle as a Dalek (1964) *www.cartoons.ac.uk*

Right: The Slyther reading *The Dalek Book* (1964) *Getty Images*

Above left: Jason King
(Peter Wyngarde) in
'A Cellar Full of Silence',
Department S (1969)
Rex Features

Above right: Terry Nation
with a script for *The Baron*
(1966) *Rex Features*

Left: John Steed (Patrick
Macnee) and Tara King
(Linda Thorson) in
The Avengers (1968)
Rex Features

Right: Lord Brett Sinclair (Roger Moore) and Danny Wilde (Tony Curtis) in *The Persuaders!* (1971) *Alamy*

Below: Poster for *The House in Nightmare Park* (1973) *BFI*

LADIES & GENTLEMEN

NAT COHEN presents an ANGLO EMI film ASSOCIATED LONDON FILMS EXTONATION production

FOR YOUR HORRIFICATION

DON'T SEE IT ALONE – BRING THE CHILDREN

FRANKIE HOWERD • RAY MILLAND

THE HOUSE IN NIGHTMARE PARK

A

EMI

THIS IS A FILM FOR THE WHOLE FAMILY – IF YOU ARE UNDER 14 YOU CAN STILL COME ON YOUR OWN – BUT ASK YOUR PARENTS FIRST

Executive Producer BERYL VERTUE · Music by HARRY ROBINSON
Screenplay by CLIVE EXTON and TERRY NATION · Produced by CLIVE EXTON and TERRY NATION · Directed by PETER SYKES
Technicolor® · Released by MGM EMI

Above: Arthur Wormley (George Baker) and Abby Grant (Carolyn Seymour) in *Survivors* (1975) with (left) Terry Nation's 1976 novel based on the series
BBC Photo Library and Orion Publishing Group

Below: The Doctor (Tom Baker) and Davros (Michael Wisher) in 'Genesis of the Daleks', *Doctor Who* (1975) *BBC Photo Library*

Above: The original crew of the *Liberator* in *Blake's 7* (1978), with left-right: Gan (David Jackson), Avon (Paul Darrow), Cally (Jan Chappell), Blake (Gareth Thomas), Jenna (Sally Knyvette) and Vila (Michael Keating) *BBC Photo Library*

Left: Servalan (Jacqueline Pearce) in *Blake's 7* (1979) *BBC Photo Library*

Terry Nation with his daughter Rebecca,
at the time of the publication of his novel
Rebecca's World (1975) *Alamy*

new ITC series, *The Champions*, filmed in 1967 and bought by NBC in America soon thereafter, though it was not screened in Britain until the autumn of 1968. Developed by Dennis Spooner and produced by Monty Berman, *The Champions* focused on three agents working for an international organisation called Nemesis, based in Geneva; in the first episode, their plane crashes in Tibet, they are rescued by mysterious monk-like figures and, as part of their recovery, are imbued with superhuman powers of telepathy, enhanced senses and phenomenal strength. This shameless borrowing from James Hilton's *Lost Horizon* (1933) was, somewhat perversely, intended to bring a sense of believability back to the ITC genre. 'Action dramas have reached the stage when the principal characters are achieving the impossible in their exploits, fights, cunning and unbelievable physical stamina,' argued Spooner. 'No one can believe that any mortal could achieve what the present day heroes manage to do and survive. But *The Champions* makes it all logical because the three characters have these out-of-the-ordinary powers.' It was a neat, counter-intuitive defence of the show's premise, but it didn't make any more comfortable the marriage of the two traditions of secret agent and superhero. More importantly, the casting was far from impressive; the three stars were less than charismatic, and none of them made much impression on the audience.

For Nation, the heroes' super-powers didn't particularly suit his preferred theme: the ability of ordinary people to rise above difficult situations by exercising ingenuity and creative improvisation. But his scripts worked well enough. In 'The Body Snatchers' the villain has seized control of a research laboratory in North Wales that has developed cryogenic freezing; having stolen the body of a recently deceased American general, he's hoping to bring the man back to life and thus acquire crucial defence secrets. (The Welsh setting allows for a rare sighting on 1960s television of a character speaking Welsh, as well as a brief, uncredited appearance by Talfryn Thomas, formerly of *Uncle Selwyn* and later to return to Nation's work.)

Stronger than that was 'The Fanatics', in which several prominent politicians have been assassinated in a spate of suicide terrorist attacks. One of our heroes, Richard Barrett (William Gaunt), infiltrates the organisation responsible for the attacks, posing as a disaffected British soldier who has been selling secrets to an enemy state on the grounds that 'No country has a moral right to exclusive knowledge on weapons of mass destruction.' The episode is lifted by a guest appearance from Gerald Harper as Croft, the evil mastermind behind the plan: 'The meek will inherit the earth? Oh no, it's the strong who'll survive, the men of courage and ideas. The mass elects a leader, yes, but the mass is a mindless organism. It destroys true progress.' 'Well, that's been the platform of every dictator,' shrugs Barrett, under-cutting one of the most hallowed traditions of the action hero, that his enemy must always deliver a bragging speech about power. The inter-ruption doesn't stop Croft, of course: 'When you've been with me a little longer, you'll know the feeling of power, real power, life and death. It's like a drug, you taste it and you want more, and you'll kill for it. You'll even die for it.' It's all good crazed stuff, though it doesn't get us any closer to an explanation of the suicide element of the operation; it's clear what Croft wants, but not what his self-sacrificing minions get out of the deal. Possibly there was a brainwashing story that got lost in the final cut, but it does leave on a slightly confused note.

The Champions is fondly remembered in some quarters, but at the time it failed to win over the critics. 'The enormous advantage that Sir Lew Grade has over his rivals among the network,' wrote Peter Black in the Daily Mail, 'is not that he knows better than they do what the public wants. It is that he doesn't mind.' He added, in reference to one of Spooner's scripts: 'I felt that a dog could have written it if he had wanted dollars more than dog biscuits. There wasn't a moment to stimulate even the simplest of minds. And this is peak-time television in one of the greatest cities in the world.' The audience, at least in America, appeared to agree and, like The Baron, the series was dropped from its network slot during the screening of the one season that was made. Its success or otherwise in Britain was more difficult to judge, since it was shown at different times in different regions. This was often the case with the ITC series, but was particularly exaggerated with The Champions; Peter Black's review was written in November 1969, when the show finally arrived in London, more than a year after it had first been screened elsewhere on the ITV network, an indication that Grade was not throwing his whole weight behind it.

Presumably, however, it was not a complete commercial failure, for Spooner and Berman immediately bounced back with two new series that were produced in tandem in order to save money: Department S and Randall and Hopkirk (Deceased). Nation wrote two of the first three episodes to be filmed of the former and was scheduled to write more before other opportunities presented themselves.

If The Champions suffered from a lack of magnetism among its stars,

Department S perhaps veered too far in the other direction. Two of the characters, Stewart Sullivan (Joel Fabiani) and Annabelle Hurst (Rosemary Nicols), were solid, unexceptional figures who could have come from any thriller series of the era, but they were entirely overshadowed by the third member of the trio, Jason King, as played by Peter Wyngarde. The original idea was that the team would be completed by a retired Oxford don named Robert Cullingford, who was also a writer of detective stories and would thus view the cases from unexpected angles. Kenneth More's name was touted for the role, but instead Berman choose Wyngarde, and the nature of the series changed entirely.

One of the great television actors of the period, Wyngarde had already appeared in various series to which Nation had contributed – including *The Baron*, *The Saint* and *The Champions* – though never in one of his scripts. Wyngarde rejected the proposed character of Cullingford, keeping only the concept of being a writer, though now it was of paperback thrillers centring on an agent named Mark Caine. The character himself was renamed Jason King, and Wyngarde created an enduring image of the 1960s playboy bachelor taken to a superbly self-parodying extreme. His camp excesses, complete with elegantly drooping moustache, coiffured hair and exquisite velvet suits and kaftans, were balanced by a Lothario image that made him an irresistible, unattainable fantasy figure for millions of female viewers. He couldn't pass a mirror without admiring his own vulpine good looks, his catchphrase was a drawled 'Fancy!' and his voice sounded like it had been aged in a cask of Amontillado. So self-assured was Wyngarde's performance that, most unusually for an action hero, he seldom won a fight – and it didn't matter.

In the scripts that Nation wrote for *Department S*, he approached the character by explicitly evoking the shade of Oscar Wilde. 'Do you have anything to declare, Mr King?' asks Stewart, and Jason replies, 'Nothing, except my genius.' On another occasion, Annabelle says, 'We still have to find the actual room,' and Jason murmurs, 'We will, Oscar, we will.' Nation's own witticisms kept up the same faux-decadent atmosphere. As Jason comes round from being knocked unconscious yet again by a villain, and complains of a headache, Annabelle suggests he take a couple of aspirin. He shudders: 'I couldn't bear the noise I'd make swallowing them.' And, inspired by King's habit of drawing the cuffs of his frilly shirts back over his jacket sleeves, Nation couldn't resist revisiting a gag from *The Saint*; Jason explains that the hero of his thrillers carries a knife up his sleeve, but that's just for fiction: 'I never carry a weapon, let alone a knife. It would fray my cuffs.' Other details are equally irresistible; of all the attempts to parody the girls in the James Bond films, none have bettered the heroine of the Mark Caine novel *Epilogue to Hong Kong*, the perfectly named Hussy Abundant. The only jarring note comes in a scene in 'A Cellar Full of Silence', which sees King, dressed entirely in black leather, dismounting from a motorbike and saying, 'I haven't been on a bike since I was a teenage rocker.' The idea that Jason King might have been a rocker rather than a mod is hard to take, though his subsequent reference to 'leather queens' may shed further light on the question.

The plots of the two episodes that Nation wrote are less relevant than details such as these, but then that was true of the entire programme; the whole of *Department S* was a magnificent triumph of style over content. The concept for the show was inspired by the mystery that had been solved by Nation in 'The Chase', on which Spooner had been script editor. 'If the *Marie Celeste* were to happen today, no one knows who would investigate it,' Spooner reasoned. '*Department S* always started like that. The "hook" was always the *Marie Celeste* sort of situation – a totally, absolutely inexplicable mystery.' Unfortunately, thanks to the structure, the ensuing fifty minutes tended to be something of a let-down, a rational solution to an intriguing conundrum, and viewers, quite understandably, found themselves less interested in the narrative than in the figure of Jason King. He was so obviously in a different league to his colleagues that a second season of the show never materialised; it was replaced by a new programme, *Jason King*, in which Wyngarde took centre stage. And what had been a superb role in the context of a team proved to be a bit too baroque and flowery to carry an entire show. By that stage, however, Nation had already flown the ITC nest, having been recruited to the staff of the biggest of all the secret agent series.

The Avengers, initiated by Sydney Newman back when he was responsible for drama at ABC, had grown out of an earlier Newman commission, *Police Surgeon* (1960) starring Ian Hendry. When that failed to get the ratings figures for which he'd hoped, Newman suggested a new series for Hendry to be titled *The Avengers*, 'an action adventure-thriller with a sense of humour', though, according to Brian Clemens, beyond the title he had few ideas of what the show might be: 'He came in and said, "I want to do a series called *The Avengers*. I don't know what it means, but it's a hell of a good title."' The star was teamed with Patrick Macnee, playing a character named John Steed, but it was not until Hendry himself departed, to be replaced by a young female companion for the cheerful but crusty-looking Steed, that the series began to acquire its distinctive identity. First with Cathy Gale (Honor Blackman, 1962–4) and then with Emma Peel (Diana Rigg, 1965–8), *The Avengers* became not merely a national but an international institution, purveying an increasingly kitsch concept of England in which all the conventions of the spy thriller were gleefully ridiculed, and in which elements from science fiction and comic book traditions were equally welcome. Roger Moore could undercut a plotline in *The Saint* with a single sardonically raised eyebrow, but *The Avengers* at its peak – which for most critics meant the Diana Rigg seasons – was so fixated on fun that the whole show seemed determined to subvert genre expectations. There was plenty of action but it was the stuff of pure fantasy.

The prime shapers of the show by this stage were Albert Fennell and Brian Clemens, but when Rigg decided to leave the series in 1967, the company decided to make a clean break in the hope of returning to a style that at least approached reality. Fennell and Clemens were fired, and replaced by John Bryce, who had been script editor and then producer in the earlier years. He recruited a Canadian actress, Linda Thorson, to be Steed's new partner, Tara King, and began to film the next season. After just three episodes, however, the results were deemed to be unacceptable and a call went out to Fennell and Clemens, the latter of whom was on holiday, touring England and Wales: 'Every time I got to another hotel there was a message saying: Could you phone? And eventually, after about two-and-a-half weeks, I did phone, and they said: Could you come back?' The two men returned to find that of the three shows already filmed, only one met with their approval, 'Invasion of the Earthmen'. And since that was written by Terry Nation, he was given the job as script editor. He was expecting at the time to be writing further episodes of *Department S*, but the chance of joining the production team on a show that had been a regular fixture in the television top ten for seven years was clearly too good a chance to miss.

'It got wilder,' was Nation's memory of that final season of *The Avengers*. 'It probably got too wild by the time we finished. There was no other market for that sort of thing. The acid test for our show was: what is the story? Now turn it on its head! Instead of seeing somebody shot, we would see the chalked outline of the body. Then somebody would walk in, get shot and fall into the chalked outline. Always turn it on its head, always make it more and more ridiculous – but then justify it.'

Despite his background in writing comedy, this kind of spoof was not the kind of thing for which Nation was primarily known, though there had been moments to suggest it could easily become part of his repertoire. The episode 'Epitaph for a Hero' in *The Baron*, for example, had opened in a cemetery after a funeral, as a woman arrives, spits in the open grave and leaves. She is followed by two men, one of whom – another of Nation's loquacious Welshmen, played here by Artro Morris – delivers an effusive eulogy: 'In this black hour of fond remembrance, when the great sorrow, dark as a raven's wing, swoops into the memory and clouds the eyes with tears as cold as the angel of death himself, we call back in gentle memories the man who was so dear. Kind, decent, honest and true friend that he was, a man of infinite goodness, his forgiveness for those he loved was endless.' During the latter part of this speech, the barely suppressed giggles of the two men have built into uncontrollable laughter, and they depart in a state of near-hysteria, as the title sequence brings a moment of pause. The story that follows is a routine bank heist, but there remains an element of strangeness. Much of the action takes place in a fairground House of Horrors that's closed for renovation, and one scene is set in a steam bath, where Mannering encounters a man complaining that it's not hot enough: 'We must have more heat, so we can get used to the flames of eternal damnation. It should be hotter, much hotter.' None of which would have been out of place in an episode of *The Avengers*.

In his scripts for the show, Nation clearly enjoyed the freedom to laugh. 'Legacy of Death' bounced ideas off John Huston's 1941 film *The Maltese Falcon*, with Stratford Johns giving a magnificent performance in the Sydney Greenstreet role (his character is named Sidney Street, in case we didn't spot the reference) as a man on the trail of 'a pearl of great price, a monstrous pearl, black as night and spawned up by some gigantic mollusc before time began, the largest, the most priceless pearl on earth'. (This is the pearl that ends up being dissolved in wine, in contravention of the words of Leslie Charteris.) The over-writing is entirely characteristic of a script in which Nation displays a glorious lack of restraint. 'We're near it now,' Sidney pants as his delirious, fevered dreams appear to be reaching fruition. 'I feel it, I smell it, all around like the perfume from some rare and exotic blossom comes the sweet smell of success. Victory is near, we have but to reach out and grasp, to take that delicate blossom in our hands and crush its petals to inhale the perfume of triumph.' Not even Steed is immune; when Tara, who is driving the two of them, asks where they're going, he replies: 'Where indeed? Philosophers have asked that question for a thousand years. Quo vadis? Whither goest thou? Man's eternal search for his destiny. You may well ask where are we going.' So she asks again: 'Where are we going?' And he answers: 'Turn left, next lights.'

In 'Take Me to Your Leader' – a shaggy dog tale in which Steed and Tara follow a talking attaché case around London – they encounter a precocious schoolgirl (played by Elisabeth Robillard) who possesses the secret key that they're pursuing, and who happily declares herself open to bribery. 'Twenty-five pounds invested in blue chip equities will show a high yield by the time I'm twenty-one,' she explains. Steed is unimpressed and reminds her that money isn't everything, to which she replies in wide-eyed innocence: 'Oh Mr Steed, don't shatter a little girl's illusions.' The episode 'Thingumajig' was less successful, concerning a mad scientist who has developed metal boxes that feed off electricity, move around of their own free will and emit a high-voltage charge that kills. The concept was fine – and Iain Cuthbertson as the scientist gave it his best shot – but the story foundered on the fact that small featureless boxes are neither frightening nor entertaining as a visual image. There was, however, room for a restatement of an argument from *The Caves of Steel* as Steed explains how vulnerable modern life is in the face of a threat to the electricity supply: 'Take a city. London, for instance. Its appetite for electricity is insatiable. It gulps up millions of kilowatts and converts them into heat and power and light.' It was a theme to which Nation was to return.

Other favourite concerns turn up in 'Invasion of the Earthmen', where Steed and Tara investigate an institution called the Alpha Academy, run on strict military lines – one might almost say as a hive – by Brigadier Brett (William Lucas), who is busily recruiting a private army of youthful soldiers. When their training is complete, he freezes them in cryogenic suspension, so that when Earth begins to explore and settle on other planets, he will have his troops ready to conquer the space colonies. It's a ludicrous proposition, of course, but Nation doesn't simply stay with the caricature of science fiction, instead expanding into a parody of his own action tales. The Academy is surrounded by a protective zone full of snares and booby-traps, snakes and scorpions, and when Tara successfully lasts for an hour outside, the Brigadier is impressed. 'I congratulate you on your powers of survival,' he tells her, and she shrugs: 'They're instinctive.' There is also a tunnel beneath the Academy, whose function is explained by one of the cadets: 'The Brigadier says everybody's got a secret fear. In that tunnel you come face-to-face with that fear.' Inevitably Tara and Steed end up in this fully equipped Room 101, where they find rats, spiders and a concrete tube designed to engender claustrophobia, as well as snares, acid pools and other hazards.

How much influence Nation had over the last season of *The Avengers*, beyond the six scripts with which he is credited, is uncertain. The show had become very much Clemens's baby and, although he was now officially the producer, he appears to have retained many of the script editor's responsibilities. He commissioned Nation to write 'Noon Doomsday', a spoof of the movie *High Noon*, but was disappointed by the result: 'He turned in a script that was really inferior. I totally rewrote it. Although Terry's got the sole credit, there's not really a word of his in any of that episode. He hadn't been rewritten like that in a long time, and it was a shock to his system. And I must say that thereafter he wrote several *Avengers* episodes and I never had to rewrite them. I forced him to get off his arse really, and do it.' No one questioned Nation's ability to write well when he tried, but even he seemed to have doubts about whether he was capable of stepping into a more supervisory role. 'I am not a good script editor,' he admitted, many years later. 'If somebody sends me a script, it could be absolutely perfect, but it wouldn't be my way of doing it, and I would tend to rewrite until it reflected my way of thinking, which is not a good thing to do.' Clemens's take was more direct: 'He wasn't suited to what I call executive decisions.'

In any event, this final season of the show was, and remains, much less celebrated than its immediate predecessors. The troubled start to the series had left Fennell and Clemens with Linda Thorson already cast as the replacement for Diana Rigg, a decision on which Clemens was lukewarm at best: 'I wouldn't have cast her. She developed into a good actress, but she was too young and she was Canadian. And Canadians notoriously don't have a British sense of humour.' In an attempt to find another companion figure (because 'Steed's got to strike sparks off someone'), he revealed for the first time their superior. Known only as Mother and played by Patrick Newell, he was a wheelchair-bound man who swung around his room by means of straps hanging from the ceiling, an image Clemens borrowed from Michael Powell's 1961 film *The Queen's Guard*. The British critics were divided both by Tara King and by Mother, though mostly the goodwill towards the show carried it through. 'The programme – arguably the best series produced by British television – is as good as ever,' was the verdict of the once and future Conservative MP, Julian Critchley, in a review in *The Times*. Dennis Spooner remembered that the imminent end of the show liberated the writers: 'We went really weird, because we knew there wasn't going to be any more.' And Clemens himself thought that the scripts for the final season were 'the best of all. Much more variety, ingenuity, originality.' It was a view shared in retrospect by Patrick Macnee, though he hadn't been enthusiastic at the time: 'They rate as some of the very best episodes that were ever made.'

In America, however, where the show had been a big hit, and had even been nominated for an Emmy in the last two seasons, the ratings fell off sharply – partly, it is argued, because it was scheduled up against *Rowan and Martin's Laugh-In*, then at the peak of its popularity. When *The Avengers* was cancelled by the American ABC network in 1969, it was clear that the show wasn't going to be recommissioned, and the last episode, 'Bizarre', ended with Steed and Tara being blasted into space, as Mother turned to the camera to reassure us: 'They'll be back, you can depend on it.'

Lew Grade's ITC was also having difficulties in America, and had been struggling to find a winning formula for some time. A string of series, including *Man in a Suitcase* (1967) and *Strange Report* (1968), as well as *The Champions* and *Department S*, had failed to make it to a second season and – despite strong overseas sales elsewhere – had met with only moderate success in the crucial American market. Meanwhile, the company's two guaranteed winners had by now finished production: *Danger Man* when Patrick McGoohan quit in order to develop the more experimental series *The Prisoner* (1967), and *The Saint* when Roger Moore finally decided in 1968 that the show had run its course. What was needed, evidently, was one unmistakably big, sure-fire hit, and in 1970 Robert S. Baker began discussions with Grade about a new series to be titled *The Friendly Persuaders* and built around the partnership of an English aristocrat and a self-made American businessman. Both would be wealthy playboys, sufficiently bored with their lives of leisure that they would be prepared to team up for the usual crime-busting adventures.

Roger Moore was always intended to play the English half of the pairing and, despite his reluctance, Grade soon had him on board, airily dismissing the actor's move into films (with the 1970 classic *The Man Who Haunted Himself*), and insisting that the earning of dollars was a patriotic duty. 'The country needs the money,' argued the newly knighted Sir Lew. 'Think of your Queen.' A more important and difficult consideration was the casting of the American actor who would join him. ITC had used American leads in series before, but they had hardly been A-list stars: Steve Forrest in *The*

Baron, Stuart Damon in *The Champions*, Richard Bradford in *Man in a Suitcase*. This time, there was to be no such skimping. Grade had authorised a budget of £100,000 per episode, making the series the most expensive drama in British television history, and he needed a major figure to sell it around the world. After some consideration of Rock Hudson and Glenn Ford, it was finally agreed that the ideal candidate was Tony Curtis, still a big name internationally, even if his screen work had, with the notable exception of *The Boston Strangler* (1968), been undistinguished in recent years. Robert S. Baker, Roger Moore and Terry Nation — the latter already recruited to be script editor and associate producer of the series — were sent to Hollywood to persuade him to do the show.

Moore's main memory of that encounter was the British trio's aware-ness that Curtis was 'the head of the anti-smoking lobby in America' at a time when they all smoked. Eventually, some way into the meeting at Curtis's house, Moore plucked up the courage to ask if it was all right to light up. An ostentatious search for an ashtray ensued, while their host used the time to pass round anti-smoking propaganda — pictures of diseased lungs and the like — to his guests. The meeting was a success, but the moral high ground so carefully established by the American star looked a little less secure when Curtis subsequently flew into Heathrow to start filming and was promptly arrested for possession of cannabis. Had he not passed a handful of pills to production executive Johnny Goodman just before going through Customs, he might have faced even more negative publicity and a harsher penalty than the small fine he actually received.

The pairing was an unqualified triumph, and the opening titles of what had now become known as *The Persuaders!* set the scene perfectly. Over the moody drama of one of John Barry's best theme tunes, a split screen shows us snapshots illustrating the contrasting life stories of the two characters. Danny Wilde (Curtis) emerges from a Bronx tenement to become a major player on Wall Street, while Lord Brett Sinclair (Moore) is seen as the product of Harrow, Oxford and the Grenadier Guards, with a particular emphasis on his sporting prowess: rowing, rugby, motor racing, even a winning ride at Ascot, however implausible that might be for a man of Moore's stature. The contrast between the products of these varying back-grounds was spelt out in the opening to 'Chain of Events', one of the stories scripted by Nation. Danny wakes up by a campfire in a field; wearing western gear, complete with fringed buckskin jacket and wide-brimmed hat, he's on a back-to-nature holiday. He starts fixing his breakfast until, two minutes into this pastoral idyll, the camera pans back to show Brett waking up. He's at the other end of the same field, in a tent equipped with every luxury from television to electric blankets, from a hot shower to a deep freeze; there's even a chandelier. 'I must admit I rather like roughing it,' he says languidly, 'but I miss the morning papers.'

Curtis brought to his character a couple of tics – 'I always try to get in close to people when I talk to them and I always keep my gloves on no matter what I'm doing' – which added to his sense of fussy restlessness, bouncing in an unpredictable orbit around the calm understatement of Moore. From the outset, there was a sense of male bonding that veered towards sexual chemistry, as the two characters bickered and bantered with each other like a divorced couple in a 1940s screwball comedy. They walk arm-in-arm down the street, they worry about breaking a nail and ruining their manicures, and they are intensely loyal and devoted to each other. They weren't as camp as Jason King, but at times it was a near-run thing. When Danny is praised for renovating a run-down cottage all on his own, he makes no comment on the plastering and structural work he's done, focusing instead on the soft furnishings: 'I picked out every little fabric you see in the place.' They were not, however, supposed to be seen as homosexual, for they are in perpetual friendly rivalry over women, most famously over Joan Collins, playing a character named Sidonie, in the episode 'Five Miles to Midnight'. Their competition however tends to result in stalemate; that particular story ends with Sidonie driving off, leaving the two men stranded in the Swiss countryside, thirty miles from the nearest town.

In the same episode, Nation gave the pair the opportunity to outline their motivations for allowing themselves to be recruited by a retired judge (Laurence Naismith) as freelance righters of wrongs, bringing justice to bear where the legal system has failed. 'I need the money,' says Danny, in echo of the self-deprecating claims of Steve Mannering in *The Baron*. 'I thought you did things for strong, noble reasons like justice and integrity and all that sort of thing,' pouts Sidonie, and Brett gives the game away: 'That is what the Judge likes to think, but I'll let you into a little secret: quite frankly, I'm having the time of my life.'

So strong are the central performances, and so focused is our attention on them, that the stories mostly fade into insignificance. Which was perhaps just as well, for they were not overburdened with originality. Most of the plots could happily have found a home in other ITC shows, though they did benefit here from the higher budget – which allowed for location shooting, some of it abroad – and from some strong guest stars. Of Nation's scripts, 'A Home of One's Own' (guests: Hannah Gordon, Talfryn Thomas) was effectively a modern western, with a man defending his homestead from villains who, as in 'The Man Outside' in *The Baron*, are engaged in smuggling forged banknotes. The aforementioned 'Chain of Events' (Peter Vaughan, George Baker) was a simple chase through the woods, with Danny being pursued by several different interest groups. And 'Someone Waiting' (Donald Pickering, Sam Kydd) saw the pre-announcement of Brett's death, much as had happened to the Saint in Nation's story 'The Time to Die'. This latter plot went back still further to Edgar Wallace's 1905 novel *The Four Just Men*, as did the show's central premise of wealthy men acting as a supra-legal force for justice. The most unlikely borrowing, though, which was surely initiated by Nation, was Walter Black's script for 'The Morning After', in which Brett wakes up with a thundering hangover to find that he's now married but has no memory of how it happened, a revival in somewhat different circumstances of the *Hancock* episode 'The Night Out'.

Influences were also discernible from *The Avengers* – the sped-up fight sequence in 'Someone Waiting' with silent movie accompaniment – and from *The Saint*: when Danny is captured in 'A Home of One's Own' and has his hands tied behind his back, he tries to burn the rope on the flame of an oil lamp, but only succeeds in burning himself. 'Ow! Always works in the movies,' he complains. And, as in *The Baron*, there is the occasional moment that is darker than one expects. 'Someone Like Me' appears to be a rerun of 'Masquerade' in *The Baron*, with someone creating a double of Brett Sinclair, until it turns out that there's no double at all, just a deeply brainwashed Brett. Unaware of what he's doing, he gets into a genuinely nasty fight with Danny on a building site, attacking his partner with a shovel and displaying not a hint of the insouciant charm that Moore brings to the rest of his performance.

The stand-out episode is 'A Death in the Family', in which a murderer in a clown mask is killing off members of Brett's family, heirs to the title of the Duke of Caith, in an attempt to get their hands on the dukedom. Moore plays three other members of the family in an explicit tribute to Alec Guinness in the film *Kind Hearts and Coronets* (1949), whose plot this borrows. Unlike that movie, the attention here is on the family rather than the killer, leading one academic study of the action genre to point out that 'what was originally a subversive narrative about usurping the existing social structure becomes a conservative narrative about preserving that social structure'. It is, however, just about possible to watch the programme without such subtexts entirely overwhelming one's pleasure at the sight of Moore in drag, particularly when he's joined by Curtis as his Aunt Sophie – the first time he'd dragged up on screen since the film *Some Like It Hot* (1959). As in the very best episodes of *The Avengers*, each of the murders is tailored to the eccentricities of the character. A crusty old general is killed by an exploding toy tank, a retired admiral is found floating in the lake, rock musician Onslow (Christopher Sandford) is electrocuted by his guitar, Roland (Denholm Elliott), a collector of rare weapons, dies from a poison dart, and the alcoholic Lance (Willie Rushton) drowns in a vat of his own wine. ('I said that wine needed a little more body,' reflects Danny.) There's also a characteristic Nation touch when Danny finds himself locked in the Sinclair family crypt and pours gunpowder from a shotgun cartridge into the lock to blow it, saying he saw someone do the same trick in the 1935 film *The Lives of a Bengal Lancer*.

It all looked like tremendous fun on the screen, tongue-in-cheek adventures with a central relationship that evoked some of the mood of Bing Crosby and Bob Hope in the *Road to . . .* films. Robert S. Baker, said Moore, 'had always wanted to make a buddy movie, and this was his chance'. Nation's contribution to this atmosphere was valued by others on the production team. 'It was a great comfort to know that Terry wasn't a temperamental type,' remembered Johnny Goodman. 'He wouldn't throw a paddy, he wouldn't suddenly go into a fit about something. Terry would simply get on with the job, and that's what made him such an attractive personality.'

But in private at least, Nation was feeling the pressure. He had a more active role in the production than on any previous series, and this time he didn't have an old friend to share the burden in the way that Dennis Spooner had on *The Baron* or Brian Clemens on *The Avengers*. 'It would drive me bananas,' he recalled. 'Like an actor in a long run. Actors find a way to handle it, but I didn't find a way to handle this – week after week trying to find new things for the same characters to do. It was tough. After a few months, I'd come home on a Friday night and say: "I'm not going back in, I'm going to quit, I can't take it anymore, it's driving me crazy." And of course on Monday morning, I'd go back in, because that's what you do.' Risking the wrath of Tony Curtis, he continued to smoke heavily. 'Making any long running TV series has its pressures, as the turnaround of episodes is always very tight,' observed Moore. 'Terry smoked to relieve the pressure, and I rarely saw him without a cigarette.'

The situation wasn't made any easier by Curtis's habit of 'making changes to his script as he went along, and turning what was a twelve-month schedule into a fifteen-month one', in Roger Moore's words. The American star came from a very different culture of filming and seemed to make little attempt to adjust to the reduced circumstances of British television. 'He was,' remembered Nation, choosing his words carefully, 'demanding. He was an American movie star, and we had not had that experience before. What he could ask for, and did ask for, was stuff like: "I need a sauna." So a sauna cabin had to be built in the room next to his dressing room. All the kind of Hollywood trimmings you'd expect.' Others in the production team felt much the same. 'Tony on the screen could be charming, elegant, whatever was required of him,' said Johnny Goodman. 'But in real life, he was a difficult man to handle, and I can't say I found the relationship particularly rewarding.' Malcolm Christopher, the production manager, was more diplomatic in his appraisal of the two stars: 'Roger was a really generous, warm, kind-hearted guy. And Tony was Tony.'

None of those tensions appeared on screen, but even so the series was slammed by the critics. Curtis 'reached new heights of mediocrity', commented Morton Moss in the *Los Angeles Herald Examiner*. 'Mostly it is lousy,' wrote Stanley Reynolds in *The Times*. 'Awful,' agreed John Weightman in the *Observer*, while his colleague on that paper, the play-wright John Mortimer, was very haughty indeed: 'Although there is not a nude in sight, they made me understand at last what Mr Muggeridge means by the "decline of standards in television". *The Persuaders!* must make Edgar Wallace turn in his grave.' It was left to the more perceptive Nancy Banks-Smith to admit the attraction of the show: 'Tooth rot perhaps but sweet temptation.' She was presumably closer to the audience's feelings, for the show was a big hit; all twenty-four of the episodes reached the top twenty in Britain, and it peaked at number one. It also sold extensively around the world, proving particularly – and enduringly – popular in Europe. At the end of 1971 Lew Grade announced that ATV's overseas sales would exceed £17 million, the highest they had ever been, and *The Persuaders!* was listed as the key series, alongside one-off shows such as a Burt Bacharach special and *Robinson Crusoe on Ice*.

And yet, with all the success it enjoyed, *The Persuaders!* again failed to make an impact in America. Screened by ABC, it didn't even finish its run before being pulled from the schedules. Several reasons were proffered for its failure, including the fact that it was up against the established *Mission: Impossible*. Curtis argued in his autobiography that 'It was more tongue-in-cheek and less violent than American audiences were used to.' In the immediate aftermath, he had complained too that there weren't enough American writers on the show and that consequently he ended up with lines that didn't ring true: 'I had to say: "Give me the gat, I am a gangster." No American gangster says that.' Perhaps not, but for British writers of Nation's vintage there was a clear precedent; Lefty, the American gangster played by Jack Train in Tommy Handley's *ITMA*, used precisely that language, his first ever line being: 'Get out your gat and shoot up the joint.'

But there was another factor at work here as well. America was becoming less receptive to imported culture, whether from Britain or elsewhere. This was to become particularly acute in the mid 1970s following the triple whammy of recession, defeat in Vietnam and the Watergate scandal; the loss of faith in core American institutions – big business, the military, the presidency – provoked a marked cultural turn inwards. The early signs of that process, however, were already visible early in the decade, evident, for example, in the way that the glam rock of David Bowie, T. Rex and Roxy Music became the first British rock and roll phenomenon since the Beatles not to make inroads in the States. On television there was a more formal expression of the same isolationist tendency; the American Federal Communications Commission ruled that from October 1971 the slot from 7.30 to 8 p.m. had to be occupied by home-made programmes. 'Multiplied by three networks over the year,' calculated the *Guardian*, 'this means that British television is to be deprived of potentially some 546 hours of American screen time in a slot frequently inhabited by British programmes.'

One solution was that pioneered by Beryl Vertue at Associated London Scripts: selling to America not the original productions but simply the show formats. Thus in 1971 Alf Garnett's Wapping in *Till Death Us Do Part* became the Queens district of New York City in *All in the Family* on CBS, and the following year the Shepherd's Bush of *Steptoe and Son* became Watts, Los Angeles in *Sanford and Son* on NBC. Johnny Speight, Ray Galton and Alan Simpson all benefited as the creators of those programmes, but more generally it seemed that the American people's infatuation with British popular culture, which had in the 1960s been so crucial to Britain's economy and to its sense of identity, was definitely on the wane. As the political climate became harsher, the demand for imported fantasy diminished.

On a personal level, Terry Nation's timing was beginning to look a little unlucky. He had been script editor for *The Baron*, one of the less successful ITC series, he had helped oversee the last ever season of *The Avengers*, and now the show on which he had his biggest production role ended after just one series. For in the absence of American sales, *The Persuaders!* was effectively doomed even before Roger Moore went off to take the role of James Bond in the movies. Lew Grade did think about commissioning a second season, with Noel Harrison replacing Moore, but Robert S. Baker talked him out of it: 'I said, "Why don't we quit while we're ahead? We've made a very good show, that's it, let's stop it now." And Lew said, "I guess you're right." And that's why we never made any more *Persuaders*.'

It was the end of the programme and the end of the era of the big ITC action adventure series. If a show as good as *The Persuaders!*, with all the money that had been thrown at it, and with two major stars in the lead roles, couldn't cut the mustard, then there was little hope for anyone else. There were to be no more Persuaders, but also no more Saints, Barons, Champions, Jason Kings or Men in Suitcases.

Chapter Ten
Darkness Descends

Lew Grade was not too badly damaged by the decline of the adventure series, and still had his biggest television hits yet to come: the star-studded biopic of *Jesus of Nazareth* (1977) and the even more star-studded comedy of *The Muppet Show* (1976). Both were huge hits in America, increasing ATV's exports still further, and Grade was promoted from the knighthood to the peerage – becoming Lord Grade of Elstree – in the resignation honours list when Harold Wilson stepped down as prime minister in 1976. By then the action shows were a fading memory, tailing off with *The Protectors* before one final flourish with the short-lived 1974 series *The Zoo Gang*.

The Protectors was made by Gerry Anderson (though with human actors rather than puppets), ran for two seasons in 1972–4, and was clearly cast from the same mould as the earlier series, with three agents engaging in the usual adventures around the better known parts of Europe. Its stars were of a higher order than those of, say, *The Champions*, even if they didn't reach the same level as *The Persuaders!*: the American Robert Vaughn, formerly of *The Man from U.N.C.L.E.*, Nyree Dawn Porter, best known from *The Forsyte Saga* as well as having been Sydney Newman's original choice for the female lead in *The Avengers*, and the relative newcomer Tony Anholt. But despite the cast, and despite a great theme song – the storming 'Avenues and Alleyways', written by Mitch Murray and Peter Callander and sung by Tony Christie – the show suffered from one crucial flaw: it reverted to the half-hour format of the 1950s swashbucklers (minus commercial breaks), leaving no room for any of the guest characters to establish themselves or for any proper plot development. Consequently it looked very much like the poor relation in the ITC family, dreaming of a glamorous lifestyle but having to get by in reduced circumstances. There was no style, no swagger, no humour, just a pale imitation of past glories, the leftovers from the 1960s served up lukewarm to a hung-over nation.

It was, in other words, perfectly suited to the impoverished era in which it appeared. For these were dark days. Many commentators in the early and mid 1970s were agreed that Britain was at best in terminal economic decline and at worst sliding into anarchy, with the trade unions the most commonly cited cause of the country's problems. In 1972, when *The Protectors* debuted, a total of 24 million working days were lost in industrial action, double the level of the previous year, and easily the worst tally since 1926, the year of the general strike. The same year unemployment exceeded the million mark, then considered a shockingly high level, and politicians and pop stars alike, from Richard Crossman to David Bowie, busied themselves evoking the imagery of Weimar Germany. And things got worse. During the second season of *The Protectors*, an international oil crisis combined with an overtime ban, which became a strike, by the National Union of Mineworkers to plunge the country into a fuel crisis, leading the government to declare a state of emergency (the fifth in four years).

Through the winter of 1973–4 new restrictions on everyday activities were introduced on what seemed like an almost daily basis; street lighting was cut, electric heating banned in workplaces and a 50 m.p.h. speed limit introduced on the motorways. At its silliest, the emergency prompted the energy minister, Patrick Jenkin, to suggest that if everyone brushed their teeth in the dark, that might save a bit of fuel; at its most serious, British industry was restricted to a three-day week. Television too was affected, with the government ordering that broadcasting end by 10.30 p.m., though that was often an academic issue for would-be viewers already blacked out by power cuts. But in this quarter at least there was some relief to come; when the prime minister, Edward Heath, called a general election for February 1974 – intended to decide once and for all who was going to govern Britain, Parliament or the trade unions – special dispensation was granted for normal broadcasting to be resumed, so that politicians might breathe the oxygen of publicity. The outcome of that election was a humiliating defeat for Heath and the return to Downing Street of Harold Wilson, a quieter, more sober figure than he had been in his 1960s heyday.

Terry Nation gently lampooned this change in government in a short story, 'Daleks: The Secret Invasion', published in 1974 in London's *Evening News*. A group of children encounter Daleks at large in London and are ushered into the corridors of power to give their accounts. One of the children recognises and points out the prime minister, leaving her brother perplexed: 'That's not Mr Heath.' She has to correct him. 'Of course it's not,' she says. 'It's Mr Wilson's turn this month.' As Nation notes drily: 'Emilie knew about politics.' She also correctly identifies a man with 'spectacles and a worried expression' as the home secretary, Roy Jenkins, though regrettably neither Wilson nor Jenkins is called upon to negotiate with the Daleks. (An encounter between the urbane Jenkins and the profoundly uncivilised Daleks would have been worth seeing.)

The heady days of the 1960s were clearly long since gone, and the country was sufficiently demoralised that it even settled for the low-level thrills of *The Protectors*, sending the show into the top twenty. Terry Nation wrote four episodes of that second season, and they were far from memorable, though 'Bagman' did feature a guest appearance by Lalla Ward prior to her incarnation as Romana in *Doctor Who*. The best of the episodes, 'A Pocketful of Posies', featured Eartha Kitt as a veteran singer on the verge of a big comeback concert, being drugged with mildly hallucinogenic stimulants by her husband and his mistress, who plan to kill her and make it look like the suicide of a madwoman. In moments that hint at the glory days of *The Avengers*, she starts experiencing hallucinations: a glass of wine disappears, a clock runs backwards, a record player starts playing the nursery rhyme 'Ring a Ring o' Roses', even though there's no record on the turntable and the machine isn't plugged in. It could all have been splendidly creepy, but here, given just twenty-five minutes, there was insufficient time to build any real sense of tension or terror.

If *The Protectors* was little more than a pale echo of the 1960s, Nation had already contributed to a largely unheralded but nonetheless effective elegy to the passing of that decade. As filming on *The Avengers* came to an end, he and Brian Clemens began planning a screenplay for a movie to be titled *And Soon the Darkness*. The credits showed the two men as co-writers though, according to Clemens, that didn't fairly represent the division of labour: 'We sat down and did this kicking around thing, blocking it out. We finished it on the Friday and I got home and I was so excited that I sat down and wrote the whole damn thing over that weekend.' The film was directed by Robert Fuest – who had directed Nation's best episode of *The Avengers*, 'Take Me to Your Leader' – and released in 1970 by Associated British Production Company, the first product of a much trumpeted programme of British releases under the aegis of the established British director Bryan Forbes.

The story takes place in a single afternoon and shows two young nurses from London – Jane (Pamela Franklin) and Cathy (Michele Dotrice) – on a cycling holiday in rural northern France. Early on, the pair discuss the death the previous week of a one-day-old baby in the hospital where they work, and the image of the death of innocence hangs heavy over the rest of the film. Neither girl speaks any French, which is something of a disadvantage since most of the people they encounter speak very little else, and the failure to communicate gradually builds an atmosphere of menace as they cycle on through small, almost deserted hamlets under big, open skies that look increasingly oppressive. 'Cette route,' warns a woman at a roadside café: 'mauvaise réputation, très mauvaise réputation.' And eventually, now split up after an argument, they discover that a young Dutch tourist was murdered here three years ago. 'She was young and pretty,' an unhelpful English woman explains. 'They always are, I suppose. Loathsome business. It was more than murder, if you know what I mean. Still, she was asking for trouble – alone on the road.' At one stage they pass through a village named Landron, and Cathy greets it sarcastically: 'Hey, swinging Landron!' And the disjunction implied by the comment seems entirely appropriate. Two young women on bicycles wearing skimpy clothing – it looks like a perfect Swinging Sixties image, except that it ends in violence and murder.

In retrospect the location of horror in an idyllic rural setting, the gleeful knocking down of the idea that the countryside might be a refuge from the sins of the city, makes *And Soon the Darkness* look like a precursor to a theme that was to become very common, with films like *Straw Dogs* (1971), *Deliverance* (1972) and *The Wicker Man* (1973), as well as novels like Thomas Tryon's *Harvest Home* (1973). That wasn't how it was seen at the time, however, and it received a critical mauling. 'I shall be charitable, and say nothing,' wrote Derek Malcolm in the *Guardian*, 'except that Robert Fuest has made a thriller which has to be seen to be believed.' John Russell Taylor in *The Times* was less generous – 'a would-be thriller of almost unbelievable ineptitude' – and James Thomas in the *Daily Express* didn't even rate the twist in the tail: 'it has all the surprise and fascination of a rent increase.' Nor did the movie fare very well at the box office.

At the time of the film's release, Nation was already engaged in the pre-production schedule for *The Persuaders!*, and the reviews were of little significance. But as that series ended, and it became clear that the days of the ITC adventurers were coming to a close, there was a renewed need to find work. With nothing obvious on the horizon, he returned to the idea of creating his own series, and began to tout around various proposals.

One of these was *The Team*, a proposed pilot for a series that would centre on a husband and wife detective partnership. It wasn't an entirely original concept, for the idea of a married couple having a shared interest in investigating crime had been around since the early days of detective fiction. Irish QC and MP Matthias McDonnel Bodkin wrote books about two separate detectives, Paul Beck and Dora Myrl, before marrying them off in the 1909 novel *The Capture of Paul Beck*. There was also *Busman's Holiday* (1937), the last of Dorothy L. Sayers's Lord Peter Wimsey books, in which the aristocratic sleuth is joined in his investigations by the former Harriet Vane, who has finally consented to marry him. More directly influential on Nation, one suspects, were Nick and Nora Charles, the heroes of Dashiell Hammett's 1933 novel *The Thin Man*, a couple who interrupt their drinking only to engage in yet more witty banter and solve crimes. The story was filmed the following year with William Powell and Myrna Loy, who proved so successful in the central roles that five sequels appeared in the next twelve years. MGM, who made the movies, clearly liked the format and launched a new married couple, Joel and Garda Sloane, in *Fast Company* (1938), based on the novel of the same title by Harry Kurnitz.

There was, then, considerable precedent for Nation's pilot for *The Team*, and there was no reason why it should not have worked. But despite approaches to several television companies, he made no progress. Perhaps the timing was wrong, coinciding too closely with the similar *McMillan and Wife*, starring Rock Hudson and Susan Saint James, which first aired in the USA in September 1971 and in the UK six months later. Nonetheless the idea did eventually bear fruit, when Brian Clemens returned to it as the basis for 'K Is for Killing', a 1974 episode in the second season of his excellent anthology series, *Thriller* (US title: *ABC Mystery Movie*). Gayle Hunnicutt and Stephen Rea starred as Suzy and Arden Buckley and, like *And Soon the Darkness*, it was co-credited to Clemens and Nation – though Clemens insisted that he didn't use Nation's storyline, taking only the essential set-up of the married couple.

More immediately productive was a meeting in December 1971, when Nation presented two proposals to Andrew Osborn, head of television drama serials at the BBC: one was a post-apocalyptic series to be titled *Beyond Omega*, the other an idea for the adventures of a Victorian investigator of the paranormal named Dr Robert Baldick. Both were received positively, and Nation was bursting with energy and eagerness when he wrote to Osborn the day after the meeting: 'I promise you I'll make both these series work, not only for myself, but to justify your confidence and enthusiasm.' After some discussion concerning fees (Associated London Scripts were asking for £1,000 for a pilot script of each, but settled for £750 instead), both pilots were commissioned, *Beyond Omega* having a delivery date of 31 January 1972 and *Robert Baldick* of 7 February.

At this point, Nation's fervour seems to have evaporated a little as he realised the scale of the undertaking to which he had committed himself. Previously he had written to a brief, following a structure already laid down, using central characters who already existed; even the pilot for *The Daleks* had been based on previous work. Now he was facing an entirely new proposition: the creation from scratch of a programme that was intended to be the foundation for an entire series, sustainable for potentially dozens of episodes. And he was committed to do it not once but twice, in the space of less than two months. Worrying too about how a series of his own creation would work out in practice (how many episodes, for example, would he write himself?), he told Osborn at the beginning of January that he didn't think he could meet the delivery dates for the two programmes and that it would take till March to get them both finished. That, replied Osborn, 'is leaving things so late as to almost constitute a crisis so far as we are concerned over production'. It was agreed therefore that the *Beyond Omega* project be withdrawn, and that Nation should concentrate solely on his script for *Robert Baldick*. Delivered almost on time, it was immediately accepted, and by June 1972 it was in production.

The title went through various permutations in its early stages, including *The Incredible Dr Baldick* and *The Amazing Robert Baldick*, before settling on its final form, *The Incredible Robert Baldick*. What didn't change, though, was the name of the protagonist, for Nation had overcome the problem of finding new names for his characters — a familiar chore for all prolific television writers — by borrowing that of a friend. The real Dr Robert Baldick, an Oxford academic specialising in French literature, agreed to his name being used for Nation's latest creation, apparently amused by the concept of being associated with a fictional character. Unfortunately, however, he died in April 1972, before the programme was broadcast, and although his widow was content for the agreement to be honoured, his son — also named Robert Baldick, and then studying for a PhD — was less happy about his name being used in this context. For several weeks in the summer of 1972, with filming already complete, the younger Baldick was in discussions with the BBC, seeking to have the show retitled and ultimately threatening to obtain a court injunction to achieve this end. While refusing to accept that there truly was a legal case here, Andrew Osborn eventually conceded that, although it was too late to change the pilot, the name would be amended — probably to Baldwick — were a series to develop. In the meantime, the uncertainty had been a major factor in the rescheduling of the programme: originally intended as the first of three shows in a short *Drama Playhouse* season, due to be shown on 23 August, it was instead placed at the end of the run on 6 September.

At the time, the rescheduling seemed of little significance. The *Drama Playhouse* strand, broadcast at 8.10 p.m. on Wednesday nights on BBC1, attracted strong audiences and had an excellent track record for launching new programmes. Four of the six pilots previously screened had spawned their own series — *Codename*, *The Regiment*, *The Befrienders* and *The Onedin Line* — and great hopes were held out for the new season, which included *Sutherland's Law* and *The Venturers* in addition to *The Incredible Robert Baldick*, all of them produced by Anthony Coburn, who had written the first ever episodes of *Doctor Who*. And indeed the ratio of winners continued: *Sutherland's Law* eventually ran to forty-six episodes spread over five seasons, while *The Venturers* managed a single season of ten episodes. *The Incredible Robert Baldick* was less fortunate; despite a repeat screening in February 1974, no follow-up to the pilot was ever commissioned.

The problems started with the programme's new broadcast date. The Olympic Games, staged that year in Munich, were entering their final week when, just before dawn on 5 September 1972, nine members of the Palestinian terrorist group Black September infiltrated the Olympic Village, shot dead two members of the Israeli team and took a further nine athletes hostage. An increasingly desperate siege lasted all day and finally ended just after midnight, when in a failed rescue attempt all nine hostages were killed together with a West German policeman, as well as five of the gunmen. It was one of the most spectacular terrorist actions the world had thus far witnessed, complete with live footage. For the first time in its history, the Olympic movement suspended competition, instead holding a memorial service to the dead athletes, before resuming in a subdued atmosphere.

British television responded, as it generally does in such situations, by rearranging its schedules in an attempt to show it was aware of the enormity of events. Among the programmes lost in the rush to demonstrate relevance was *The Incredible Robert Baldick*, its broadcast postponed to a 9.25 p.m. slot on Monday 2 October, where it was sandwiched between the *Nine O'Clock News* and *International Show Jumping* from the Empire Pool, Wembley. It was watched by a fair-sized audience of 6.6 million viewers, but it looked a little isolated in the schedules, and undoubtedly suffered from being up against the popular ITV agony-aunt series *Kate*, then in the midst of its third season, and the might of *News at Ten*. Whether it would have fared better in its original time slot – taken instead by *Sutherland's Law* – is arguable, but the rescheduling certainly didn't help its cause.

The fact that the show didn't grow into a series was regrettable, for despite some flaws its premise was eminently sound. Dr Robert Baldick (played by Robert Hardy) is a mid-Victorian scientist of enormous private wealth – presumably inherited, since he's a baronet living in a manor house in Baldick Park – who is also an independent investigator of mysteries. 'He cannot resist the inexplicable,' explains one of his assistants. 'Almost any happening qualifies for his interest so long as it is out of the ordinary. He's a man of insatiable curiosity.' The man adds that his employer prefers to be known as Dr Baldick rather than Sir Robert: 'After all, he does have the highest scientific qualifications in the country.' (This is not, it has to be said, Nation's best writing; even allowing for the necessity of setting the scene and establishing character in a pilot, there is a prosaic quality to it, quite apart from the silliness of those 'highest scientific qualifications in the country'.) Baldick is accompanied by his valet, Thomas Wingham (Julian Holloway), who happens to be an expert researcher with a sound grasp of archaic languages, and by his gamekeeper, Caleb Selling (John Rhys-Davies), who can bring his knowledge of nature to bear on the case in hand. A thoroughly meritocratic type of Victorian, Baldick treats these two not as servants but as colleagues, albeit junior colleagues who are never quite up to speed, though this is largely because their master shares Sherlock Holmes's habit of not revealing what he has deduced until after the denouement: 'All in good time, Thomas, all in good time!'

Armed only with intelligence and enthusiasm, and adorned with the facial hair considered appropriate for the nineteenth century (Caleb has the edge on the others, sporting a pair of sideburns that would have been envied by early 1970s pop stars like Ray Dorset of Mungo Jerry and Trevor Bolder of the Spiders from Mars), the three heroes travel to the site of their investigations in Baldick's private train, a luxuriously furnished affair known as the Tsar, since it was originally built for Nicholas I of Russia. Their only other companion is a pet owl named Cosmo.

All of this is attractive and appealing, suggesting one of the fifty-seven varieties of Edwardian detective that had recently been collected by Hugh Greene in book form as *The Rivals of Sherlock Holmes* (1970), a volume which had subsequently inspired the Thames Television series of the same title. Among the characters featured there was William Hope Hodgson's Carnacki the Ghost-Finder, who investigated seemingly paranormal events, some of which had rational explanations while others turned out to be supernatural manifestations. Carnacki was the last in a line of psychic doctors dating back to Sheridan Le Fanu's Dr Hesselius in the 1860s and reaching maturity in the Edwardian era with Algernon Blackwood's Dr John Silence and others, before starting to look merely quaint and out-of-date in the aftermath of the First World War and the rise of Freudianism. Robert Baldick can be seen as sitting squarely in this now defunct tradition, while also sharing something with William Hartnell's incarnation of the Doctor: another Edwardian figure intent on bringing his intellect and curiosity to bear on unknown situations.

The pilot episode, 'Never Come Night', is similarly promising, with an eclectic blend of Gothic, detective, fantasy and science fiction genres. It starts in Hammer Films style on a dark and stormy night with the death of a servant girl, savagely beaten to death in a ruined abbey. The local squire and the vicar call in Baldick, for this is not the first violent death in the vicinity of the abbey. 'Local legend has it that the deaths go back into prehistory,' explains the vicar. 'There are written records covering the last two hundred years, and documented proof of at least forty-three deaths.' As he excavates the site, Baldick argues that there is something in the place itself that stores up fear: 'An accumulation of terror that has festered in men's minds for all of time and has given this place a real power of evil.' That power is unleashed on those who venture too near during hours of darkness, manifesting itself in the form of the victim's personal phobia. The dead servant girl, for example, had a fear of being beaten, thanks to an abusive father, while Baldick himself, terrified of cobwebs since he was a child, finds himself alone at night in the abbey becoming enveloped in a web. (In the original proposal, the vicar also had a fear of snakes, and the squire of leeches.)

Summoning up all his reserves of will, Baldick is able to rationalise his fear and thus overcome it sufficiently that he can carry out his intention of burning the place down. He concludes that the evil here pre-dates humanity, and the suggestion is of a supernatural force, though the final scene opens up an alternative, rational explanation that could take us into the realms of science fiction. For Baldick has discovered, in the course of their digging, a strange object; made of an unknown metal, it comprises some kind of electrical circuit and a keyboard of mysterious design. 'Something from the past,' ponders Baldick. 'Or the future?'

There are elements here reminiscent of Nigel Kneale's 1958 television drama *Quatermass and the Pit*: the depiction of a localised evil pre-dating humanity and requiring excavation, the explanation of paranormal events as the product of alien technology, even the deconstruction of place-names. The abbey is set in Duvel Woods, which were originally known as Uvel, the Middle English for evil, just as Hobbs Lane in *Quatermass and the Pit* was originally Hob's Lane, Hob being an old name for the Devil. There is too, in this tale of a 'physical manifestation of a mental condition', a memory of the house of horrors created by Nation in the *Doctor Who* story 'The Chase', a place that 'exists in the dark recesses of the human mind'. And, of course, Nation's recurrent interest in phobias is central to the plot. The fear of cobwebs and spiders expressed by Baldick had been a key part of the original script for 'The Chase', with the Doctor explaining to Ian that such phobias derive from early memories: 'All your life, you have believed that a spider running across your hand is an unpleasant experience. As an intelligent adult, you know it can't hurt you. Despite that, your earliest childhood memories dominate. You have an unfounded – pre-conditioned – fear of spiders.' This was dropped from the screened version of 'The Chase', but Nation was reluctant to lose anything, and the idea resurfaces in *Robert Baldick*.

But perhaps the most obvious association in the mind of a modern viewer is with Nigel Kneale's *The Stone Tape*, a similar blend of science and the supernatural, in which the walls of an old mansion record the violence that has happened there. Any such resemblance, however, was entirely coincidental. Kneale's play (directed by Peter Sasdy, who had earlier made 'The Caves of Steel' and 'A Kiss Before Dying') was not broadcast until Christmas 1972 on BBC2, and had not even been commissioned when Nation delivered his script.

Despite all the potential of the character, the pilot episode didn't entirely convince. For the most part it was a stylish, well-produced piece. A crane shot of the drive to Baldick Park was impressive enough to have come from an ITC production, while Baldick's private train – courtesy of the Severn Valley Railway – was shown in all its finery, steaming through the

English countryside, almost as though it were a period parody of the luxury cars we had seen in those action hero series. ('Should add the railway nuts to the horoscope consulters and swell the ratings even further,' wrote critic Clive James in the *Observer*.) But there was a strange lack of drama at both beginning and end that fatally undermined the piece. The title sequence was so casual that it had no theme tune and used captions that looked like an amateur slideshow, while what should have been the climactic burning of the abbey was low key to the point of being perfunctory. Nor was the final reveal of the unearthed object from the future given the weight that it deserved, hurried over as though time had got the better of the director.

A more serious difficulty, since those problems could be addressed in later episodes, was the casting of Robert Hardy as Baldick. A respected, highly competent actor, Hardy was solid and believable, but was simply too smooth a presence for a character who needed a fair degree of eccentricity if he was ever going to become an audience favourite. There was insufficient intensity, an absence of quirk, in the depiction. The ghost-finder Carnacki in Thames's *The Rivals of Sherlock Holmes* the previous year had been portrayed by Donald Pleasance, and Baldick similarly needed someone rather less emollient than Hardy. Nor did the two sidekicks add sufficient colour to the proceedings, either in the writing or in the acting.

Even so, there was confidence in the project at the BBC, an expectation that a series would result. And in many ways it seemed appropriate for a time when nostalgia was very much in the air. The huge success of *The Forsyte Saga*, a series made by the BBC in 1967 from the novels by John Galsworthy, had been followed by several other period dramas at the beginning of the new decade, including *Upstairs Downstairs* and *The Onedin Line*. It wasn't just on television, for some of the most iconic 1960s brand names were also reaching back into Britain's past for inspiration: the Biba fashion label, which had done so much to popularise the mini-skirt, was now finding inspiration in Victoriana and art deco, while the quirky products of Portmeirion Pottery were being replaced by images culled from nineteenth-century illustrations to create the Botanic Garden range, one of the great export successes of the time. Laura Ashley was making a name for herself with romantically rustic clothing designs, and the day was not far off when Edith Holden's *The Country Diary of an Edwardian Lady* would become a publishing and marketing phenomenon. The slow death of 1960s idealism was matched by a rise of revivalism in every corner of popular culture, and there was no obvious reason why *Baldick* should not benefit in the retreat from the present.

Nation spent some time negotiating what his position would be in the event that the show took off. Having learnt from his experience with the Daleks where the real money was to be made in television, he was determined to maximise his earnings should opportunity come knocking again. His contract for the show licensed the format and characters to the BBC in return for a fee of £85 for each episode on which he wasn't the writer, rising to £100 per episode after the first twenty-six had been made. He reserved the film, publishing and merchandising rights (though the BBC would receive a small cut of these), and he insisted on being appointed series consultant, explaining: 'This position would simply allow me to have the authority to comment on, make suggestions, to be consulted and generally assist in the development of any series that might result from the pilots. This, I assure you, is no lust for power. It is merely to allow me to have a voice in the progress of the series. After all, no one will care more deeply about the shows than I.' (This was to become a familiar comment.) It was further determined that the words 'Series created by Terry Nation' – a credit to which he had aspired for years – would appear as a single caption in the titles, and would be included in the *Radio Times* listing. He even signed a separate book deal with the publishers Weidenfeld & Nicolson, though the failure to secure a series meant that the proposed volume never appeared.

The BBC's decision not to exercise its option was a major setback for Nation. After a decade of writing for other people's series, it looked in the first months of 1972 as though he had finally broken through with his own project. He had aspired to that credit – 'Series created by Terry Nation' – for years and briefly it had seemed to be within his grasp, before again slipping through his fingers. *Uncle Selwyn* had originally been intended as a pilot, but never got past the single drama stage, *The Daleks* hadn't even got that far, and now *The Amazing Robert Baldick* had similarly failed. The following year, he received yet another commission that never materialised. He was paid by the BBC to write two episodes of a series to be entitled *No Place Like Home*, set in Ireland with two retired couples, one English and one American. This was talked about as a series of twelve episodes, and the first two scripts – 'The Accident' and 'Everything in the Garden Is Lovely' – were delivered, sent for rewrites and accepted, before that project too was abandoned.

By then, however, Nation was less concerned, for he was greeted on his return to the BBC fold, nearly seven years on from 'The Daleks' Master Plan', by offers of new work. In April 1972 he was commissioned to produce a *Doctor Who* storyline, which would become 'Planet of the Daleks', and the following month the *Beyond Omega* proposal was revived under another title; he was offered £750 to write a pilot script for a potential series to be called *The Survivors*.

That latter commission proved to be the last contract he signed under the auspices of Associated London Scripts. In early 1968 ALS had merged itself with the Robert Stigwood Organisation, though two of the founders, Spike Milligan and Eric Sykes, remained behind and kept the offices at Orme Court. Thereafter it began to drift away from the single business of being an agency. Beryl Vertue, who had represented Nation for so long, was becoming involved in production, working on the 1966 film *The Spy with the Cold Nose*, written by Alan Galton and Ray Simpson, and then serving as executive producer on Eric Sykes's *The Plank* (1967) and the movie version of *Till Death Us Do Part* (1969), all of which were made by a new sister company, Associated London Films. 'I stopped being an agent, because I wanted to be a producer,' she explained. 'Then in the end we decided we wouldn't have an agency at all.' At the start of the 1970s, as Vertue's interests moved elsewhere, it increasingly fell to Pam Gillis to negotiate on behalf of Nation, but in 1972 he left ALS altogether and became instead the client of Roger Hancock, younger brother of Tony, who had by now formed his own agency; he was to remain here for the rest of his life.

'Roger was a legend,' remembered the comedy writer Barry Cryer, who had been represented by Hancock since the mid 1960s. 'He was very tough – his clients were everything. But he had so many friends. I never heard a bad word about him on a personal level.' It was an opinion shared by others. 'Off work, he was very charming, very amusing,' noted Alan Simpson, while *Doctor Who* producer Barry Letts, who encountered Hancock from the other side of the negotiating table, recalled him and Nation as a double-act: 'They played good guy, bad guy. Roger Hancock was a very fierce agent and made sure he got the best, best deal for Terry.' And Terrance Dicks, who described Hancock as 'a Rottweiler', saw the success of the partnership in this meeting of opposites: 'I think Terry knew he was so easy-going that he had his agent to protect him.' As Cryer made clear, Hancock's relationship with his clients was based on absolute trust; Cryer himself never signed a contract, merely shaking hands on a deal that was based on a simple premise. 'He said: If you get pissed off with me, you walk away. If I get pissed off with you, I walk away.' That arrangement lasted until Hancock's retirement.

The benefits to Nation were soon to be manifest in better contracts with the BBC, but the connection with ALS was not entirely at an end. In 1973

Associated London Films produced a new film, a horror comedy titled *The House in Nightmare Park*, starring Frankie Howerd and co-written by Nation and Clive Exton, the latter also from the ALS stable.

Again, just as the idea for *The Team* had revisited *The Thin Man*, so this new venture was rooted in the Hollywood of Nation's youth, for it came fairly directly from *The Cat and the Canary*, originally a stage play written by John Willard, but best known as a 1939 film, starring Bob Hope as a wise-cracking, cowardly actor. He and a motley and eccentric collection of family members gather in an old, dark house to hear the reading at midnight of a dead man's will, and to chase after an inheritance that centres on a fortune in diamonds, hidden on the estate. Over the course of the ensuing night, we discover that there's a vein of hereditary madness in the family, which might explain why the characters are being killed off one by one. The story had been reworked in 1961 by Robert S. Baker and Monty Berman as *What A Carve Up!*, with Kenneth Connor and Sid James; the source material here was credited as being Frank King's novel *The Ghoul*, which accounted for the setting of the Yorkshire Moors, but the influence of *The Cat and the Canary* was unmistakable.

So too was it in *The House in Nightmare Park*, which again featured a rambling, eccentric family gathered in a remote mansion in pursuit of a cache of diamonds hidden somewhere on the estate, as they are successively murdered. Into this situation comes Frankie Howerd as a dreadful Edwardian actor, hired – so he believes – to provide entertainment based on his dramatic readings from Dickens, though it transpires that he too is a member of the family and unwittingly holds the key to the location of the diamonds. Despite its creaky and derivative plot, much of the film is very successful, with some classic Howerd lines. 'Do I play the piano?' he says indignantly. 'Does Paganini play the trumpet?' Asked how he takes his whisky, he requests 'just a threat' of soda. And when he finally discovers the truth about the diamonds, he bends over to explore a secret cavity in the floor and is horrified to see a snake rearing up between his legs: 'Please make it a crusher not a biter,' he murmurs. Delivered in Howerd's most fervent voice, it's a line that works beautifully at the time, even if it defies rational analysis.

The best moment though comes with the revelation that when the family was stationed in India, they used to have a variety act, Henderson's Human Marionettes, in which the sibling children dressed as, and behaved like, dolls. Now middle-aged adults, they dress up again for a rendition of their party piece, which is genuinely disturbing. At the end of it one of the brothers, Ernest (Kenneth Griffith), is found dead, stabbed in the back while portraying a golliwog. It's a sequence that could have come straight from *The Avengers*, and indeed the film's director, Peter Sykes, had worked on a couple of episodes for that series, including Nation's 'Noon Doomsday'. As well as Griffith, who hadn't acted in a Nation script since *Hancock*, the cast included Hugh Burden, Rosalie Crutchley and Ray Milland, who had once been a pupil at the same Cardiff school as Nation. But it was Howerd who dominated the proceedings. 'It was very much written with Frankie in mind,' according to Verity Lambert, again the executive producer, while Nation and Exton were credited as the producers. (They even formed a company for the occasion, Extonation, though it did no further business.)

'I was grateful the film received the first unanimously good press I'd had for a picture in a long, long time,' remembered Howerd. 'You expect, naturally, some divergence of opinion, but as I recall it, not one critic panned *The House in Nightmare Park*.' He was right; the movie got tremendous reviews. 'As good an attempt as anyone has made to employ the elusive gifts of Frankie Howerd,' said David Robinson in *The Times*; 'his funniest film role', agreed the *Daily Mirror*; while 'for much of the time' it had Ian Christie of the *Daily Express* 'quite helpless with laughter'. Derek Malcolm in the *Guardian* thought that the creators had 'obviously tried for more than routine comedy and have, at least in part, succeeded', and in the *Observer* George Melly declared that it was 'as British as nailing a kipper to the underside of an unsympathetic seaside landlady's dining-room table'.

There was perhaps an element of nostalgia in this reception. Howerd had first become a star more than a quarter of a century earlier, with *Variety Bandbox*, and his persona had changed very little in the intervening years, so that he was now a reassuring presence at a time when familiar comforts were much in demand. For Nation, about to embark on some much darker work, it was an unexpected footnote to his career as a comedy writer, his first piece of overt comedy for a decade. It also proved to be his last, but it did earn him some of the best notices of his career.

Chapter Eleven

Dalek Renaissance

In 1971, as producer Barry Letts and script editor Terrance Dicks planned the ninth season of *Doctor Who* for the following year, they came to the conclusion that the proposed opening wasn't quite strong enough. 'We had a story from Louis Marks about guerrillas from the future, which was good, but we felt didn't have the "wow" factor that you want for your first show,' remembered Dicks. 'And suddenly one of us – I think probably me – had the brilliant idea: let's put the Daleks in, let's make the villains behind the villains be the Daleks. Which was fairly easy to do. But incredibly, I forgot that the Daleks were Terry Nation's copyright.'

In fact it wasn't the copyright as such that had been forgotten. Letts sent a memo to the copyright department in April 1971 asking them to clear the use of the Daleks in what became 'Day of the Daleks', and Nation later signed a contract authorising their appearance (his fee had gone up to £25 per episode by now). To mark the broadcast, Nation also contributed an unfinished story for a *Radio Times* competition; readers were invited to submit an ending as well as illustrations, with the prize being a model Dalek. But Dicks and Letts had perhaps forgotten the arrangement whereby Nation was to be given the first option of writing any story featuring his creations, and they went to Pinewood Studios – where he was working on *The Persuaders!* – to apologise. Over lunch it was agreed that Nation would write a Dalek story for the following season, smoothing over any hurt feelings and resolving the situation to everyone's satisfaction. 'He said, "Let's have a bottle of champagne." And we thought he was celebrating because the Daleks were coming back,' remembered Letts. 'Until he actually came to the studio and we realised he always drank champagne, because the Daleks had made him so rich.'

The Daleks had never quite gone away, of course, even though the last new serial had been in 1967. There was still the occasional cheque for an overseas sale (sometimes very small indeed: in 1971 Nation received £3.12 when 'The Chase' was sold to Ethiopian television), and there were still payments for the use of Daleks in other programmes, from the quiz show *What's the Sense?* through to *Look — Mike Yarwood!*, the BBC's vehicle for the up-and-coming impressionist. In 1973 Roger Hancock even managed to get a £10 fee for the use of a Dalek voice on Jimmy Savile's show *Clunk-Click*, an agreement which seemed to lack natural justice since the voice was invented not by Nation but by Brian Hodgson. But by that stage Hancock was rapidly proving that his reputation as a determined agent was well founded. There was a continual barrage of letters to the BBC pointing out uses that hadn't been cleared and demanding payment; he secured, for example, £75 for an appearance on Savile's other show, *Jim'll Fix It* in 1975.

The point of this endless hassling over Dalek appearances was not simply the money, but the desire to keep a tight grip on the creatures' image. Back in February 1964 a Dalek had featured in a sketch on the children's show *Crackerjack*, and later that year one had appeared in Roy Kinnear's sitcom *A World of His Own* (written by Nation's old collaborator, Dave Freeman), but that was before their true value had become apparent. Since then there had been a definite attempt to ensure that they were not used in comedy situations, Nation rightly fearing that their cultural power would be diminished if they were publicly treated with ridicule. 'Peter Vincent and I once wrote a sketch, "Dalek Theatre: Romeo and Juliet",' remembered Barry Cryer. 'Dalek Juliet was on the balcony and Dalek Romeo down below. And of course you knew he was never going to climb up to the balcony, he kept crashing off the wall. And Terry put the block on it. He wouldn't have it performed. He guarded the Dalek thing very fiercely.'

The one exception to this rule came in 1975 in a sketch for Spike Milligan's BBC2 series *Q6*. The sketch was prefaced by a voice-over explaining that we were about to see a portrayal of everyday life in a modern mixed marriage. A domestic scene of a clichéd 1970s housewife laying the table for dinner is rudely interrupted by her husband breaking through the door. He's a Dalek, though curiously one with a Pakistani accent, who proceeds to smash the room up and to exterminate the household pets and even his mother-in-law, each death being greeted with the catchphrase, 'Put him in the curry.' It was, by Milligan's recent standards, a coherent and focused sketch, embodying his comment on the subject of racial tensions in Britain: 'You can't solve the problem so you might as well laugh at it.' Milligan's biographer Humphrey Carpenter described the sketch as one 'in which Spike's racist humour suddenly becomes irresistible', and certainly it became one of the most celebrated of the series. It also, of course, mercilessly made fun of the Daleks, both with its summary of a day in the life – 'Exterminating is hard work,' he complains – and in the very appearance of a child Dalek. Had it been by anyone else, Nation would certainly have prevented its appearance, but he was more than conscious of his debt to Milligan, and he allowed it as a personal favour, accepting no fee in return.

The fact that there were programmes to chase about their usage of the Daleks indicated how much a part of the cultural furniture the creatures had become. In the wake of the Louis Marks story, the Daleks again became an annual fixture on *Doctor Who*, and Roger Hancock made clear to the BBC that he at least recognised their value to the corporation. When, following that lunch at Pinewood, Nation signed a contract to write a storyline for what would become 'Planet of the Daleks', he received no fee, just a commitment to £400 per episode if it were accepted; the following year, however, the first deal under Hancock's guidance saw an advance of £100 paid for the storyline of 'Death to the Daleks', deductable from the £450 per episode he would then receive. Elsewhere, while the heyday of Dalekmania may have passed, there was a rise again in the amount of merchandising available – 132 products were reported to exist by 1974, shortly to be joined by the Dalek's Death Ray ice lolly from Wall's – and there were odd echoes of the past. Back in 1964, when Alec Douglas-Home was prime minister, he was portrayed in a cartoon as the Alek; a decade later, he was foreign secretary in Edward Heath's government, and a correspondent to the *Guardian* was suggesting that he be renamed Dalek Hugless-Doom.

While 'the second coming of the Daleks', as Nation called it, lacked the fever and fervour of the initial craze, it also looked more sustainable; this time, there was a very real possibility that they might not disappear so readily. The creatures' status as a mainstream cult really took root in these years, though there were still some parts of the establishment that they struggled to penetrate. When a young student named Charles Braham, whose family were neighbours and friends of the Nations, asked if he could borrow one of the Dalek props from the Amicus movies for use in rag week fund-raising at the art college he was attending, Nation agreed on the proviso that he got the thing insured. 'I must have visited twenty-five small insurance offices,' remembered Braham. 'Have you ever tried to get insurance for a Dalek?' Unable to convince anyone that the request itself wasn't simply a rag week stunt, and finding no one willing to give a quote, he ended up persuading the college to underwrite the cost of any damage.

In Nation's absence there had been changes at the BBC, primarily the embrace of colour broadcasting, which started on BBC2 in 1967 and reached *Doctor Who* in time for the 1970 season. It was still, however, only available to a minority, fewer than 2 per cent of the licences issued that year giving their holders the right to receive colour transmissions; not until 1977 did colour licences outnumber black and white. Although many ITC shows had, of course, been made in colour, that had been for export reasons alone, and was of no benefit to the British viewer. The change in what was by now the nation's favoured recreation became for some symbolic of a generational shift in the country. 'I am a modern man,' proclaimed Tony Blair during the 1997 campaign that saw him elected as prime minister. 'I am part of the rock and roll generation – the Beatles, colour TV. That's the generation I come from.'

There had been changes too at *Doctor Who*, with the number of companions whittled down from the original three to just one, and a move towards a slightly older viewer. What had been – despite Sydney Newman's protestations – very definitely a children's show, that also happened to attract a wider audience, was now aimed much more obviously at the family. It was calculated that nearly three-quarters of viewers in the early 1970s were adults, many of whom had grown up with the programme, and the more mature content was causing some concern. Mary Whitehouse, founder of the National Viewers' and Listeners' Association, who campaigned against obscenity, blasphemy and violence on television, already had her sights set on *Doctor Who* (for having transgressed in the third of those categories), and in 1972 the BBC Audience Research Department published a report identifying the show as the BBC's most violent drama series. There was a consequent and immediate impact on Nation's own writing; when he proposed ending 'Planet of the Daleks' with a massacre of the surviving Thals, he had to be warned off by Terrance Dicks: 'In the present climate of opinion, we have to be very careful about violence, massacres and gloom.'

Other developments derived from Nation's own work on the series. When he had last written for the show, it was still making detours into historical drama, but that came to an end in 1967 with 'The Highlanders'. There was a brief reversion in 1982 with 'Black Orchid', but apart from that it was bug-eyed monsters all the way; the Daleks had finally rewritten *Doctor Who*'s original mission statement. The tentative linking together of different storylines that Nation had begun when the Doctor explained the relationship in time between the events of 'The Daleks' and 'The Dalek Invasion of Earth', had evolved so that a reasonably coherent mythology was building, most notably with the introduction of the concept of Time Lords in 'The War Games' (1969), written by Terrance Dicks and Malcolm Hulke. We now knew something of the Doctor's background and nature. It was also Nation who had, with Mavic Chen, introduced the theme of the megalomaniac scoundrel, hell bent on controlling the known universe, which had become a staple of the series. In Robert Holmes's 'Terror of the Autons' (1971), this reached its seeming pinnacle with the Master (played by Robert Delgado), a rebel Time Lord intended as the arch-enemy of the Doctor, though Nation was soon to add his own recurrent super-villain to the programme's pantheon.

There had, too, been a slight shift in structure, so that each serial was now given a single name (in the early years no overall title had been shown on screen for the stories, each episode being individually titled). It was a development that somewhat spoilt Nation's convention of revealing a Dalek in an incongruous setting as the last scene in the first episode of a story; since we already knew from the opening titles that Daleks were scheduled to appear, there was not much surprise to be had from the revelation. He continued with his format regardless. Most significant of all, there was a new Doctor, with the introduction of regeneration; indeed there was a second new Doctor, since Nation had missed the Patrick Troughton incarnation altogether, and returned to the show to find Jon Pertwee in possession of the TARDIS.

'I had known Jon for a long time and I knew what he was trying to do with the part,' Nation said later. 'We were in the height of the 007 period, and everybody was trying Bond movies; I think that's how Jon saw the role: a little more dashing, a little more daring, and a little more physical.' Pertwee's own description was slightly different: 'I played him as the flamboyant dandy, really the folk hero figure.' But there was too a simplifying of the character. Hartnell's irascible Doctor had been a decent man but appallingly self-centred, prepared to abandon Barbara to her fate in 'The Daleks', dismissive of the Thals' pacifist beliefs, happy to leave his granddaughter behind in the year 2164 in 'The Dalek Invasion of Earth', despite her clear reluctance. Pertwee's Doctor was a much more responsible figure of liberal authority, lacking the ambiguities and most of the arrogance. Indeed he's not far removed from the action heroes for whom Nation had been writing, both in attitude and style (the floppy shirt cuffs protruding from the velvet jacket would not have looked wrong on Jason King himself). It is perfectly possible to see the Pertwee era of *Doctor Who* as a continuation of the ITC adventure shows by other means.

Nation's script for 'Planet of the Daleks' displayed little sense of these changes. In fact, the most commonly levelled charge against the story became that it replayed many of the incidents and plot twists from 'The Daleks' itself: the jungle setting, the hiding of a person inside a Dalek shell, the Doctor being captured by the Daleks, and so on. Even the Thals, who hadn't been seen since the first serial, were back. But this was an era before home video players, let alone DVDs, a time when repeats were rare. It was even before the paperback imprint Target Books began publishing their series of novelisations of old serials, which provided the first opportunity to catch up on the past. ('One of the reasons for the success of the books was that if you missed a *Doctor Who*, you missed it,' observed Terrance Dicks, who wrote many of the novels. 'You were never going to see it again. There were virtually no repeats.') In this context, concerns about recurring plot devices meant little; it had been nearly ten years since the first serial and television memories simply weren't that long.

So we see again the Thals and the Daleks engaged in deadly combat, this time on the planet Spiridon, an inhospitable place with 'vegetation that's more like animal life than plant. Creatures hostile to everything, including themselves.' There is also a sentient life-form in the shape of the native Spiridons, who have perfected the techniques of invisibility (like the Visians in 'The Daleks' Master Plan'), hence the presence of the Daleks on their planet, seeking to learn the secret. In the last shot of the first episode, the Doctor and a Thal spray a dead invisible creature with cans of spray-paint to reveal what it is; the Doctor exclaims, in Pertwee's horrified, sibilant whisper: 'Daleks!'

As it turns out, there isn't a great deal of invisibility in the story. The Doctor's companion, Jo Grant (Katy Manning), has an encounter with a rebel Spiridon named Wester, but the rest of his species — who have been enslaved by the Daleks — tend to wear heavy furs because it's such a cold planet, making them perfectly visible, while the Daleks themselves find that the process uses too much power, so they too remain visible after the first episode. Likewise, the deadly vegetation isn't an issue for very long, making only a belated reappearance in the last two minutes of the final episode. There is a clear sense that Nation is making this up as he goes along and losing track of what he's already written. Terrance Dicks had asked for the scripts to be submitted one at a time, so that he could comment on them during the writing process, and Nation's self-confessed reluctance to rewrite became apparent when a second Thal mission arrives on Spiridon at the end of the second episode with a female Thal named Rebec on board. 'She turned up late because Terry Nation had forgotten there was supposed to be a female in the crew,' remembered Dicks. 'So I sent him a memo saying, "What happened to the female?" And she arrived by the next spacecraft. He was an old pro, Terry, he could always cope with that kind of thing.'

The same problem recurs throughout the six episodes, a lack of coherence that undercuts some typically inventive ideas, particularly in relation to the planet's climate. Spiridon has at its core liquid ice, which occasionally explodes out of ice volcanoes (the phenomenon of cryo-volcanoes was then unknown, the first evidence of their existence coming from observations of one of Neptune's moons in 1989), and is so cold that at night all the wildlife huddles together on the Plain of Stones, where large rocks have absorbed the heat of the day and release it slowly during the hours of darkness. There are also, following the influence of *The Time Machine* and *The War of the Worlds*, more borrowings from the early science fiction of H.G. Wells. The invisibility theme clearly derives from *The Invisible Man* (1897), as well as reprising 'The Invisible Invaders', a comic strip in the book *The Dalek World*, while the anti-gravitational mat that allows Daleks to rise vertically has something in common with the mysterious substance Cavorite that facilitates space travel in Wells's *The First Men in the Moon* (1901). Meanwhile there's an army of ten thousand Daleks in cryogenic suspension waiting for the order to attack the galaxy (not dissimilar to 'Invasion of the Earthmen' in *The Avengers*), and a plan to release a bacteria bomb to kill off all life on Spiridon, the public profile of biological weaponry having supplanted that of the neutron bomb since the days of the first serial.

So packed with incident and ideas does the story become that at one point in the fifth episode the Doctor has to stop for a brief recap to make sure we're up to speed: 'First of all, we've got to stop the Daleks releasing their bacteria. Second, we've got to make sure their army stays inactive. And third, we've got to generally put an end to their chances of invasion of other planets.' 'Well, how are we going to do all that?' worries Jo. The Doctor admits, 'I haven't the faintest idea.' Neither, one suspects, did Terry

Nation. But it's just the kind of challenge that both he and the Doctor relish, since it means that a plan is needed. And perils, problems and plans were what Nation liked best.

The Daleks are, of course, duly destroyed, leaving just enough time for a final message from the Doctor to the survivors of the Thal mission. 'Throughout history, you Thals have always been known as one of the most peace-loving peoples in the galaxy,' he tells them. 'When you get back to Skaro, you'll all be national heroes. Everybody will want to hear about your adventures. So be careful how you tell that story, will you? Don't glamorise it. Don't make war sound like an exciting and thrilling game.' (The message would presumably have been different if Nation had been allowed the slaughter of the Thals that he'd originally planned.)

It may not have been the most original piece of work that Nation ever produced, but 'Planet of the Daleks' was a big hit. Benefiting from extensive publicity about his return to *Doctor Who*, it attracted the largest audience — 11 million viewers for the first episode — the series had enjoyed since the story 'Galaxy 4' back in 1965. It also won good reviews. 'Even though the Doctor has defeated the Daleks countless times, they still represent the ultimate bogeymen,' wrote Stanley Reynolds in *The Times*. 'The Daleks are the boss space horrors, something to get the children hiding behind the sofa in happy anticipation of twenty-five minutes of fear. Saturday's episode, written by Nation himself, more than justified one's faith in the Daleks' intrinsic menace.'

The fact that serious newspapers were prepared to review the show was a recent development. There had long been a split between generations on the subject of the Daleks. A contributor to a BBC audience research report at the time of 'The Daleks' Master Plan' caught it perfectly. 'I cannot for the life of me see what my children find so fascinating about this rubbish, but fascinated they certainly are,' he noted. 'They go absolutely mad about the Daleks, God knows why.' The same continued to be true to some extent in the 1970s; the chat show host Michael Parkinson was baffled that his children should be frightened by such 'harmless things', while acknowledging that 'like all kids they've made Dalek noises around the house and played at exterminating'. But there was now a growing recognition that the Daleks were here to stay and that, however elusive their appeal, they were something special.

Huw Wheldon once declared that the four greatest achievements of television were *Quatermass*, *Maigret*, Gilbert Harding and the Daleks. Now

Richard Boston, television critic of the *Observer*, was prepared to go considerably further. 'It is, I suppose, beyond dispute that *Doctor Who* is the best thing that has ever been done on television,' he wrote in 1974. 'But what has above all distinguished the programme is not the Doctor or the Brigadier or the TARDIS or the music or even the screaming girls but the Daleks.' He went on to compare them to Billy Bunter, Jeeves, Tarzan, Sherlock Holmes and Superman as 'creations of prose fiction and comic strips that, like Frankenstein's monster, have grown out of the creator's control'. In short: 'they are among the immortals, the only products of television that have passed straight into mythology (with the possible exception of Robert Dougall).'

'Planet of the Daleks' was followed by 'Death to the Daleks', written in 1973 and broadcast in February 1974. The first episode went out five days before the General Election that swept the Conservative government of Edward Heath out of office, and — amid the chaos and power cuts of the three-day week — there was something particularly apt about a story that starts with the TARDIS stranded on the planet Exxilon, drained of all power, with the Doctor having to resort to an oil lamp for illumination. (For long-time Nation-watchers, there was a happy memory here of *Uncle Selwyn*, which had centred on the dying trade in oil lamps.) The loss of power is also suffered by the Daleks, who have similarly arrived on Exxilon, leaving their weaponry neutralised and forcing them into an alliance with the Doctor and his companion — now plucky journalist Sarah Jane Smith (Elisabeth Sladen) — and with a small human group, the latter having come in search of a rare mineral that can cure a plague affecting Earth and its Outer Worlds.

This suspension of hostilities is not welcomed by all, as one of the humans makes clear: 'My father was killed in the last Dalek war. I hate the thought of working with them.' In the reluctance to collaborate with the old enemy, one might again see shades of current affairs, with the controversy over Britain's entry into the European Economic Community, an event that was often portrayed at the time in terms of the Second World War. (THE BIGGEST SELL-OUT SINCE MUNICH and UNCONDITIONAL SURRENDER were two of the headlines chosen by the left-wing newspaper *Tribune* to cover the story.)

But, as ever with Nation, these concerns were no more than glanced at in passing as the story rushed on, and here more so than ever, for at just four episodes 'Death to the Daleks' was the shortest serial he had yet written for *Doctor Who*. The reduced length worked greatly to its benefit. In the longer stories there had always been a sense of sagging in the middle, what Terrance Dicks referred to as 'the curse of the six-parter' (let alone the twelve parts of 'The Daleks' Master Plan'), but here, with the ideas coming thick and fast, the serial is entirely driven by the narrative. Credit is also due to Dicks as the script editor, who felt the need to give Nation a slight nudge to prevent him repeating himself. 'The main necessity,' he wrote, following a meeting between the two men, 'is to avoid any resemblance to your previous show, i.e. a group of fugitives hunted through the jungle by Daleks. Instead of jungle, think of bleak, rocky, foggy quarry.'

The central concept, however, was genuinely new. 'The idea of a city that is a living organism,' as Nation put it in a letter to Dicks. 'A non-animal life, a truly monstrous monster.' In the programme, an Exxilon explains to the Doctor the ancient history of his race: 'They built a City that would last through all of time. They used their sciences to make the City into a living thing. It could protect itself, repair itself, maintain itself. They even gave it a brain. It then had no need of those who created it. Our people had created a monster.' Long ago, the Exxilons had been an advanced people, travelling the universe, and the Doctor even suggests that they visited Earth, passing their knowledge on to humans – a jokey reference to the theories of the Swiss pseudo-scientist Erich von Däniken, whose book *Chariots of the Gods?* (1968) had become a best-seller by positing the theory that extraterrestrials were responsible for ancient construction projects. As a consequence of building the sentient City, however, the Exxilons have reverted to the level of a Stone Age tribe, worshipping the City as a god. It's an excellent notion, a logical extension, perhaps, of the all-embracing womb-like cities of *The Caves of Steel* (the mention of Earth's colonies on the Outer Worlds suggests that Nation may have had the book in mind), and for once the special effects were flawless, with the construction of the model of the City entirely appropriate to the conception.

Both 'Planet of the Daleks' and 'Death to the Daleks' had their moments, but the creatures' limitations still suggested that there was only a finite number of variations to be wrung out of them. They had not, of course, been created with longevity in mind, and their career thus far paralleled two of the biggest film brands of Nation's childhood: Universal's Frankenstein and MGM's Tarzan. Both of those series had started with a strong opening feature (*Frankenstein*, *Tarzan the Ape Man*) that was intended to stand alone but was followed by an even better sequel (*Bride of Frankenstein*,

Tarzan and His Mate), before each descended into repetition and self-parody, to diminishing artistic and box-office returns. Both characters then faded from the screen, only to be revived in later years by others with a purer vision and a determination to reinvigorate the myth, even if in Tarzan's case, he had to wait half a century for Hugh Hudson's *Greystoke: The Legend of Tarzan, Lord of the Apes* (1984). There was a danger that the Daleks had gone down precisely the same path. A peak had been reached with 'The Dalek Invasion of Earth' and, although there had been good things in subsequent stories, a sense of treading water was becoming unavoidable.

Breaking the pattern, however, it was Nation himself who was to reinvent the mythology, though he needed a little prompting before he explored more deeply the creatures' potential. Commissioned to write another Dalek storyline, he submitted a proposal that was greeted with something less than enthusiasm by Terrance Dicks and Barry Letts: 'It's a very good story. The only snag is you've sold it to us three times already.' Unfazed by the accusation that his recycling of plots was starting to catch up with him, Nation replied, 'Yes, you're quite right. I'd better do you something else, then.' As the discussion continued, it was Letts who came up with the killer suggestion: '"You know, Terry, you've never shown us the genesis of the Daleks. Why don't you have a go at that?" And he said, "Oh yes, that'd be great." And he not only picked up the idea, he picked up the title as well.'

The resulting serial, 'Genesis of the Daleks', was broadcast in the spring of 1975 and became one of the best known of all *Doctor Who* stories, being repeated several times over the coming decades, both in its original six-episode form and in an edited 89-minute omnibus edition (the latter version also being broken down into two parts). A novelisation, written by Terrance Dicks, was published in 1976 by Target Books, the biggest-selling of the 150 or so titles in the series, and an audio version was released on record, comprising excerpts from the original soundtrack linked with narration by Tom Baker. Nation's earlier Dalek stories had already achieved a longevity that seemed to be denied their rivals, with the Peter Cushing films enjoying re-screenings on television and in the cinema, and with the David Whitaker novelisation of the first serial; now 'Genesis' was to become an even more familiar presence. When *Doctor Who Magazine* conducted a poll of its readers in 1998, 'Genesis' was voted the best *Doctor Who* story of all time. It was an opinion that Nation himself shared: 'I think it was a smashing set of episodes, I loved them. David Maloney directed it and he found production values that hadn't been there for ages. It seems to me that if you ask, "What's the best *Doctor Who* series ever?", from my point of view, "Genesis" would be it.'

Certainly it has one of the very best openings to a story. Into a mist-clad, deserted wasteland come what look like troops from the trenches of the First World War. Some are machine-gunned in slow motion to the ground, others continue to advance past the camera and onwards. As they disappear into the mist, the Doctor (newly reincarnated as Tom Baker) materialises, to be confronted by a Time Lord (John Franklyn-Robbins), who has a mission for him. The combination of the new Doctor's motley outfit and the Time Lord's all-in-one black garment with jester-style hood (taken from Ingmar Bergman's *The Seventh Seal*), set in the context of the warfare we've just seen, gives the sequence a disturbingly surreal quality. So does the Doctor's behaviour, evoking nothing so much as the familiar image of the ageing secret agent as he accepts his task: 'All right. Just one more time.' Thereafter things get more solid, if no less disturbing. The Doctor, together with his companions – Sarah Jane has been joined by Surgeon-Lieutenant Harry Sullivan (Ian Marter) – has been sent to the planet Skaro in the pre-dawn of the Daleks, his mission to prevent the emergence of the creatures, or at least to shape their nature into a less destructive form.

'I think this war's been going on a very long time,' reflects the Doctor, as he looks at the incongruous mixture of weaponry, both ancient and modern. 'They probably started out with the most modern equipment, but no longer have the resources, have to make do.' Indeed this turns out to be the centuries-long conflict, of which we heard in the first story, between the Thals and the Kaleds – the latter being the original humanoid form of the Daleks before they retreated into their protective shells. Now, however, we get a glimpse of its reality, with some scenes that made for gruesome viewing in what was supposed to be a children's show, particularly the shot of a trench manned by corpses, propped up against banks of sandbags, guns in their hands, to make it look as though the position is defended. The Doctor and Harry are captured by Kaled troops, encountering first a general named Ravon (Guy Siner) and then a security commander from the elite forces, Nyder (Peter Miles), and the Nazi imagery that has always accompanied the Daleks is here made explicit. The Kaleds wear black uniforms and click their heels as they give each other Hitler salutes (not the outstretched right arm, but the jerking up from the elbow of the forearm, palm out). Just in case there is any doubt, Nyder wears black leather gloves and, around his high-necked tunic, an Iron Cross. 'I think the imagery was suggested by the script,' remembered director David Maloney of the Nazi accoutrements, 'but I certainly didn't regret it afterwards.'

Nyder explains that there is also a third group on the planet, the Mutos, who are 'the scarred relics of ourselves. Monsters created by the chemical weapons used in the first century of this war. They were banished into the wastelands where they live and scavenge like animals.' They had to be expelled, says Nyder, because 'We must keep the Kaled race pure. Imperfects are rejected.' He speaks too in awestruck admiration of Davros, the greatest of all Kaled scientists, and the episode ends with Sarah, stumbling away from a group of Mutos to come across Davros for the first time. Together, she and we witness a moment of destiny, as the wizened, wheelchair-bound scientist unveils the first Dalek in the history of the universe.

It's a great episode, as good as *Doctor Who* ever got, and arguably Terry Nation's finest achievement. There are some of his characteristic touches, but they are given new and violent twists. Sarah Jane is separated from her companions, as ever in a Nation story, but only because she's been left for dead in a trench full of corpses; the familiar iconography of the Second World War is invoked, but is fused with images both from earlier periods and from the future to create a picture of perpetual conflict (Nation cited Wells's 1936 film *Things to Come* as an influence here); even the traditional final-scene reveal of a Dalek is trumped by the debut appearance of Davros the Creator.

The figure of Davros dominates the remainder of the tale. He is the leader of the Elite, a group of scientists who are housed outside the main city dome in a place known as the Bunker, and who represent an alternative centre of power in Kaled society, a sort of scientific SS. Through his research on the genetic mutations thrown up by the chemical weapons used in the war, he has concluded that there is no way back for his race. He has therefore accelerated the workings of evolution, as a Kaled explains, 'to establish our final mutational form. He took living cells, treated them with chemicals and produced the ultimate creature.' He then developed the travel machines that would house these creatures and thus bequeathed to the universe the Daleks. He's a magnificent addition to both the Dalek mythology and *Doctor Who* more generally, following on from the likes of Mavic Chen, Tobias Vaughn (in the 1968 story 'The Invasion') and the Master and raising the stakes still higher as the ultimate in deranged but charismatic megalomaniacs.

As Nation pointed out, 'any crazy old mad professor is wonderful to have around'. Such characters had been stock figures in horror and science fiction since Mary Shelley's *Frankenstein*, but Davros also has some very specific associations. Most immediately, the image of a wheelchair-bound deranged Nazi scientist drew on Peter Sellers's title role in Stanley Kubrick's film *Dr Strangelove* (1964). There's a hint too of Leslie Charteris's Dr Sardon from 'The Man Who Liked Ants', another scientist who was keen to speed up the evolutionary process. But even closer is another of the classic H.G. Wells novels, *The Island of Dr Moreau* (1896), in which, on an isolated island in the South Pacific, the eponymous scientist pursues a combination of vivisection, plastic surgery and education to turn animals of various sorts into passable imitations of human beings, almost in parody of evolution. The resulting creatures live wild on the island, but are in constant danger of reverting to their animal natures, kept in line only by fear of Moreau and by constant recitation of the Law he has imposed on them: 'Not to go on all-fours; that is the Law. Are we not Men?' they chant. 'Not to eat flesh nor fish; that is the Law. Are we not Men?' Much of this is echoed in 'Genesis of the Daleks', both with the Mutos out in the wastelands and with artificially created monsters. 'Davros's early experiments were with animals,' we are told. 'Some of the things he created were horrific. And they're still alive.' When Sarah is captured by Mutos, one of them insists that she is what they term a Norm, and must therefore be killed: 'Kill her! It is the Law. All Norms must die.'

A common thread running through the tradition of the mad scientist had been the implication that creator and created share a single nature. That was, for example, the basis of Dr Jekyll and Mr Hyde, and the first film version of *Frankenstein* (1910) had acknowledged the element of the doppelganger with a scene in which the monster fades away while standing in front of a mirror, though his reflection remains; when Frankenstein subsequently looks in the mirror, he sees only the monster's reflection looking back at him. Davros – 'This thing that was half-man and half-Dalek,' as Nation described him – takes the shared identity to a logical conclusion. The description of him in the script was quite explicit: 'Davros is contained in a specially constructed self-powered wheelchair. It has similarities to the base of a Dalek.' We never discover what it was that so scarred and destroyed the scientist's physical body, but the chair has been developed as a life-support mechanism, leaving him effectively a cyborg. 'The only really human feature we ever see of Davros is an ancient, withered hand that plays across the switch-packed surface of the control panel that stretches across the front of the chair.' (The focus on the hand also echoes *Dr Strangelove*.)

The realisation of Davros – designed by Peter Day, with the face created by sculptor John Friedlander, both from the BBC Visual Effects Department – followed that prescription, adding a hint of the Mekon, Dan Dare's arch-enemy, in the expansive cranium. It was a superb piece of work. Since the commissioning of the serial, both Barry Letts and Terrance Dicks had left the show, replaced by producer Philip Hinchcliffe and script editor Robert Holmes, neither of whom had any fondness for the Daleks at all. They were, however, stuck with the story. 'So I thought that we'd better do something bloody good with the Daleks,' said Hinchcliffe, 'because people had seen them ad nauseam. They were silly things, running around on castors. So I just tried to inject more atmosphere.' The strength of the design was complemented by the performance of Michael Wisher, the first and best of the actors to take the role. In his hands the character emerged as a worthy opponent for the Doctor, a Professor Moriarty to his Sherlock Holmes. 'The courage and resourcefulness of a hero figure,' Nation once wrote, 'is directly related to the strength and ruthlessness of his opponent.' Nowhere was this more true than with Davros. And from the Doctor's point of view, he at last had a representative of the Daleks with whom he could engage, the first one with a face, a name, and a voice capable of expressing an emotion beyond insecure hysteria.

The conflict between the two reaches its peak in the second half of the story, which, as in other Dalek tales by Nation, features discussions of morality. The Doctor attempts to reason with Davros as a fellow man of science: 'If you had created a virus in your laboratory, something contagious and infectious that killed on contact, a virus that would destroy all other forms of life, would you allow its use?' Davros replies, thoughtfully at first but with increasing levels of self-abandon: 'Yes. Yes. To hold in my hand a capsule that contains such power, to know that life and death on such a scale was my choice. To know that the tiny pressure on my thumb, enough to break the glass, would end everything. Yes. I would do it. That power would set me up above the gods. And through the Daleks, I shall have that power.'

For he is not at heart a scientist at all, but the ultimate arch-villain of the thriller tradition, the power-crazed would-be dictator, who dismisses his opponents as weak-willed and feeble-minded: 'They talk of democracy, freedom, fairness. Those are the creeds of cowards, the ones who will listen to a thousand viewpoints and try to satisfy them all. Achievement comes through absolute power. And power through strength.' Intrigued though he is by the Doctor, ultimately he dismisses him for the same reason: 'You have a weakness that I have totally eliminated from the minds of the Daleks so they will always be superior,' he sneers. 'You are afflicted with a conscience.' He is even prepared to betray his own people to the Thals, in order to thwart an attempt by higher-minded Kaleds to curtail his activities: 'Today the Kaled race is ended, consumed in a fire of war, but from its ashes will rise a new race, the supreme creature, the ultimate conqueror of the universe – the Dalek!'

We have encountered his kind before in Nation's writing. The character Croft in 'The Fanatics', an episode of *The Champions*, for example, with his suicide squads and his lust for power. Or the professional revolutionary Theron Netlord (John Carson) in 'Sibao' in *The Saint*, who seeks world domination through organising the oppressed nations of the world: 'For a thousand years they have been searching for a leader to take them to their rightful place in the world.' Or possibly Curt Hoffman (Robert Hardy) in 'A Memory of Evil' in *The Baron*, a neo-Nazi whose ambitions might seem to make him a candidate for the presidency of the European Union: 'The whole of Europe. A dozen countries, all scrambling for the seats in the halls of power. If they were one country, with one leader, then they would have enough manpower and resources to conquer the world.' There were to be more such figures to come, but never was the character manifest in such pure, unadorned form as Davros.

All of this is building towards the climactic scene in the final episode. The Doctor places explosives in Davros's laboratory, with the intention of destroying the genetically mutated Kaleds who will become the Daleks, but then hesitates over whether to detonate the charge. 'Do I have the right? Simply touch one wire against the other and that's it: the Daleks cease to exist. Hundreds of millions of people, thousands of generations can live without fear, in peace, and never even know the word "Dalek".' As Davros has correctly identified, the possession of a conscience brings with it moral uncertainty. 'If I kill, wipe out a whole intelligent life-form, then I become like them. I'd be no better than the Daleks.' He spells out the dilemma in its simplest form: 'If someone who knew the future pointed out a child to you and told you that that child would grow up totally evil, to be a ruthless dictator who would destroy millions of lives, could you then kill that child?'

The quandary is resolved when he is distracted from his task and a Dalek subsequently passes over the wires, making the connection that detonates the explosives. As Tom Baker pointed out: 'It's the villains exploding themselves because, of course, the moral hero which I play can never actually press the button. He just sets up a situation in which they actually take the decision because good conquers evil in melodrama. It's not like in real life.'

But there are sufficient numbers of Daleks already in existence to ensure that the race will survive, and as the Thal forces blow up the entrance to the bunker, sealing the creatures inside, the creations turn on their creator in time-honoured fashion, apparently killing Davros himself. Through a television monitor, the Daleks are seen accepting their fate in the sure and certain knowledge of their survival: 'We are entombed, but we live on. This is only the beginning. We will prepare. We will grow stronger. When the time is right, we will emerge and take our rightful place as the supreme power of the universe.' Unusually for *Doctor Who*, the story ends on a note of failure. The Doctor had been sent to prevent the emergence of the Daleks, and the best he has managed to do has been to delay them a little, by no more than a thousand years in his own estimation. As a rule, *Doctor Who* opted for happy endings, for the restoration of normality after the removal of a deadly threat; here there was simply a temporary cessation of hostilities.

The bleakness of the ending was fully in keeping with a serial that had been resolutely downbeat for much of its course. Suitably exercised by the third episode, Mary Whitehouse wrote publicly to the BBC to complain about the story: 'Such was the level of violence that I believe this particular episode should not have been screened before 9 pm. It is difficult to imagine the effect it must have had on any pliable mind under the age of fourteen.'

As ever in the six-part serials, there is a certain flabbiness around the middle, sequences of action that detract from rather than augment the main story. And there are absurdities that have to be endured for the sake of the plot. We are expected to believe that the main Kaled and Thal cities are still, after a thousand years of war, linked by a network of service ducts, allowing the Doctor and his companions (and even Davros) to pass between the two with the same ease that Biggles's arch-enemy, Erich von Stalhein, displayed when moving between German and British camps in *Biggles Flies East* (1935). There is also an unfortunate encounter with some giant clams, the fruits of one of Davros's experiments. Despite the flaws, however, the great majority of the serial works splendidly, eclipsing not only the recent Dalek adventures but also the classic stories from the 1960s.

It also contradicted entirely the history of the Daleks as seen in previous television serials and elsewhere. In the 1960s comic strips, the equivalent of the Kaleds, though they were not given that name, were short humanoid figures with blue skin, and the scientist who created the machines was named Yarvelling. An alternative account of the origins was offered by Nation in 'We Are the Daleks!', a short story he contributed to a *Radio Times* special, published to mark the tenth anniversary of *Doctor Who* in 1973; here alien scientists were said to have taken early humans to a planet named Ameron, accelerated their evolution and created from them the Daleks.

None of this related to 'Genesis'. But then *Doctor Who* was not at this stage particularly obsessed with consistency. Explaining the programme's attitude, Terrance Dicks cited the maxim 'history is what you can remember', from the anti-history textbook *1066 and All That* by W.C. Sellar and R.J. Yeatman, commenting: 'Continuity on *Doctor Who* was what I could remember of the past and what future script editors could remember about what I'd done. *Star Trek*, I believe, had a bible, in which everything was laid down. We never did that on *Who*. There are varying accounts of almost everything. And I really don't care. I always say: if they're asking questions about inconsistencies, the show's not good enough. They shouldn't have time to think about that.' Of course, he was quite right; the discrepancies made no difference to viewers' entertainment, and this new account of the origin of the species became happily accepted as the correct version.

Reinvigorated by the possibilities opened up by 'Genesis', Nation was quick to talk up his creatures to the press, suggesting that he hadn't entirely abandoned his dream of a stand-alone series. 'I see no limit to their lifespan,' he enthused. 'I would think that it's possible the Daleks could survive even beyond *Doctor Who*. This is something we've talked about: if he ever runs out of steam the Daleks could have a programme of their own.' The passion wasn't shared by others on *Doctor Who*. In keeping with their dislike of the creatures, Philip Hinchcliffe and Robert Holmes next commissioned a non-Dalek story from Nation, which became 'The Android Invasion', screened later in 1975. Before that was broadcast, however, he had finally realised his long ambition to see a credit that read: 'Series created by Terry Nation'.

Chapter Twelve

Journal of a Plague Year

Back in December 1971, when Terry Nation had met Andrew Osborn to discuss potential programme ideas, it had been *The Amazing Robert Baldick* that had first found favour, perhaps because of the nascent nostalgia boom that came to dominate so much of the decade. But other currents running through popular culture, following the upheavals of the late 1960s, were to make his other proposal that day, originally entitled *Beyond Omega*, a more viable proposition.

There was, in the first instance, a trend away from industrialisation and towards ruralism, a movement initially manifested in the world of youth culture, and in the growing appeal of hippy communes, particularly in the West Country and Wales. The example was followed, in a milder form, by rock musicians. Previously the first objective of a new band had been to rehearse a live set and get out on the road as swiftly as possible, but when in 1967 Stevie Winwood left the Spencer Davis Group to co-found Traffic, the group's initial move was instead to a cottage in a small Berkshire village, where they spent some months jamming and writing, before releasing the fruits of their labour on vinyl. By 1970, when Led Zeppelin retreated to a remote Welsh cottage to write their largely acoustic third album (there was no electricity in the place), the idea of serious musicians seeking inspiration far from the urban centres of the music industry was becoming one of the great clichés of the time. And gradually the same tendency became visible in the country more generally, beyond the bounds of music and youth culture.

In 1975 the BBC launched *The Good Life*, one of the most popular sitcoms of the era, celebrating a suburban expression of the instinct to get away from the rat-race in favour of a more natural lifestyle. The same year the pop artist Peter Blake and his wife, Jann Haworth, moved to Somerset to found, with several others, the Brotherhood of Ruralists, seeking to reconnect to an older tradition of art rooted in the English landscape. It wasn't a huge success. 'The critics were very much against it,' Blake explained later, 'and other artists thought we were kind of sentimental and silly.' But it was another symptom of a feeling that modern culture, with its emphasis on city-based life, had lost its way. Given that this was the high point of the brutalist concrete housing estates, from the Barbican in the City of London to Broadwater Farm in Tottenham, the appeal of an escape to Arcadia was self-evident, even if there were cultural suggestions — including *And Soon the Darkness* — that all was not quite as lovely in the country garden as it might look to a city-dweller.

Allied to this trend was the rise of environmentalism, which found official expression in the declaration of 1970 as European Conservation Year, and which concerned itself at this stage with issues such as those outlined by Prince Philip: 'Problems of overpopulation, environmental pollution, depletion of finite resources and the threat of widespread starvation.' Effectively this was the flip-side of ruralism: underpinning the optimism of the move to the country with a sense of potential catastrophe arising from contemporary life, and with both tendencies expressing a rejection of modernism. The boom in ecological campaigning did not last long, withering in the cold winds that blew through the economy in the late 1970s and early 1980s — though the arguments survived to re-emerge later in the century — but for a brief period environmentalism was taken very seriously. And, as ever with such issues, the BBC was very keen to demonstrate relevance by responding to new social concerns; the most celebrated early result was *Doomwatch* (1970), a drama series concerning environmental and technological problems that was created by Kit Pedler and Gerry Davis, who had earlier invented the Cybermen for *Doctor Who*. (A 1972 film of *Doomwatch* was scripted by Clive Exton and directed by Peter Sasdy.)

Some of this thinking was undoubtedly behind the BBC's com- missioning in May 1972 of a pilot episode for the post-apocalyptic *Beyond Omega* project, now retitled *The Survivors* and ultimately to be made as simply *Survivors*. Nation had a great deal of other work on at the time — 'Planet of the Daleks' had just been commissioned, followed by 'Death to the Daleks', there were episodes of *The Protectors* to write, *The Amazing Robert Baldick* was in pre-production and *The House in Nightmare Park* was also in the pipeline — and it wasn't until October of the following year that he received the second half of his payment, due on delivery of the pilot script. Thereafter things moved considerably faster. The pilot was accepted and the project expanded into a series, expected to run for ten episodes in mid 1975, with the theme succinctly identified as: 'Bubonic plague sweeps the world, killing all but a handful of people who escape to the country with absolutely nothing and who start civilisation again from scratch.' Contract negotiations were concluded by January 1974, with Nation receiving a fee of £850 per script, plus £50 per episode as the creator (£100 for each episode written by someone else) and an additional £50 per episode as script consultant. He also retained the film and merchandising rights and signed separately a publishing contract for a novel based on the series.

At the heart of Nation's thinking about this new series was a sense of the fragility of civilisation. He had researched the Black Death, the pandemic that killed around half the population of Europe in the fourteenth century, but had concluded that the modern world was even more vulnerable. 'In those days, the Death travelled through Europe and Asia at the speed of a man on a horse because that was the fastest means of locomotion,' he noted, but today it would 'travel at the speed of a jet plane. In twenty-four hours it would be in every major city in the world.'

Bringing this potential defencelessness into focus was the epochal moment in 1969 when human beings first set foot on the Moon, an achievement which was at least partially responsible for the growth of environmentalism. The images sent back of Earth as seen from its nearest neighbour revealed our planet to be a much more delicate entity than it had previously appeared, while the barrenness of the Moon itself served to emphasise the precious rarity of life. Nation, however, drew another lesson from the episode: the huge gap that space exploration illustrated between the scientific possibilities of humanity as a species, and the technological ignorance of the individuals within that species. We were the first known beings to have consciously escaped from their own planet, and yet the complexities of modern life had alienated most people in the developed world not merely from the intricate technologies that we now took for granted, but from the most basic skills that had allowed the emergence of society in the first place. The interdependence of humanity, the division of expertise, meant that no one individual – nor even a small group of individuals – could live a genuinely self-sufficient life in any form that would be recognisable to contemporary culture. The premise of the series, a cataclysmic event that produces the near-extinction of humanity, was intended to illustrate this gap between individual and society; it was summed up in the *Radio Times* listing for the first episode, using the words of one of the characters: 'Incredible, isn't it? We are of the generation that landed a man on the moon and the best we can do is talk of making tools from stone.'

There was also a personal dimension to this concern. However impressive Lynsted Park might be as a house, there were also problems. 'We are at the end of the electricity and water mains,' Nation told the *Daily Mirror* in 1964. 'If somebody in the village uses extra electricity, our lights go out.' In later interviews he was to cite this as part of the motivation for *Survivors*: 'We had a big house in the country at the time and I was becoming more and more aware of the difficulties in just surviving in a big house with running water, electricity and all that. I was also aware of how little I knew. I didn't know how to preserve food, I didn't know how to make anything, and I suddenly realised that I and my whole generation were virtual victims of a tremendous industry.'

With this in mind, he attempted to introduce a note of self-sufficiency to Lynsted Park, though, as he happily acknowledged, his contribution to the experiment was in directing, rather than running, the project, the burden of which fell squarely on his wife, Kate. 'We had geese, chicken, sheep,' he remembered. 'I would say, "Why don't we get some goats?" and before I knew it there were goats up there, trying to knock us down every time we moved. She tried baking bread, but the truth was if you needed it, you would go down to the store and get it, but I was just fascinated, seeing it done.' He was attracted to the ideas contained in John and Sally Seymour's influential book *Self-Sufficiency* (1970), even if he lacked the commitment to follow them through too far. 'My wife was exhausted,' he admitted. 'This poor woman was living this *Survivors* thing while I was sitting up in this room. I'd come down and say, "God, what a day I had today!" and she'd say, "*You* had a day?"' With a daughter, Rebecca, and an infant son, Joel (born in 1973), to look after, it's a tribute to Kate's supportive nature that she went along with the idea at all. 'She slaved through the years of that, and afterwards she said, "You know, I want your next show to be about this couple who live on a yacht in the south of France, and they've got servants, and they're terribly rich." She'd had enough of surviving.'

If this was the starting point for *Survivors*, Nation also discovered during the writing process that he was revisiting a key theme that had run through much of his previous work. 'It is only since I started work on this new series,' he said, 'that I have realised my writing has previously been dominated by the business of survival: the people in those other series survived because of their extreme cleverness, wit or ability.' In an interview with the *Daily Express*, promoting the show, he stressed the same point: 'I've been thinking about this for twenty years. I've written *The Saint* and *The Persuaders!* – people always against the odds.'

Perhaps these weren't the best examples that Nation could have chosen from his previous work, for the ITC series featured resourcefulness in very specific situations; when John Mannering or Simon Templar improvise their way out of danger, it demonstrates quick thinking in a moment of high stress, not the long-term methodical planning required in a society that has collapsed completely. But there were certainly precedents in his work, starting with the title of the show itself. It harked back to the original storyline for 'The Daleks', which had been called 'The Survivors' (as broadcast, the second episode of the serial bore that title), and had also been set in the aftermath of an apocalypse that destroyed almost all civilisation on the planet. Indeed the theme of a largely depopulated planet was a regular one, from the neutron bomb in 'The Daleks' to the solium radiation device yet to come in the *Blake's 7* episode 'Countdown'. And there are perhaps echoes of other plagues in 'Planet of the Daleks' and 'Death to the Daleks'.

More directly, the original script for 'The Daleks' Master Plan' had included discussion of sending planets back in time to a primitive past. 'The Earth can start again,' Mavic Chen was to have reflected, 'but without the shackles of infantile philosophies like democracy. It will be a new and virgin land which can be shaped.' Similarly in the original scripts for 'The Dalek Invasion of Earth', one of the characters recounts how the invasion was prefaced by the dropping of bacteria bombs, killing most of humanity with a deadly virus; when there were insufficient numbers of humans left to carry the disease, it faded away, and those who were left grouped themselves into small communities, working the land and fighting off attacks from marauding gangs. The arrival of the Daleks has interrupted this process, but as the possibility of defeating the invaders becomes a reality, attention turns again to the rebuilding of society. David, one of the resistance fighters, emphasises that agriculture is the way forward: 'It's the land that matters, isn't it? The world's saturated itself with science.' He later talks of soil as 'The most valuable thing we have, the basis of all life.' Little of this made it into the televised version of the serial, but there were definite resonances to be heard in *Survivors*. Even in the minor details of 'Invasion' there were elements that would recur in the later series; we were to be told of radio hams linking some of the groups of survivors together, while Susan's response when she learns that humans are fighting each other for food and supplies tersely summarises one of Nation's chief concerns: 'Survival at all costs.' The timing was not far removed either; the first draft of 'Invasion' set the action in 2041, with the Doctor calculating that Earth must have succumbed to the Daleks in the 1970s.

But if Nation drew on elements of his earlier work for *Survivors*, they were to be transformed into something much more convincing here. Perhaps buoyed by the new-found critical respectability of the Daleks and the unusually good notices for *The House in Nightmare Park*, Nation began to enjoy something of a purple patch, writing – in addition to 'Genesis of the Daleks' – seven episodes of what turned out to be the thirteen-week series of *Survivors*, among them some of his best work. In particular the opening three episodes, which link together into a continuous narrative, are hugely effective, a sustained two-and-a-half-hour tale that for the first time allowed him the leisure to develop character, as well as to explore his favourite concerns in some depth. In the absence of the cliff-hanger endings that were demanded every twenty minutes or so in *Doctor Who*, the pacing is less forced, and the moments of action and high drama emerge more naturally from the narrative. This was new territory for a writer who had come from comedy into children's science fiction and action adventure stories, and there was nothing in his list of credits to guarantee that it would work, but it was a challenge to which Nation proved himself more than capable of responding.

He did so largely by changing his writing style. In reference to a scene in 'Planet of the Daleks', Terrance Dicks once pointed out: 'The thing about Terry Nation scripts is that he had this technique where he puts the characters into a bad situation, and almost immediately makes things worse. So you're climbing up the tunnel and then the ice is coming up behind you. And when you reach the top, the doors start closing.' The same approach was evident in *The Baron* and *The Persuaders!* as well as – allowing for genre differences – in his early comedy writing; incidents were heaped one on top of another for dramatic effect, not always as a logical consequence of one another. In *Survivors*, however, he abandoned his familiar structure in favour of a more straightforward linear tale.

The story opens in the familiar television world of a village full of half-timbered, thatched cottages, almost a parody of an Agatha Christie com-munity in the Home Counties. There are already signs that an epidemic is disrupting normal life as a wealthy housewife, Abby Grant (Carolyn Seymour), waits for her husband David (Peter Bowles) to come home on a commuter train that doesn't arrive. When he does finally appear, having completed his journey from London by bus, the implication is that this is typical of the situation one expects in modern Britain. It could be 'a bad snow fall or a rail strike', comments Abby, though David is still furious at the lack of service: 'I've never seen anything like it. It'll take them literally days to get things sorted out. Not that I saw anybody doing anything about it.' Intercut with this portrayal of near-normal frustration is the story of Jenny Richards (Lucy Fleming), a young woman living in London whose flatmate has come down with the mystery virus. It is largely through her experiences that we get a glimpse of how bad the situation really is, as she goes to a hospital seeking help for her friend, only to be shocked at the number of patients seeking admission. 'The home secretary has ordered us to keep up the fiction,' she's told by a doctor. 'With the speed this thing is travelling, we have no way of stopping it. In a few days the dead will outnumber the living, the cities will be like open cess-pits.'

This theme of the dangers of the city is reinforced by Abby's own reflections as she fixes a belated supper for her husband. 'You know, I never thought what happens to a city. If it all breaks down, all at the same time. There's no power, there's no lighting or cooking, and food, even if you get it into the city, you can't distribute it. Then there's water, sewage – yeuch! – things like that.' She concludes: 'The city's like a great big, pampered baby, with thousands of people feeding it and cleaning it and making sure it's all right.' The echoes of *The Caves of Steel*, with its analysis of urban insecurity, are unmistakable. 'New York must spend every ounce of effort getting water in and waste out,' a character had observed in Asimov's novel. 'The balance is a very delicate one in a hundred directions, and growing more delicate every year.' The consequence is that humanity has become dependent on the city itself: 'Earthmen are so coddled, so enwombed in their imprisoning caves of steel, that they are caught forever.' It was a theme that had surfaced elsewhere in Nation's work, most notably in the sentient city of 'Death to the Daleks'. Here, however, it's not a science fiction projection into the future, but a simple recognition of the situation that modern humanity has already created for itself.

By this stage the gloom is gathering. As the lights go out, it descends even into the cosy kitchen that should be Abby and David's refuge from the world. And we know that bad times are coming. In 'Planet of the Daleks' Nation had employed a basic device of dramatic irony, showing the Doctor being treated by the Thals for a fungal infection received when one of the plants spat at him; without treatment, the fungus will grow and spread over his body to engulf him completely. We then cut to Jo who notices fungal growth on her hand, though she doesn't know what it is or that she needs immediate treatment. The same technique is used here: we learn from the depiction of Jenny's flatmate that the symptoms of the disease include sweating and swellings under the arms, and that the prognosis is certain death, so when Abby pads perspiration from her face and feels gingerly under her arm, we recognise – even though she doesn't – that she has been infected. Sure enough, she soon falls into unconsciousness.

Five days later she wakes up – one of the very few to recover from the plague – to find that she is alone in what seems like a dead world. Her husband's corpse is in the living room and when she goes out into the village, there is no one left alive, just a church with, it is suggested, the pews full of the dead. As she leaves the church, she looks up to the heavens and prays, 'Oh God, please don't let me be the only one.'

With her husband and neighbours gone, she drives to the boarding school where her son, Peter, was a pupil. Again she finds initially nothing but death and silence, though there is also a faint glimmering of hope; Peter's bed is the only one in the dormitory not occupied by a corpse. Eventually she finds a single survivor, Dr Bronson (Peter Copley), a teacher who initiates the discussion that will dominate the series: how do the few members of humanity who have come through this deadly epidemic begin to build a new world? Abby's suggestion that there's plenty of stuff lying around just waiting to be used is dismissed as mere 'scavenging', and Bronson goes on to explain how difficult it's going to be to survive the aftermath of the epidemic, learning from scratch how to make everything. Electric lighting isn't simply about generating power, he points out, but about extracting metal from the earth and refining it to make wires, as well as blowing glass to make a light bulb; in reality, most of us couldn't even make a candle.

This is the argument that Abby takes with her as the focus of the story widens in the second episode, 'Genesis', to show others beginning to make plans for the future. She makes contact with a small group led by Arthur Wormley (George Baker), a trade union leader in the old world who's looking now to the future. 'There's odd people moving around all over the country, aimless, lost. They'll make contact with each other, start forming into groups. Somebody's got to unite those groups, bring them under central control. They'll want leadership, guidance, they'll want somebody in authority.' It's a role he clearly relishes: 'I think God might have spared me to help those of us that are left. That's my skill, that's my talent: organisation.' When challenged by Abby about his practical abilities, he says modestly that he has the skills to knock up a simple table, but she queries the claim: 'Right from scratch? You'd fell the timber? With what? An axe or a saw. The steel for the saw has been made in a foundry, the iron ore has been dug from the ground, and the fuel to smelt it with has been mined. Now, what happens when the last axe-head cracks and the last saw breaks?' She then restates Dr Bronson's analysis: 'Our civilisation had the technology to land a man on the moon, but as individuals we don't even have the skill to make an iron spearhead. We are less practical than Iron Age man.' But still he remains more concerned with establishing 'the rudiments of government' as the first objective. When he responds to an attack on the house he has commandeered by having one of the intruders shot dead, Abby makes her excuses and leaves.

The episode ends as she joins forces with the other two central figures in the first season, Jenny and an engineer named Greg Preston (Ian McCulloch), the former eager for human contact, the latter revelling in the freedom of having no responsibilities for anyone else. They have also, separately, encountered other variations on the theme of survival. On the one hand there is a Welsh tramp, Tom Price (Talfryn Thomas), who has a naïve faith that salvation will come from America: 'The Yanks'll have something, don't worry. In the war, they give us the stuff then. The Yanks'll fix us up, don't worry.' On the other hand there are Anne Tranter (Myra Frances) and Vic Thatcher (Terry Scully), who have holed up in a quarry, accumulating vast quantities of stores from nearby towns to use as security. 'I don't think we're going to be too badly off,' reflects Anne. 'You see, from now on money isn't going to mean anything. The rich will be the ones who've got things.' In her past life she had servants and she sees no reason why she can't buy the labour of others now: the essential law of property relations will surely continue.

These conflicting ideas of how society should be rebuilt dominate the early stages of the series, generating much of the action. When Abby, Jenny and Greg go to a supermarket for supplies, they are interrupted by an armed gang of Wormley's men. 'There was a state of martial law declared,' one of them explains. 'Looters can be shot on sight.' Our trio win this encounter, but later find that the sanctuary they have established in a church has been smashed up by Wormley's thugs. Abby is deeply shocked by the violence: 'I thought that those of us who were left would come together, I mean really come together. There wouldn't be national interests, nor political, just a total unity and a sense of purpose. And that one thing we have in common – that we are survivors – should have been enough.'

These episodes were being written in highly charged political times – Edward Heath's government had just fallen, following its confrontation with the miners – and the overtones are unavoidable. Abby accuses Wormley of acting like a feudal baron, using the familiar title then accorded to trade union leaders, and when one of his henchmen brags, 'We are the authorities now,' it has the resonance of a quote attributed to Hartley Shawcross, the attorney general in the post-war Labour government: 'We are the masters now.' Given his background and Kate's parentage, Nation's sympathies were with the miners in their dispute with the government, but the political position of his central character – her belief that in a time of absolute crisis there should be a coming together – resonated with a current more often heard on the centre-right at this period.

The Labour home secretary, Roy Jenkins, believed at the start of 1975 that the situation in Britain had become bad enough that it was time for a government of national unity and that the nation was ready for it. 'He wants a coalition government and expects to see one in the first half of this year,' it was reported, with Jenkins making clear that whoever led this alliance, he expected to take over very swiftly. Other politicians, mostly in the Conservative and Liberal parties, were coming to the same conclusion, and even the Queen seemed to share the feeling. 'Different people have different views about our problems and how they should be solved,' read the text of her 1973 Christmas broadcast. 'Let us remember, however, that what we have in common is more important than what divides us.' That passage was deleted at the request of Heath, attempting to keep the monarch out of the political debate, but he himself had some sympathy with the concept of coalition.

The motivation behind this desire was the hope that a coalition government might provide a unified voice in opposition to precisely the kind of union leader represented by Arthur Wormley and, in real life, by

Jack Jones, the general secretary of the Transport and General Workers Union, who was identified in an opinion poll as being the most powerful man in the country. At a time when trade union power was the most contentious issue in British politics – it had brought down successive governments in 1970 and 1974 and was to do so again in 1979 – Wormley's previous occupation was a very deliberate choice. His name also suggested a cross between Arthur Scargill and Joe Gormley, the two most prominent figures in the National Union of Mineworkers.

There was too, in the depiction of Wormley's militia, a nod towards certain right-wing figures of the era, the likes of General Sir Walter Walker and Colonel David Stirling, who were calling for the formation of private armies of 'volunteers on call to the government in the event of a crisis'. They may have been fantasists, but the state of the nation was sufficiently chaotic to lend some credence to their vision. 'Two years ago we could have easily faced a coup in Britain,' said Jack Jones in 1977, looking back on the period when the first season of *Survivors* was being broadcast. 'There was talk of private armies being assembled. There was talk of the end of democracy.'

The fact that Abby, Jenny and Greg spent time discussing the future direction of the community they wished to establish, and the society they wanted to see emerge, annoyed some critics. 'Just as Doctor Who, when chased by marauding Daleks, will gather his witless assistants around him for a time-wasting conversation,' wrote Clive James in the *Observer*, 'so the Survivors, while being pursued by a ravening carload of hooligans with guns, pause for a metaphysical interchange rivalling *The Symposium* in duration.' But, as so often, James's comments missed the essence of the drama: the arguments over the nature of society arise from, and comment upon, the action. And, as the cornerstone of the series, the debate was continued in later episodes written by Nation.

In 'The Future Hour' the trio, now settled down in a large manor house with various others they have collected on the way and trying to establish an agrarian community, encounter itinerant trader Bernard Huxley (his name conflating those of the protagonist and the author of *Brave New World*), played by Glyn Owen. Huxley leads a convoy that scavenges in towns for food, hardware and other household goods, which they then sell to the various scattered settlements, offering to take gold in exchange, in anticipation of society eventually settling down and needing to re-establish a currency. His obsession with collecting gold is roundly mocked ('He's a nutcase,' says one character; 'Bananas,' agrees another), though the idea that a precious metal might one day become a useful symbol of exchange is as logical as Wormley's wish to form a government. Others are also to express their opinions on what counts as currency in the new world. 'Cartridges – the money of the future, you mark my words,' says Tom Price, while elsewhere petrol becomes the most valuable commodity.

A more perceptive comment on Huxley's values comes from Emma Cohen (Hana Maria Pravda), when she's told that he won't let a pregnant woman in his convoy keep her child, because he doesn't want to be burdened with it. 'Burdened with it?' she exclaims. 'Who does he think's going to feed him in his old age?' And when, following a dispute, the community faces an armed confrontation with Huxley's men, its liberal values are made explicit in Greg's instructions: 'There's to be no shooting. Not unless they start it.'

Even in 'Something of Value' there is room for discussion, though much of the episode is a siege story, with Greg trapped in a barn defending a tanker of petrol against three armed men. The situation is tense and exciting enough that it could have come straight from *The Baron*, except that here it's preceded by a stranger arriving at the manor house with news of what's going on elsewhere. 'There seems to be a narrowing down of choices. Groups that have set up small communities, like you here, people grafting away to become self-supporting,' he explains. There are still some wandering nomadically, but others have entrenched themselves with their stores in armed camps. 'Things must get worse before they get better. Groups are setting up but they have different ideas and they're becoming afraid of one another. That makes them insular.' And Nation's original thread – the frail interdependence of the modern world – is expressed by one of the men trying to steal the community's petrol. 'Have you any idea what this country used to spend on imported food?' he asks rhetorically. 'Billions, billions of pounds. There wasn't a single day in your life when you didn't eat something that was brought in from abroad: grain, chocolate, rice – the list goes on and on – sugar, coffee, yes and including that tea you're swilling down.' His comrade, who has been protesting all the way through this diatribe ('Yes, yes, all right, don't go on about it'), sums up his lack of interest in such philosophising as the first man walks away: 'Know-all!' In a different context, it could be Tony Hancock and Sid James bickering.

That conversation comes in the penultimate episode of the first season, and the second man's dismissive attitude suggests that the argument has moved on; there has been a shift in the series away from the past – we are now nearly a year on from the epidemic – and towards practical preparations for the future. There is a form of evolution at work here, a struggle among ideas in which only the fittest will survive. And there's a clear direction emerging. The initial pluralism of societies is resolving into a straightforward conflict between two opposed visions: the rule of force on the one side, and a rough and ready cooperative democracy on the other. To put it another way, the clash is between different concepts of leadership, a theme that preoccupied Nation throughout his work.

All his heroes, from the Doctor to the Saint and the Baron, are portrayed as natural leaders. 'A man of forty, tough and rugged', was Nation's description in 'The Dalek Invasion of Earth' of the resistance fighter Tyler. 'Very strong face. A determined man with the qualities of leadership.' But so too are their opponents, the massed ranks of megalo-maniacs and would-be dictators represented at their apex by Davros; there is never any question as to their leadership abilities, only the direction in which they are expressed. The key distinction is between those who actively seek power and those who will reluctantly accept it being passed to them, the gulf between Arthur Wormley's faux-modest 'it's up to somebody to take the power to lead' and Abby Grant's honest self-appraisal: 'I couldn't be a leader. I can't be responsible for other people's lives. I couldn't do it.' Despite their different starting positions, both are accepted as the leaders of their groups. 'Nobody doubted her authority, and no one even considered challenging it,' Nation wrote of Abby in his novel of *Survivors*. 'That she was their leader never occurred to her.'

But the nuances are more subtle here than in *Doctor Who* or the ITC shows. Wormley is evidently descended from the villains of popular fiction, surrounded by thugs acting as a private army, as was Squires (Bernard Lee), the baddie in 'The Body Snatchers' in *The Champions*, or Brigadier Brett in 'Invasion of the Earthmen' in *The Avengers*. And the name of his militia group – the National Unity Force, or NUF – carried associations not merely of the initials of contemporary trade unions (NUM, NUR, NUS, etc.), but also of Oswald Moseley's British Union of Fascists. Yet his ideas are not dismissed out of hand. He may be a dictator, but he believes he's acting in the best interests of his own community, and he's a much more carefully shaded character. When he argues for the need to stop people hoarding supplies so that they might instead be distributed fairly, the scene comes immediately after we've seen Vic Thatcher and Anne Tranter stockpiling goods for purely selfish reasons. Given the extreme situation in which the survivors find themselves, the need for strong leadership is ever more apparent and urgent. And although Wormley's expansionist ambitions are portrayed as morally objectionable, his core philosophy is not far removed from that of Jimmy Garland, a character portrayed far more sympathetically.

Played by Richard Heffer, Jimmy Garland, the 14th Earl of Waterhouse, is one of Terry Nation's great creations, the ultimate embodiment of the boys' adventure stories he read as a child. As a fourth son, Garland had no expectation of ever inheriting the earldom or the estate, Waterhouse, that went with it, but in the wake of the epidemic, he is the sole survivor and he feels that his hour has come at last. His only problem is that the ancestral home has been commandeered by a group of survivors led by a man named Knox (Peter Jeffrey), and he's now engaged in a one-man war to reclaim what he considers his rightful inheritance – indeed the episode that introduces him is titled 'Garland's War'.

Before the plague, he tried to keep himself amused galloping around the globe, desperately seeking out expeditions to the Amazon, the Zaire river, the poles, anywhere that offered him the hope of excitement. Yet he was forever chafing at the bit. 'Wherever white man had not trod before, I was there. But my kind were rather running out of world,' he explains. 'You'd scale some unconquered peak, get to the top and like as not find a television camera. Hack your way through darkest jungle and come face-to-face with a film crew shooting nature pictures. There just wasn't much left.'

'You should have been born two hundred years ago,' remarks Abby Grant, and Garland puts her right: 'Oh, no. Now's the time to be alive, now's the best time of all.' His intention is to replace Knox and establish himself at the head of a neo-feudal society. 'I am better equipped and trained to administer the running of an estate than any of them,' he insists. 'I suppose it might sound paternal, but it would always be benevolent. I'd put as much into that society as anyone else, and they'd all have a say in what went on.' This is what his family has been doing for centuries and he sees no reason to stop now. 'Wouldn't it be better just to join them?' Abby asks. 'Do you have to be the leader?' He simply looks at her, raising his left eyebrow as though he were Simon Templar. She laughs: 'Yes, I suppose you do.'

For Abby has fallen under the spell of this impossibly good-looking hero, living in a secret den in the woods, revelling in his booby-traps and ambushes, staying always one step ahead of Knox's men. He hunts his own food, keeps a decent drinks cabinet and is romantic enough to light two cigarettes at once and then pass one to her, in the time-honoured manner popularised by Paul Henreid in the 1942 film *Now, Voyager*. (In the novel of *Survivors*, Knox lights his own cigarette before offering one to her, a basic breach of etiquette that – in the lexicon of a smoker like Nation – signals he is not to be trusted.) While aristocratic pedigree ought perhaps to mean nothing in this fearful new world, it takes more than a global epidemic to wipe out generations of breeding, and anyway Garland's vision of Waterhouse as 'a self-supporting estate' is perfectly in tune with Abby's own thoughts for the future. Quite rightly, he's also a man of honour. When Abby negotiates a ceasefire so that the two rivals might attempt to negotiate a settlement, Knox is confident that Garland will come unarmed: 'He's given his word. That's one thing we can depend on.' Which naturally allows Knox to break his own word and have Garland seized, despite Abby's protests. 'Oh, to hell with promises!' he says. 'Those are old standards: a man's word being his bond, contracts, treaties. Things like that don't apply anymore, we just do or say whatever is expedient. There are no Queensbury Rules for survival.' As the Doctor before him has found out, and Roj Blake will later discover, decency is often the weak point in the armour of a hero.

The episode ends with Abby asking Garland to come away with her. But he refuses, because 'Nothing's settled yet, the war's not over.' He clearly understands the convention observed by the old 1920s thriller heroes, the likes of Richard Hannay or Bulldog Drummond, that a real man doesn't win his woman with words, but with deeds. 'Shall I see you again?' she asks. He promises, 'I'll find you.'

And of course he does. In 'A Beginning', the final episode of the first season, he returns, literally riding in on a white charger (it's named Jasper, even if that is the name of the archetypal Victorian villain), to whisk Abby off to a picture-postcard country cottage on his estate, which he keeps for those times when he needs some privacy. While we've been away, following events with Abby and the others, Knox has broken his neck in an accident and the people at Waterhouse have come to Garland asking for his guidance, thereby allowing him to emerge as the rightful moral leader he was destined to be. Wearing riding boots and a burgundy blouson, unbuttoned to reveal a manly chest and a medallion, he shows Abby what she's been missing. 'You need looking after,' he tells her. 'What do you fancy? There's rabbit – I expect you're rather fed up with that. Venison, but it's a bit high. What I can offer you is my speciality: oxtail with haricot beans.' When we cut back to them, they're sharing a post-coital glass of champagne (he's wearing a silk dressing-gown now) and he's trying to persuade her to stay with him, using a neat line in post-apocalyptic pillow talk: 'The world's a marvellous place. It always was, it was the people that turned it sour. We could help to sweeten it.' He's also good at a kind of existential romanticism: 'I know how to face facts. We must be what we are, do what we must do.' When Abby wonders whether they can just leave their communities behind, he replies: 'They can do without me, just as your people can do without you. All that's indispensable is what *we've* got: you and me.'

Abby can hardly fail to be tempted by such a fabulous offer, but at the very end of the episode, it's swept into irrelevance by the news that there has been a sighting of her son, Peter, for whom she spent much of the first half of the series looking, and for whose survival she has never quite given up hope. Hopes have been raised and dashed throughout the story – Abby went to Waterhouse in the first place because she'd heard there were boys there of Peter's age – but this time it seems the news is both positive and genuine.

It was a surprisingly cheerful note on which to end a series that had been dark and downbeat for the majority of its run. The show had been a moderate success, attracting an audience big enough to warrant the commissioning of a second season, though the critics were for the most part lukewarm. Praise came from Shaun Usher in the *Daily Mail* – 'At times, Nation mastered the H.G. Wells format, so effective in *War of the Worlds*, by which extraordinary events are set in actual, small-scale landscapes' – but the *Guardian* was ambivalent ('impressive, creepy, but a bit comic-strippy'), with its reviewer Nancy Banks-Smith, a normally reliable guide, distinctly underwhelmed: 'a perfectly passable pastime,' she concluded, but 'you wouldn't accuse it of being ambitious.' And Stanley Reynolds in *The Times* was disappointed: 'It has slowed down considerably since the initial episode,' he wrote, five shows in. 'I had hoped for some perhaps classic SF from Terry Nation, and it has just not been forthcoming.'

Perhaps Reynolds's mistake was expecting science fiction at all, for the show didn't fall comfortably into that bracket. The title sequence showed a scientist dropping a flask, presumably containing the virus, followed by a montage of air travel shots and passport stamps, to indicate the rapid spread of the contagion around the world, before a bloodstain seeps over the image to fill the screen. The imagery is thus drawn from the thriller genre rather than from science fiction, and even then it applies only to the opening; the tone for the remainder is more akin to an historical drama, albeit one set in a future history of deindustrialisation. *Survivors* makes absolutely no attempt to explore the science fiction potential of the story.

Instead the world we encounter, once we have left London behind in the first episode, is an entirely recognisable contemporary Britain. Much of the series was filmed on location, and the shots of deserted English countryside gave it a beautiful if slightly unsettling feel, the emptiness emphasised by the absence of incidental music (omitted because a strike at the BBC meant the production schedule was absurdly tight). The scale may have been small – 'the Four Shetland-Pony Riders of the Apocalypse', as Shaun Usher described it – but it was entirely effective. And the low budget meant that, as with all the best BBC dramas of the era, the focus was entirely upon the script and the actors. Many of these latter, incidentally, had already appeared in Nation's work, perhaps inevitably given the diversity of his career thus far: Talfryn Thomas was making his fourth appearance, but there were also Lucy Fleming from 'Invasion of the Earthmen', Glyn Owen from 'Imposter', Hana Maria Pravda from *And Soon the Darkness*, George Baker from 'Chain of Events', and Peter Copley and Peter Jeffrey from an episode each of *The Saint* ('The Sign of the Claw' and 'The Crime of the Century' respectively). The landscape, and the people within it, were familiar, but the texture was deeply disquieting.

The distance that Nation had come as a writer over the last fifteen years was highlighted when the episode 'The Future Hour' was scheduled immediately after a rare television screening of *What a Whopper* ('written by Terry Nation,' noted the *Guardian*, 'who's seen to better effect in the next programme'), but the overall tone of pessimism was not unprecedented. Ever since he had encouraged his most famous monsters to run rampant through the streets of swinging London in 'The Dalek Invasion of Earth', Nation had been exploring ever darker material and, left to himself, *Survivors* too would have been even more bleak. He wrote seven episodes and helped create the shape of the overall series, but four episodes were also contributed by another writer, Jack Ronder, and two by Nation's old friend Clive Exton, writing here under the pseudonym M.K. Jeeves.

There was no problem with the latter – Exton was a great television writer and one of his scripts, 'Law and Order', is among the most celebrated of the *Survivors* episodes – but Ronder's work seemed to go against the grain of Nation's vision. It was not simply that he wrote the episodes that saw the community established, giving a more domestic focus to the story, but that the emphasis was a little wayward. In his story 'Revenge', Vic Thatcher and Anne Tranter meet again for the first time since she left him for dead in their quarry hideaway (his legs had been crushed under a tractor), and the episode rapidly descends into melodrama with Anne, a character full of interesting potential, now cast in the simple role of soap opera bitch. The wheelchair-bound Vic, meanwhile, has been given the job of teaching the children in the community, and there is the beginning of a discussion about what should constitute education in these circumstances — whether learning sums is necessary, for example, or the history of ancient Rome — but such concerns are soon forgotten when Anne tries to murder him before he can exact his revenge on her.

It was a long way from the harsh reality that Nation heard about from his cousin, a paratrooper captured by the Germans at the 1944 Battle of Arnhem and marched off to the east. 'One night, many years afterwards when he was drunk, he told me about it,' remembered Nation. 'This was survival, he said, when your best friends, the people you care for, became your enemy. If they had a potato in their pocket, you'd want to steal it because that was survival. I knew the drive to live was very powerful and that's what I wanted to investigate.' In 1972 he had talked about his ambitions for his own work, suggesting a certain impatience with the restrictions he felt under and a desire to move away from escapism: 'I'd like to be able to write a show that made people turn off on occasions, to feel some emotion, either hate or loathing or fear or disgust or something. But really to feel something again. I would just like to outrage and shock and horrify and make people know they're watching something on television, to know at least that they're alive.'

Survivors was a starker piece of work even than 'Genesis of the Daleks', but it never lived up to his aspirations, and was never likely to, given its time slot of 8.10 p.m. on a Wednesday evening, before the 9 p.m. watershed that was intended to demarcate family viewing from more adult themes. There wasn't much appetite at the BBC for such an extreme tone anyway. Even as Nation was writing the pilot in 1973, the corporation pulled the plug on Nigel Kneale's fourth and final *Quatermass* story, which had already started preliminary filming, ostensibly for budgetary reasons but also, as Kneale saw it, because the depiction of a near-future Britain torn apart by rival gangs of thugs, vigilantes and security forces was too much for the BBC to take; it 'didn't suit their image at the time; it was too gloomy'. Nation was aware that he had created a great series and couldn't help but be disappointed with its realisation: 'This one was, I thought, important, and I'd like to have done it better, I'd like it to have been a better show.'

Even if the production didn't quite live up to his concept, however, Nation did have the satisfaction of having finally brought to the screen an original series of his own. After nearly two decades of false starts, dating back to *The Fixers* on radio, and fifteen years after the BBC passed up on *Uncle Selwyn* as a pilot for a proposed television series, *Survivors* was unequivocally his creation, and it had been commissioned for a second season. As it turned out, however, he was to have no further involvement with the show, having fallen out with the producer, Terence Dudley, who was, he declared, 'thick as a board'. Perhaps even worse, he had also fallen out with an old friend and colleague, Brian Clemens, over claims that he had stolen the idea for *Survivors* in the first place.

Chapter Thirteen

Surviving

Terry Nation's problems on *Survivors* started with the selection of a producer for the series. *The Incredible Robert Baldick* had been produced by Anthony Coburn, and Nation discussed the new project with him, since it too was originally intended for the *Drama Playhouse* slot. As it turned out, however, that strand didn't come back for a fourth season, and anyway *Survivors* rapidly progressed beyond the level of a pilot into a fully fledged series. Coburn left for other shows, and in his place came Terence Dudley, who had earlier produced series such as *Cluff* and *The Men from Room Thirteen*, though his most recent and relevant success had been *Doomwatch*, several episodes of which he also wrote.

Perhaps it was Dudley's aspirations to writing that helped sour the relationship with Nation, for he came to the series with very definite ideas about how it should be shaped, and few of them matched the original vision. 'I fell out instantly with the producer, Terence Dudley,' remembered Nation. 'He didn't see it at all. Not at all.' The problems, he said, began very early on, and he used to cite a pre-production meeting at which Dudley insisted that, in the event of such a massive disaster, the BBC would continue to broadcast. This argument was, in Nation's view, indicative of the man's inability to grasp the concept of the series fully, though one might feel that he exaggerated the level of what he viewed as naivety. Dudley's point was not entirely fanciful, as Nation, to whom the radio had been so important during the war, might perhaps have recognised. A couple of years after *Survivors*, the government and the BBC began working together on plans for how to respond to a nuclear attack, and even got as far as scripting the initial announcements: 'This is the Wartime Broadcasting Service,' it was to begin. 'This country has been attacked with nuclear weapons . . .' It was not unreasonable to assume that, faced with civil disorder following a deadly pandemic, the government would see broadcasting as being among its highest priorities, an essential part of keeping alive at least the illusion of authority.

Nation evidently won the argument, for the BBC is conspicuous by its absence in the series, but it didn't set the two men off on a good footing. And others involved in the series noticed that Dudley was not a man who easily forgot disputes. Carolyn Seymour, around whose character of Abby the entire first season revolved, ran into problems with the producer even at the stage of contract negotiations. 'It was a tortuous affair, because I was pushing the envelope a little bit and we were asking for a little bit more money than they were used to paying,' she recalled. 'That was one of the problems, that he lost ground, and he had to give up some things he didn't want to give up.' Others too fell foul of Dudley, including Clive Exton and the writer Michael J. Bird, who had been commissioned to write three scripts but left the project after the first episode he submitted was rejected.

From Nation's point of view, a large part of the problem was that there was no script editor to act as a buffer between himself and the producer. Officially he himself was being retained as script consultant, but – isolated in Lynsted Park, with a heavy writing schedule – his ability to shape the continuing storylines was extremely limited. And while Dudley might have conceded the point about the BBC, much of what emerged on screen was determined by him. It was significant, for example, that the discovery at the end of 'A Beginning' that Abby Grant's son Peter is probably still alive was not in Nation's original script for the episode. Its late addition allowed the season to end on an optimistic note, as well as preparing the ground for Abby's departure from the series altogether, a development which Carolyn Seymour believed was already in Dudley's mind long before she learnt of it.

The disputes with Dudley meant that for Nation the creation of *Survivors* was not a particularly happy experience, and the bitterness was evident in interviews given years later. 'He wanted to get the electricity turned back on. That was their main aim by the third episode. I could have fought him, and I could have won on every possible occasion, but I was trying to write the episodes, and it gets so exhausting to fight every inch of the way.' Nation was probably overstating his ability to emerge victorious from any conflicts, but the note of weariness was genuine enough. Pennant Roberts, who directed five episodes of the first season, remembered him chiefly for his absence: 'He was basically quite a shy man, who kept himself very much to himself down in Kent.'

Nation's enthusiasm for the series was not increased when Brian Clemens initiated a court case against him for allegedly stealing his idea in the first instance. While the two men were working together on *The Avengers* and *And Soon the Darkness*, said Clemens, 'I came up with this idea called *The Survivors*, about a holocaust that destroyed the world and what the people did. I couldn't get it off the ground with London Weekend Television, but then I should think a year later, suddenly I read in the papers that the BBC is doing a series called *The Survivors*, and it was absolutely my idea. What pissed me off – I didn't mind him stealing the idea – was that he was so lazy he didn't even change the title!' To make matters worse, he thought the series that emerged did no justice to the concept at all: 'They did it ever so badly. It became a sort of tract on how to survive. Oh, it was awful.'

The lawsuit was brought in the spring of 1975 and dragged on for nearly a year before, in May 1976, Clemens decided that the only beneficiaries were going to be the lawyers and he abandoned the case. 'After I spent a few thousand pounds, I realised it was a bottomless pit,' he said. 'I pulled away.' Since it never reached a full court hearing, it is impossible to know what Nation's defence against the accusation of plagiarism would have been, but one can perhaps assume that he would have been able to cite large parts of his own previous writing to demonstrate that *Survivors* fell clearly into that body of work, from the title onwards. (Though it should be noted that there is no copyright in titles.)

Nor was the idea itself particularly original. Many post-apocalyptic fictions had concerned themselves with the fate of human society in the wake of near-extinction, from Jack London's *The Scarlet Plague* (1912) through George R. Stewart's award-winning *Earth Abides* (1949) to John Christopher's *The Death of Grass* (1956) and John Wyndham's *The Day of the Triffids* and *The Chrysalids*, traces of all of which can be seen over the course of the series, whether deliberately or not. Indeed the estate of John Wyndham might have had cause to look quizzically at the series, for there are some very obvious nods to *The Day of the Triffids*, which also featured the proliferation of small communities in the wake of an apocalyptic event, an attempt to impose martial law by the Emergency Council for the South-Eastern Region of Britain, and a widespread belief that help would come from across the Atlantic: a 'Micawber fixation on American fairy godmothers'. Much of the thinking articulated by Nation is foreshadowed in the same book. 'There won't always be these stores,' a character explains, arguing that the survivors must go 'back and back and back until we can – *if* we can – make good all that we wear out'. Wyndham's novel ends with a colony of survivors on the triffid-free Isle of Wight looking across the Solent at a land under enemy occupation. Similarly the suggestions of empty streets in *Survivors* are familiar from H.G. Wells's *The War of the Worlds*, while the 1953 film version of that book featured a church full of the dead, an image that recurred in Arthur Conan Doyle's *The Poison Belt*: 'The church was crammed from end to end with kneeling figures,' notes Malone the narrator, one of only five people to have survived the end of humanity (as it seems). 'It was a nightmare, the grey, dusty church, the rows of agonised figures, the dimness and silence of it all.'

Given the literary precedents, alongside Clemens's feeling that 'I didn't think they made the series I wanted to do,' it's not easy to see how a charge of copyright infringement could have been made to stick, even if he were correct that Nation was inspired by his concept. But the episode ruptured the friendship between the two men, and they remained estranged for nearly two decades until Clemens brought the dispute to an end in the mid 1990s. 'I wrote to Terry and said: Look, I want to bury the hatchet; we were always good friends before. And he wrote back and said: God, I wish I'd written this letter to you.' They continued to correspond for the last couple of years of Nation's life.

Combined with the disputes with Terence Dudley, this distressing affair did little to endear Nation to the idea of further work on *Survivors*. Even before the first season ended in July 1975, a second had been commissioned and Dudley was writing to Nation, discussing which actors should be retained: 'All the regulars are available with the exception of Carolyn Seymour. Her availability in future is very much in doubt and I think we should forget about her.' The final plot twist of 'A Beginning' had suggested that Abby wouldn't be making a reappearance, but the decision still came as a kick to Seymour: 'It was a shock, it was a blow, I certainly was horrified.' Abby was not the only casualty of Dudley's new approach to the series. 'Thinking hard about Garland,' he wrote to Nation, 'I feel that the character has limitations and that he will counter audience identification. I think the "Roger Moore" cardboard is ideal for the hokum series with the stylish tongue in cheek approach. Audiences for this sort of thing escape in fantasy and are voyeurs of the antics of superman.' Arguing that the bulk of the correspondence he received from viewers was about how they identified with the everyman normality of the characters, Dudley dumped Garland and began to shape the future direction of the series so that it depicted a more settled farming community.

At this stage, in late 1975, Nation was still officially part of the team. He withdrew from the role of script consultant, but was pencilled in to write four episodes in the forthcoming season, and was even commissioned to write two of them, with half-fees being paid upfront. And the letters from Dudley continued to arrive, all of them perfectly friendly and courteous, though they remained unanswered. It wasn't until January 1976, when the delivery dates for the two scripts had passed with no sign of anything having been written, that Dudley allowed himself to express his true feelings in an internal memo. 'In my judgement Terry Nation can't give the programme the sort of scripts it needs at present. He is unhappy writing "character" and "atmosphere" which is the requirement,' he claimed, adding a hint of his own frustrations from their previous collaborations: 'I don't want, as in Series One to commission scripts from him that have to be drastically re-written by me.' There is little to support such a claim – save that infelicitous resolution to Abby's quest tacked on to the end of the first season – but it was an indication of how strained the relationship had become. The commissioned episodes were cancelled, with an agreement that the advances already paid were to be recovered from the royalties due to Nation over the coming season.

A further twenty-five episodes of *Survivors* were made over the course of two seasons in 1976 and 1977. Nation had no involvement at all, though he was, of course, still being paid his format fees. (Roger Hancock's negotiating was paying dividends; when the BBC suggested a payment of £175 per episode for the third season, Hancock held out for and won £200 – even allowing for inflation, this represented an increase of nearly 40 per cent on the first contract.) With both Nation and Clive Exton having left, the only writer to survive was Jack Ronder, his scripts augmented by contributions from Don Shaw, Martin Worth and Roger Parkes – all of whom had worked on *Doomwatch* – as well as an episode apiece from Roger Marshall, a veteran of *The Avengers*, and from Terence Dudley himself, who was unquestionably the most influential figure in the series, the one constant factor running through all three seasons. There were also three scripts by the actor Ian McCulloch, whose character, Greg Preston, emerged as the most powerful figure in the absence of Abby. 'I was happier with the same format and the same style that Terry Nation did,' he was later to say. 'It was an action adventure as far as I was concerned, and when it got into what I consider the feebler plots, the more philosophical plots, I found them drawn out, boring, banal.' Convinced that the show had lost its way, he was reluctant to return for the third season at all, and only agreed to appear in the two episodes that he scripted, though his presence looms large throughout.

The post-Nation *Survivors* had a very different feel to the original. It opened with a fire that wrote out some of the peripheral characters, and saw Greg and the now-pregnant Jenny set up a new community with Charles Vaughan (Dennis Lill), a former architect who had appeared in one of Jack Ronder's episodes the previous year. Much of this second season was concerned with the maintenance of their settlement, the practical difficulties of establishing a sustainable technology, and there was noticeably less action than in Nation's work. But certain episodes, such as 'The Chosen' and 'New Arrivals', both written by Roger Parkes, continued to explore alternative social structures and the nature of leadership. There was also Ronder's excellent two-part story 'Lights of London', depicting a rat-infested city, where five hundred survivors huddle in the Oval cricket ground and – following the example of *The Day of the Triffids* – plan their escape to the Isle of Wight. They are ruled over by yet another power-hungry leader, Manny (Sydney Tafler), and the blackouts and the scenes set in Tube tunnels evoke the Blitz in a way that even Nation should have appreciated. Manny ends his broadcasts to his people with the catchphrase 'TTFN', the sign-off popularised by the charlady Mrs Mopp in Tommy Handley's *ITMA*, even though his authoritarianism clearly places him on the wrong side of such imagery.

The third season took another turn again. Greg had departed for Norway in a hot air balloon at the end of the previous year, promising to return, and the survivors moved on from the settlement they had so painstakingly established, spending most of the twelve episodes on the road. Again there were some strong and celebrated episodes: Don Shaw's 'Mad Dog' and Ian McCulloch's 'The Last Laugh', in the latter of which Greg becomes infected with smallpox and acts as a kind of suicide bomber, harbouring within himself a biological weapon as he inveigles his way into the camp of yet another warlord. But there was also a certain lack of focus, as well as a not entirely convincing restoration of elements of pre-plague civilisation: steam trains are put back in action, it is discovered that the Scottish Highlands have been largely unaffected by the infection and, in the final episode, the National Grid is switched back on to provide power.

The series did, however, end on a suitably intriguing note as the laird, McAlister (Iain Cuthbertson), sits down to a romantic candlelit dinner with his housekeeper, candles now being once again an optional extra rather than a necessity. The implication is that, after all the discussions on social organisation and all the different structures we have encountered, it is the quasi-feudal society of the pre-plague Highlands that has survived best of all. It was an image not far removed from Nation's evident attraction to Jimmy Garland's hereditary claim, but if he recognised it as such, it did nothing to assuage his scorn at the restoration of power with the switching on of the hydro-electric plant. 'They seemed to think that if you get the electrical systems turned back on, everything would be just hunky,' he mocked. 'Which was silly.'

By now the series had departed entirely from Nation's original vision. Despite his comments about the need to relearn basic technologies, the truth was that he wasn't much interested in the practicalities of how that would work, but rather in the psychology and human drama of surviving the collapse of civilisation. He toyed with the principles of self-sufficiency without being committed to exploring the implications. Beyond that, his concerns lay in humanity's instinctive drive to ensure the continuation of the species, as opposed to the survival of individuals. The idea of getting the lights switched back on had no appeal to him, however symbolic it seemed in the mid 1970s, with the power cuts of the Heath years still fresh in the country's memory. Nation's model was essentially that of the western, the struggle against nature and the attempt to establish a morality in a lawless land.

His conception of how the story might have developed was hinted at in the novel he wrote based on the first season, which was published in 1976. Not strictly a novelisation, since Nation had no access to the episodes written by Ronder and Exton or to the characters developed therein, it opens with an extended treatment of the first three instalments, before diverging sharply from the television narrative. The core of the book, however, remains the tale of Abby Grant. In this context it should be acknowledged that having Abby as the central figure was an unusual development at the time, a fact of which Nation was justifiably proud. 'I'm one of the few people who had an adventure show with a woman as the lead,' he noted in retrospect, 'because I saw she was mother, she was the future, she was all of those things.' At the time, perhaps reflecting on his own limited experience of self-sufficiency at Lynsted Park, he argued that the choice of a female protagonist was a simple recognition of reality: 'Women are better survivors than men. They are tougher than men physically and psychologically.' Carolyn Seymour shared much the same perspective. 'I become a matriarch because I'm the only one with a sense of purpose,' she told the press. 'It's very good propaganda for Women's Lib, and I'm all for that – in a gentle way.'

But while the central characters remain strong, there is in the novel no significant development, despite the extra space available. As a television writer, and as a devotee in childhood of the thriller genre, Nation remains wedded to action and dialogue, allowing little scope for interior depictions of his characters; we seldom know what they think, only what they express in words to others. Perhaps the one exception is Greg, whose reluctance to commit himself is more convincing on the page, and who does emerge as a more believable figure. His detachment, his sense of relief at having unwanted responsibilities lifted from his shoulders by the plague, is more thoroughly fleshed out, but again this tends to be through his own words, with even the smallest changes resonating. 'I was wrong, Jeannie,' he says to the dead body of his wife, who has perished in the epidemic. 'I thought you were the sort of bitch who would survive just to spite me.' The word 'bitch' was not in the television script and adds considerable weight to his comments, even though it remains an unlikely thought to articulate aloud to a corpse.

It is not a wholly successful book. Too episodic, too reliant on dialogue, it largely confirms Nation's own assessment: 'I don't come easily to prose, I don't find prose an easy form to write in.' Even in the moments when the writing almost breaks free from its origins to achieve its own identity, there are still traces of the staccato rhythms of a television script:

> Some roads had almost vanished, and passage along many was all but impossible. Weeds and saplings and briar buried the land and what stood on it. Only the small pockets of cultivated ground around the communities remained. Like islands in a rising green sea. The survivors found the limits of their worlds at the edges of their small holdings. They ate, and they worked. And they worked to eat. The demands of maintaining that cycle allowed them little else.

Even so, there are good things about the book. The tone throughout is low-key and unsensational, despite the much more pessimistic – or, one might argue, realistic – narrative. Vic Thatcher, left abandoned in the quarry with his legs crushed, dies alone, rather than being found alive months later, while Abby carries out euthanasia on a member of the community with terminal cancer, and other survivors resort to cannibalism: 'When there was nothing left, some conquered their disgust at eating human flesh and lived on.' Most shocking of all, Jimmy Garland, whose war with Knox is recounted in the novel (though at a different point in the timeline) doesn't live long enough to ride in to whisk Abby away, but instead dies of a wound that turns gangrenous. In a way of which Terence Dudley would probably have approved, his death isn't even depicted directly, but only mentioned in passing by Abby later on. Meanwhile the threat posed by Arthur Wormley's National Unity Force looms larger than it did on television; the community has to learn to live with the ever-present risk of attack.

This grim note, apart from being closer to Nation's original concept, is also indicative of a general attempt to make the material more adult, in contrast to the television version, which had been criticised by some as juvenile. ('It goes down very well indeed with children,' noted Nancy Banks-Smith in the *Guardian*.) That hadn't been Nation's intention, but he had been restricted by the pre-watershed scheduling and by conventions over which he had no control. Most absurdly, the BBC had refused to allow a shot of Abby and Jimmy Garland in bed together, since they weren't married, reflecting a moralistic attitude that permeated British broadcasting at the time; in 1977 the ITV sitcom *Robin's Nest* had to get special dispensation from the Independent Broadcasting Authority to show an unmarried couple living together. It was perhaps in retaliation that the novel shows Abby, alone in her bed, masturbating to the image of Garland, though it's not a very convincing passage. *Survivors* was already Nation's first serious work to attempt a love interest; venturing into sex scenes was perhaps a step too far.

There is, however, one major exception to the harsh tone, a genuine lightening of the original. Clive Exton's episode 'Law and Order' had depicted the community celebrating May Day with a party, after which the former tramp Tom Price rapes and murders one of the women while he's drunk. He then frames a simple-minded resident, and the rest of the community try the man in an ad hoc court, find him guilty and execute him, before some of them discover their mistake. It's a shocking development, coming completely out of the blue and seemingly out of character, and Nation subsequently provided Price with an element of redemption, having him die a heroic death in 'The Future Hour'. In the novel, without benefit of Exton's plot, there is no rape, no murder and no need for self-sacrifice. Instead Nation lets Price live on and takes a much more generous view of the character. Far from being a killer, Price is here simply a roguish Welsh fantasist, 'a man to whom lies came more easily than truth'. He's always keen to seek refuge in fiction, so that when he reveals his knack for snaring rabbits and wins the praise of the others, he can't help but spin yarns about having been the head gamekeeper to Lord Glamorgan, with twenty men working under him. And when the group decide to arm themselves, he begins to reminisce 'about his past campaigns, his heroism and the medals that recognised it'. He remains an outsider in the group, but he is at least tolerated and accepted.

Nation was later to explain that Price was based on a man he knew in his local village, a part-time poacher who did some casual cash-in-hand work, who he thought would find a niche, however catastrophic the situation: 'this guy had scrounged around, he'd done an odd job here, an odd job there, he'd steal something, and he was a survivor right from the beginning.' But there were also surely memories of Nation's own Welsh childhood, his preference for a good tale over prosaic reality, almost as though he were imagining an alternative reality for himself in which he never became successful, never discovered a legitimate outlet for his story-telling. As Price picks up a flash car in the immediate aftermath of the plague, he imagines the response it would have elicited from his old acquaintances. 'Damn! Look at that! There's old Pricey in a bloody Rolls-Royce!' he says aloud with, we are told, 'his Welsh ancestry strong in his voice'.

The biggest change made in the novel, however, lies in the ending. Five years on from the advent of the plague, Abby has come to the conclusion that the British climate simply isn't amenable to the level of subsistence farming required, let alone to building something more durable. So she proposes to the group that they relocate: 'I want to cross into Europe and move down to the Mediterranean. Probably Italy.' It's an argument whose foundations had been laid by Greg some time earlier: 'In this country we have only about six months when the ground is workable. In that time we have to grow enough to eat day by day, enough to set aside for a six-month winter. Provide winter feeding for our stock. Collect fuel. There's no way it can be done.' However daunting the prospect of such a move, the alternative of remaining, with the ever-present danger from Wormley's

NUF, proves too much for the survivors and, reluctantly, they agree to the undertaking. And so the community uproots itself and begins the long trek to the south coast, where they hope to find the means to cross to France.

There, just outside Dover, with most of the group having already sailed, Abby finally comes face-to-face with her long-lost son Peter, for whom she has spent so much time searching in the wake of the outbreak. And, before he realises who she is, he shoots her dead.

If it's a somewhat melodramatic conclusion to the novel, as fanciful in its way as Garland's appearance on a white charger, it is at least in tune with the sense of hopelessness and the haphazard violence that has punctuated the whole story. Abby's journey began when she woke up from her bout of the disease to find her husband dead (a particularly severe shock in the screen version, since it meant the loss of the ever-likeable Peter Bowles), and death has stalked her ever since, an unpredictable interruption to life. Nation's artistic vision was becoming increasingly dark, although – given his chosen medium of populist television – the bleakness manifests itself in a slightly different manner to that of much contemporary fiction.

There weren't, for example, the moral ambiguities and confusions of John le Carré's novels, where the well intentioned find themselves corrupted by the actions demanded of them. Rather Nation's work still presents an essentially black-and-white world where there is little confusion about who are the good guys and who the villains, even if the baddies are more subtly written than before. This is not a post-apocalyptic world in which society and community collapse altogether – as in Barry Hines's television drama *Threads* (1984), where even language falls apart in the aftermath of a nuclear attack – for there is still an optimism about humanity and morality. But there is also an abandonment of any suggestion that virtue might bring its own reward. The senseless brutality and bloodshed were almost reminiscent of the new generation of horror writers led by James Herbert, author of the best-selling *The Rats* (1974), *The Fog* (1975) and *The Survivor* (1976), except that in Herbert's novels it is always clear who the victims are going to be; characters appear, have their life histories sketched in and are dispatched within the space of a few pages. With Nation there is no such certainty who will survive. A hero is as likely to die suddenly as a villain, and Abby Grant's death, just at the moment of escape to a better future, just when she has discovered that her son has survived against all the odds, is the most startling manifestation of the theme.

Rather less convincing is the way in which the departure for Europe feels as though it's tagged on to the end. The whole episode is covered in barely thirty pages, and one can't help thinking that it would have made for a more coherent narrative if the group had embarked upon the project earlier, if the trek towards sunnier climes had been explored at greater length. Or, indeed, if they had got further than merely crossing the Channel, which was, Nation explained in later interviews, how he'd wished the story to develop. 'Really what I wanted was to have them go back to the valley of the Indus. They have to go across the English Channel to France, and then find some way across the Mediterranean, and this was on a gigantic scale which we could never do on television.'

He was right, of course, that it was entirely impractical for a television drama, but he spoke too about writing 'the novel of the length I wanted to do'. And this certainly was within his control, though not perhaps within his powers, for a book on the epic scale he was suggesting was an under-taking of a very different nature to anything he'd ever written. What did emerge was a hybrid that didn't convince as a novel in its own right, while being too far removed from the television storyline to satisfy many viewers. By sticking too closely for too long to the scripts he had already written, by staying with the objectivity of television rather than the subjectivity of prose fiction, Nation sacrificed the integrity of a novel that could have stood alone.

The book was published in hardback by Weidenfeld & Nicolson (who were to have published *The Incredible Robert Baldick*) and in paperback by Futura, and sold well enough to merit a sequel, particularly in light of the television series being commissioned for a third season. *Survivors: Genesis of a Hero* emerged in 1977, though it had no involvement from Nation himself, and was written instead by John Eyers. Unable to use the continuing story from television, he starts at the point where Nation's book left off, on the beach near Dover where Peter Grant has just shot his mother. The narrative then follows Peter as he rises through the ranks of the National Unity Force, before he falls foul of court politics and defects to a rival society in Wales. It's an entertaining romp through post-industrial barbarism, but has nothing to do with the television series or with Nation's conception. (Only one other book ever appeared under the name of John Eyers, a spin-off from the ITV series *Special Branch* titled *In at the Kill*, published in 1976, and it is generally accepted that it was a pseudonym.)

Nation's awareness of his own limitations when it came to writing prose, however, needs to be balanced by the success of the only other novel he wrote. *Rebecca's World*, published in his *annus mirabilis* of 1975 – when 'Genesis of the Daleks' and the first season of *Survivors* also made their appearance – was a children's book, named for his daughter, to whom, he announced, he was assigning all the royalties. It's the tale of a small girl named Rebecca, who is accidentally transported via a transmitter beam to another planet, rather in the manner of Lewis Carroll's Alice falling down a rabbit-hole. The world on which she finds herself has four suns and a wide variety of wildlife, including Silkies (bat-like creatures that spin silk as they fly), Swardlewardles (who breathe out laughing gas to render their prey helpless) and Splinter Birds (who remove splinters from people). Sadly, however, there is little now for the latter to do, for this is a world in which all the trees have been chopped down in order to feed the vast furnaces making the glass out of which the buildings, and most other things besides, are constructed. This has had unfortunate consequences for the population, since it turns out that it was only the presence of the trees that kept at bay a tribe of evil, shapeless monsters called GHOSTS (the capitalisation is Nation's own). Without the trees the GHOSTS can now prey on the people at will.

Rebecca soon acquires three companions: a deeply depressed man named Grisby, who has a Hancock-like obsession with his feet (they are, he insists, 'the sorest pair of throbbers in the entire history of feet'), an unemployed spy named Kovak, who believes he's a master of disguise, though he always remains instantly recognisable, and a would-be super-hero named Captain 'K', whose only power comes from his possession of the last stick of wood on the planet that isn't owned by the all-powerful Mr Glister. It was the Glister family who discovered how to make glass and who now control the whole planet. When the magical power of the trees became apparent, the Glisters had the last remaining specimens chopped down and the wood made into planks, from which were constructed GHOST shelters. Now, whenever the GHOSTS attack, the populace swarm into these shelters to hide, for which privilege they are charged by the grasping and wicked Mr Glister. 'Nature has endowed me with all the finest qualities a man can have,' he brags. 'I am a splendid liar, a marvellous cheat and a magnificent bully. I have made myself rich by being vicious and cruel.' There is, however, one small ray of hope. A map exists showing the location of one last tree, hidden deep in the Forbidden Lands, guarded by GHOSTS and accessible only by passing through a series of challenges and trials. And so Rebecca and her three new friends set out in the hope of saving the world.

Apart from the echoes of the Alice stories, there are also nods to *The Wizard of Oz* – a small girl and her three ill-assorted companions set off on a quest, albeit from a glass city rather than to an emerald one – and there is even a hint of the Daleks when the GHOSTS, believing that they have destroyed the last remaining tree, become hysterical in their demands that the people bow down before them. 'We are the victors!' they shriek. 'The supreme power of this planet!' And, of course, the theme of a world in which technology has triumphed over nature to the detriment of the inhabitants parallels much of Nation's thinking in *Survivors*.

The structure too is recognisably Nation. Ever since 'The Daleks', he had regularly used the device of his hero arriving on a planet in the midst of a story and having another character bring him up to speed on the history of the place. Even *Survivors* had started with the epidemic in full sway, with much of the background sketched in after the fact. The same is true here, as Rebecca's new friends fill her in on how they got to this parlous position. Similarly the perils and predicaments that they face, as well as the plans they concoct to escape, are characteristic of his work, though, as so often, it is the villain who commands centre stage. Glister is a wonderfully evil creation, a monstrously caricatured capitalist who becomes self-indulgently maudlin when he thinks about the poor. 'Call me silly and sentimental if you will,' he tells Rebecca with a sob in his voice, 'but one day I hope that everybody in this world will be penniless, hungry and in rags. With poverty on that scale I could love them all.'

The book was well received – 'a pleasant, entertaining and imaginative tale for 8 to 12s', thought the *Daily Express* – and in April 1976 it featured on the children's story-telling series *Jackanory* on BBC television, read. in five fifteen-minute episodes by Bernard Cribbins, who had a decade earlier battled the Daleks in the second Peter Cushing movie. It ran to more than a dozen printings and attracted a great many enthusiastic readers, both among children and teachers, the latter finding that it lent itself admirably to being read aloud to a class. Perhaps it was appropriate that the best prose writing of a man who worked almost exclusively in television was more suited to oral delivery than it was to solitary reading. 'I'd been reading children's stories to my daughter and to my son, and I get really very bored with some of them,' he explained. 'And I wanted a book that was going to please the adult who read aloud and please the child who was listening to it.' In common with much of Nation's work, it continued to find new audiences after his death, being released in 2010 as an audio CD, read by Paul Darrow, while early editions became highly sought after collectors' items, partly in tribute to the beautiful illustrations by Larry Learmouth.

But if 1975 was mostly a series of triumphs for Nation, he didn't exactly end the year in style. November saw the broadcast of 'The Android Invasion', his first non-Dalek story for *Doctor Who* in over a decade, and perhaps his least celebrated of all. Its low critical standing is perhaps a little unfair, for it starts tremendously well, with the TARDIS landing on what is assumed to be Earth ('Oak trees don't grow anywhere else in the galaxy,' reasons the Doctor), just outside a picture-postcard village that Sarah Jane Smith recognises as Devesham. Almost immediately the travellers find themselves in an altercation with men who wear white isolation suits and helmets and who shoot with their fingers; they also witness a soldier running off a cliff to his certain death for no apparent reason. Escaping their pursuers, the Doctor and Sarah make their way into the village, only to find it entirely deserted, until a flatbed truck arrives, from which disembark dozens of villagers who behave as though they have been brainwashed. The Doctor goes off to investigate at the nearby Space Defence Centre, leaving Sarah in the local pub, where unfortunately she is discovered – by the very soldier they had earlier seen killing himself. Nor is the Centre immune to the strangeness.

It's a great first episode, the image of the abandoned English village reminiscent of an episode of *The Avengers* or, more particularly, one of the best *Department S* stories, Donald James's 'The Pied Piper of Hambledown'. To confirm the impression, the Doctor comments that it's all a bit like the *Mary Celeste*, the original reference point for *Department S*. And while the title of the story, 'The Android Invasion', seems to give the game away, there are other details to suggest this might not be simply a reprise of the 1956 movie *Invasion of the Body Snatchers*; most puzzling of all, it appears that every coin in the vicinity is from the same year. As the story progresses, it turns out that they aren't actually on Earth at all, but on Oseidon, a planet occupied by a race of rhinoceros-looking aliens named the Kraals, who are planning to invade Earth to escape the rising radiation levels at home, and have built this replica village for the purpose of a training exercise. The invasion of the androids has not yet happened, and it can still be prevented if only the Doctor and Sarah can get back to Earth in time to deliver a warning, a process made more difficult by the fact that they have temporarily lost the TARDIS.

Thereafter, the story degenerates rapidly. Nation returns to his idea from 'The Chase' of having an android Doctor, and adds a duplicate Sarah to be on the safe side, both of whom add some nice complications, but much of the remainder of the tale involves a great deal of aimless rushing around. And at the centre of it all is a yawning hole where there should have been an explanation of why the Kraals went to so much trouble recreating Devesham. For once it is revealed that the Kraal plan is to release a virus on Earth that will kill all humans within three weeks (a not unprecedented theme in Nation's writing), the existence of the imitation village becomes entirely inexplicable. Nor is it clear why the Kraals then proceed to destroy their creation, since they are planning on leaving the planet anyway. The lack of logic is not unique in Nation's work for *Doctor Who* – or elsewhere – but here it is actively intrusive; his tendency to leave loose ends, evident as far back as *What a Whopper* and the *Hancock* episode 'The Assistant', renders the story somewhat meaningless. There are, as ever, some tense and exciting moments, but never before had there been such a sense of him having lost interest in a story quite so quickly and comprehensively. The serial still commanded audiences averaging more than eleven and a half million over the four episodes, far in excess of anything *Survivors* achieved, and higher than any of the more celebrated stories from the same season, but Kenneth Williams had it about right when he noted in his diary after the second episode: '*Doctor Who* gets more and more silly.'

By this stage, however, Nation was not much concerned by the reception of 'The Android Invasion', for he had already pitched a new idea to the BBC, and had been commissioned to write a pilot. And this time, scarred by the experience of *Survivors*, he was determined to keep a tighter grip on his creation.

Chapter Fourteen

Fighting the Federation

At conventions and in interviews in the last decade of his life, Terry Nation often told the story of how *Blake's 7*, his last major work, came into being and of his absolute confidence in the concept. 'I said to my wife: "I'm going to pitch this show today, and I know they're going to do it."' His account of the subsequent meeting evokes an era at the BBC that has long since passed. 'I wanted to do another science fiction show, a good, rousing adventure series in space,' he remembered. 'I went and pitched the idea. I said, "The Dirty Dozen in Space", and they said, "Yeah, let's do it!" It was just like that, truly. We went on a bit further and I said: "The leader is a little more Robin Hood." But that was it. Then I went home and I got a call from my agent. He said that the BBC had been in touch and said they would do it, but I had to write the first thirteen episodes.'

It sounds like an implausibly easy way to get a series made, but such things were not unheard of in the mid 1970s, in the days before bureaucracy took a firm grip of the corporation. Around the same time, David Croft and Jeremy Lloyd, then riding high with their sitcom *Are You Being Served?*, approached the head of comedy at the BBC with an idea that, said Croft, 'was so hot that I didn't want to tell him what it was', for fear of word getting out and the idea being plagiarised. 'To his eternal credit, he didn't protest or ask for a script. He told me to go ahead and do it.' The resulting pilot, *Come Back Mrs Noah*, starring Mollie Sugden as a Yorkshire housewife sent into space in the year 2050, resulted in a short series. Although it was a resounding flop, its very existence demonstrated the freedoms accorded to those with a proven track record. Over at ITV in its heyday, things could be even more straightforward. When Patrick McGoohan tried to explain his concept for a new series called *The Prisoner* to Lew Grade, the head of ATV interrupted him mid-flow. 'I don't understand one word you're talking about,' said Grade. 'The money will be in your company's account on Monday morning.'

It was true, then, that commissioning policy allowed for a much greater degree of individual decision-making on the part of executives than in later years, but even so Nation's familiar version of the origins of *Blake's 7* did not quite tell the whole story. More accurate was his 1982 account of a meeting with the BBC which was coming to an inconclusive end when he was suddenly struck by an idea for a series. 'It is set in the third century of the second calendar,' he improvised. 'A group of criminals is being transported to a prison planet. Under the leadership of a wrongly convicted patriot, they escape and get hold of a super spacecraft, then begin to wage war against the evil forces of the Federation.' He claimed that, when asked for a name, he spontaneously came up with the title *Blake's 7*. The whole thing, he added, was not so much a flash of inspiration as 'the product of desperation'.

Again, however, his memory of events, this fully formed vision of the plotline of *Blake's 7*, shouldn't be taken at face value. A memo recording his meeting on 9 September 1975 with Ronnie Marsh, the head of drama series at the BBC, shows that he pitched two separate ideas. The first concerned Dan Fog, an American who has been a policeman and a district attorney, and is also the author of a book titled *Criminal Investigation*. Now in his fifties, he becomes a professor of criminology at Oxford, moving to Britain with his younger, second wife and finding himself involved in a series of adventures through his contacts with the police and the higher reaches of government. Intended to be a 'witty, glossy thriller', it was surely conceived with at least one eye on the American market, still the great unrealised dream. It did not, however, make any further progress, perhaps because the idea of an expert being called in when all other agencies have failed seemed too reminiscent of the special agent series of the 1960s, at a time when both American and British television were moving into more straightforward police shows with *Columbo*, *Kojak* and *The Sweeney*. (The idea of an Oxford don of mature years who's also an author was strongly reminiscent of the character Robert Cullingford in the original proposal for *Department S*.)

The second proposal was received more warmly. Nation may well have pitched the idea as 'the Dirty Dozen in space', but the memo of the meeting records no such phrase, instead describing *Blake's 7* as 'cracking Boy's Own/kidult sci-fi, a space western-adventure, a modern swashbuckler'. The same note summarised the proposed plotline: 'Group of villains being escorted onto a rocket ship (transported) which goes astray and lands on an alien planet where inhabitants are planning to invade and destroy Earth. Possibly live underground.'

A script for a fifty-minute pilot was immediately commissioned, but Nation's recollection that he was expected from the outset to write all thirteen episodes of the first series was incorrect. The pilot was approved and a second episode commissioned in June 1976; this was delivered in September, more than a year after the initial meeting. By November he had been commissioned to write the first seven episodes, but still the BBC did not envisage him completing the whole series: 'it is our intention to commission other writers for later episodes although Terry Nation has agreed to write further scripts towards the end of the strand of thirteen programmes.' It was not until December 1976 that the BBC agreed in principle to him writing all thirteen episodes, and not until the following May – twenty months after the pilot had been commissioned – that a contract was signed for the remaining five shows. The initiative, it seems, came from Nation himself rather than from the BBC; determined not to repeat the experience of *Survivors*, it was he who insisted on writing the whole season, so that he didn't lose control of his work again. Meantime Roger Hancock had been busily negotiating a better deal on the fees, so that the £975 paid for the pilot had become £1,200 for each script from episode three onwards.

The resulting series inevitably faced comparison with *Star Trek*, the American science fiction series which began airing in Britain in 1969 – after production had ceased – and which had steadily acquired a cult following. There were points of similarity. In both shows a small crew on a highly advanced spacecraft (the *Enterprise* in *Star Trek*, the *Liberator* in *Blake's 7*) roam a galaxy dominated by a political structure known as the Federation, and encounter alien races and cultures in a series of weekly adventures. The differences, though, were more significant than the resemblances. Above all there were questions of tone and of the status of the protagonists. The United Federation of Planets in *Star Trek* is an essentially progressive force, envisaged as a kind of galactic United Nations, whereas the Earth Federation in *Blake's 7* is a repressive regime existing somewhere between the worlds depicted in George Orwell's *1984* and Aldous Huxley's *Brave New World*. The *Enterprise* is on an official mission 'to explore strange new worlds, to seek out new life and new civilisations', but the *Liberator* is on the run, fighting rearguard actions and engaging in guerrilla attacks on key installations. It is the difference, perhaps, between the rampant optimism of 1960s America and the doubt-ridden, nervous state of Britain in the 1970s, where few believed that the immediate future offered much hope for improvement. Even with his love of story-telling, Nation couldn't avoid the inherent negativity of his vision.

There was a similar discrepancy between *Blake's 7* and the movie that Nation cited as its inspiration, Robert Aldrich's 1967 film *The Dirty Dozen*. Both featured groups of convicted criminals embarked on a desperate mission against a fascist state, but there was a gulf between the idea of military prisoners recruited by the American army to operate behind enemy lines in the build-up to D-Day, on the one hand, and Blake's gang of renegades on the other. In *Blake's 7* there is no official force for good in the struggle against fascism, no higher authority on which to call.

More pertinent was Nation's other reference point: Robin Hood, the greatest of all English myths, the noble-born hero who makes himself an outlaw in order to fight a guerrilla war in the name of justice, the rights of the oppressed and the restoration of honest governance. Just as important as Robin's campaign is the company he keeps. The Merry Men are popularly depicted mid-feast, quaffing flagons of mead and laughing uproariously as they gather round an open fire on which a whole deer is being spit-roasted. This very English revolutionary has no time for Spartan self-denial when there's drinking, singing and general roistering to be had. It's a seductive image that has run through the national culture for centuries, and variations on the theme turn up throughout Nation's work, from *The Fixers* through *The Saint* and *The Persuaders!* to Jimmy Garland in *Survivors*. Even the Doctor – however crotchety William Hartnell was, however severe Jon Pertwee could be – is essentially cut from the same cloth: the fight against the Daleks is always conducted with a twinkle in the eye. *Blake's 7* was to be Nation's final expression of the myth, with some very deliberate echoes of Robin Hood, in terms both of character (Olag Gan is clearly derived in part from Little John) and of costume.

And yet there was the same dark twist to the tale. Robin was sustained by the knowledge that one day King Richard would return to reclaim his land from the evil Prince John and his henchmen, represented by the Sheriff of Nottingham, but for Blake and his companions there is no such king over the water, no real hope of ultimate victory, only the fact of resistance against overwhelming odds. 'Virtually all revolutionary movements, once established, are outlawed by the establishment,' Nation wrote in a document setting out the themes for the second season. 'If their cause is just, they generally emerge to overthrow the authorities and themselves become the establishment. So it is with Blake. Except that Blake will never achieve that final objective.'

Trapped in perpetual opposition and lacking any official sanction, the outlaws are cast in a different light. 'If you grew up when I did,' Nation reflected, 'it was simple to read stories about Robin Hood, and Robin Hood was the good guy, Prince John was the bad guy – very simple.' In the late 1970s, however, with Irish and Arab terror attacks dominating the news, Blake's campaign against the Federation ran the risk of looking more like terrorism than resistance. It wasn't an angle that Nation had consciously considered but he did concede that it was a reasonable interpretation: 'What set out to be a good, rousing adventure yarn started turning into something different.'

Other currents also fed into the show's concept. Paul Darrow, who starred as Kerr Avon through all four seasons and became a close friend of Nation, claimed that the name of the protagonist derived from that of the British spy, George Blake, who was sentenced in 1961 to a record forty-two years in jail, but who escaped after serving just five years and fled to the Soviet Union. 'Terry Nation, while not necessarily approving of his politics,' noted Darrow, 'liked Blake's style and stole his name.' There was also, however, a more obvious association with Sir Percy Blakeney, the hero of Baroness Orczy's classic adventure novel *The Scarlet Pimpernel* (1905), an Englishman who, with a band of followers, stages operations to rescue condemned aristocrats from the guillotine during the French Revolution. Indeed Blakeney might be seen as one of the key templates for Nation's heroes, with 'his reckless daring, his mad bravery, his worship of his own word of honour' and his inspired improvisations in moments of danger: cornered by his arch-enemy in an inn, he fills his snuff-box with pepper and offers it to his adversary. When asked why they risk their own lives to save strangers, one of the gang brushes aside suggestions of heroism in the same self-deprecating terms that the Baron and Lord Brett Sinclair would later evoke. 'Sport, Madame la Comtesse, sport,' drawls Lord Antony Dewhurst. 'We are a nation of sportsmen, you know, and just now it is the fashion to pull the hare from between the teeth of the hound.' Orczy's novel was required reading for boys in Nation's childhood and its influence was apparent in much of his writing; at one point in *The Persuaders!* Danny even refers to Brett as 'the Scarlet Pumpernickel'.

Given this rich pedigree, it was unfortunate that Blake emerged as one of Nation's less entertaining heroes. 'He was supposed to be swashbuckling and dashing and all those things,' regretted Nation, 'but I never found it, I never really gave him a chance.' He is sincere, committed to his cause and concerned for the well-being of his crew, but there is a lack of the devil-may-care hearty bravado that was surely required, and no compensating charisma. 'To a man of my spirit, opportunities are duties,' declares Rudolf Rassendyll, hero of Anthony Hope's *The Prisoner of Zenda* (1894), and it was that defiant embrace of life that Blake should have embodied as a kind of Jimmy Garland in space. Instead, as played by Gareth Thomas, a doleful-faced actor with a vague resemblance to Tony Hancock, he was, observed Shaun Usher in the *Daily Mail*, 'a thoroughly decent, rugger-playing chap, rather than a maverick anti-Establishment man-of-the-future'. Thomas himself became disillusioned with the role, and ultimately left the series that bore his character's name. 'One of the many reasons why I left *Blake's 7* was because I wasn't really quite sure where else I could go with it,' he reflected. 'I mean, within the bounds of what could happen in the series, I felt I'd explored most avenues of Blake.'

That development, however, was for the future. When the first episode of *Blake's 7* was broadcast on the first Monday of 1978, it was clear who was intended to form the centre of the story. As in *Survivors*, the first three episodes form a single, sustained narrative and, as normal with Nation, the back-story is established early on. Some four years before the start of the opening episode, 'The Way Back', Roj Blake was the leader of a revolutionary group on Earth, seeking the overthrow of the Federation, but was captured by the authorities. Not wishing to create a martyr for the cause, they brainwashed him, blocking out existing memories through intensive therapy and implanting new ones, before bringing him to court in a show trial, where he confessed his crimes and professed his loyalty to the Federation; they then removed his memory of the trial itself. Now living a normal, unexceptional life amid a population kept in 'a state of drug induced tranquillity', he is taken to a meeting of a new rebel group, who are desperate to recruit him to their cause, as a powerful symbol of resistance. But the meeting has been betrayed and Federation troops arrive to break up the illegal gathering.

'Do not attempt to resist arrest,' urges the group's leader, recalling the pacifism of Temmosus, leader of the Thals in the first Daleks story. 'No matter what the provocation, we must not resort to violence.' Like

Temmosus, he's promptly shot down along with everyone else, save Blake himself, the sole surviving witness to the massacre. Faced once again with the problem of what to do with this thorn in its side, the Federation frames Blake on a charge of sexually assaulting children and has him banished to a far distant planet, Cygnus Alpha, which – like Desperus in 'The Daleks' Master Plan' – is a penal colony. The episode ends with him on board a prison ship, setting off for exile.

Since we will seldom return to Earth in the ensuing series, our understanding of the Federation is largely shaped by what we have seen in this first episode. It's a curiously ambivalent picture. The first impression is of the borrowings from other science fiction dystopias, debts not only to the work of Orwell and Huxley, but also to the 1971 film of Anthony Burgess's *A Clockwork Orange* – in the flashbacks of Blake's brainwashing – and to one of Nation's favourite sources, Isaac Asimov's *The Caves of Steel*: the city here is another sealed dome, there are tensions between Earth and the more sparsely populated Outer Worlds, and there is a largely ineffectual dissident faction that meets in secret. But beyond the surface impression of futuristic totalitarianism, life under Federation rule remains almost entirely unexplored; we don't see the daily life of the population, what they do for entertainment, how the media operates, what the basis of the economy is, even whether there are political parties. Ultimately Nation has little interest in exploring the nature of a future society, merely wishing to establish the existence of an evil empire against which his heroes can rebel. As with the Daleks, he is evoking a militarism that harks back to the Nazis.

Yet even this is not quite such an absolute as it seems. When Blake is charged, he is assigned a lawyer named Varon to defend him. Although the guilty verdict is pre-ordained, Varon himself is an honest and honourable man who comes to believe in Blake's story of the massacre and in the trumped-up nature of the charges, even though to do so means challenging everything he believes. 'If it were true, do you realise the implication of what you're saying?' he asks. 'It would mean there was corruption at a high level of the administration.' Ultimately the truth does him no good, for both he and his wife are killed, but the fact that such people can exist and thrive within the Federation is an indication that it is not quite as monolithic in its evil as first appears. There will be further suggestions that not everyone in the Federation hierarchy is corrupted by power, and that there remain checks and balances within the system. In the second episode, 'Space Fall', the captain of the prison ship disapproves, albeit feebly, of the murderous actions of a subordinate officer, and when we first meet the brutal Space Commander Travis, he is facing a disciplinary inquiry concerning a massacre he ordered on the planet Auros; his methods, another senior officer says, represent 'the philosophy of an assassin, not a Federation officer'. This, it turns out, is not the stark simplistic evil of the Daleks, but a more subtly delineated society, in which the structures and legal forms are those of a democracy sinking into dictatorship with an increasingly powerful and autonomous security state. In the words of Kasabi, formerly a senior officer in the administration: 'The Federation is degenerate.'

These nuances, however, are overshadowed by the most shocking abuse of power in 'The Way Back' — not the massacre of the dissidents, nor the killing of Varon, nor even the treatment of Blake, but the fact that, in order to frame Blake, false memories are implanted in children, so that they will testify to having been sexually abused by him. The ramifications aren't developed, but presumably the psychological effect of such a process is no different to a real assault. The charge of paedophilia was a particularly resonant one at the time. In 1976 the home secretary, Roy Jenkins, had asked the Criminal Law Revision Committee to look at whether the age of consent should be reduced and there were plenty of academics and experts, including the likes of future health secretary Patricia Hewitt, who supported a reduction to fourteen years of age. Briefly it appeared as though the liberalising culture of the 1960s might find a new direction to explore, and a campaigning body called the Paedophile Information Exchange sprang up to promote the cause. Then the moment passed and a media panic ensued, focused particularly on child pornography; even as the first season of *Blake's 7* was being broadcast in 1978, the legislation that became the Protection of Children Act — heavily promoted by Mary Whitehouse — was passing through Parliament. To bring such issues on to television in an early-evening drama was an intriguing decision, even though the explicit references to Blake's alleged crimes were toned down from the original script.

In characteristic Nation fashion, much of what has been established in the first episode disappears very rapidly. The child-sex conviction does not feature in later episodes, though this was a conscious decision by the production team, recognising that the public mood had become much more sensitive to the issue; when Blake's trial is revisited in 'Voice from the Past', a second-season episode written by Roger Parkes, it is conspicuously not referred to. Less deliberately, the brainwashing, which had provided such a strong visual image in the first episode, appears to have been negated by Blake's subsequent experiences, so that by the time he's on the prison ship bound for Cygnus Alpha he has reverted to his revolutionary self. When someone comments that at least he's alive, he responds vehemently: 'No! Not until free men can think and speak. Not until power is back with the honest man.'

Meanwhile he is beginning to acquire the companions who will take us through the rest of the first season: a smuggler named Jenna Stannis (Sally Knyvette), who is also an expert pilot; a cowardly thief and locksmith named Vila Restal (Michael Keating); a convicted murderer named Olag Gan (David Jackson); and Avon, a computer expert who came close to stealing five million credits from the Federation's own systems. It is the latter who will prove Blake's chief rival as leader of the group, espousing a very different value system. 'Wealth is the only reality,' proclaims Avon. 'And the only way to obtain wealth is to take it away from somebody else.' He joins the others in staging an attempted mutiny on board, but only with some reluctance. 'You're a civilised man,' urges Blake, trying to appeal to his self-interest. 'On Cygnus Alpha that will not be a survival characteristic.' Avon's casual reply – 'An intelligent man can adapt' – suggests a greater degree of self-confidence than he actually displays, for despite his protestations of independence, he remains at Blake's side, more or less loyally, for the next two seasons.

Blake's ability to convince others, however, is less impressive. He, Jenna and Avon successfully escape from the prison ship, taking control of the sophisticated *Liberator*, which has been found abandoned, drifting like the *Mary Celeste* through space, and – at Blake's insistence – make their way to Cygnus Alpha to rescue their fellow convicts. Using the teleportation facilities on the ship (as in 'The Keys of Marinus', these involve the use of bracelets), Blake ventures down on a reconnaissance mission to the surface and, discovering a blighted and benighted planet, concludes that the prospects for recruiting crew members are good: 'From the little I did see, they won't take too much persuading.' But when he attempts to do so, he succeeds in convincing only four that their future lies with the *Liberator* rather than with the primitive religious cult presided over by Vargas (played by Brian Blessed in a typically unrestrained performance). Of those four, two are killed, leaving only Vila and Gan to join. One further crew member, the telepath Cally (Jan Chappell), turns up in a later episode and, together with the *Liberator*'s computer, Zen (voiced by Peter Tuddenham), these comprise the seven characters who make up the series title.

If what we see of Blake gives little indication that he is a charismatic, inspirational leader, the same is not true of his arch-enemies, representing the Federation in its most extreme manifestation. 'Authors, unless they are careful, fall in love with their big villains,' wrote the critic Richard Usborne, and Nation had clearly saved much of his creative energy for a splendid brace of baddies, who don't appear until episode six, but who then become an ever greater presence as the season progresses. Even before they speak, Supreme Commander Servalan (Jacqueline Pearce) and Space Commander Travis (Stephen Greif) are a striking pair. He's dressed entirely in black leather, with a patch over one eye and a laser gun built in to his prosthetic left hand (the injuries are from a previous encounter with Blake), while she's clad in clinging white dresses and furs, like a cross between Hans Christian Andersen's Snow Queen and the White Witch of C.S. Lewis's Narnia, or even Lady Arabella March in Bram Stoker's feverish last novel, *The Lair of the White Worm* (1911). There's also a hint in her name of Chauvelin, the principal foe of Blakeney, the Scarlet Pimpernel, and of Severin, the narrator of Leopold von Sacher-Masoch's *Venus in Furs* (1870), though her abrupt switches between tactile flirtation and cruel disdain rather recall Wanda, the heroine of that novel. Ambitious, scheming and utterly ruthless, the two of them swagger through their episodes in the manner of the very best – and campest – pantomime rogues.

As head of the Federation's armed forces, Servalan turns to Travis, the man who apprehended Blake the first time around, and charges him with the mission of tracking the rebel down again. The crew of the *Liberator* have begun to attack outposts of the Federation – a campaign made possible by possession of a ship that can outgun and outrun any in their enemy's fleet – and there is growing concern that Blake could wreak serious damage on the empire. Some of the governments of the outlying planets are already talking about leaving the Federation, for if it can't provide security from a marauding gang of guerrillas, then its usefulness must be called into question. There is also the danger that Blake's actions are acting as a beacon for the discontented. 'Stories of his exploits are still circulating,' frets Servalan. 'They excite people. The fact that he is still free gives them hope, and that is dangerous, Travis. Hope is very dangerous.' Or, in the words of another senior figure of the Federation: 'Any damage to the Federation is attributed to Blake. The smallest incident is exaggerated out of all proportion until it becomes a major event. Blake is becoming a legend. His name is a rallying call for malcontents of all persuasions.' It is as though he has come to occupy the supposed position of Emmanuel Goldstein in *1984*, alleged to be the leader of the Brotherhood, the organisation fighting the ruling party.

Quite how these stories are circulating, however, is something of a mystery, for the rebel movement seems singularly ill-organised and misguided. The meeting in the first episode heard calls for a programme of civil disobedience in order to tie up Federation forces on Earth, thereby allowing the Outer Worlds to pursue their campaigns for independence. It was a perfectly logical strategy that only fell down when it came to proposing the sabotage of food production; starving the people into rebellion is seldom a winning tactic. In 'Time Squad' the resistance on the planet Saurian Major was so ineffectual that it has been entirely wiped out, with the exception of Cally. And in 'Project Avalon' a key rebel leader is captured and submitted to an interrogation machine that will extract information against her will, leaving Blake to stage a rescue attempt before the beans are spilt: 'Avalon knows all the resistance movements in this star sector – places, names, everything,' he explains. One cannot help but wonder at the incompetence of an organisation that would allow so much sensitive information to be in the possession of a single person, rather than distributed through a network of cells; by contrast, the Brotherhood in *1984* operates on the principle of no one person having contact with more than three or four others. As in 'The Dalek Invasion of Earth', Nation's attraction to the romanticism of resistance outstripped any practical concerns.

Despite the flawed logic, the conflict between Blake and the double-act of Servalan and Travis provides a focus for the series that drives the narrative forward and provides many of the most effective sequences. In particular, the episode 'Duel' finds Nation at his very best. Federation pursuit ships have cornered the *Liberator* in the vicinity of an unknown planet and seem certain this time to kill their quarry, when both Blake and Travis find themselves transported against their will to the surface of the planet. Here they encounter two beings, Sinofar the Guardian (Isla Blair) and Giroc the Keeper (Patsy Smart), the powerful and mysterious survivors of a thousand-year war that has destroyed the planet, whose role now is to teach others about the nature of aggression. 'You both know how to kill,' Sinofar tells the two antagonists. 'But here you must take a life. There will be no machines to make the act unreal. You must touch the life you take.'

Blake and Travis, with just one companion each and armed only with a knife, are sent separately into a forest to track each other down and fight to the death. The conflict ends with Blake triumphant but refusing to kill his enemy, admitting that he would enjoy it too much, and Sinofar returns him to the *Liberator*, apparently satisfied that he has understood the lesson: that the instinct for violence should not be indulged. Travis, of course, learns nothing at all from the experience.

Some of this is familiar ground. 'With each generation there were fewer of us. The dead vastly outnumbered the living. And still there was no victory for either side,' explains Sinofar, as she recounts the history of her world. And then the ultimate weapon was created and used. 'It wasn't a victory, it was only the end of the war. We were left with a planet made barren by radiation. Our children were monsters, or died, or were never born.' The resemblance to Skaro is unmistakable, though the phrasing here is both more elegant and elegiac. The concept of the duel had also occurred earlier in Nation's work; in 'Invasion of the Earthmen' in *The Avengers*, two of the cadets were sent out on a night survival exercise, with instructions that they were to hunt each other and that only one could return. There were echoes too of 'Arena', a 1967 episode of *Star Trek*. But the power of 'Duel' rests elsewhere, in the suggestion that violence is an integral part of human nature and evolution, touching on the theories of scientists like Robert Ardley and Konrad Lorenz, whose work was popular at the time. (Nation had cited Ardley's 1961 book *African Genesis* in the novel of *Survivors*.)

There were other moments in the first season of *Blake's 7* that returned to favourite Nation scenarios, perhaps not surprisingly given the pressure of writing all thirteen episodes. 'It was a hell of a workload for him,' said Chris Boucher, the script editor of the series, 'it was a hell of a strain.' Boucher reworked many of the drafts, with further contributions from producer David Maloney, but there was no doubt that the process pushed Nation harder than any commitment since the days of being script editor on *The Persuaders!*. 'During those thirteen weeks,' he remembered, 'I ran entirely out of ideas, and I'd sit around and walk for days, saying, "There are no more ideas, that's it! I've shot it all, and it's gone." But then something comes up and you get an opening scene, and then you get the feeling that something's there.'

Sometimes the borrowings worked rather well. The climax to 'Project Avalon' comes when the woman that Blake believes to be Avalon turns out to be a robot replica, armed with a phial containing a deadly virus that will kill the crew of the *Liberator*, a neat blend of Philip K. Dick's 'Imposter' and *Survivors*. Earlier in the episode, as Blake tries to work out a way into the heavily guarded complex where Avalon is being held, his first thought is typical Nation: 'What about ventilation shafts?' Such a means of access has proved invaluable in earlier stories, particularly in *Doctor Who*, but it turns out that this planet has an unusual climate and is entering its Long Cold, a winter that lasts for eight and a half Earth years, with massively sub-zero temperatures, and the ventilation shafts are closed off for the duration – one Nation cliché renders another obsolete. In 'Deliverance' Avon, Vila and Gan are welcomed on the planet Cephlon as the fulfilment of a long-standing prophecy on a formerly advanced world that has fallen into savagery, and the references to Erich von Däniken from 'Death to the Daleks' return. 'We're not really gods from the skies, you know,' protests Gan. 'We're just men from a spacecraft.'

On other occasions the influences are less successful. In 'Bounty' we meet Sarkoff (T.P. McKenna), the exiled former president of the planet Lindor, who has a fondness for the past to rival that of the Medievalists in *The Caves of Steel*. Some of the details are nicely done – he plays a 78 rpm gramophone record of Tommy Steele's 'Singing the Blues' and murmurs: 'Echoes of a more civilised age' – but the effect is rather that of an uninspired, budget episode of *The Avengers*, seeking to be quirky and offbeat and failing. (Nation later explained that some of the plotline was influenced by the Syrian intervention in Lebanon in 1976, though he admitted 'that 99.9 per cent of people who see that show won't see any political significance at all'.)

More explicit still are the echoes in 'The Web', which revisits the episode 'The Velvet Web' in 'The Keys of Marinus'. Here the consciousnesses of several scientists survive in a single entity called Saymon, who is suspended in a glass tank on a life support system, and who operates by proxy through humanoid assistants. For good measure, the story also throws in elements of Wells's *The Time Machine* and *The Island of Dr Moreau*. Saymon has been developing techniques of genetic engineering banned elsewhere in the known universe, and has created not only the beautiful assistants, but a race of ugly, stunted creatures called Decimas, a mutant strain of which has evolved, capable of thought and emotion. These mutant Decimas have turned hostile and are attacking the laboratory complex that houses Saymon. In retaliation Saymon wishes to release a lethal dose of radiation into the atmosphere to kill the creatures. But to carry out his plan he needs additional power cells from the *Liberator*, in exchange for which he will release the ship, currently trapped in a massive cosmic web. It's a moral dilemma reminiscent of that faced by the Doctor in 'Genesis of the Daleks': can Blake condemn an entire race to death in order to save himself and his crew? And, as in 'Genesis of the Daleks', Nation sidesteps the issue by having the Decimas break into the lab and kill the occupants.

Then there is 'Mission to Destiny', a stand-alone episode that is essentially a murder mystery story of a man beaten to death on board a spaceship. There are no witnesses and the only clue is a number, 54124, written by the victim in his own blood as he lay dying. It takes the intelligence of Avon to recognise that what looks like a number is actually a series of letters: SARA, the name of one of the crew members. 'We wanted to show that we could do an Agatha Christie story in space,' reflected Nation. 'It had all the mystery elements in it, and years later I thought, "What a dummy! I could have made a first-class movie out of that." It would have been the first space murder mystery.' He might also have mentioned that it bore a strong resemblance to a Leslie Charteris story that he had adapted as 'The Inescapable Word' for *The Saint*, which likewise features a murder victim leaving behind a cryptic message written in his own blood, in this instance the letters COP. Suspicion is directed at a former police officer, until Simon Templar learns that the dead man was of Russian origin and deduces that he had in his death throes reverted to his native alphabet. The Russian letters COP translate to the English SOR, thus pointing the finger at a character named Professor Soren. Even that was not strikingly original, being rooted in the first Sherlock Holmes story, *A Study in Scarlet*, in which a dying man scrawls the letters RACHE in blood; the police assume he was trying to implicate a woman named Rachel, until Holmes points out that 'rache' is the German word for 'revenge'.

In the final episode of the season, 'Orac', the crew of the *Liberator* triumph over Servalan and Travis in the race to acquire the ultimate computer from its creator. At the age of eighteen Professor Ensor (Derek Farr) invented a component called a Tarial cell, which became an integral part of every computer in the known universe. Now in exile, he has developed a supercomputer named Orac, in a rare outbreak of futurology by Nation. 'It is a brain, a genius,' enthuses Ensor. 'It has a mind that can draw information from every computer containing one of my cells. Orac has access to the sum total of all the knowledge of all the known worlds.' But Ensor is a dying man, and possession of the computer passes to Blake, who only then discovers that it also has the personality of its creator: a crotchety, impatient old man who has little but contempt for those less intelligent than himself. 'This wasn't a polite computer,' as Nation pointed out. In fact Orac (again voiced by Peter Tuddenham) is not far off being a rebirth of William Hartnell's Doctor, always Nation's favourite incarnation of the Time Lord.

If the first season of *Blake's 7* sometimes feels like a run-through of Terry Nation's greatest hits, it's none the worse for that. Since his move from comedy to drama, he had written more than 120 television programmes and his ability to tell a good story had not deserted him. The characters, as rich as those in *Survivors*, included some of his most memorable creations, particularly Servalan and Travis, but also Vila who has a good line in jokes about his own cowardice: 'I plan to live forever. Or die trying.' Most intriguing of all is Avon, whose professed lack of concern for anyone else, maintained throughout with a straight face, is steadily undermined by his interactions with the others. He banters with Vila and, although he makes no secret of his desire to take over the *Liberator*, he tends ultimately to defer to Blake, seemingly aware that he is not yet ready for leadership. When, in 'Deliverance', Blake asks him what it felt like to be treated as a god on Cephlon, he throws back the question with a tone of studied neutrality: 'Don't you know?' And Blake replies, with some insight: 'Yes. I don't like the responsibility either.'

When the BBC conducted an audience research report after the first season, Avon emerged as the most popular character among the *Liberator* crew, followed in order by Blake, Jenna, Vila, Cally and Gan. The same research showed an impressive reaction index rating that averaged at 67, and a definite interest in having the show continue; asked whether they wanted to see a second season, 73 per cent of the sample replied positively. While not a spectacular ratings success, it had been solidly successful, averaging an audience of 9.2 million and reaching the weekly top thirty in the final episode; scheduled against *Coronation Street* on ITV, hardly the most desirable time slot, it had managed steadily to build an audience.

Less impressed were the critics, though this came as no great surprise. *Doctor Who* had become acceptable by virtue of its age, but still popular science fiction was seldom the recipient of critical praise, and Nation's new show was no exception. '*Blake's 7* has turned out to be rather a run of the mill space adventure,' said the *Daily Express*, while Peter Fiddick in the *Guardian* thought it was 'a mix of olde-world space jargon, ray guns,

Western-style goodies and baddies, and punch-ups straight out of *The Sweeney*'. Stanley Reynolds in *The Times* was more enthusiastic, though his comments came after just four episodes, before the arrival of Servalan and Travis: 'Terry Nation's new series is straight with real villains, and it is nice to hear the youngsters holding their breath in anticipation of a little terror. Television science fiction has got too self-consciously jokey lately.' And there was one comparison that could not be avoided, whether for good or ill. 'I suppose the *Star Wars* boom sparked it off,' reflected Clive James in the *Observer*. 'Suddenly it seemed like a good idea for the Beeb to have its own space opera. Well, here it is. Activate main garbage tubes! Stand by for gunge disposal!' Or, in the words of Shaun Usher in the *Daily Mail*: 'For all those adults who pretend not to watch *Doctor Who*, and find it a shade too jokey and cliff-hanging, *Blake's Seven* will have to do. And considering that it has the kind of budget *Star Trek* devoted to coffee breaks and *Star Wars* spent on trailers, it could be a lot worse.'

George Lucas's film *Star Wars* had been released in Britain the month before *Blake's 7* debuted, having already been a runaway box-office hit in America. Its huge budget and ground-breaking special effects raised the bar for subsequent screen treatments of science fiction, far beyond a level with which the British film industry, let alone British television, could compete. 'I enjoyed and admired the film, but came away from the screening green with envy,' admitted Nation, after attending the press preview. He recognised that his own work had to take a very different tack. 'When we did *Blake's 7* we realised we had to have interesting stories because our effects would win us no friends. When the space ship went through a black hole it was someone shaking a piece of black card.' David Maloney, who went with him to the screening, concluded, 'Well that's us finished, we can't possibly match that, we're dead.' The possibility of achieving higher production values had in fact been raised early on, when the American media company Time-Life approached the BBC, seeking to put money into the show in return for world rights, but the option was rejected by Alasdair Milne, later to be become director general of the corporation but then the director of programmes. 'I do not accept,' he wrote authoritatively in a memo, the same month *Star Wars* was released, 'that there is going to be a great surge of interest in science fiction series in America.'

For many of its fans, part of the appeal of *Blake's 7* was precisely that low-budget production, a defiantly British response to American overkill. Some of the design and special effects were as good as anything the BBC had yet produced – particularly the *Liberator* itself, created by Roger Murray-Leach – but the approach to television drama had not essentially changed from the early days of *Doctor Who*. This was still 'a kind of strange, bastard medium,' in the words of David Maloney, 'which lay between the theatre and film'. Maloney, who had earlier directed 'Planet of the Daleks' and 'Genesis of the Daleks' and who produced the first three seasons of *Blake's 7*, was another who had come to *Doctor Who* with a background in theatre. As he suggests, there remained a certain staginess to the series.

Within its limitations, however, the first season of *Blake's 7* was a personal triumph for Nation, whose resolve to write the whole thing had been entirely vindicated. There were weak moments, but he had avoided the problems he encountered on *Survivors* of having his image of the show diluted by others. The volume of work this entailed meant he had even less involvement in the actual production than normal, but he did this time have a sympathetic producer and the result was exactly what he had set out to create: 'a modern swashbuckler'. In many ways it was the ultimate Terry Nation creation, a variation on the ITC action adventure stories set on the alien planets of *Doctor Who* and with the more subtle characterisation of *Survivors*. There's also Servalan, a monster almost to rival Davros, there are good jokes, the plot developments and action are relentless and a fight is seldom more than a few minutes away.

Equally characteristic of Nation, there is, running underneath the romping fun, a vein of pure pessimism in its depiction of the future; there's no sense of hope or progress in this vision of things to come. 'With its drugged, dejected masses crushed by tyrants,' noted Shaun Usher, it 'seemed to picture the future as being much the same as the present, Lord help us, only worse.' And, while not straying from his wish to entertain the audience, Nation was developing a new sense of moral ambiguity. In *Survivors* he had begun to introduce a little shading to his villains, suggesting that there might be a need in extremis for the authoritarianism of Wormley and Knox; here he left the arch-villains pure at heart in their evil, but created a cast of 'heroes' that included a murderer, a thief, a smuggler and an embezzler. Blake may have been framed, but there is no suggestion that any of the others were anything but criminals.

The season ended on a note of negativity that seemed perfectly in tune with the preceding episodes. Blake and his comrades bring the all-seeing computer Orac on to the *Liberator* and find that it's so powerful and has access to so much information that it can effectively predict the future, extrapolating from the present to see the ensuing chains of events and their ultimate consequences. And, in a wonderful cliff-hanger of an ending, Orac reveals to the crew images from the future of the *Liberator* exploding in space.

Chapter Fifteen

The Story Continues

The experience of the Dalek craze had convinced all parties – Terry Nation, Roger Hancock, the BBC – of the value of merchandising, and approaches were made early on in the development of *Blake's 7* to more than a dozen companies with ideas for everything from a video game to ice cream, from colouring books to jigsaws. However proud Nation had been of his work on *Survivors*, he was aware of the limited spin-off opportunities involved in that series and was keen to remedy the situation. 'I knew I wanted to do another science fiction show,' he said later, 'because of having had all sorts of ancillary successes with the Daleks and *Doctor Who*, like merchandising and so on.' Unlike *Doctor Who*, however, *Blake's 7* was not primarily aimed at children and few such opportunities materialised; many of the licences that were signed were never followed through, foundering on a lack of available imagery at an early enough stage. There was moreover little public appetite for those products that did make it to the shops: jigsaws, a two-inch-long replica of the *Liberator* from Corgi Toys, and the Blake's 7 Neutron Space Rifle, the latter capable of firing table tennis balls.

More encouraging were sales of related literature. There was now clearly a market for novelisations, as demonstrated not only by Nation's own *Survivors*, but even more by the success of the *Doctor Who* books published by Target. The first of these had been a reprint of David Whitaker's version of the first Daleks serial, and a further twenty titles had been added by the time two other Nation stories, *The Genesis of the Daleks* and *The Planet of the Daleks*, appeared in 1976. Nation had no involvement in either – both were written by Terrance Dicks – though of course he benefited from their sales. 'Basically you get half the money and do none of the work,' observed Chris Boucher, whose *Doctor Who* serials were also adapted by Dicks; 'which sounds reasonable enough to me.' Suitably inspired, Roger Hancock had, by

December 1976, negotiated deals for a *Blake's 7* novelisation, to be published in hardback by Arthur Barker and in paperback by Sphere.

Nation was by now committed to writing all thirteen episodes for the first season and had no time or appetite to add a book to his workload, so instead Sphere turned to an established science fiction writer, Trevor Hoyle, who had just completed his *Q Trilogy* of novels. 'Terry was happy to have someone take the chore off his hands,' remembered Hoyle, who worked from draft scripts of the first four episodes, augmented by phone conversations and meetings with Nation, to produce *Blake's 7*. He followed that with *Project Avalon*, published by Arrow Books, which rounded up a further four first-season scripts, and with *Scorpio Attack*, taken from the fourth season, which came out under the BBC's own imprint, completing a hat-trick of publishers. There were also three annuals, starting in 1979, from World Distributors, the company responsible for the successful *Doctor Who* annuals, and a monthly magazine from Marvel, that lasted for nearly two years from October 1981.

What was notable about all these publications was that they identified themselves on their covers as being part of 'Terry Nation's *Blake's 7*', with Nation's name rendered in a facsimile of his signature. This was even true of *Scorpio Attack*, which contained none of his plots at all. The same styling was not used on screen. Indeed David Maloney rejected a suggestion from Hancock that, from the second season, the credit 'series created by Terry Nation' should be changed to 'series devised by Terry Nation'; after consultations with Chris Boucher, this was felt to give too much recognition to Nation's continuing contribution. But the trend was evident elsewhere. When, in 1979, Target brought out a cheaply produced paperback about the Daleks, edited by Terrance Dicks (it contained a history of the species, various puzzles and games, and a reprint of the 1974 short story, 'Daleks: The Secret Invasion'), it was titled *Terry Nation's Dalek Special*, with his name again in his own handwriting. Similarly World Distributors brought out a series of four Dalek annuals from 1976, and they too were billed as *Terry Nation's Dalek Annual*.

'People knew about Terry and the Daleks,' reasoned Dicks, 'so there was a commercial value to having his name on the books, although he had very little to do with them.' But there was something more deliberate at work here, a conscious attempt to turn Nation himself into a brand. 'I had a very good agent and he insisted on it. I wanted to associate the name with the product,' Nation explained. 'It was a calculated effort really, selling a product. I was the product.' It's hard not to see this as preparatory work in a planned campaign to try again the recurring dream of conquering America; by identifying Nation so overtly with his successful creations of the Daleks and *Blake's 7*, it was hoped to raise his profile, enabling him to approach the US television industry from a position of strength.

Meanwhile there was a new series to write, and this time Nation was no longer to be responsible for the whole thing. 'I wanted the weight off me a little,' he was later to comment. 'I was tired by that time.' Instead he was contracted to write five episodes, the remainder being split between Chris Boucher, who also remained the script editor, and a trio of other experienced writers: Allan Prior, Roger Parkes and Robert Holmes. Three scripts were duly delivered, but when it came to what was intended to be the double-part season finale, Nation found he'd simply run out of steam. 'Terry said that he had made several efforts to write part 12 but was defeated,' recorded David Maloney in an internal memo, 'this being his seventeenth script for *Blake's 7*.' Instead the season finale was written by Boucher, who was now more involved in shaping the series.

Born in 1943, Boucher was – like Nation – an only child who had started his professional career writing jokes, in his case for *Braden's Week*, the BBC consumer show that spawned Esther Rantzen's *That's Life*, and for the comedian Dave Allen. before moving into sitcoms with, among others, a pilot, *Slater's Day* (1974) for Yorkshire TV, that starred Nation's old friend John Junkin but didn't get commissioned as a series. By the time he came to *Blake's 7* as script editor (after Robert Holmes turned the job down), he had had three serials screened on *Doctor Who*, but his new role was a major step forward in his career and he ended up writing nine episodes as well as remaining on the production team throughout. The pressure on Nation to produce the first season meant that Boucher had a greater involvement in rewriting than was normal for a script editor, but it was a relationship that seemed to work for both men. 'He didn't seem hugely protective, but then he was a pro from way back,' observed Boucher, while Nation was more generous in his praise than he could sometimes be for those who changed his work: 'Chris Boucher did a splendid job overall. I would not have approved of every change he made, but that was what he was being paid for. I think he did it terribly well.'

Nation did, however, retain considerable influence over the direction of the series, and for the second season Hancock negotiated payments of £240 format royalty for each episode written by anyone else, plus a script consultancy fee of £50 per episode – the result was that of the money Nation received for the season, nearly 40 per cent came from episodes written by others. There was also a payment of £500 for a concept and theme for the season, and Nation produced a document summing up what had been done thus far and outlining what should happen next. '*Blake's 7* is a space *adventure*,' he emphasised. 'It is filled with action and adventure. This must be our yardstick by which we judge all future stories.'

The overarching theme for the second season, he said, should be Blake's attempt to launch 'a bold and stunning strike against the oppressors. Something that will stiffen the spines of the waverers and give them the courage to join in the fight. One spectacular event that will both damage and humiliate the enemy.' This would occupy several of the thirteen episodes and would provide the cliff-hanger finale, in which Blake finally locates Star One, the 'city sized space station' that is the command centre of the entire Federation, only to discover that it is about to be attacked by an alien empire. 'The aliens intend to destroy life on all the Federation planets and repopulate with their own kind. Must Blake now save the Federation?' This, of course, was the two-part storyline that Nation never managed to write, but his idea did form the basis of the season cliff-hanger, 'Star One'. (Early on, according to Boucher, Nation had tentatively suggested introducing the Daleks at this point: 'We stamped on that idea very firmly.')

The other key theme that Nation wanted to run through the second season was the feud between Blake and Travis, who was still seen at this point as being the arch-enemy. Travis was to be dismissed from the service of the Federation but, obsessed by his desire for revenge, was to continue the pursuit of Blake, aided unofficially by Servalan. This storyline was followed, but it suffered from the absence of Stephen Greif, who had made Travis such a splendidly excessive figure. 'I kept piling it on,' said Nation of the character and of Greif's portrayal. 'I was sending it up slightly but he played it with such panache and reality that it didn't seem overloaded at all.' Greif's decision to leave the show at the end of the first season left a gap that was only partially filled by his replacement, Brian Croucher, who was dealt an almost unplayable hand. It was 'an unenviable task', observed Paul Darrow, to have to take on another actor's character. 'Poor Brian was on a hiding to nothing.' The double-act with Servalan was no longer a partnership of equals, and Travis was killed off in the final episode of the season, slain not by Blake but, significantly, by Avon.

For the balance of power was shifting within the series. The rivalry between Blake and Travis was supposed to form the core of the story, personalising Blake's doomed struggle with the Federation, but both characters were gradually being eclipsed by Avon and Servalan respectively. It was their relationship that came to dominate memories of the series, largely because, as Darrow pointed out, they were the ones who brought an element of sexuality to the screen: 'Servalan hit on any male that moved and Avon kissed a lot of girls before blowing them away.' Fifteen years after the series ended, Elizabeth Coldwell, editor of the erotic magazine *Forum*, was still celebrating the sexual subtexts of the show, with the 'show's dominant, arrogant anti-hero Avon always dressed in tight black leather', and Servalan, 'science fiction's only prime-time dominatrix', whose 'sadistic love of cruelty and ability to wander over any alien landscape in ridiculously high stilettos caused disruption in many an adolescent trouser area'. There was, she pointed out, 'a scything sexual tension' between the two.

This relationship was to emerge more fully in the third and fourth seasons, but already there were signs that the characters were coming to dominate the storylines, though each for slightly different reasons. Servalan herself never changed, since she was already so far over the top there was nowhere else for her to go. 'I never really saw her as possessing any great depth or detail somehow,' said Boucher. 'She was an archetype. She was Terry's villainess and he wrote her as a villainess.' Her growth was simply a result of Jacqueline Pearce inhabiting the part with ever more commanding authority and sheer relish. Avon, on the other hand, developed new sides to his character. Having originally been introduced as an unemotional computing expert, he had evolved into an action hero, though a particularly ruthless one: he's the only Nation hero happy to shoot his enemies in the back and to kill women as well as men. Balancing this contempt for the conventions of the genre, he also acquired new subtleties, particularly in the episode 'Countdown', a Nation story for season two that was arguably his finest script for the entire series.

Much of the first half of the episode is an entirely characteristic Nation plot. The people of the planet Albian wish to secede from the Federation but are kept in check by the threat of a solium radiation device, a weapon that when triggered will cause the destruction of all life on the planet. As Avon explains: 'Once in fission, it creates intense radiation, it destroys living tissue instantly.' But isn't it, wonders Vila, a little extreme to threaten to destroy the planet in reprisal for rebellion? Avon has to clarify: 'But they don't blow it up, that's the point. Solium itself produces a very small explosion and the radiation fallout decays rapidly. They could wipe out a whole population and still leave the buildings and the installations intact. In less than a day there is no trace of any radiation.' It is, snorts Blake, 'typical Federation policy – things are more important than people.' (It's also, a viewer might be forgiven for thinking, a typical Nation concept: an improved neutron bomb, as previously seen in 'The Daleks', though given renewed resonance at a time when the proposed deployment of American neutron bombs in Europe was proving highly controversial.) Albian rebels take over the command complex, but the device is triggered and it starts counting down to the ultimate explosion. Avon thinks he can disable the device, but first they have to find it.

Thus far, this is almost self-parody, Nation's love of ticking time-bombs taken to its ultimate level, with the entire episode structured around a countdown. But he has some twists to come. It transpires that the coup has been organised by a mercenary, a man named Del Grant (Tom Chadbon), brought in by the resistance to coordinate the uprising, when they realise they aren't up to the job themselves. Our appetite to meet the man is further whetted by Avon's revelation that he knew Grant of old, and that the last time they met, Grant made it clear that he wanted to kill him. This back-story is sketched in with a conversation on to which we effectively stumble, as though eavesdropping:

AVON: That last day, when it was all over, did they hurt her?
GRANT: They kept her under interrogation for nearly a week. They tried everything, but she never broke. If she'd spoken, told them what they wanted to know, she'd be alive now.
AVON: She should have told them.
GRANT: She held on because she believed in you. She didn't know that you'd run out and leave her to face it alone.
AVON: That was not the way it was.
GRANT: I know exactly how it was. She died under Federation torture. But it was you who killed her.

It's a beautifully taut piece of writing, a complete story in under a hundred words, with all the elegant simplicity one might find in a 1940s movie. When the conversation is resumed later on, the impression is heightened, as Avon seeks to give his side of the story of the dead woman, Anna. He was, he says, buying escape visas for the two of them from an underworld dealer who double-crossed him. Avon killed the dealer, but was himself shot and lay unconscious for over thirty hours, during which time Anna was captured. There was nothing he could do for her. But still he remained, risking his own freedom, until word was received of her death and, all hope having been lost, he finally used his forged visa to flee the city. 'You expect me to believe that?' challenges Grant, and Avon replies: 'Not particularly. But it happens to be the truth. If there had ever been a time when I could have given my own life to save her, I would have done it. The only grain of consolation that I have is that Anna knew that.'

This truly is the romance of the resistance, the doomed martyrdom of a *Casablanca*, except that here the heroic words are delivered not with the bruised machismo of a Humphrey Bogart, but in Avon's precisely enunciated, emotionally neutral tones. The disjunction between his sarcastic superiority and the spirit of self-sacrifice he evokes is surprisingly effective. And there is also our knowledge that Avon and Anna were not part of any resistance movement fighting selflessly against the Federation, but rather criminals engaged in the theft of millions of credit from bank computers.

Being Nation, of course, there is much else happening both here and elsewhere, for these conversations are undertaken in conditions of extreme stress, as the timer continues to count down. The solium device has been located by now, buried in a block of ice, deep in the frozen polar wastes of the planet, and Avon and Blake have been beamed in to defuse it. While they race against time to save the lives of the six million people who live on Albian, they also seek a resolution to their personal, historical conflicts. And all the time, the ice is thawing, with huge blocks dropping around them because, as ever, there's always something new to add to the danger of the situation.

Neither of Nation's other two episodes for the second season came close to matching 'Countdown', though there were some strong ideas in both. The first episode, 'Redemption', resolved the cliff-hanger from 'Orac' at the end of the previous season, by taking the *Liberator* back to its original makers, hitherto unidentified. They turn out to be a network of computers, known collectively as the System, ruling a group of three planets that used to be in a state of perpetual warfare. 'Now there's no war, no famine . . .' explains a humanoid worker. 'And no freedom,' interrupts Blake. It's a telling exchange, for on the face of it, there's little to choose between the System here and *Doctor Who*'s Conscience of Marinus some fifteen years earlier. Except that in 'The Keys of Marinus' the Doctor had automatically sided with the machine, while Nation's new hero has no hesitation in identifying with the oppressed. Meanwhile, the solution to how the *Liberator* was going to escape its inevitable destruction, as foreseen by Orac, was resolved very neatly; in fact it is a sister ship, identical in all respects, that is blown up.

In 'Pressure Point' Blake's gang return to Earth, with the intention of hitting Control, the much vaunted central information computer of the Federation. The plan is to link up with a resistance group led by a woman named Kasabi (Jane Sherwin), though by the time they arrive the rebels have already been killed or captured, leaving only Kasabi's daughter at large, and she promptly betrays Blake in the hope of saving her mother. It's all in vain, of course, for Kasabi has fallen into Servalan's hands and it transpires that there is history between the two. Kasabi was once a senior Federation officer, training classes of cadets, until Servalan, one of her students, reported her to the authorities for teaching treason.

After a dangerous — and not very convincing — journey into the fortified base where Control is said to be housed, Blake finally achieves his objective. But he discovers that he, and everyone else, has been deceived: in one of Nation's best plot twists, there is nothing there but an empty room. Control isn't here at all, hasn't been for thirty years, and they've all been tricked into attacking a decoy target. 'It's the great illusion, Blake,' taunts Travis. 'You give substance and credibility to an empty room, and the real thing becomes undetectable, virtually invisible.' (If only the resistance displayed this level of strategic thinking, their cause might not be so hopeless.)

The episode is chiefly remembered, however, for the death of one of the original crew. As the gang escape from the complex, Gan is fatally injured though he does at least end on an heroic note. 'Go! I'm not worth dying for,' he urges the others in time-honoured fashion, as he's trapped in a tunnel. It's a sudden and entirely unexpected development, but one which Nation had long intended. 'It was Terry's instinct,' explained Chris Boucher, 'that you had to convince the audience that everyone really was under threat, and so the only way to do that was to kill someone.' Nation himself portrayed it as a simple shock tactic: 'We made the decision that we needed a major publicity jolt. There is nothing like a death in a show.' There was a suggestion that his eye had fallen first on Vila, though in his preparatory paper for season two he had clearly identified Gan and Cally as the weak links, confirming the BBC's audience research that these were the least popular characters with viewers.

The killing of Gan tied in with the random, meaningless deaths that had been such a feature of the *Survivors* novel, even if it went against what Nation claimed had been his philosophy ever since he'd been obliged to resurrect the Daleks: 'From that time on, I have always said, "Whatever happens, whatever we do, we do not kill off any of my characters. You always give them a little swab of hope somewhere."' In fact, there had long been a high mortality rate among his characters, from Sara Kingdom in 'The Daleks' Master Plan' to Tom Price in *Survivors*. But the underlying truth remained: however happy he was to dispense with individuals, he ensured that the format would never again be jeopardised – the ending of 'The Daleks' would not be reprised.

As if to make the same point, the second season of *Blake's 7* was followed later in 1979 by 'Destiny of the Daleks', the first new Daleks serial on *Doctor Who* for over four years and the last story that Nation would write for the creatures. It included the return of Davros, last seen in 'Genesis of the Daleks' apparently being killed by his own creations, his body buried deep in the Kaled bunker on Skaro. But, whatever our assumptions, we hadn't actually seen the scientist die and Nation had been careful to keep his options open, insisting in his script that the light on Davros's life support should be seen to be still switched on. That detail didn't in fact appear on screen, but Nation never lost sight of his intentions. 'There is a legend that people tell in space,' explained the 1978 *Dalek Annual*. 'It is said that Davros had built into his life-support system a device that would keep him in a condition of suspended animation; that the spark of life could never die. Some people believe that if his body is ever recovered he could again be brought to full and active life . . .'

The story concerned a centuries-long stand-off between the Daleks and a race of androids called the Movellans. Both have huge battle fleets waiting for the most propitious moment to launch an attack, but since both races are governed exclusively by logic, and both are dependent on computers, the moment never arrives – any move by one is predicted and pre-emptively countered by the other, leaving the forces in a perpetual stalemate. 'Two vast computers so evenly matched they can't outthink one another,' as the Doctor puts it. And so the Daleks have returned to Skaro, their former home, long since abandoned, in order to find Davros, that he might reprogram their computers. 'That's why they came back for you,' exclaims the Doctor to Davros, as the penny drops. 'They remembered they were once organic creatures themselves, capable of irrational, intuitive thought, and they wanted you to give it back to them, to get them out of their trap of logic.' The Movellans, meanwhile, are here to prevent the Daleks from achieving their objective.

The discovery of the cobweb-shrouded Davros (played here by David Gooderson), kept alive in long-term suspended animation by his secondary and back-up circuits, is the highlight of the story and is couched in religious imagery. 'So, the long darkness has ended and the eternity of waiting is over,' he declares as he recovers. 'The resurrection has come, as I always knew it would.' The almost blasphemous language is countered by a subsequent scene in which the Doctor holds Davros hostage, threatening to blow both of them up with an improvised explosive device if the Daleks make any move. It's an idea that leaves the Daleks puzzled: 'Self-sacrifice illogical,' they argue, 'therefore impossible.' There's also a nice moment when one of the creatures mentions the Supreme Dalek, which throws Davros entirely. He evidently hadn't considered the idea that the hive might have developed a social structure in his absence: 'Supreme Dalek! Hah! That is a title I shall dispute most vigorously. I created the Daleks, it is I who will guide their destiny. I am the Supreme Commander.'

Beyond the reappearance of Davros, however, and his survival for future stories, it is not one of the more memorable Dalek tales, and there is some doubt about how much involvement Nation had in the final result. '"Destiny of the Daleks" needed top-to-bottom rewriting,' said Douglas Adams, the script editor. 'When you did a Dalek script, it had to be done by Terry Nation – a canny fellow, and very charming. He had to get paid for the script, but the script that he brought forward was a couple of explosions, and a couple of people running up a corridor. You had to turn that into a story.' Ken Grieve, the director of the serial, had much the same memory: 'To be honest, Douglas wrote about ninety-six per cent of it with [series producer] Graham Williams. And myself a little. Terry Nation came up with the ideas, but the hard work was done by Douglas.' There is clearly some exaggeration in such accounts, since the broadcast serial did not depart as substantially from Nation's original twelve-page storyline, let alone from his script, as they imply. But the influence of Adams can be detected, and not always in ways of which Nation approved.

Adams had taken over the role of script editor on *Doctor Who* in late 1978, at a time when his own star was definitely in the ascendant. In March that year Radio 4 had broadcast his science fiction comedy *The Hitchhiker's Guide to the Galaxy*, which had attracted an enthusiastic following – it was repeated twice that year – and would go on to spawn a sequel, several books, a television series and ultimately a movie. To celebrate the fact, he inserted a self-indulgent reference into 'Destiny of the Daleks', with the Doctor seen reading a book titled *The Origins of the Universe* by Oolon Colluphid, a figure from *Hitchhiker's*. Adams also, less happily, added some gags about the design of the Daleks, so that the Doctor jokes about how he'll be received by the creatures. 'Oh, I'm sure they'll welcome me with open ar . . . I mean, they would welcome me with open arms if they had arms,' he says to Davros. 'Please, please, no offence meant at all.' And when he climbs up a rope to escape the pursuing Daleks, he throws back a taunt: 'If you're supposed to be the superior race of the universe, why don't you try climbing after us?' This was precisely the humour that Nation had striven for so long to avoid, the reason why he had blocked Barry Cryer and Peter Vincent's sketch about a Dalek Romeo and Juliet. The appearance of jokes within *Doctor Who* itself was deeply deplored by Nation.

There was also some confusion about the nature of the Daleks themselves. They are repeatedly referred to as 'robots', while their portrayal as creatures governed entirely by logic doesn't chime with what we already know of them. Their long-standing tendency to hysterical, repetitious boasting always suggested an emotional insecurity, while as far back as 'The Dalek Invasion of Earth' we saw the Black Dalek keeping the Slyther as a pet; the idea may evoke the image of a concentration camp commandant, but it reveals a degree of sentimentality that makes a nonsense of the central plot of 'Destiny'. Nation's original storyline for the serial made no mention of the theme of two robotic races locked in a logic trap; instead the Daleks have come after Davros in search of missing circuitry. According to the story's producer, Graham Williams, the change came after a meeting he and Adams had with Nation; there they recommended him a short story by Isaac Asimov with a similar theme, which he then picked up on.

But while Nation's own contribution to the below-par standards of 'Destiny' can't be ignored, it was clearly Adams who was the more culpable. Nation's revenge came in 'Aftermath', the opening episode of the third season of *Blake's 7*. The Intergalactic War between the Federation and the alien forces, presaged in 'Star One', has produced a narrow victory for the Federation, but survivors have been scattered in all directions, and Avon escapes in a capsule to a planet named Sarran, where he bumps into

Servalan, an encounter that occasions no surprise on his part. 'It has a perverse kind of logic to it,' he explains, parodying Adams's Improbability Drive in *Hitchhiker's*. 'Our meeting is the most unlikely happening I could imagine. Therefore we meet. Surprise seems inappropriate somehow.'

For the new series of *Blake's 7*, which began in January 1980, there were substantial changes in the cast. Travis had been killed in 'Star One' and both Blake and Jenna had disappeared in the Intergalactic War, presumed dead, Gareth Thomas and Sally Knyvette having separately declined new contracts. 'I upset Terry enormously when I left the series,' remembered Thomas. 'Later on, I realised I really had hurt him a lot, and I was deeply upset about that.' The circumstances were different, but there was a sense of history repeating itself. *Survivors* had lost its lead character with the departure of Abby, and slipped away from Nation's vision; was *Blake's 7* going to go the same way?

During negotiations for the second season, Roger Hancock had asked that 'the copyright in any new characters created by other writers for the series will become the property of Lynsted Park Enterprises Ltd', in an attempt to keep the series firmly in Nation's grip; memories of the loss of control over *Survivors*, and the consequent difficulties of the novelisation, were still fresh. The BBC had rejected that suggestion out of hand, but did concede for the third season that Nation would at least be given advance information about any new running character that he didn't himself create. In the event, the new additions to the regular crew made their debuts in episodes scripted by Nation and he was able to direct their characterisation. Del Tarrant (Steven Pacey), intended as a fearless pilot, was modelled on the heroes of RAF Fighter Command in the Battle of Britain, and Dayna Mellanby (Josette Simon) was a weapons designer capable of producing high-tech armaments despite her own more traditional tastes. 'I like the ancient weapons: the spear, the sword, the knife,' she explained. 'They demand more skill. When you fight with them, conflict becomes more personal, more exciting.'

More immediately striking was the meeting of Servalan and Avon. Having emerged as the most intriguing figures in the previous season, they now came together on centre stage, with Servalan proposing a coalition. The Federation has lost its command centre on Star One and is in disarray, but the two of them – together with Orac and the *Liberator* – could build a new Federation over which they could jointly rule. For a moment it looks as though the implausible alliance might be on: they kiss but, just as she thinks she has won him over, he seizes her by the throat and throws her to the ground, spurning her offers of power and sex. The enmity between the two will come to dominate much of the remainder of the series.

The change in personnel, and in their relative significance, came at a crucial moment in the show's run. The previous season had been rescheduled to 7.20 p.m. on a Tuesday evening, pitching it against the hugely popular American import *Charlie's Angels*, which might reasonably be expected to attract many of the same potential viewers, and the result had been a collapse in audience share. Viewing figures averaged just 7.1 million, a loss of more than two million from the first season, and on one occasion an episode had slipped out of the weekly top 100 altogether. Restored to its original Monday night slot, however, the third season saw the lost audience restored, while nearly half the episodes reached the top thirty. This was despite the absence of Roj Blake, whose name the show continued to bear. It looked as though Nation had created a format that was as sustainable as a soap opera — half of the original characters had now disappeared, and still it survived.

The cause was inadvertently helped by the political transformation that had occurred since season two. In May 1979 the exhausted and largely discredited Labour government that prime minister James Callaghan had inherited from Harold Wilson was voted out in a General Election, and a Conservative administration led by Margaret Thatcher began what turned out to be a generation in office; the Conservatives were still in power when Nation died eighteen years later. In an era when there were few women in political life, let alone domineering right-wing women, Thatcher was seen in some quarters as possessing a cruel seductiveness: 'Elle a les yeux de Caligule, mais elle a la bouche de Marilyn Monroe,' in the words of French president François Mitterrand. Even as the numbers of strong women multiplied on television — from police chief Jean Darblay in *Juliet Bravo* to animal trainer Barbara Woodhouse — the comparisons between Servalan and the prime minister did not go unnoticed. When in 1980 the *Guardian* diary column asked its readers to suggest nicknames for Thatcher, there were, among such offerings as Scoldilocks, Maggiavelli and Attila the Hen, several nominations simply for Servalan.

Nation's own writing for the third season was again limited to just three episodes, though he was still involved in discussions to develop running themes. In the event, the continuing storylines he suggested — particularly a search for Blake — were dropped, and the episodes that resulted lacked the narrative thread that had previously been a feature of the show. There remained, however, the concept of a season cliff-hanger in 'Terminal', the last contribution that Nation was to make to the series; indeed it was the last thing he ever wrote for British television.

Happily it's a fitting swansong. The setting is an experimental artificial planet named Terminal, set up as a replica of Earth to study the evolution of life and populated by a primitive ape-like species. These creatures are assumed to be the ancestors of humanity, and are hence called Links, though this turns out to be an error, as Servalan gleefully points out: 'The planet's evolution was massively accelerated. It developed through millions of years in a very short time. The creature you saw is not what man developed from; it is what man will become.'

There's a hint here of the film *Planet of the Apes* (1968), but essentially we are back on ground prepared by Nation in 'The Keys of Marinus', 'Genesis of the Daleks' and the short story 'We Are the Daleks!', with artificially accelerated evolution, and in territory explored in 'Death to the Daleks', with the refusal to accept that evolution necessarily means progress. Except that Nation's concerns were now emerging into a cultural climate that seemed more receptive. The American rock group Devo had become cult stars with their espousal of the theories of de-evolution on their 1978 album *Q: Are We Not Men? A: We Are Devo!* (its title echoing the Law in *The Island of Dr Moreau*), while Ken Russell's 1980 film of Paddy Chayefsky's novel *Altered States* depicted a scientist experimenting with biological de-evolution through the use of psychedelic drugs and sensory deprivation. Dystopian visions of the future were far from unusual, but the embrace of evolutionary regression seemed ever more appropriate as memories of 1960s liberalism faded in the face of a reactionary move to a much harder political right in both Britain and America. By coincidence ITV had, a couple of months earlier, finally aired Nigel Kneale's *Quatermass* story that the BBC had rejected earlier in the decade, showing a Britain where society has completely fallen apart. In the midst of the nightmarish violence are a hippy cult left over from the 1960s, the Planet People, angrily rejecting the scientific faith represented by Professor Quatermass. 'Stop trying to know things,' one of them exclaims.

There had been a minor variation on this theme in one of Nation's other scripts for season three, 'Powerplay'. Here Vila finds himself on a planet named Chenga, populated by two tribes, the Primitives and the Hi-Techs. Both are descended from the original settlers, having adopted very different visions of the society they wish to build and the technology they are prepared to use. Much of the action on Chenga is played for laughs, including a scene in which Vila tries to scare off potential attackers by adopting different voices and pretending to be a heavily armed force (a routine lifted directly from 'The Threatening Letters', a 1958 episode of *Hancock's Half Hour*). But there is also an element of wishing to have the last, ironic word on *Survivors*, the series that Nation felt was taken from him; the Primitives have followed Abby Grant's prescription of returning to sustainable technology, and yet are clearly not destined for survival.

The account of de-evolution in 'Terminal', however, is merely the backdrop to the main story. Avon, who took over command of the *Liberator* when Blake disappeared, has learnt that Blake is still alive and well and living on the artificial planet. He takes the ship there and discovers Blake in an underground bunker, hooked up to a life support system though fully conscious. But it's a trap. Servalan has lured Avon here to offer him a deal: she will give him Blake in exchange for the *Liberator*. He agrees, unaware – as is she – that the unknown cloud of particles that the ship flew through en route to Terminal has already begun to corrode its fabric. The crew teleport down to join Avon, and Servalan, having revealed that 'Blake' is actually a computer simulation and that the real man is dead, takes the reverse route on to the *Liberator*, just in time for it to explode from the effects of the particle cloud.

The production team expected that this would be the end of the entire series. Nation had gone out in style, destroying the ship that had given the band of rebels their one advantage over the Federation, as well as the computer Zen, who had been effectively part of the cast ('I have failed you,' it says plaintively as the *Liberator* begins to disintegrate), though its rival, Orac, had survived. 'I was fascinated with the idea of cancer in a machine,' said Nation. 'I suppose I wanted to give the machine the same vulnerability as a man.' He had also, as far as the viewers could tell, killed off Servalan and, having teased us with an apparition, finally laid Blake to rest. The surviving crew were left stranded in a bunker on a dangerous planet with no means of escape. Even so, as Nation pointed out in a covering letter to David Maloney when sending in the script: 'You'll notice that I have left the door open for series four, should public demand ever drive us to it.'

As it turned out, it wasn't public demand that did the trick; rather it was approval from the BBC hierarchy. 'Terminal' was such a strong episode that Bill Cotton, the controller of BBC1, phoned up while it was being broadcast and insisted that an announcement be made during the credits that the series would return the following year.

By this stage, however, Nation himself had already departed. His letter to Maloney, enclosing the script for 'Terminal', had ended on a valedictory note: 'We've had three seasons of Blake together and I thank you most sincerely for everything you've done for the show. Apart from odd moments of creative blackouts, I have enjoyed it. What I value very much is the relationship we have had over such a long haul. I very much hope we'll work together again.' He wasn't even in the country to see 'Terminal' being broadcast. 'I actually missed that episode on its original transmission,' he remembered later, 'because I was already in the United States.'

Chapter Sixteen

To America and Beyond

By the end of the 1970s Nation was reaching a critical point in his career. Now in his late forties, he was a major figure in popular television in Britain, coming off two successful series of his own devising, and with the Daleks confirmed as a continuing, integral part of *Doctor Who*. Like Ray Galton and Alan Simpson and Johnny Speight, his erstwhile colleagues at Associated London Scripts, he had become a name in his own right, even if this was partially achieved in spite of the BBC; they might have refused to put his name above the titles, but the merchandising of *Blake's 7* and the Daleks was doing its best to redress the balance. Within his field, there was little more that Nation could achieve on television at home.

For someone in his position twenty years earlier, the logical next step would have been into the movies, but the British film industry was now at its lowest ebb, with even the established box-office brands failing. Hammer had made its last horror film, *To the Devil a Daughter*, in 1976, while the Carry On series had petered out with the substandard *Carry On England* (1976) and *Carry On Emmanuelle* (1978). Lew Grade, obliged to retire from his television empire at the age of seventy, had moved instead into film-making, but ITC's touch was less sure when it came to the cinema and the company came a cropper with the hugely expensive flop *Raise the Titanic* (1980). Less celebrated companies were also struggling: Amicus had a three-year gap before its final production, *The Monster Club* (1980), and Associated London Films, ALS's sister company, had made its last big-screen picture with *Steptoe and Son Ride Again* in 1973.

Nation did try to develop a film project in 1978, to be titled *Bedouin*. 'It's a marvellous adventure story to be shot in the desert,' he explained at the time. 'I think twelfth century – the Crusaders.' There was to be a strong vein of fantasy running through it, going back to an earlier theme of ancient wisdom: 'The von Däniken kind of thinking. I disapprove of him entirely, but is there a wisdom somewhere that could have been from another source?' Discussions were held with a production company in Geneva, but it came to nothing.

The opportunities for new challenges in Britain seemed slight, and if he was ever going to make a serious attempt to break America, clearly it had to be soon, before age caught up with him. There was some encouragement that the tide might be turning in favour of his style of writing. In 1977 *Doctor Who* had finally found a home in the States on the Public Broadcasting Service, and even on some commercial channels, and by the end of the decade it had begun to build a cult following. By 1984 it had become established enough to warrant coverage in *Time* magazine.

And so, in 1980, Nation and his family moved to Los Angeles for what was initially intended to be a two-month trial. He celebrated his fiftieth birthday in Hollywood.

In his absence, the unexpected commissioning of a fourth season of *Blake's 7* resulted in a very tight production schedule, complicated further by the departure of producer David Maloney, to be replaced by Vere Lorrimer, who had already directed a dozen episodes of the series. There was too a change in the cast. Jan Chappell, who played Cally, decided not to return, so was killed off-screen in the first episode, leaving just two of the original crew members – Avon and Vila – on board a new ship, the much less impressive *Scorpio*, joined by a new comrade, Soolin (Glynis Barber). Jacqueline Pearce, on the other hand, whose involvement was initially doubtful, did return, via a somewhat tortuous plotline that meant Servalan was posing for some time under the alias Sleer to no discernible dramatic advantage.

Lorrimer visited Nation in Los Angeles to discuss the direction of the fourth season, but it was more a matter of courtesy than of serious consultation, and Nation was far from impressed with the results: 'I didn't have anything to do with the last [series], which I hated. I've seen some of them and I think, again, that they missed it.' There was, he argued, an inherent problem with other writers taking over his characters: 'I believe that I wrote *Blake's 7* (and *Survivors* and the Daleks) better than anybody else, simply because I invented them. I knew them deeply and more intimately than anybody else. I knew what I was trying to achieve.' It was a complaint that he had made repeatedly when others had taken on his creations, though it was hard to see how it could be avoided, given the collaborative medium in which he worked.

Even Nation, however, could not help but admire the last episode of season four. Written by Chris Boucher and broadcast in the Christmas week of 1981, 'Blake' was a great piece of television. Again Avon has discovered that Roj Blake is still alive, this time on an obscure, lawless planet named Gauda Prime, raising hopes that he might return as the unifying figurehead for the resistance. And this time the reports are true. Blake is indeed alive, but Avon, mistakenly believing that he has betrayed the rebel cause and gone over to the Federation, shoots him. Federation guards arrive, kill all the others – Dayna, Vila, Soolin, Tarrant – and surround Avon, who stands astride the corpse of Blake and raises his gun to shoot, as he breaks into a smile. The image freezes, and as the credits roll, we hear the sound of a gun battle on the soundtrack.

Few series have ever dared go out on such a triumphantly negative note. But then few series have been prepared to sacrifice characters in the way that *Blake's 7* had. The ending was entirely in keeping with what had gone before; indeed its conclusion echoed its start four years earlier with a Federation massacre of rebels. Blake had now been killed off for the third and final time, on this occasion – it appeared – with every other member of the cast. The only missing element was Servalan herself, a fact which reportedly upset Jacqueline Pearce, though dramatically it was a wise decision not to include her in the episode: this was a tale of grim fatalism, no place for her brand of warped glamour.

'I did admire enormously the dramatic moments of Avon standing over Blake's body and raising the weapon and starting to smile,' admitted Nation, 'which I think was sensational but dumb.' He also claimed that the production team 'purposely did not let me know what was happening', calculating that he would have disapproved of this radical gesture, this slaughter of so many characters, in contradiction of 'my old axiom: Never kill anything off.' But when his initial anger at what had been done faded, he reasoned that at least we hadn't definitively seen Avon die. There was no reason why he couldn't make a return, if the possibility for further episodes arose. Boucher made the same point: 'It was an ending in itself, but it wasn't necessarily the end of the programme. If *Blake's 7* had returned for a fifth series, then the episode would now be regarded as a cliff-hanger, following in the tradition previously laid down by Terry Nation.' For now, however, there was no doubt that it was the end of *Blake's 7* – this time there was no last-minute reprieve from a BBC executive. Viewing figures had fallen (the season averaged 8.5 million viewers, down from 9.5 million the previous year) and no one appeared to have an appetite to continue.

Meanwhile, back in Hollywood, Nation appeared to have fallen on his feet. He became involved in a proposed series titled *The Young Arthur* and discovered the delights of the development deal, an entirely unknown concept in British television. 'They paid me a lot of money, gave me an office and a secretary and paid my expenses,' he explained. 'The idea was that I was to come up with episode and series ideas for television.' The contract, with Columbia Television, was followed by similar deals with 20th Century Fox, MGM and Paramount. But *The Young Arthur* never got made, nor did anything else, and gradually the joy of receiving a regular wage began to pale. 'I was very frustrated by it,' he admitted. 'I just didn't want to work at the studios anymore, so I quit and waited for people to say, "Good God, he's available!" But nobody did.'

In fact very little of Nation's later writing ever appeared on American television. There was work to be done doctoring other people's scripts, but it was not until 1985, when he contributed to a new series titled *MacGyver*, that he got an on-screen credit at all. He was listed as producer for three episodes and also wrote the pre-title sequence for three, supplying five-minute stories that had no connection with the main plot of the following episode. MacGyver, played by Richard Dean Anderson, was a secret agent who relied more on his wits than on weaponry, allowing Nation a chance to indulge his love of an action hero making use of everyday objects; in prelude to the episode 'Target MacGyver', our man rescues a kidnapped general using only a collection of saucepans, a bag of ice, some cooking oil and a garden hose. It was all perfectly agreeable and the show was, eventually, a huge success, running to 139 episodes over seven seasons, but it was no match for the wit and style of ITC in the 1960s. And Nation's contributions were all made within the first ten episodes, before it really took off.

He was now inhabiting a very different world to that of the BBC, where he could wander into the office of his friend, Ronnie Marsh, pitch an idea for *Blake's 7* and walk out with a commission for a pilot that evolved into a series. 'What is difficult in the United States is that you work for twenty-seven masters each time,' he complained. 'You have several producers, you have the studio, you have the actors, and all of them seem to be asking for something different. It drives you insane.' But the stakes were so much higher, and the rewards so much greater, that the temptation to continue playing the game was almost irresistible. 'If you make a smash-hit here –

had *Blake's 7* been made here and had the same level of success – I would be a multi-multi-millionaire,' he said. 'These are the glittering prizes in the United States. It's not just the fact that you have a good audience out there, it's the fact that you are making vast amounts of money, and people kill for less.' As MacGyver once observed: 'Typical! Just when you're getting ahead, somebody always changes the odds.'

The idea of a two-month trial period had long since been overtaken by events, and in 1983 the Nations burnt their bridges with the sale of Lynsted Park. The family was now settled in Los Angeles and it would remain his home until his death, however unsatisfying it was in creative terms.

By the end of the decade he had notched up just two more screen credits. One was an episode of the short-lived series *A Fine Romance*, also known as *Ticket to Ride* and not to be confused with the British sitcom starring Michael Williams and Judi Dench. Titled 'The Tomas Crown Affair', it was, unsurprisingly, a parody of the 1968 movie *The Thomas Crown Affair* and featured a dentist (played by David Rappaport) concealing a smuggled diamond inside the tooth of Michael Trent (Christopher Cazenove). Nation, in an interview conducted at the time of writing, described it as 'a kamikaze episode. You know it's going to go down and nobody's going to watch it – not even me!'

On a slightly happier note, there was *A Masterpiece of Murder*, a television movie screened in 1986 that he co-wrote with Andrew J. Fenady. It told the story of an ageing private detective and an equally ageing crook teaming up in pursuit of an art thief, and while it may not have set many pulses racing, it was notable for teaming up the veteran actor Don Ameche with Bob Hope, the comedian to whom Nation had listened so avidly on the American Forces Network as a child during the war. Nation didn't originate the storyline, and he never cited the piece in interviews as any kind of achievement, but if, thirty-five years earlier when he was trying to establish himself as a stand-up in South Wales, he'd been shown a vision of his future self, living in Hollywood and writing for Bob Hope, he would surely have considered it the wildest, most fantastic success story. 'He absolutely loved that,' remembered Kate Nation. 'These were idols to him. He was just like a kid with a new toy.' Unfortunately, the reality was not as impressive as the dream. 'Hope is game, but painfully past his prime', noted one review, adding that 'the script is never more than mediocre.'

Apart from working on other people's scripts, Nation also spent time trying to bring his own work to the screen. In the mid 1980s this primarily meant a remake of *Survivors*, which he wished to relocate to America. The new Abby would be living in the north-east of the country, with her son, Peter, in Los Angeles. The story would thus come closer to his original concept of a trek across vast distances, with a makeshift convoy of 'strange vehicles crossing empty America, where there are little pockets of survivors here and there, all doing different things'. There had always been a strong element of the frontier western in his episodes of the BBC original and in his novel; this new version would emphasise the theme still further, tapping into 'the American ethos of the wagon train – there's always that great urge to push west for the Americans'.

It was an inspired idea, and there's no reason why it shouldn't have worked, at least commercially. One suspects that, had it been made, it would have ended up a more cheerful affair than Nation might have wished, but revisiting America's greatest myth could have fitted well into the more bullish cultural climate of the country in the 1980s, during the years of Ronald Reagan's presidency. There were, however, other changes in the culture of the times that made the idea of a post-plague drama less appealing to executives. 'We were so close to getting it on one occasion,' remembered Nation, 'and then AIDS reared its head, and everyone was terrified to do anything with it. They didn't want to be associated with it.' That, at least, was his explanation, though there were plenty of other factors militating against him: neither he nor the series itself had any real track record in the States, and it was asking a lot of US television executives to put their money on an outsider when he was touting what appeared at first sight to be such a depressing concept. The made-for-television nuclear disaster movie, *The Day After*, may have achieved record audience figures when it was aired in 1983, but it didn't spark any enthusiasm for other similarly downbeat dramas.

With the abandonment of that project, Nation turned instead to the idea of trying to revive *Blake's 7*. The series had finally been screened in America and, like *Doctor Who*, it had acquired a cult following, sufficient to warrant the presence of Nation, Paul Darrow and others at fan conventions. By 1989 Nation was talking about making a series 'next year', and outlining his thoughts as to how it would work. This time it was not a remake he had in mind, but a continuation of the story from where it had been left off in 'Blake'. We hadn't seen Avon die, so he was to return, a decade or so on from that final episode, exiled on an island on a remote planet, like Napoleon on Elba. He appears to have changed sides, making broadcasts in support of the

Federation and against an outlaw called Blake, who may or may not be the real Blake: 'It may be simply that anybody who leads the fight against the Federation *becomes* Blake; "Blake" has now become a title.' But in reality Avon is merely awaiting his opportunity to return to the fray, his chance to relive Napoleon's final campaign in the Hundred Days. 'That's the kind of thing I have in mind,' Nation said. 'Avon comes out of nowhere and scares everybody to death. Of course, in the end, he cannot win. Like I said, Avon dies.'

This proposal made no progress either, as Nation admitted in a 1992 interview: 'Nothing has been happening, although I'll never say never again.' But it was still in his mind and he was even suggesting that he might bring back Vila as well. More significantly he was now talking about the vague hope that the BBC might take up the idea, as though he had lost any faith in doing anything further on American television. '*Points of View* got more letters for *Blake's 7* than any other series, so there is a demand,' he argued. 'I'm ready to go with it, and we'll give it to them, but I have no idea. The BBC doesn't talk to me, I don't talk to them, not for any other motive than we just don't talk together.'

He was certainly right about the enduring popularity of the programme. In 1983 the BBC had reported that – with the exception of breakfast television, which had been launched that year – the subject that attracted the greatest amount of correspondence from viewers was *Blake's 7*. More than two thousand letters were received asking for the return of the series. The BBC dismissed the letters as being 'part of an organised lobby', which was true, but it was nonetheless a tribute to the enthusiasm that the show continued to inspire. When in 2000 the British Film Institute polled more than 1,500 people in the industry to find the best British television programmes ever made, *Doctor Who* came in third, behind *Fawlty Towers* and 'Cathy Come Home' from Sydney Newman's *The Wednesday Play*. But when the BFI then asked the public to vote for their own favourites, *Doctor Who* rose a place to number two, kept from the top position only by *Blake's 7*. Admittedly the turnout was very low, the 113 nominations for *Blake's 7* accounting for nearly twenty-five per cent of the votes cast, but it was testament to the loyalty of fans that such a campaign could still be mounted, a generation on from the ending of the show.

Unusually for a science fiction series, a great deal of this support came from women. 'When the *Blake's 7 Magazine* was launched it was hoped it would sell to maturing *Doctor Who* fans,' noted Paul Darrow. 'It didn't. A survey was undertaken and it revealed that most readers were in the twenty-two to thirty range, with a significant number of older people. Ninety per cent were female.' He observed the same phenomenon when attending his first fan convention in Chicago.

Although the proposals to bring back *Survivors* and *Blake's 7* continued to fall on stony ground, seeds were still being sown. And it was a tribute to the roles that Nation had created that, in both instances, a good deal of the running was made by the series' lead actors. Paul Darrow became heavily involved in the attempts to relaunch *Blake's 7*, while Ian McCulloch developed – with Nation's approval – a concept for a new series of *Survivors*. Set some fifteen years on from the original, this would show a rudimentary society having evolved but coming under attack from an external power, bent on imperialist domination. He got as far as writing a pilot script and outlines for a further twelve episodes before the idea was rejected by the BBC on the bizarre grounds that it would be racially offensive.

This was, it should be noted, the same corporation that, within very recent memory, had happily broadcast *The Black and White Minstrel Show*, only ending the programme in 1978, around the same time that Bill Cotton had thrown the dance troupe Ruby Flipper off *Top of the Pops* on the grounds that 'the British public didn't want to see black men dancing with white women'. By the end of the 1980s, however, the BBC had belatedly become sensitive to multicultural sensibilities in the country, even if it remained unsure of its ground. So when McCulloch explained his suggestion that the raiding parties assaulting Britain came from Africa, the BBC panicked and rejected it out of hand 'because they thought it was racist'. It was an absurd argument, but McCulloch didn't entirely lose faith. He returned with a reworked proposal in the mid 1990s, though again without success.

But if all these projects came to naught, and if Nation's writing career in America was little more than a long series of professional disappointments, there were compensations. The income generated by the Daleks had ensured that he and his family could live comfortably, and the rise in popularity of conventions gave him the sort of personal acclaim that writers seldom enjoy. 'I retain an enormous affection for the Daleks,' he wrote in 1988. 'They have rewarded me in many ways, and not least amongst these benefits have been the opportunities to meet fans all over the world. They are dedicated and wonderful people, and I am extremely grateful to all of them.' Among those fans, helpfully enough given the celebrity-based hierarchy of Hollywood, were some big names, as Nation's obituary in *The Times* pointed out: 'American aficionados of *Doctor Who*, such as Steven Spielberg, made "the Dalek Man" welcome.' And, according to Kate Nation, the daily working routine was not always disagreeable. 'He loved it. He loved going out to the studios to his office, getting involved with people, because writing can be very solitary.' She added, however: 'He didn't get a lot on – he didn't like that part of it.'

Nation wasn't missing a great deal at home. As an old socialist, who had grown up in the depression of the 1930s in South Wales, he was unlikely to have taken with any enthusiasm to living in Margaret Thatcher's Britain. Nor was British television a particularly happy place in the 1980s for the kind of programmes that he wrote. There had been a brief attempt to pour new wine into old bottles with *The New Avengers* (1976) and *Return of the Saint* (1978), but neither was entirely convincing, and when Brian Clemens found a durable action adventure vehicle in *The Professionals* (1977), it owed more to the grittiness of *The Sweeney* than it did to the fantasies of Steed and Simon Templar.

Science fiction was also struggling. The huge success of *Star Wars* prompted the making of further Hollywood epics with the likes of *Star Trek: The Motion Picture* and *The Black Hole*, both in 1979, and the following year ITV bought in two American series whose high-gloss production values, while not quite on the scale of *Star Wars*, were a long way from the make-do-and-mend approach to which British fans had become accustomed on television. *Battlestar Galactica* was screened on Thursdays, while – in an act of virtual sacrilege – *Buck Rogers in the 25th Century* was broadcast on Saturday evenings, up against *Doctor Who* itself. Worse still, it began to win the ratings war. In response the BBC moved *Doctor Who* in 1982, after eighteen years in the same slot, screening it twice weekly on Mondays and Tuesdays. By 1985 it was back in its proper place at a Saturday teatime, though in its new format it now lasted forty-five minutes rather than its traditional twenty-five.

More importantly, the entire episode had demonstrated the BBC's loss of faith in the brand. The chief villain emerged as Michael Grade, the nephew of Lew Grade and now the controller of BBC1. He was later to say that he thought the show 'was rubbish, I thought it was pathetic. I'd seen *Star Wars*, *Close Encounters of the Third Kind* and *E.T.* and then I had to watch these cardboard things clonking across the floor trying to scare kids.' The option of increasing the budget to keep pace does not seem to have been seriously considered, even though the revenue from merchandising and foreign sales was by now said to be seven times higher than the production costs. Instead, after that 1985 season, the programme disappeared entirely for eighteen months. When it did return it was for a series of much briefer seasons that migrated from Saturdays to Mondays and then to Wednesdays, and attracted ever smaller audiences. The last storyline to be seen by more than seven million viewers was 1985's 'Revelation of the Daleks', written by Eric Saward; by the time of Ben Aaronovitch's 'Remembrance of the Daleks' (1988), which – as part of the show's silver jubilee season – took the story right back to the junkyard in Totters Lane, the figures were barely scraping past five million and were set to plunge further. The final episode of *Doctor Who* was broadcast in December 1989 and, although there was no formal announcement of the end of the show, it was clearly understood what was happening. 'We were told to wait and see about a new season,' remembered the last script editor, Andrew Cartmel, 'but it was definitely a flavour of "you'll have to wait a very long time".' Having lost both BBC support and its public, the series was finally cancelled, ending an extraordinary 26-year run.

Unable to match the special effects-driven scale of Hollywood, television science fiction in Britain reverted to comedy, following the lead of David Croft and Jeremy Lloyd's *Come Back Mrs Noah*, Douglas Adams's *The Hitchhiker's Guide to the Galaxy* and the saga of Captain Kremmen, first heard on the Capital Radio programme of disc jockey Kenny Everett. The two latter eventually made the transition all the way from radio via television to film. Of those that followed, *Red Dwarf* (1988) was clearly in a class of its own, but there was too a host of other British-made science fiction comedies on television, many of them scarcely remembered: *Metal Mickey* (1980), *Kinvig* (1981), *Luna* (1983), *They Came From Somewhere Else* (1984), *The Groovy Fellers* (1989), *Mike & Angelo* (1989), *Kappatoo* (1990), *Watt on Earth* (1991), *Space Vets* (1992) and *WYSIWIG* (1992). One of the few serious attempts to produce a science fiction series, a BBC adaptation of John Christopher's trilogy *The Tripods* in 1984–5, was cancelled at the end of its second season, a decision again made by Michael Grade, while Chris Boucher's *Star Cops* (1987) didn't get beyond a single season.

Many of Nation's contemporaries were also finding the changed climate of British television less amenable than it used to be. Gerry Anderson launched a new puppet series, *Terrahawks*, which ran for thirty-nine episodes between 1983 and 1986, but failed to inspire in the way that *Thunderbirds* and *Stingray* once had (and would again). Dennis Spooner wrote for *The*

Professionals and *Bergerac* though, like Nation, he really yearned for American success; the closest he came, before his untimely death in 1986, was when a story developed by him and Brian Clemens was used for an episode of *Remington Steele*. Clemens himself thrived more than most; an attempt to create an American version of *The Avengers* didn't work out, but he did find success in the States with episodes of *Darkroom*, *Father Dowling Investigates* and *Perry Mason*, before helping to create the British series *Bugs* (1995) and reviving *The Professionals* as *CI5: The New Professionals* (1999). And Clive Exton co-wrote the much-reviled movie *Red Sonja* (1985), starring Brigitte Nielsen and Arnold Schwarzenegger, before finding mainstream success adapting literary work for series like *The Ruth Rendell Mysteries*, *Jeeves and Wooster* and *Poirot*.

Meanwhile, the luminaries of Associated London Scripts were being made to feel decidedly unwelcome, not by the new generation of comedians – many of whom revered the old masters – but by unimaginative executives who valued birth certificates higher than curricula vitae. When, in 1985, Eric Sykes won a special award at the Festival Rose d'Or in Montreux for his long contribution to comedy, he took the opportunity to pitch some ideas for new programmes to Bill Cotton, only to be told: 'Your day's gone Eric. We're now into alternative comedy.' Two ALS graduates – Nation's old writing partner, Dave Freeman, together with John Antrobus – later wrote *Carry On Columbus* (1992), an attempt to revive the old brand with many of the new comedians (Alexei Sayle, Julian Clary, Rik Mayall and others), but it wasn't a great success.

There was, though, at least one bright spot in 1986, when the BBC finally got around to repeating some classic episodes of *Hancock's Half Hour* on television and found that it had a top ten hit on its hands all over again. Perhaps unexpectedly, it was Beryl Vertue, who had started out as ALS secretary, who emerged from a quiet decade in the 1980s to be one of the key figures in 1990s television, producing the sitcom *Men Behaving Badly* (1992) and the excellent, if underrated, George Cole comedy *My Good Friend* (1995). Her company, Hartswood Films, was also responsible for the acclaimed series *Coupling* (2000), produced by her daughter, Sue Vertue, and written by her son-in-law Steven Moffat, who would later take over the reins of the revived *Doctor Who*.

None of this suggests that Britain would have provided a congenial environment for Terry Nation. He was still offered the opportunity to write new Daleks stories for *Doctor Who*, but consistently declined, though he did insist on script approval and made changes where he felt his creations were in danger of being damaged. 'My agent and I have guarded the Daleks tremendously,' he said in 1995. 'We've never allowed them to be used as figures of fun, and we've tried always to stop anyone looking inside them.'

In the wake of the cancellation of *Doctor Who*, Nation's interest in the programme was reawakened. With the backing of Columbia Pictures, he and Gerry Davis, co-creator of the Cybermen and *Doomwatch*, put together a bid to revive it with the idea of targeting the American market. That venture collapsed with Davis's death in 1991, but there were many other proposals floating around in the early 1990s for a revival of the show, either as a television series or a one-off film. In those discussions, the Daleks and Davros featured heavily, though *Doctor Who*, the television movie that finally resulted in 1996, focused instead on a battle between the Doctor and the renegade Time Lord, the Master. The film starts on Skaro where the Master has been sentenced to death by the Daleks, and the intention had been to employ the creatures in a self-contained prologue, but financial restrictions prompted a rewrite and the Daleks were confined to being voices off screen. Nation, however, didn't come out of the deal too badly. 'We were forced to pay Terry $20,000,' noted executive producer Philip Segal, 'and as it happened, Universal and Fox made me shorten the Dalek introduction to cut the budget.' Clearly Roger Hancock's tenacity remained undiminished. And it was somehow inevitable that the closest Nation came to getting one of his creations back on screen – and in America, to boot – was not with *Survivors* or *Blake's 7* but with the Daleks.

The cultural climate of British television was to change again, becoming more receptive to Nation's style of programme, but for some time the flames were kept burning in other media. In 1988 Nation lent his name to *The Official Doctor Who & the Daleks Book*, written by John Peel, a writer whom he then authorised to produce the novelisations of 'The Chase' and 'The Daleks' Master Plan', which had long been absent from the list of Target *Doctor Who* novels. It was Peel too who wrote the first of the *New Adventures* novels in 1991, a series of original stories about the Doctor published by Virgin Books. *Blake's 7* was also attracting new fiction, with Tony Attwood's novel *Afterlife* published in 1984 and *Avon: A Terrible Aspect* (1989), written by Paul Darrow as a prequel to the series exploring his character's origins. A decade later came two radio plays, written by Barry Letts and broadcast on BBC Radio 4. *Blake's 7: The Sevenfold Crown* and *Blake's 7: The Syndeton Experiment* reunited many of the original cast – including Darrow,

Jacqueline Pearce and Michael Keating – though they weren't greeted with a great deal of enthusiasm.

Together with the proliferation of videos and then DVDs and with a continuing high level of fan club and convention activity, particularly in relation to *Doctor Who*, there were times in the 1990s when it seemed – for those who cared – as though the shows associated with Nation had never gone away. But there was still a gap between the hardcore fan community and the mass audiences for whom the programmes had originally been written. All that was to change in 2005 with the revival of *Doctor Who* as a BBC1 series on early Saturday evenings. The new incarnation was an instant ratings-winner, updated to attract a new generation while retaining enough of the original features to satisfy those who remembered it the first time round.

The most significant of those features, for most older viewers, was always going to be the Daleks, but for some time it was unclear if they would be making a return at all. For several months in 2004, after the revival was announced, the media were full of stories about the protracted negotiations between the BBC and the estate of Terry Nation – now represented, since Roger Hancock's retirement, by his son, Tim – which were said to be foundering on questions of the updating of the creatures and the fees that would be due to the estate. Rumours and counter-rumours spread; there were reports at one stage that a figure of a quarter of a million pounds had been agreed to license the Daleks (leading to complaints about how the BBC was spending its money), before it was abruptly announced that the talks had broken down. The corporation issued a statement that 'Mr Hancock had demanded unacceptable levels of editorial control', while Hancock was quoted as protesting: 'We want to protect the integrity of the brand.' There was a suggestion that in their new incarnation, the Daleks would be 'too evil'.

It was a story that gripped both the quality press and the tabloids, though the country's best-selling paper, the *Sun*, made most of the running. It launched one of its self-proclaimed campaigns, reporting with enthusiasm a protest march in Southampton, staging its own stunts (it had acquired a Dalek prop) and rounding up publicity-hungry politicians to add a quote: '*Doctor Who* without Daleks is like fish without chips,' opined Tim Collins, the Conservative Party's education spokesperson. And then came the inevitable press release to reveal that the dispute had been resolved and that the creatures would indeed be back on the screen to battle their arch-enemy, the Doctor ('thanks to the *Sun*'s campaign'). As the *Daily Telegraph* noted, somewhat cynically: 'Whoever's in charge of the PR for the new *Doctor Who* series has been doing a knockout job.'

The result of this saga came in the sixth episode, 'Dalek', written by Robert Shearman. 'This was the one we'd all been waiting for,' wrote Charlie Catchpole in the *Daily Express*, and the story of the Doctor (played by Christopher Eccleston) encountering the last surviving Dalek in the universe, now trapped in a private collection of space artefacts, was generally considered to have been a success, though there were qualifications. 'For thirty pant-shittingly wonderful minutes, BBC1's new *Doctor Who* was the best thing on telly. Ever,' announced Ian Hyland in the *Sunday Mirror*. 'Then they went and spoilt it with a load of symbolic, sentimental, one world, one universe, war-what-is-it-good-for nonsense.'

Certainly the sequence that saw the Dalek infuse itself with the DNA of the Doctor's companion, Rose (Billie Piper), and thereby experience emotion, as well as the opening up of the casing to reveal the organic creature within, went far beyond anything that Nation himself had ever written. But it wasn't out of character. 'Destiny of the Daleks' had failed to convince because it treated the creatures as simple robots, losing sight of the organic life-form inside the metallic shell; 'Dalek' paid due respect to the fact that these were sentient beings, aware of what they had lost in their artificial evolution. Their nature as the embodiment of hate-fuelled evil is enhanced by the possibilities opened up by Shearman's script, and adds to Nation's legacy.

There were other elements that also made for happy memories of the past. The Doctor's description of the Daleks as 'the ultimate in ethnic cleansing' was an appropriate updating of Nation's invocation of the neutron bomb in the first serial: current political imagery had always been part of the story. There was something pleasingly nostalgic too about the way that Mediawatch-UK, the latest incarnation of the National Viewers' and Listeners' Association set up by Mary Whitehouse, objected to the episode even before it was broadcast. And still there was the great mystery of why the Daleks remained so attractively frightening for children. Russell T. Davies, who had earlier written the acclaimed series *Queer as Folk* and who, as overseer of the new series, was instrumental in bringing *Doctor Who* back to the screen, was asked about their appeal and simply shrugged: 'It's a bit like asking "why is the dark scary?" I don't know. It just is.'

As *Doctor Who* went from strength to strength, spawning another great outbreak of merchandising spin-offs for the programme and for the Daleks themselves, attention turned to another of Nation's creations, and in November 2008 a six-part revival of *Survivors* began airing on BBC1. It wasn't quite a remake, for the rights had been acquired to Terry Nation's novel rather than to the original series, but the essence remained the same, merely updated to a world even more dependent on technology than it had been thirty years earlier: this time, the collapse of the mobile phone network causes deep disquiet.

The changes that were made revealed intriguingly how television had adjusted its perception of society over the past two decades. Abby is still in search of her son, Peter, but he's absent from home not because he's away at public school, but because he's on a school field trip; Tom Price is a convicted criminal rather than a comic tramp, for homelessness was now seen in a much more concerned light; Greg Preston is played by a black actor, and two Muslim characters are added. Arthur Wormley has disappeared, since no one would any longer believe in a trade union leader having any political authority, and is replaced by Samantha Willis, a government minister who makes the last official broadcast before the power shuts down, promising a swift restoration – in the characteristic terminology of the New Labour era – of 'your government'. And Jimmy Garland has changed entirely; he's still trying to get back in his house, but there's no aristocratic title, no Boys' Own celebration of adventure, no glamour; instead he comes across, in the words of Andrew Billen in *The Times*, as 'a raving, grimacing maniac'.

Created and (mostly) written by Adrian Hodges, the series achieved respectable viewing figures and returned for a second six-week season in early 2010, before being cancelled. By this stage, there was little left resembling Nation's original work, and nothing that quite matched the high standards set by the first episode of season one – which also happened to be the one that most closely followed Nation's template.

There was a certain irony that, after all those years of trying to get remakes of his work on to American television, it was Nation's old employers at the BBC who ended up reviving *Doctor Who* and *Survivors* after his death. But then, even with the controversial management reforms in the early 1990s of John Birt, the director general, and Marmaduke Hussey, chair of the board of governors (the pair of them famously denounced as 'croak-voiced Daleks' by playwright Dennis Potter), the corporation remained a more open institution than the American broadcasters, more willing to take the occasional risk.

The truth was that Nation was never temperamentally suited to the world of the American networks. He was in his element when sitting at a typewriter, creating absurdly difficult situations and resolving them. When he tried moving into a more executive role, he required the support of a trusted colleague – Dennis Spooner on *The Baron*, Brian Clemens on *The Avengers* – if he wasn't to find himself struggling to keep his head above water, as when he was both script editor and associate producer on *The Persuaders!*. And the experience of American television was harder than anything he had encountered in Britain. 'I'm not sure I want to work at this level,' he admitted in 1989, 'because it's a killer level. I find I look for a little more ease now, I look for a little gentler way of life.' There was still the same dream – 'I'd also love, as a Brit, to have a smash-hit American show' – but he knew that it was becoming increasingly unlikely. 'I don't know whether a writer ever retires,' he reflected in 1995. 'I've not written anything recently, that's true. If I could just raise the energy level a little, there's so many things I want to do.'

By now, though, he was ill with emphysema, assumed to be the consequence of his long smoking habit. And although he spoke about wanting to write a *Blake's 7* novel to continue the story from the end of season four, he knew that it wasn't going to happen. Just as he wasn't suited to being an executive, he lacked the single-minded application to write a convincing full-length novel. In any event he was aware that time was running out and, as he said, with self-conscious irony: 'You can't live with past triumphs.'

It had been a long, successful and influential career, centring on that fifteen-year period from 'The Daleks' to *Blake's 7*. The move to America had, in professional terms, been a mistake, resulting in an equally long period that proved unproductive and frustrating, but there were, by the end of his life, clear signs that his work was not going to be forgotten. Anyway, he had at least got there, he had made it to the Hollywood that he had dreamed of when he was a child back in South Wales. And he surely would have found something very satisfying about the fact that, just a few hundred yards from the street where he grew up in Llandaff, there now stands Broadcasting House, home of BBC Wales, the company that produces the new incarnation of *Doctor Who* and its associated works. Exactly fifty years after Nation had been obliged to leave Cardiff to seek his fame and fortune in

London, the revival of *Doctor Who* ensured that writers and actors, directors and designers would be making the same journey in reverse.

Terry Nation died in Pacific Palisades, Los Angeles on 9 March 1997. He was sixty-six years old.

Closing Credits

The kind of television show that Terry Nation wrote for has never been critically acclaimed. Of the series on which he worked, the only one that is accepted without reservation as a major piece of work, a national institution even, is *Doctor Who*, grown respectable through sheer longevity, part now of the shared childhood experience of the majority of the British population. *Blake's 7* and *Survivors* have their passionate defenders, but few professional commentators would consider them alongside contemporary television works such as Mike Leigh's *Abigail's Party* (1977) or Alan Bleasdale's *Boys from the Blackstuff* (1982). The only other exception is perhaps *The Avengers*, which narrowly missed making the top fifty when the British Film Institute drew up its list of the best British television shows of the twentieth century. As for the rest of the 1960s action adventure series, they were disparaged by critics at the time and, even when they have in later years come under the gaze of academics specialising in cultural studies and the mass media, they have tended to be regarded as windows on their world, rather than as works in their own right.

Terry Nation never tired of explaining: 'My intention always is to entertain because if I fail to do that, I think I've failed to reach an audience. But within the context of primarily entertaining, I like to say some things that I believe are valid and good and honourable. I hope it's subversive in that sense.' He was perfectly well aware, however, that this was not the path to critical respectability. 'Oh, I'm never taken as a serious writer,' he said. 'I don't mind that too much.'

The same has long been true, of course, of popular fiction more generally. Far-fetched tales of exaggerated heroes and villains may be the bedrock of literature, but they have always been seen as slightly unworthy when compared to high art. Even in this context, however, popular television – and particularly the escapist side of it – was a special case, not simply overlooked but attacked vehemently from the outset. Unlike previous media it was so visible, so intrusive that it could not be disregarded.

In the 1920s and 1930s the great and the good in society could pretend the Saint and Bulldog Drummond didn't exist, simply by averting their gaze as they passed the bookstalls at railway stations, and by not venturing into the circulating libraries run by Smith's and Boots that supplied the working class with their reading matter. The arrival of the broadcast media in the shape of radio suggested that a new world was coming, but the monopoly exercised by the BBC, particularly in its pre-war incarnation, did its best to keep popular entertainment under a benign, paternalist control. Millions might choose to tune into Radio Luxembourg, but there was no official recognition of this fact by the establishment. Standards got looser during the war, but in 1946 came the consolation of the Third Programme, a cultural enclave devoted to classical music, lectures and serious drama.

Less easily avoided was the growing popularity of American culture, a distressing development that went hand-in-hand with the USA's eclipse of Britain as the world's major power. In an attempt to combat this pernicious influence, the post-war Labour government under Clement Attlee set up the Arts Council of Great Britain, building on wartime initiatives. 'Let every part of Merry England be merry in its own way,' urged the Council's founding chairman, the economist John Maynard Keynes. And in case the subtext wasn't clear, he spelt it out: 'Death to Hollywood.' In similar vein, the Communist Party of Great Britain, still an influential political force at the time, staged a conference in 1951 under the title 'The American Threat to British Culture'. The contemporary campaign against American comics followed along the same lines: a defence of British culture irrespective of what the British people might choose for themselves. But still it was possible for those of delicate sensibilities to avoid contamination by choosing to visit the state-subsidised, Eurocentric opera and ballet, while shunning the cinema of Hollywood.

Television, though, was a very different matter, once the BBC monopoly had been broken by the independent companies. The entertainment favoured by the masses was now being beamed directly into the most genteel of drawing rooms and it was becoming increasingly difficult to ignore its irksome presence. Some did so by resisting for as long as possible the purchase of the new television sets that could receive the commercial stations, and thereafter by pretending that the button to change channels did not exist: as late as the 1970s, it was still the practice in many normal middle-class homes to have an unofficial ban on watching ITV. Research in 1974 showed that the working class spent 59 per cent of their viewing time watching ITV; the comparable figure for the upper middle class was just 34 per cent. In the first decade and more of independent television, the proportions had been even more pronounced.

Confronted by the menace of ITV, and with its audience figures in free fall, the BBC couldn't resist indefinitely and the contagion couldn't be contained. If it was going to offer any resistance at all to the onward march of ITV, and maintain its unique claim to the funds of the licence fee, the BBC would have to compete on the field of populism. Thus began the process of what would, fifty years later, come to be referred to as dumbing down. With the likes of *The Ted Ray Show*, the corporation tentatively began the embrace of variety programmes, which had long been looked upon with disfavour (even in pre-broadcast days, there had been a definite social and class divide between the 'legitimate' theatre and the music hall), though BBC television did not yet try to match the brassy pleasures of *Val Parnell's Startime* or *Sunday Night at the London Palladium*.

There were by the end of the 1950s criticisms of popular television in general, but it was ITV in particular that came under intense and sustained attack. Those on the right criticised the appalling decline of artistic standards, while those on the left railed against the duping of the working classes with game shows, variety and lowbrow drama. Few were prepared to argue, as did the Labour politician Richard Crossman, that the public had a 'right to triviality' if it so chose, and fewer still were prepared to defend ITV as providing a legitimate expression of popular culture. The assault reached a peak with the Pilkington Report in 1962, published the month before Terry Nation's first television drama was screened on ITV. 'The disquiet about television,' opined Pilkington (or rather, Richard Hoggart, who provided the intellectual backbone of the committee), 'is mainly attributable to independent television and largely to its entertainment programmes.'

On the other side of the argument, there was Lew Grade, the principal target of Pilkington, who was baffled by all the criticism. 'I was determined to prove that British programmes were the best in the world,' he protested, 'and I did it. Look at the sales figures!' It would be absurd, of course, to claim that audience share should be the sole criterion for judging the value of entertainment, but equally absurd to ignore it altogether. Like pop music, which defined itself by the relative weekly sales of various records, television was designed to provide entertainment for large numbers of people, and viewing figures at least provided a crude measure of its success in this direction. Furthermore, Grade's defence of exports went some way to answering the charge of Americanisation: selling British programmes to the States was surely as valid a response to Hollywood as was Keynes's allocation of tax revenues to the Royal Opera House, or the Communist Party's belated endorsement of folk music and Morris dancing.

In any event, competition between ITV and the BBC, whatever the reservations, proved to be beneficial to both. Despite all the fears, Britain had by chance stumbled upon a near-perfect structure for television. With just two mainstream channels, each dependent on a different source of funding, competition was centred on programming, not on chasing advertising revenue. Meanwhile the establishment of BBC2 – the one positive outcome of Pilkington – allowed an outlet for the new, the experimental and minority interests, including the science fiction championed by Irene Shubik. For twenty-five years from the launch of BBC2 in 1964, through the first incarnation of Channel 4, up to the dawn of the multi-channel satellite future, this was the golden age of British television.

Terry Nation was a key part of that era. He didn't create *Doctor Who* (despite a famously inaccurate answer in the game Trivial Pursuit), but there is little doubt that without the boost given to the series by the Daleks, it would have faded away within a year. And *Doctor Who* was significant not merely as a show in its own right, but because it laid the foundation for what would become BBC1's most important institution: the family-orientated schedules of Saturday evening.

Traditionally Saturdays hadn't been seen as a major prize. The legal restrictions on Sunday trading meant that it wasn't considered a particularly advantageous time for advertisers on ITV, just as Christmas tended to be of little value to the commercial channel in the days when shops closed on bank holidays: what was the point of encouraging people to buy things when they couldn't act on your suggestion? So there were, for example, no soap operas broadcast on Saturdays. But when London Weekend Television was launched in 1968, promising to break with ITV's populism and to provide sophisticated programming for the more discerning weekend viewer, the BBC saw its opportunity and began to target Saturday evenings with straightforward entertainment. Within a few years it had secured complete control of the ratings, with a string of guaranteed crowd pleasers: *The Generation Game, The Two Ronnies, The Dick Emery Show, Match of the Day*. From *Doctor Who* through to the late-night chat on *Parkinson*, Saturday evenings belonged to BBC1.

And it's that Saturday evening programming that tends to induce the greatest nostalgia among those who lived through the 1970s, when viewing figures were at their highest. When Jack Kibble-White and Steve Williams wrote an *Encyclopaedia of Classic Saturday Night Telly* in 2007, they pointed out it was unlikely that they would produce 'a follow-up looking at, say, Tuesday night's output; mainly because no one really remembers which shows were regularly transmitted on that day of the week'. The foundation stone for the BBC's domination of Saturday nights was *Doctor Who*, the programme whose success was assured by Terry Nation. When the show returned to British screens in 2005, eight years after Nation's death, it was a foregone conclusion that it would find its place again early on Saturday evenings, trying to catch a family audience that could be passed on to the remainder of the schedule, while evoking memories of the golden age.

But even during those years, there remained for many commentators the well-worn suspicion of populist drama, the reluctance to accept that Terry Nation might have a point when he claimed that 'the function of people in television should be to take people away from all their daily toil'. At the heart of his belief, as well as at the core of the critical hostility, was a love of telling stories, a conviction that the essence of entertaining fiction is to keep the reader wanting to turn the page, or the viewer wanting to see what happens next.

'I'd get very uneasy if a whole page went by and nothing was happening except people talking,' Nation explained. 'So if I had a situation where people were going to talk for three pages, I would put a bomb there, and it was going to be ticking. Now you can keep your dialogue, because you can keep coming back to that bomb – will they find it in time?' From the point of view of the script editor, this sometimes presented problems. 'If Terry sent you an hour's script, you couldn't cut half of it out, because Terry would look at the story as a whole, and it would be impossible to lose any of it,' commented Dennis Spooner. He reached out for a similar example of the ticking bomb: 'If Terry had done a sequence with a dustbin, it would fit in, it would hold a bomb or something, and you couldn't take the scene out. Whatever Terry put in was relevant to the story.'

There would be other work for a script editor. Nation was sometimes said to be weaker on dialogue than some of his contemporaries, though this wasn't a view necessarily shared by the actors who delivered the lines. 'It was not difficult to learn his dialogue because it was true,' reflected Roger Moore. 'Things are easy to learn when they're well written. Noel Coward was like that – to do Coward it was very easy to learn the dialogue because it flows. And Terry could do that too.' But the rush of story-telling, the love of improbable plot developments was undoubtedly Nation's greatest strength. Perhaps it owed something to his method of writing, to his dislike of going back to rework his material. He would place his characters in impossible situations of peril and then have to find a way to extricate them from under the pile of problems he had created. 'I didn't want anybody to be bored,' he said. 'I put in more and more. I put in a lot of stories which I would then have to resolve.' His experience of writing the stories, as he smoked furiously and spoke the dialogue out loud to himself, commenting on the action, was thus not dissimilar to that of his audience watching them, unsure what might happen next, eager to see how on earth it could all be wrapped up before the closing credits rolled. These were tales designed to be seen in weekly episodes, to provide such exciting enter-tainment that the viewers would want to come back for more.

It has long been the case with popular fiction that, for the most part, the successful practitioners are those who identify with their audience – not in terms of political perspective or social experience, but in terms of genuinely liking the genre in which they're working. It's notable too that many of the works most readily taken to heart by the public have been written at speed. Matthew Lewis wrote his three-volume Gothic classic *The Monk* (1796) in the space of ten weeks, Robert Louis Stevenson said that the first draft of *Doctor Jekyll and Mr Hyde* took him three days, while Henry Rider Haggard, having read Stevenson's *Treasure Island*, decided he could do better and knocked out *She* (1886) in six weeks, 'written at white heat, almost without rest'. The year before the Daleks were born, Anthony Burgess had taken three weeks to write *A Clockwork Orange*.

So it was with Nation's most enduring work. In formal terms, 'The Daleks' is far from his best piece of writing. But the speed at which he produced it allowed him to tap into his love of adventure tales, to produce his own take on them. Working reluctantly, but out of necessity, for children's television enabled him to bypass any pretensions to being taken seriously as a writer and to channel the literature that 'I lapped up when I was a boy'. There was, as ever with such runaway hits, a strong element of luck, but the years of consuming H.G. Wells, Arthur Conan Doyle and W.E.

Johns had prepared the ground for fortune. And, however impressive the design of the Daleks in look and sound, the essence of their appeal was there in his scripts.

But the design of the Daleks was certainly part of Nation's luck. He had chosen to work in the most collaborative of writing environments and was ultimately dependent on others to realise his stories. It often produced a conflict within him, as with so many other screenwriters. On the one hand, the presence of script editors and producers and directors absolved him of the need to rework and rewrite; there was always someone else to do the polishing. He claimed that he didn't care what happened to the scripts after they left his typewriter: 'I delivered something into the hands of other professionals, now let them go ahead with it.' But underneath that professed disregard was a feeling that things would be better if he had more control. 'If I had my way, I would be down there and I'd hem the dresses and paint the scenery and put the make-up on the actors and then act it all myself. But you can't do that.' He never quite reconciled himself to the contribution of others, always complaining that no one else cared as much about his creations – whether it were the Daleks, *Survivors* or *Blake's 7* – as he did. And he was, inevitably, at the mercy of others. Some of his best stories are to be found in *The Baron*, intricate, taut little thrillers that are little remembered because the production lacked the gloss and the glamour of *The Saint* or *The Avengers*.

Given his approach to writing, and the sheer quantity of material he turned out, it is hardly surprising that Nation repeated himself from time to time: those ticking bombs, for example. 'Terry Nation had a thing about bombs,' reflected Terrance Dicks. 'You can rely on a bomb turning up in every Terry Nation script, somewhere or other.' But then he was far from alone in having his obsessions and his familiar tricks.

The last series from the pen of Dennis Potter, for example, one of the most acclaimed and revered of all television writers, was *Cold Lazarus* (1996), a science fiction piece set four hundred years in the future, in which scientists are accessing the memories contained in a disembodied head that is held in cryogenic suspension. It's an intriguing piece of work that contained much that would have looked very familiar to Nation. Helmeted security guards gun down members of a resistance group, the head floats in a tank, echoing the imagery of the *Blake's 7* episode 'The Web' (or even 'The Keys of Marinus'), and a flirtatious, megalomaniac woman seeks to create a disturbing half-hour virtual-reality serial that will enable her corporation to sell anti-anxiety pills; just to make clear that Potter knows his references, she insists that it should have 'No bug-eyed monsters'. But, this being Potter, no one is much surprised when the memories that the scientists tap into turn out to be those of a boy growing up in the Forest of Dean in the 1930s, nor that the boy is sexually assaulted and later becomes a writer.

That was the key difference between a writer such as Potter and one such as Nation. In all his most celebrated and lauded work, Potter wrote from his own experience. He may have drawn explicitly on popular culture with the music and detective fiction of the 1930s in, say, *The Singing Detective*, but the psoriatic arthropathy from which his central character, Philip E. Marlow, suffers is the same condition that Potter himself had.

There is no equivalent in Nation. When he includes a disability, it tends to be immobility. Time and again his work includes characters trapped in wheelchairs: Dortmun in 'The Daleks Invasion of Earth', Lucien in 'A Memory of Evil' (*The Baron*), Mother in *The Avengers*, as well as Steed in 'Noon Doomsday' and Baron von Orlak in 'Legacy of Death' from the same series, Davros in 'Genesis of the Daleks', Vic Thatcher in *Survivors*. While a couple of these weren't actually his creations – Mother came from Brian Clemens, while it wasn't Nation who put Vic Thatcher in an improvised wheelchair – it is clearly a recurring image. But it's not drawn from life, and nor is there any consistent theme. Dortmun leads the resistance against the Daleks, but the scientist who created the monsters is also confined to a chair. There is nothing to be read into these cases except that Nation recognised the dramatic potential of a character with limited mobility. And that he was influenced by other fiction. Much of the enduring power of *Treasure Island*, for example, is derived from the disabilities of Blind Pew and the one-legged Long John Silver. More directly there were recent cinematic examples of characters in wheelchairs, Blanche (Joan Crawford) in Robert Aldrich's *Whatever Happened to Baby Jane* (1962) and Peter Sellers's eponymous antihero in *Dr Strangelove*. Nation's reference points were almost always to be found in the literature and cinema that he enjoyed or admired. One of the few pieces of work that was inspired directly by his own life was the writing of *Rebecca's World* for his daughter.

Beyond the familiar images, there was also in Nation's work a coherent vision, a set of recurring themes that identify his preoccupations. From Skaro onwards, we find ourselves repeatedly witnessing the decay of societies, whether through conflict, decadence or disease. And from 'The Dalek Invasion of Earth' onwards, many of those societies are under enemy occupation, places of repression, collaboration and personal betrayals; Nation never forgot the fears of his nine-year-old self, sheltering from the bombing raids that were intended to prepare the ground for a Nazi invasion of Britain: 'As a wartime child, I grew up when bombs were dropping and men were trying to kill me.' The horrors of the time shaped his adult writing. 'Much of sci-fi promises a bright future – even if my view is rather bleak,' he once reflected, and it was a portrayal that grew ever bleaker as Britain's economic and social decline became more pronounced, as the optimism of his post-war youth faded. Even when the country was congratulating itself on its swinging international image, he was writing tales of dissent; the Doctor may have thwarted the evil plans of the Daleks in 'Invasion', but the images that linger are of slave labour camps and of aliens occupying the streets of London.

However dark his creations became, they were always balanced by two redeeming features. First there was the element of humour, whether it were the tongue-in-cheek fun to be had with genre expectations in *The Saint* or the sarcastic wisecracks of Vila in *Blake's 7*. Second, there was the moral consistency, the absolute belief in the need for honour, honesty and decency; though these virtues were not necessarily proof against the random violence of life, they were nonetheless to be admired and cherished. Nation's villains – Davros and the Daleks, Servalan, Mr Glister – are wonderfully captivating creatures, but his heroes too are inspiring fantasy figures, from the Doctor and *The Persuaders!* to Abby Grant and Jimmy Garland. Even in the case of his most morally ambiguous hero, there's ultimately no doubt that Avon is really an old-fashioned swashbuckling good guy, the kind with whom Nation himself, as a child, would have identified.

But if Nation's mature work was firmly in the old thriller tradition of his childhood, it didn't mean that he added nothing to that tradition or that he wasn't responsible for technical innovations. Most influential was his popularisation of the story arc and the season cliff-hanger within television series.

The traditional format for popular dramas had been established in the USA where the need to syndicate shows to local stations meant that each episode was expected to stand alone; there was no guarantee that episodes would be shown in a particular order, and it was therefore considered wise for there to be no continuing storylines. The ITC series followed this lead, so that the essential situation in a show like *The Adventures of Robin Hood* remained unchanged from episode to episode. Even in the American series *The Fugitive* (1963), where a broad storyline ran throughout, as Dr Richard Kimble sought to prove his innocence, there was little in the way of continuing plot development; and when ratings fell low enough that the series was cancelled, it merely meant that an ending was added to tie up the loose ends. Structurally nothing much had changed since the nineteenth-century penny dreadfuls, when James Rymer's *Varney the Vampire* (1845) had run in instalments for the best part of three years, until falling sales figures brought it to an abrupt end after 220 chapters.

There were, of course, other models used for television – the soap and the drama serial, where there was a continuing narrative thread – but science fiction and action adventure shows remained firmly wedded to the existing format. The key exception was the special case of *Doctor Who*, which was a series of serials: each episode of a six-part story followed on from the previous one, with cliff-hanger endings built into each. It was not, however, until Nation's 'The Dalek Invasion of Earth' that the first links were established between those serials, establishing the concept of continuity across the whole series. Others built on his work, but his was the first stone.

It was *Blake's 7*, though, that was the real game-changer. In his notes for the second season, Nation spelt out his thoughts on what would later be referred to as a story arc. 'Whilst we remain a series and not a serial,' he wrote, 'it is important to have a progressive theme and an ultimate goal. This theme will be dealt with in five or six key episodes. We should have some passing reference to the theme in all other episodes.' By the end of Nation's life, this had become standard practice, with shows like *The X-Files* (1993), *Star Trek: Deep Space Nine* (1993) and *Babylon 5* (1994), but back in 1978 it was far from being an obvious idea. Nor was it normal to end a season with a major cliff-hanger that would be resolved next year; the era of the 'who shot J.R.' storyline in *Dallas* had not yet arrived. Nation played a key role in establishing these elements of modern television fantasy shows, with *Blake's 7* being cited as an influence by American creators such as J. Michael Straczynski (of *Babylon 5*) and Joss Wheldon (*Buffy the Vampire Slayer*). Straczynski even toyed with the idea of having guest appearances by *Blake's 7* stars in his show, a cross-pollination that again Nation had attempted, with his suggestion that the Daleks might appear on *Blake's 7*. The stylistic flourishes of Dennis Potter were more obvious in their reinvention of what television could do, but have ultimately proved far less influential than Nation's work.

Despite these technical innovations, Nation's career is ultimately defined by the Daleks, a fact of which he was more than aware, and which he happily accepted. Some of those whose work was overshadowed by a single popular success – Conan Doyle with Sherlock Holmes, Burgess with *A Clockwork Orange* – were keen to repudiate their creations, but Nation never gave any indication that he regretted the monsters' extraordinary popularity. Towards the end of his life, he reflected on the generation that had grown up watching the Daleks. 'They'd watch from outside the room, through a crack in the door, or from behind the couch,' he mused. 'It frightened them, but they wouldn't miss it for the world. It must be thirty years ago we're talking, so those little kids are now parents with children of their own, growing up and still sitting behind the couch watching. I find that quite amazing.'

The longevity of the Daleks has depended on the fact that they have changed very little since their first appearance in 1963. Many of those who influenced Nation as a child created characters who were initially on the wrong side of the law – Edgar Wallace's Four Just Men, Leslie Charteris's Saint, John Creasey's Baron – but who crossed back over the line to become official or semi-official figures of respectability. In moral, if not legal, terms Avon followed their example. The Daleks never did. That was their greatest strength, even if it was the same inflexibility that also made the idea of them having their own series so implausible; they were and are the perfect supporting villains, rather than lead characters in their own right.

The failure to secure backing for the *Daleks* proposal, however damaging to Nation's ego at the time, should not be a cause of much regret. Nor should the non-appearance of some other proposals, such as *The Team* or *No Place Like Home*. On the other hand, *The Fixers* would have been an interesting addition to his portfolio of programmes. As indeed would 'The Red Fort' – Nation never did write any historical stories, and it would be intriguing to see how he handled the proposition. Tales of British heroism during the Indian Mutiny were commonplace in his childhood, but might have found very different expression in the hands of a socialist writing in the wake of Indian independence. But the greatest loss is surely that of *The Incredible Robert Baldick*, a character that deserved much more than a single pilot.

Nation himself, however, expressed very few public regrets over missed television opportunities, content that he had created some of the most enduring characters on British television and originated some of its finest dramas, particularly with 'Genesis of the Daleks', the early episodes of

Survivors and *Blake's 7*. Instead, when asked in 1989 what his ultimate lifetime ambition was, he gave an entirely different answer: 'To have written a book as good as *The Bonfire of the Vanities*. I'd love to write a *good* book, one I was truly proud of.' Perhaps, after all, he too didn't quite realise that his contribution to popular television, these shows that attracted such huge audiences at the time and that inspired such continuing affection, was in the same class as serious literature. Or perhaps it was simply that he'd only recently finished reading Tom Wolfe's novel and it was the first thing that came into his head at the end of a long interview.

Back in 1974, speaking to the *South Wales Echo*, he had similarly reflected on what he would consider a permanent achievement. 'I suppose that all writers want a bit of immortality. I would be very happy to settle for one day seeing the word Dalek in the dictionary. So as a writer's memorial, I'd like that.' He would, no doubt, be delighted that the *Oxford English Dictionary* did indeed come to include the word 'Dalek', defining it as: 'A type of robot appearing in "Dr. Who", a BBC Television science-fiction programme; hence used allusively.' It was a flattering inclusion – even if the definition was inaccurate, since Daleks aren't robots at all, and even if the citations also repeated his own myth that he 'named them after an encyclopaedia volume covering DAL-LEK'. But then, as Nation used to say: 'A good story is a good story.'

Appendix: The Works of Terry Nation

A. Radio

All My Eye and Kitty Bluett (BBC, 1955) – 13-week series written by Terry Nation and Dick Barry, produced by Alastair Scott Johnston

The Frankie Howerd Show (BBC, 1953–5) – contributions to 1955 series written by Terry Nation and Dick Barry, produced by Alastair Scott Johnston

Floggit's (BBC, 1956–7) – two series and Christmas special, totalling 35 episodes, written by Terry Nation, John Junkin and Dave Freeman, produced by Alastair Scott Johnston and Bill Gates

Calling the Stars (BBC, 1957) – one episode of series written by Terry Nation and John Junkin, produced by John Simmonds

Variety Playhouse (BBC, 1953–63) – 1957 series written by Terry Nation and John Junkin, produced by Alastair Scott Johnston; further sketches in 1958 series

Fine Goings On (BBC, 1951–8) – 1958 series written by Terry Nation and John Junkin, produced by Bill Worsley

It's a Fair Cop (BBC, 1961) – eight-week series written by John Junkin and Terry Nation, produced by Herbert Smith

B. Television

The Idiot Weekly, Price 2d (Associated Rediffusion, 1956) – five-part series written by Spike Milligan and Associated London Scripts, including Terry Nation, John Junkin and Dave Freeman, produced by Dick Lester

Friday the 13th (BBC, 1957) – one-off sketch show written by John Junkin and Terry Nation, produced by George Inns

Val Parnell's Startime (ATV, 1958) – variety show with some contributions written by John Junkin and Terry Nation, produced by Val Parnell

The Ted Ray Show (BBC, 1958–9) – two series comprising seven episodes and a Christmas special, written by John Junkin and Terry Nation, produced by George Inns

The Jimmy Logan Show (BBC, 1959–60) – 12-part series of which eight episodes, plus a one-off special, written by John Junkin and Terry Nation, produced by George Inns and Bryan Sears

Out of this World (ABC, 1962) – produced by Leonard White, story editor Irene Shubik
  'Imposter' – wr. Terry Nation from a story by Philip K. Dick, dir. Peter Hammond
  'Botany Bay' – wr. Terry Nation, dir. Guy Very
  'Immigrant' – wr. Terry Nation from a story by Clifford Simak, dir. Jonathan Alwyn
No Hiding Place (Associated Rediffusion, 1959–67) – produced by Ray Dicks
  'Run for the Sea' (1962) – wr. Terry Nation, dir. Ian Fordyce and Richard Sidwell
Hancock (ATV, 1963) – executive producer Bernard Delfont, dir. Alan Tarrant
  'The Assistant' – wr. Terry Nation from a story by Ray Whyberd (Ray Alan)
  'The Night Out' – wr. Terry Nation
  'The Reporter' – wr. Terry Nation
  'The Writer' – wr. Terry Nation
Wish You Were Here (BBC, 1963) – one-off variety show presented by Eric Sykes with linking
    material written by Terry Nation
Doctor Who (BBC, 1963–89) – prod. Verity Lambert, John Wiles, Barry Letts, Philip
    Hinchcliffe, Graham Williams
  'The Daleks' (1963–4) – seven-episode serial wr. Terry Nation, dir. Christopher Barry
    and Richard Martin
  'The Keys of Marinus' (1964) – 6-episode serial wr. Terry Nation, dir. John Gorrie
  'The Dalek Invasion of Earth' (1964) – 6-episode serial wr. Terry Nation, dir. Richard Martin
  'The Chase' (1965) – 6-episode serial wr. Terry Nation, dir. Richard Martin
  'Mission to the Unknown' (1965) – one-off episode wr. Terry Nation, dir. Derek
    Martinus
  'The Daleks' Master Plan' (1965–6) – 12-episode serial wr. Terry Nation and Dennis
    Spooner, dir. Douglas Camfield
  'Planet of the Daleks' (1973) – 6-episode serial wr. Terry Nation, dir. David Maloney
  'Death to the Daleks' (1974) – 4-episode serial wr. Terry Nation, dir. Michael E. Briant
  'Genesis of the Daleks' (1975) – 6-episode serial wr. Terry Nation, dir. David Maloney
  'The Android Invasion' (1975) – 4-episode serial wr. Terry Nation, dir. Barry Letts
  'Destiny of the Daleks' (1979) – 4-episode serial wr. Terry Nation, dir. Ken Grieve
Uncle Selwyn (Associated Rediffusion, 1964) – play in the *ITV Play of the Week* series written by
    Terry Nation, directed by David Boisseau
Story Parade (BBC, 1964–5) – produced by Eric Taylor, story editor Irene Shubik
  'The Caves of Steel' (1964) – wr. Terry Nation from a novel by Isaac Asimov, dir. Peter
    Sasdy
  'A Kiss Before Dying' (1964) – wr. Terry Nation from a novel by Ira Levin, dir.
    Peter Sasdy
The Saint (ITC, 1962–9) – produced by Robert S. Baker and Monty Berman, script
    supervisor Harry H. Junkin
  'Lida' (1964) – wr. Terry Nation from a story by Leslie Charteris, dir. Leslie Norman
  'Jeannine' (1964) – wr. Terry Nation from a story by Leslie Charteris, dir. John Moxey
  'The Revolution Racket' (1964) – wr. Terry Nation from a story by Leslie Charteris, dir.
    Pat Jackson

'The Contract' (1965) – wr. Terry Nation from a story by Leslie Charteris, dir. Roger Moore

'The Inescapable Word' (1965) – wr. Terry Nation from a story by Leslie Charteris, dir. Roy Ward Baker

'The Sign of the Claw' (1965) – wr. Terry Nation from a story by Leslie Charteris, dir. Leslie Norman

'Sibao' (1965) – wr. Terry Nation from a story by Leslie Charteris, dir. Peter Yates

'The Crime of the Century' (1965) – wr. Terry Nation from a story by Leslie Charteris, dir. John Gilling

'The Man Who Could Not Die' (1965) – wr. Terry Nation from a story by Leslie Charteris, dir. Roger Moore

'Invitation to Danger' (1968) – wr. Terry Nation, dir. Roger Moore

'The Desperate Diplomat' (1968) – wr. Terry Nation, dir. Ray Austin

'The Time to Die' (1968) – wr. Terry Nation, dir. Roy Ward Baker

'Where the Money Is' (1968) – wr. Terry Nation, dir. Roger Moore

Out of the Unknown (BBC, 1965–71) – producer and script editor Irene Shubik

'The Fox and the Forest' (1965) – wr. Terry Nation from a story by Ray Bradbury, with additional material by Meade Roberts, dir. Robin Midgley

The Baron (ITC, 1966–7) – produced by Monty Berman, script editor Terry Nation

'Epitaph for a Hero' (1966) – wr. Terry Nation, dir. John Moxey

'Something for a Rainy Day' (1966) – wr. Terry Nation, dir. Cyril Frankel

'Red Horse, Red Rider' (1966) – wr. Terry Nation, dir. John Moxey

'Masquerade'/'The Killing' (1966) – wr. Terry Nation, dir. Cyril Frankel

'And Suddenly You're Dead' (1966) – wr. Terry Nation and Dennis Spooner, dir. Cyril Frankel

'Portrait of Louisa' (1966) – wr. Terry Nation, dir. Roy Ward Baker

'There's Someone Close Behind You' (1966) – wr. Terry Nation and Dennis Spooner, dir. Roy Ward Baker

'Storm Warning'/'The Island' (1967) – wr. Terry Nation, dir. Gordon Flemyng

'A Memory of Evil' (1967) – wr. Terry Nation and Dennis Spooner, dir. Don Chaffey

'The Seven Eyes of Night' (1967) – wr. Terry Nation, dir. Robert Asher

'Night of the Hunter' (1967) – wr. Terry Nation, dir. Roy Ward Baker

'So Dark the Night' (1967) – wr. Terry Nation and Dennis Spooner, dir. Robert Tronson

'Roundabout' (1967) – wr. Terry Nation, dir. Robert Tronson

'The Man Outside' (1967) – wr. Terry Nation, dir. Roy Ward Baker

'Countdown' (1967) – wr. Terry Nation, dir. Robert Asher

The Avengers (ABC, 1961–9) – produced by Albert Fennell and Brian Clemens, story editor Terry Nation

'Legacy of Death' (1968) – wr. Terry Nation, dir. Don Chaffey

'Noon Doomsday' (1968) – wr. Terry Nation, dir. Peter Sykes

'Invasion of the Earthmen' (1969) – wr. Terry Nation, dir. Don Sharp

'Take Me to Your Leader' (1969) – wr. Terry Nation, dir. Robert Fuest

'Thingumajig' (1969) – wr. Terry Nation, dir. Leslie Norman

'Take-Over' (1969) – wr. Terry Nation, dir. Robert Fuest

The Champions (ITC, 1968–9) – produced by Monty Berman, script supervisor Dennis
  Spooner

'The Fanatics' (1968) – wr. Terry Nation, dir. John Gilling

'The Body Snatchers' (1969) – wr. Terry Nation, dir. Paul Dickson

Department S (ITC, 1969–70) – produced by Monty Berman, story consultant Dennis
  Spooner

'A Cellar Full of Silence' (1969) – wr. Terry Nation, dir. John Gilling

'The Man in the Elegant Room' (1969) – wr. Terry Nation, dir. Cyril Frankel

The Persuaders! (ITC, 1971–2) – produced by Robert S. Baker, script editor and associate
  producer Terry Nation

'Take Seven' (1971) – wr. Terry Nation, dir. Sidney Hayers

'Someone Like Me' (1971) – wr. Terry Nation from a story by Robert S. Baker, dir. Roy
  Ward Baker

'Chain of Events' (1971) – wr. Terry Nation, dir. Peter Hunt

'A Home of One's Own' (1971) – wr. Terry Nation, dir. James Hill

'Five Miles to Midnight' (1972) – wr. Terry Nation, dir. Val Guest

'A Death in the Family' (1972) – wr. Terry Nation, dir. Sidney Hayers

'Someone Waiting' (1972) – wr. Terry Nation, dir. Peter Medak

The Incredible Robert Baldick (BBC, 1972) – play in the *Drama Playhouse* series, written by Terry
  Nation, directed by Cyril Coke, produced by Anthony Coburn

The Protectors (ITC, 1972–4) – produced by Gerry Anderson and Reg Hill, script editor Tony
  Barwick

'Bagman' (1973) – wr. Terry Nation, dir. Johnny Hough

'Baubles, Bangles and Beads' (1973) – wr. Terry Nation, dir. Jeremy Summers

'Route 27' (1974) – wr. Terry Nation, dir. Don Leaver

'A Pocketful of Posies' (1974) – wr. Terry Nation, dir. Cyril Frankel

Thriller (ATV, 1973–6) – created by Brian Clemens

'K Is for Killing' (1974, US title: 'Color Him Dead') – wr. Brian Clemens and
  Terry Nation, dir. Peter Moffatt

Survivors (BBC, 1975–7) – produced by Terence Dudley

'The Fourth Horseman' (1975) – wr. Terry Nation, dir. Pennant Roberts

'Genesis' (1975) – wr. Terry Nation, dir. Gerald Blake

'Gone Away' (1975) – wr. Terry Nation, dir. Terence Williams

'Garland's War' (1975) – wr. Terry Nation, dir. Terence Williams

'The Future Hour' (1975) – wr. Terry Nation, dir. Terence Williams

'Something of Value' (1975) – wr. Terry Nation, dir. Terence Williams

'A Beginning' (1975) – wr. Terry Nation, dir. Pennant Roberts

Blake's 7 (BBC, 1978–81) – produced by David Maloney, script editor Chris Boucher

'The Way Back' (1978) – wr. Terry Nation, dir. Michael E. Briant

'Space Fall' (1978) – wr. Terry Nation, dir. Pennant Roberts

'Cygnus Alpha' (1978) – wr. Terry Nation, dir. Vere Lorrimer

'Time Squad' (1978) – wr. Terry Nation, dir. Pennant Roberts

'The Web' (1978) – wr. Terry Nation, dir. Michael E. Briant

'Seek-Locate-Destroy' (1978) – wr. Terry Nation, dir. Vere Lorrimer

'Mission to Destiny' (1978) – wr. Terry Nation, dir. Pennant Roberts

'Duel' (1978) – wr. Terry Nation, dir. Douglas Camfield

'Project Avalon' (1978) – wr. Terry Nation, dir. Michael E. Briant

'Breakdown' (1978) – wr. Terry Nation, dir. Vere Lorrimer

'Bounty' (1978) – wr. Terry Nation, dir. Pennant Roberts

'Deliverance' (1978) – wr. Terry Nation, dir. David Maloney and Michael E. Briant

'Orac' (1978) – wr. Terry Nation, dir. Vere Lorrimer

'Redemption' (1979) – wr. Terry Nation, dir. Vere Lorrimer

'Pressure Point' (1979) – wr. Terry Nation, dir. George Spenton-Foster

'Countdown' (1979) – wr. Terry Nation, dir. Vere Lorrimer

'Aftermath' (1980) – wr. Terry Nation, dir. Vere Lorrimer

'Powerplay' (1980) – wr. Terry Nation, dir. David Maloney

'Terminal' (1980) – wr. Terry Nation, dir. Mary Ridge

MacGyver (ABC, 1985–92) – produced by Henry Winkler and John Rich

    'The Golden Triangle' (1985) – opening gambit wr. Terry Nation, dir. Donald Petrie

    'Thief of Budapest' (1985) – opening gambit wr. Terry Nation and Stephen Downing, dir. Lee H. Katzin

    'Target MacGyver' (1985) – opening gambit wr. Terry Nation, dir. Lee H. Katzin

A Masterpiece of Murder (20th Century-Fox, 1986) – written by Andrew J. Fenady and Terry Nation, directed by Charles S. Dubin

A Fine Romance (ABC, 1989, UK title: *Ticket to Ride*)

    'The Tomas Crown Affair' – wr. Terry Nation

C. Cinema

And the Same to You (Monarch Productions, 1959) – directed by George Pollock, screenplay by John Paddy Carstairs, adapted from the play *The Chigwell Chicken* by A.P. Dearsley, with additional material by John Junkin and Terry Nation

What a Whopper (Viscount Films, 1961) – directed by Gilbert Gunn, screenplay by Terry Nation, based on an idea by Trevor Peacock and Jeremy Lloyd

Dr Who and the Daleks (Amicus, 1965) – directed by Gordon Flemyng, screenplay by Milton Subotsky, based on the BBC television serial by Terry Nation

Daleks' Invasion Earth: 2150 A.D. (Amicus, 1966) – directed by Gordon Flemyng, screenplay by Milton Subotsky with additional material by David Whitaker, based on the BBC television serial by Terry Nation

And Soon the Darkness (Associated British Productions, 1970) – directed by Robert Fuest, screenplay by Brian Clemens and Terry Nation

The House in Nightmare Park (Associated London Films/Extonation, 1973) – directed by Peter Sykes, screenplay by Clive Exton and Terry Nation

D. Literature

David Whitaker & Terry Nation, *The Dalek Book* (Souvenir/Panther, 1964)

David Whitaker & Terry Nation, *The Dalek World* (Souvenir/Panther, 1965)

Terry Nation, *The Dalek Pocketbook and Space-Travellers Guide* (Souvenir/Panther, 1965)

Terry Nation & Brad Ashton, *The Dalek Outer Space Book* (Souvenir/Panther, 1966)

Terry Nation, 'We Are the Daleks!' in *Radio Times Doctor Who Special* (BBC, November 1973)

Terry Nation, *Rebecca's World: Journey to the Forbidden Planet* (G. Whizzard/Andre Deutsch, 1975; pbk edn: Red Fox, 1991)

Terry Nation & Terrance Dicks, *Doctor Who and the Daleks Omnibus* (Artus, 1976)

Terry Nation, *Survivors* (Weidenfeld & Nicolson, 1976; pbk edn: Futura, 1976; repub: Orion Books, 2008)

Terry Nation, 'Daleks: The Secret Invasion' (*Evening News*, 1974), republished in Terrance Dicks (ed.), *Terry Nation's Dalek Special* (Target, 1979)

John Peel & Terry Nation, *The Official Doctor Who and the Daleks Book* (St Martin's Press, 1988)

E. Stage

Off the Cuff – 15-minute sketch as part of revue staged at the Irving Theatre, London in 1956

The Curse of the Daleks – written by Terry Nation and David Whitaker, first staged at Wyndham's Theatre, London in December 1965

References

Material derived from interviews – whether in person, by telephone or by email – is indicated as being personal communications with the mark 'PC'.

Quotes taken from files in the BBC Written Archives Centre are indicated by the preface BBC WAC and then the file reference number.

Many of the novels cited that are out of copyright – by H.G. Wells, Arthur Conan Doyle and others – are available in so many editions that page references would be less than helpful; instead any references are to chapters.

Quotes from television, film and radio are my own transcriptions – my apologies for any misquoting or wayward spelling.

The following abbreviations are used for television shows and stories written by Terry Nation:

'Android' – *Doctor Who*: 'The Android Invasion' (1975)
Baron – *The Baron* (1966–7)
B7 – *Blake's 7* (1978–81)
'Chase' – *Doctor Who*: 'The Chase' (1965)
'Daleks' – *Doctor Who*: 'The Daleks' (1963)
'Death' – *Doctor Who*: 'Death to the Daleks' (1974)
'Destiny' – *Doctor Who*: 'Destiny of the Daleks' (1979)
Dept S – *Department S* (1969)
'Genesis' – *Doctor Who*: 'Genesis of the Daleks' (1975)
'Invasion' – *Doctor Who*: 'The Dalek Invasion of Earth' (1964)
'Marinus' – *Doctor Who*: 'The Keys of Marinus' (1964)
Persuaders – *The Persuaders!* (1971–2)

'Plan' – *Doctor Who*: 'The Daleks' Master Plan' (1965)
'Planet' – *Doctor Who*: 'Planet of the Daleks' (1974)
Saint – *The Saint* (1962–9)

INTRO: Vote Dalek!

p. 3 **Terry 'Daleks' Nation** – Peel, *Starburst*, 1995
p. 3 **I have always been** – Cook and Wright, *British Science Fiction Television*, p. 121
p. 3 **I set out to write** – *Daily Mirror*, 11 December 1964
p. 3 **Stories must be strong** – Nation, 'Blake's 7: Series Two'
p. 4 **If he'd been writing** – Molesworth, *Terror Nation*
p. 4 **I thought he was** – 'Invasion', DVD commentary ep. 4
p. 4 **an encyclopaedia** – *Daily Mirror*, 11 December 1964
p. 4 **absolute rubbish** – Frost, *Today*, 1973
p. 4 **notices of his death** – *Sun*, 12 March 1997; *Times*, 13 March 1997
p. 4 **more TV scripts** – *South Wales Echo*, 2 March 1974
p. 5 **what people want** – *Guardian*, 31 January 1966
p. 5 **heroes constantly on the move** – Usborne, *Clubland Heroes*, p. 89
p. 5 **too much character** – Symons, *Bloody Murder*, p. 238
p. 5 **exaltation of idea** – Amis, *New Maps of Hell*, p. 28

p. 5 he had read the novels – Buchan, *Huntingtower*, ch. 1

p. 6 a story-telling medium – Ferris, *Sir Huge*, p. 249

p. 7 the nicest guy – Terrance Dicks, PC

p. 7 I've never really met – Molesworth, *Terror Nation*

p. 7 He was an intelligent – Roger Moore, PC

p. 7 lovely, rich, pastoral voice – Molesworth, *Terror Nation*

p. 7 Tall, handsome, relaxed – *Guardian*, 31 January 1966

p. 7 Look, we're just about – Terrance Dicks, PC

p. 7 Terry was larger – Deb Boultwood, PC

p. 8 Saturday afternoon – Butler, *The Durable Desperadoes*, p. 162

p. 8 I work directly – Ophir, Gies and Best, *Horizon*, 1989

p. 8 Terry's first drafts – Molesworth, *Terror Nation*

p. 8 I've known him – Stevens and Brown, 'Chris Boucher', *DWB* 108

p. 8 He had a habit – Terrance Dicks, PC

p. 9 Terry had talent – Brian Clemens, PC

p. 9 Terry was very ambitious – Groves, *The Terry Nation Story*

p. 9 I have never – ibid.

p. 9 Between the mid '60s – Cornell, Day and Topping, *The Avengers Dossier*, p. 4

p. 9 the same problem – Peel, *Starburst*, 1995

p. 10 same social experiences – Brian Clemens, PC

1 A Boy's Own Story

p. 11 to be an actor – *TV Times*, 7 February 1964

p. 13 unemployment descended – Lewis and Lewis, *The Land of Wales*, p. 57

p. 13 foraging parties – Summers, *Edge of Violence*, p. 64

p. 13 a time of soup – ibid., p. 73

p. 13 stiff and starchy – Elsie White, quoted by Harry Greene, PC

p. 13 a different planet – Pill, *A Cardiff Family in the Forties*, p. 94

p. 14 far-left socialism – *Guardian*, 31 January 1966

p. 15 There were all sorts – Stan Stennett, PC

p. 15 I'm a prolific writer – Groves, *The Terry Nation Story*

p. 15 three halfpence – Orwell, *The Road to Wigan Pier*, ch. 5

p. 16 He played truant – Groves, *The Terry Nation Story*

p. 16 I grew up – Fleming, *Starburst*, 1979

p. 16 horror fiction – Ophir, Gies and Best, *Horizon*, 1989

p. 16 quiet islands – Quicke, *Tomorrow's Television*, p. 29

p. 17 I do not pretend – Blythe, *The Age of Illusion*, p. 46

p. 18 very influential – Brian Clemens, PC

p. 18 For over five hours – *South Wales Echo and Express*, 2 January 1942

p. 18 read a newspaper – *Times*, 4 January 1941

p. 18 common Nation trait – Cornell, Day and Topping, *The Avengers Dossier*, p. 260

p. 19 a wartime child – Ophir, Gies and Best, *Horizon*, 1989

p. 20 round the compartment – Buchan, *The Island of Sheep*, ch. 1

p. 21 as the hero – Ophir, Gies and Best, *Horizon*, 1989

p. 21 what was credible – Harry Greene, PC

p. 21 lack of imagination – DVD production text, 'Daleks' ep. 3: 'The Rescue'

p. 21 the American shows – Ophir, Gies and Best, *Horizon*, 1989

p. 21 We listened closely – Muir, *A Kentish Lad*, p. 146

p. 22 personal pantheon – Monkhouse, *Crying With Laughter*, p. 102

p. 22 Youngsters with an ambition – Wyn Calvin, PC

p. 22 there they were – Ophir, Gies and Best, *Horizon*, 1989

p. 23 The glossy paper – Pickard, *I Could a Tale Unfold*, p. 116

p. 24 England I dream of – Thompson, *Sunshine on Putty*, p. 23

p. 24 **reputation for comedy** – Wyn Calvin, PC

p. 24 **to be a comedian** – Ophir, Gies and Best, *Horizon*, 1989

p. 25 **dressed beautifully** – Harry Greene, PC

p. 25 **turn out more cogs** – Summers, *The Raging Summer*, p. 83

p. 25 **instant recognition** – Harry Greene, PC

p. 25 **he was the epitome** – ibid.

p. 26 **a rather good comedian** – Nazarro, *Doctor Who Magazine*, 1989

p. 26 **I used to be a member** – *South Wales Echo*, 2 March 1974

p. 27 **Terry was doing** – Groves, *The Terry Nation Story*

2 Goings On

p. 28 **I auditioned** – Nazarro, *Doctor Who Magazine* 1989

p. 28 **His first break** – *Guardian*, 31 January 1966

p. 28 **writing comedy scripts** – Harry Greene, PC

p. 29 **encourage new writers** – Beryl Vertue, PC

p. 29 **tenacity, initiative and guts** – *South Wales Echo*, 27 May 1955

p. 29 **encouragement and advice** – BBC WAC RCONT1

p. 29 **many a humorist** – Sykes, *If I Don't Write It, Nobody Else Will*, p. 216

p. 30 **We never heard the names** – *Times*, 30 March 1963

p. 30 **novel in every respect** – Askey, *Before Your Very Eyes*, pp. 93–4

p. 30 **one hundred gags** – Kavanagh, *Tommy Handley*, p. 110

p. 30 **I never got a credit** – Wilmut, *Kindly Leave the Stage!*, p. 131

p. 31 **Pre-Ted Kavanagh** – Muir, *A Kentish Lad*, p. 120

p. 31 **their ambition** – *South Wales Echo*, 27 May 1955

p. 31 **When Ray and I started** – Alan Simpson PC

p. 31 **the advent of television comedy** – Sykes, *If I Don't Write It, Nobody Else Will*, p. 326

p. 32 **mutual protection society** – McCann, *Spike & Co*, p. 19

p. 32 **usual agency commission** – ALS contract for Dave Freeman dated 26 September 1955, signed by Eric Sykes

p. 32 **If you got stuck** – McCann, *Spike & Co*, p. 33

p. 32 **an altruistic manner** – Beryl Vertue, PC

p. 32 **the great value** – McCann, *Spike & Co*, p. 33

p. 33 **a rotten show** – Ophir, Gies and Best, *Horizon*, 1989 op. cit.

p. 33 **ordeal by fire** – Peel, *Starburst*, 1995

p. 33 **Everybody wrote** – Alan Simpson, PC

p. 33 **very double-barrelled** – Beryl Vertue, PC

p. 33 **a lovely man** – Ray Galton, PC

p. 34 **hairy tweeds** – McCann, *Spike & Co*, p. 32

p. 34 **Terry tried to be** – this and following quotes: Alan Simpson, Beryl Vertue, Ray Galton, PC

p. 35 **not cut out** – Keith Waterhouse, *Daily Mail*, 9 March 2006

p. 35 **you can write** – McCann, *Spike & Co*, p. 32

p. 36 **We feel that** – Nation's letter and Alastair Scott Johnston's covering note, BBC WAC RCONT1

p. 36 **We were beginning** – McCann, *Spike & Co*, p. 38

p. 37 **They were unafraid** – Groves, *The Terry Nation Story*

p. 37 **Peter Sellers series** – ALS letter to Dave Freeman dated 16 February 1956, signed by Beryl Vertue

p. 38 **They cleared the potato sacks** – McCann, *Spike & Co*, p. 33

p. 38 **You'd go to lunch** – ibid., p. 34

p. 40 **Nice cupper tea** – *Observer*, 26 August 1956

p. 41 **I should like you to know** – BBC WAC RCONT1

p. 41 **a small pier** — *Observer* 18 May 1958

p. 42 **He has been in and out** — *Radio Times*, 18 May 1961

p. 42 **Ealing-film-type music** — *Observer*, 28 May 1961

p. 42 **voracious appetite** — Sykes, *If I Don't Write It, Nobody Else Will*, p. 268

p. 42 **It did okay** — McCann, *Spike & Co*, p. 98

p. 43 **witty and topical** — BBC WAC T12/391/5 The Ted Ray Show

p. 44 **He didn't like me** — Logan, *It's a Funny Life*, p. 158

p. 44 **They made me sick** — ibid., p. 159

p. 44 **at least two years** — ibid., p. 162

p. 46 **very depressed state** — *South Wales Echo*, 2 March 1974

3 The Lads Themselves

p. 47 **progressive comedy** — Carpenter, *Spike Milligan*, p. 186

p. 47 **This is shit** — Monkhouse, *Crying With Laughter*, p. 97

p. 48 **inclined by stage experience** — *Times*, 1 January 1958

p. 49 **crudely farcical** — Bignell and O'Day, *Terry Nation*, p. 13

p. 50 **sweetness and naivety** — *TV Times*, 7 February 1964

p. 50 **The play sucked** — Tony Tanner, PC

p. 50 **proved very successful** — *South Wales Echo*, 2 March 1974

p. 50 **incredibly well received** — Peel, *Starburst*, 1995

p. 50 **a queer jumble** — *Guardian*, 11 February 1964

p. 50 **well in period** — *Daily Mirror*, 11 February 1964

p. 50 **big three** — *New Musical Express*, 10 March 1961

p. 51 **There's Adam Faith** — Galton and Simpson, *Hancock's Half Hour*, p. 109

p. 51 **family comedy** — Owen and Burford, *The Pinewood Story*, p. 92

p. 51 **British appetite** — quoted in Ross, *Sid James*

p. 52 **dire** — *Independent*, 10 March 2003

p. 52 **Howard and Marjorie** — *The Stage*, unknown date in 1956

p. 53 **I have decided** — Hancock and Nathan, *Hancock*, p. 111

p. 53 **all comics loathe** — *Guardian*, 18 February 1972

p. 54 **Without any discussion** — Oakes, *Tony Hancock*, p. 95

p. 54 **more salubrious** — Sykes, *If I Don't Write It, Nobody Else Will*, p. 352

p. 54 **To my amazement** — Goodwin, *When the Wind Changed*, p. 366

p. 54 **wonderful audience** — Ophir, Gies and Best, *Horizon* 1989

p. 54 **collapse in giggles** — Goodwin, *When the Wind Changed*, p. 366

p. 54 **visibly shaking** — ibid,. p. 367

p. 55 **finished the writing** — Hancock and Nathan, *Hancock*, p. 128

p. 55 **cold food** — Ophir, Gies and Best, *Horizon*, 1989

p. 55 **Matt's compartment** — Goodwin, *When the Wind Changed*, p. 458

p. 55 **the fellatio** — Williams, *Diaries*, p. 424

p. 56 **best-ever scriptwriters** — Oakes, *Tony Hancock*, p. 6

p. 56 **I was never** — Ophir, Gies and Best, *Horizon*, 1989

p. 56 **hiding to nothing** — Ray Galton, PC

p. 56 **quite so common** — *Daily Mail*, 3 January 1963

p. 57 **unnecessarily nasty** — Goodwin, *When the Wind Changed*, p. 365

p. 58 **Hancock fancied himself** — Oakes, *Tony Hancock*, p. 13

p. 58 **wine snob** — Ophir, Gies and Best, *Horizon*, 1989

p. 59 **You bastard** — Hancock and Nathan, *Hancock*, p. 130

p. 59 **I have sometimes** — *Guardian*, 4 January 1963

p. 59 **It is all very funny** — *Times*, 4 January 1963

p. 59 **If we had never** — *Observer*, 6 January 1963

p. 59 **unpalatable truth** — *Daily Mail*, 4 January 1963

p. 60 **I expected it** — *Daily Express*, 10 January 1963

p. 60 **The series was doomed** – Hancock and Nathan, *Hancock*, p. 132

p. 60 **My second look** – *Daily Mirror*, 1 March 1963

p. 60 **no happy moments** – Fisher, *Tony Hancock*, p. 385

p. 61 **strange three weeks** – Hancock and Nathan, *Hancock*, p. 133

p. 61 **Hancock in rags** – ibid., p. 134

4 Into the Unknown

p. 62 **in a dream world** – Jennings, *The Paul Jennings Reader*, p. 68

p. 62 **The wonderful thing** – *Radio Times*, 3 December 1964

p. 63 **This is free television** – Quicke, *Tomorrow's Television*, p. 25

p. 64 **a cross between** – Shubik, *Play for Today*, p. 9

p. 64 **non-conformist outsider** – White, *Armchair Theatre*, p. 31

p. 64 **Sydney was noisy** – ibid., p. 79

p. 64 **a suave character** – *Observer*, 12 February 1961

p. 64 **great impresario** – Shubik, *Play for Today*, p. 31

p. 65 **The policy I adopted** – Norden, Harper and Gilbert, *Coming to You Live!*, pp. 59–60

p. 65 **I am proud** – *Daily Express*, 5 January 1963

p. 65 **I've always been a sucker** – *Observer*, 22 April 1962

p. 66 **too remote** – David Butler, 'How to pilot a TARDIS' in Butler, *Time and Relative Dissertations in Space*, p. 22

p. 67 **In the late 1950s** – Ballard, *Miracles of Life*, p. 184

p. 67 **Ninety-five per cent** – *Times*, 13 September 1958

p. 67 **baffling characteristic** – *Guardian*, 3 April 1961

p. 67 **true literature** – Ballard, *Miracles of Life*, p. 194

p. 67 **man-eating** – Amis, *New Maps of Hell*, p. 70

p. 67 **more vitality** – *Observer*, 28 September 1952

p. 68 **a pet subject** – Shubik, *Play for Today*, p. 54

p. 68 **everyone is interested** – *Daily Mail*, 20 June 1962

p. 69 **I can't really remember** – Ray Galton, PC

p. 69 **I don't remember him** – Beryl Vertue, PC

p. 69 **one of the most subtle** – *Times*, 16 February 1960

p. 69 **I had nothing** – Peel, *Starburst*, 1995

p. 70 **galactic El Dorado** – Simak, 'Immigrant', p. 219

p. 70 **a doctorate on Earth** – ibid., p. 275

p. 70 **only one thing** – ibid., p. 276

p. 70 **an ingenious** – *Times*, 4 August 1962

p. 71 **level of writing** – *Times*, 4 August 1962

p. 71 **the most intelligent** – *Kinematograph Weekly*, 9 August 1962

p. 71 **the most accomplished** – *Yorkshire Evening Post*, 25 July 1962

p. 71 **the series as a whole** – *Daily Mail*, 24 September 1962

p. 71 **That was a great moment** – Groves, *The Terry Nation Story*

p. 71 **'DUSTBIN' MAN** – *Daily Mail*, 19 April 1963

p. 71 **a sort of anthology** – Shubik, *Play for Today*, p. 42

p. 71 **too derivative** – Bignell and O'Day, *Terry Nation*, p. 14

p. 72 **most interesting and amusing** – Shubik, *Play for Today*, p. 57

p. 72 **individualism and initiative** – Asimov, *The Caves of Steel*, p. 92

p. 72 **The balance** – ibid., p. 96

p. 72 **first became a city** – ibid.

p. 73 **Do you fear robots** – ibid., p. 173

p. 74 **A fascinating mixture** – *Listener*, 16 July 1964

p. 74 **highly successful** – *Times*, 13 June 1964

p. 74 **find no fault** – *Daily Telegraph*, 6 June 1964

p. 74 **highly polished** – *Times*, 13 June 1964

p. 74 **I actually sat back** – Fleming, *Starburst*, 1979

p. 75 **I am confident** – BBC WAC RCONT18

p. 75 **The rabbits may hide** – Bradbury, 'The Fox and the Forest', p. 157

p. 75 **one of the most** – Ward, *Out of the Unknown*, p. 110

p. 76 **remorseless pursuit** – *Guardian*, 23 November 1965

5 Life on a Dead Planet

p. 77 **children's science fiction** – Hoey, *Sunday Best*, 6 February 1972

p. 77 **How dare they?** – Nazarro, *Doctor Who Magazine*, 1989

p. 77 **your calibre** – *South Wales Echo*, 2 March 1974

p. 78 **an inverted cone** – Goodwin, *When the Wind Changed*, p. 367

p. 78 **It was never intended** – Butler, *Time and Relative Dissertations in Space*, p. 44

p. 78 **senile old man** – Norden, Harper and Gilbert, *Coming to You Live!*, p. 71

p. 78 **friends of friends** – Howe, Stammers and Walker, *Doctor Who: The Sixties*, p. 11

p. 79 **When I first read** – *South Wales Echo*, 2 March 1974

p. 80 **Terry came round** – Deb Boultwood, PC

p. 80 **a flash of inspiration** – Frost, *Today*

p. 80 **two-syllable word** – *South Wales Echo*, 2 March 1974

p. 80 **I don't have many friends** – ibid.

p. 80 **this brilliant idea** – *Guardian*, 2 May 2008

p. 81 **frog-like animal** – Peel and Nation, *The Official Doctor Who and the Daleks Book*, p. 186

p. 81 **They are invulnerable** – Wells, *The War of the Worlds*, Book One, ch. 11

p. 82 **on the style of** – Norden, Harper and Gilbert, *Coming to You Live!*, p.71

p. 82 **Fear breeds hatred** – 'Daleks' ep. 4: 'The Ambush'

p. 83 **ready-made army** – 'Daleks' ep. 5: 'The Expedition'

p. 83 **I had a bad time** – *Guardian*, 31 January 1966

p. 83 **both hemispheres** – Peel and Nation, *The Official Doctor Who and the Daleks Book*, p. 192

p. 84 **they have realized** – ibid., p. 193

p. 84 **master of the planet** – 'Daleks' ep. 6: 'The Ordeal'

p. 84 **cheap-jack** – Norden, Harper and Gilbert, *Coming to You Live!*, p.71

p. 84 **David Whitaker and I** – DVD commentary, 'Daleks' ep. 2: 'The Survivors'

p. 84 **machine-like creatures** – dalek6388.co.uk/the-daleks-the-dead-planet.htm

p. 85 **anything mechanical** – Giddings, *Cusick in Cardiff*

p. 85 **The first time I saw them** – DVD commentary, 'Chase' ep. 1: 'The Executioners'

p. 85 **never take off** – Norden, Harper and Gilbert, *Coming to You Live!*, p. 73

p. 85 **cinema-goer** – Nazarro, *Doctor Who Magazine*, 1989

p. 86 **I saw Hattie** – Le Mesurier, *Lady Don't Fall Backwards*, p. 60

p. 86 **inside each of these** – 'Death', ep. 2

p. 86 **simply the vehicles** – *Manchester Daily Express*, 21 November 1964

p. 86 **peripatetic machine** – Amis, *New Maps of Hell*, p. 26

p. 86 **the human form** – Asimov, *The Caves of Steel*, p. 134

p. 86 **They were original** – Terrance Dicks, PC

p. 86 **tremendous contribution** – Nazarro, *Doctor Who Magazine*, 1989

p. 86 **rough notes** – *Guardian*, 31 January 1966

p. 86 **pepper pot** – Giddings, *Cusick in Cardiff*

p. 87 **The only interest** – 'Daleks' ep. 6: 'The Ordeal'

p. 87 **Only one race** – 'Daleks' ep. 7: 'The Rescue'

p. 87 **I can understand** – DVD production text, 'Daleks' ep.2: 'The Survivors'

p. 87 **That bloody Nation** – Goodwin, *When the Wind Changed*, p. 367

p. 87 **enormous contributors** – Ophir, Gies and Best, *Horizon*, 1989

p. 87 **I've been reading** – Peel, *Starburst*, 1995

p. 88 **on the map** – DVD commentary, 'Invasion' ep. 2: 'The Daleks'

p. 89 **After that first episode** – Ophir, Gies and Best, *Horizon*, 1989

p. 89 **I would be very grateful** – this and subsequent viewers' letters: BBC WAC Teli/c/781/5948

p. 90 **blond faeries** – DVD production text, 'Daleks' ep. 3: 'The Rescue'

p. 90 **They're amoral** – *Daily Mail*, 28 December 1964

p. 90 **those metal bodies** – *Guardian*, 6 October 1972

p. 90 **he couldn't see it** – *Guardian*, 9 July 1976

p. 91 **Adults can see** – *South Wales Echo*, 2 March 1974

p. 91 **a model community** – Baden-Powell, *Scouting for Boys*, p. 171

p. 91 **the destined ruler** – Charteris, *The Happy Highwayman*, p. 176

p. 91 **their rightful** – ibid., p. 189

p. 91 **It seems to me** – Wyndham, *The Day of the Triffids*, pp. 243–4

p. 92 **termites and wasps** – Nigel Kneale, *Quatermass and the Pit*, ep. 4: 'The Enchanted' (BBC TV)

p. 92 **settled more issues** – Heinlein, *Starship Troopers*, p. 28

p. 92 **Things come together** – Terrance Dicks, PC

p. 92 **Every writer** – Terrance Dicks, PC

p. 93 **slightly magical** – Nazarro, *Doctor Who Magazine*, 1989

p. 93 **I wish I could** – *South Wales Echo*, 2 March 1974

p. 93 **The one recurring dream** – Fleming, *Starburst*, 1979

p. 93 **I was now a hit** – Ophir, Gies and Best, *Horizon*, 1989

p. 93 **in God's name** – Frost. *Today*

6 Dalek Invasion

p. 94 **bug-eyed monsters** – Norden, Harper and Gilbert, *Coming to You Live!*, p. 72

p. 94 **the travellers** – *Radio Times*, 6 February 1964

p. 94 **We had no intention** – *Daily Mirror*, 13 March 1964

p. 94 **the Keys of Marinus** – Nazarro, *TV Zone* #35

p. 95 **judge and jury** – 'Marinus' ep. 1: 'The Sea of Death'

p. 95 **six feet tall** – *Daily Express*, 5 April 1964

p. 96 **elementary** – 'Marinus' ep. 5: 'Sentence of Death'

p. 97 **I was a new agent** – Beryl Vertue, PC

p. 97 **My instructions are** – BBC WAC RCONT18

p. 97 **breaking new ground** – Nazarro, *Doctor Who Magazine*, 1989

p. 98 **fastest selling** – *Smith's Trade News*, 28 November 1964

p. 98 **great pride** – Nazarro, *Doctor Who Magazine*, 1989

p. 98 **the real invasion** – *Guardian*, 30 December 1964

p. 99 **We would stock them** – *Aberdeen Evening Express*, 21 December 1964

p. 99 **Within days** – *Daily Mail*, 12 December 1964

p. 100 **I was going to give** – *Daily Mail*, 14 December 1964

p. 100 **Dalek of defence** – *Guardian*, 15 October 1966

p. 100 **Rescue men** – *Guardian*, 11 January 1966

p. 100 **Next year** – *Orange County Evening News*, 13 January 1965

p. 101 **I-am-a-Dalek** – *Guardian*, 31 October 1965

p. 101 **We started the merchandising** – Beryl Vertue, PC

p. 101 **great commercial operator** – Nazarro, *Doctor Who Magazine*, 1989

p. 101 **formed lately to deal with** – *Guardian*, 1 October 1966

p. 101 **outbreak of merchandising** – Terrance Dicks, PC

p. 101 **a manor house** – Beryl Vertue, PC

p. 102 **good parties** – DVD commentary, 'Invasion' ep. 4: 'The End of Tomorrow'
p. 102 **loads of champagne** – Deb Boultwood, PC
p. 102 **invented a life** – Brian Clemens, PC
p. 102 **He is proud** – *Guardian*, 31 January 1966
p. 102 **They became such a** – Frost, *Today*
p. 103 **Is any of this money** – Goss, *Daleks Beyond the Screen*
p. 103 **an ex-gratia payment** – *Daily Mirror*, 30 April 2005
p. 103 **Envy, I think** – Terrance Dicks, PC
p. 103 **according to Television Centre** – *Daily Sketch*, 24 November 1964
p. 103 **Tall, dark and shapely** – *Daily Mail*, 28 November 1964
p. 103 **I don't want** – ibid.
p. 104 **I remembered Conan** – Frost, *Today*
p. 104 **What happened on Skaro** – 'Invasion' ep. 2: 'The Daleks'
p. 105 **howl of anguish** – *Daily Mail*, 28 November 1964
p. 105 **Our switchboard** – *Glasgow Sunday Mail*, 22 November 1964
p. 105 **Terry and all of us** – Molesworth, *Terror Nation*
p. 105 **We're old, child** – DVD production text, 'Invasion' ep. 5: 'The Waking Ally'
p. 106 **The appalling thing** – Kevin Brownlow and Andrew Mollo, *It Happened Here* (Rath Films, 1965)
p. 107 **My two children** – BBC WAC Teli/c/781/5948
p. 107 **Not all human beings** – 'Invasion' ep. 4: 'The End of Tomorrow'
p. 107 **What's the point** – 'Invasion' ep. 3: 'Day of Reckoning'
p. 107 **world you have come into** – DVD production text, 'Invasion' ep. 4: 'The End of Tomorrow'
p. 108 **One day** – 'Invasion' ep. 4: 'The End of Tomorrow'
p. 109 **this awful panting** – Nikkel and Dougherty, *Information*
p. 109 **huge, black jellyfish** – DVD production text, 'Invasion' ep. 4: 'The End of Tomorrow'
p. 109 **up in the sky** – 'Invasion' ep. 2: 'The Daleks'
p. 109 **The Earth rebelled** – 'Invasion' ep. 6: 'Flashpoint'
p. 109 **I just felt** – DVD commentary, 'Daleks' ep. 7: 'The Rescue'
p. 110 **Writers have to be** – *Daily Mail*, 28 November 1964
p. 110 **I met Terry** – Molesworth, *Terror Nation*

7 Action Men

p. 112 **If you didn't want** – Tinker, *The Television Barons*, p. 62
p. 112 **Is this the man** – ibid., p. 50
p. 112 **We have two scripts** – *Guardian*, 11 October 1966
p. 112 **Lew was a wonderful** – Moore, *My Word Is My Bond*, p. 142
p. 113 **half-hearted attempt** – ibid., p. 103
p. 113 **Money** – Moseley, *Roger Moore*, p. 129
p. 113 **After many years** – Butler, *The Durable Desperadoes*, p. 259
p. 113 **I am not here** – Osgerby and Gough-Yates, *Action TV*, pp. 18–19
p. 113 **Rumhattan cocktail** – 'Judith' in Charteris, *Saint Errant*
p. 114 **terror to the underworld** – Charteris, *The Saint Goes On*, p. 19
p. 114 **The human race** – Charteris, *The Happy Highwayman*, p. 173
p. 115 **tongue in cheek** – Chapman, *Saints and Avengers*, p. 109
p. 115 **only foreigners** – Watson, *Snobbery with Violence*, p. 230
p. 115 **I made a decision** – La Riviere and Cock, *The Saint . . . Steps Into Television*
p. 115 **I used to carry** – *Saint*, 'Jeannine'
p. 115 **the fat cigars** – quoted in Watson, *Snobbery with Violence*, p. 211
p. 116 **foreign-looking birds** – ibid., p. 230
p. 116 **We're the last** – *Saint*, 'The Man Who Could Not Die'

p. 117 **I think he felt** – Groves, *The Terry Nation Story*

p. 117 **I was given** – Peel, *Starburst*, 1995

p. 117 **the story of pearls** – Charteris, *Saint Errant*, p. 88

p. 118 **Whenever people get killed** – *Saint*, 'The Revolution Racket'

p. 119 **If you're smart** – *Saint*, 'The Contract'

p. 119 **such a lot to do** – Butler, *The Durable Desperadoes*, p. 124

p. 119 **I know the rules** – *Saint*, 'Where the Money Is'

p. 120 **We always called a lift** – Brian Clemens, PC

p. 120 **a number of things** – *Observer*, 17 October 1965

p. 121 **work with Bob** – Moore, *My Word Is My Bond*, p. 139

p. 121 **I remember Monty** – interview included in *Baron* DVD box set

p. 121 **I wasn't allowed** – DVD commentary, 'Invasion' ep. 5: 'The Waking Ally'

p. 122 **have the writer in** – Brian Clemens, PC

p. 122 **odd sort of balance** – Terrance Dicks, PC

p. 122 **As story editor** – *Fantasy Empire* #4, 1982

p. 122 **met Nation once** – Bignell and O'Day, *Terry Nation*, p. 42

p. 122 **never around** – DVD commentary, 'Marinus' ep. 3: 'The Screaming Jungle'

p. 122 **Nation never appeared** – Peel, *Starburst*, 1995

p. 123 **As a theatre actor** – DVD commentary, 'Chase' ep. 2: 'The Death of Time'

p. 123 **all the credits** – Brian Clemens, PC

p. 124 **anti-radiation gloves** – 'Daleks' ep. 2: 'The Survivors'

p. 124 **Our shows were** – Moore, *My Word Is My Bond*, p. 135

p. 124 **a Hammer set** – Peel, *Starburst*, 1995

p. 124 **if Associated Television** – Chapman, *Saints and Avengers*, p. 111

p. 124 **number one in Finland** – *Guardian*, 2 March 1965

p. 125 **We put out** *The Saint* – Tinker, *The Television Barons*, p. 50

p. 125 **I have sold everything** – *Observer*, 31 December 1967

p. 125 **ITC was basically** – Chapman, *Saints and Avengers*, p. 11

p. 125 **Mayfair bachelor** – Creasey, *The Baron Returns*, p. 7

p. 126 **Ronald Colman** – Creasey, *Red Eye for the Baron*, p. 23

p. 126 **used the profit** – Creasey, *The Baron Returns*, pp. 28–9

p. 127 **psychological change** – ibid., p. 9

p. 127 **only three men** – *Baron*, 'The Killing'

p. 129 **Lucille Ball** – interview included in *Baron* DVD box set

p. 130 **If nothing else** – Ray, *My Turn Next*, p. 48

8 Dalek Empire

p. 133 **the most famous writer** – Nazarro, *Doctor Who Magazine*, 1989

p. 134 **culture poured out** – *Daily Worker*, 16 September 1954

p. 134 **British domination** – Booker, *The Neophiliacs*, p. 231

p. 134 **favourite fictional hero** – *Time*, 19 October 1962

p. 135 **life in England** – Mortimer, *Paradise Postponed*, pp. 142–3

p. 135 **American TV companies** – *Sun*, 3 August 1965

p. 135 **the thing that attracted me** – Hearn, *Stripped for Action*

p. 136 **full-grown culture** – Davies, *Dalekmania*

p. 136 **sex and violence** – Pirie, *A New Heritage of Horror*, p. 133

p. 136 **few modern films** – *Guardian*, 9 August 1965

p. 136 **likely to do more harm** – *Guardian*, 2 August 1965

p. 137 **Shoddy** – *Observer*, 22 August

p. 137 **The money came in** – Davies, *Dalekmania*

p. 137 **Grown-ups may enjoy it** – *Times*, 21 July 1966

p. 137 **We're in a stick** – Goss, *The Thrill of the Chase*

p. 137 **Yogi Bear** – bbc.co.uk/doctorwho/classic/episodeguide/chase/detail.shtml, retrieved 11 September 2010

p. 138 **These are tiny men** – DVD production text, 'Chase' ep. 2: 'The Death of Time'

p. 139 **I think Terry** – BBC WAC T5/1241/1

p. 139 **the dark recesses** – DVD production text, 'Chase' ep. 4: 'Journey into Terror'

p. 139 **one of those stories** – Charteris, *Saint Errant*, p. 181

p. 140 **about a saint** – ibid., p. 189

p. 140 **While the premise** – Chapman, *Saints and Avengers*, p. 135

p. 140 **Allow the possibility** – Walpole, *The Castle of Otranto*, Preface to 1st edn

p. 140 **realms of fiction** – BBC WAC T5/1241/1

p. 141 **You had your eye** – Nazarro, *Doctor Who Magazine*, 1989

p. 141 **The Mechanoids** – *Fantasy Empire* #4, 1982

p. 142 **Daleks don't like** – 'Chase' ep. 4: 'Journey into Terror'

p. 143 **If I was a producer** – Nazarro, *TV Zone* #35

p. 143 **007 of space** – Pixley, 'The Daleks Master Plan'

p. 144 **the rarest mineral** – 'Plan' ep. 2: 'Day of Armageddon'

p. 144 **the most dangerous** – 'Plan' ep. 3: 'Devil's Planet'

p. 144 **modelled on Stalin** – though an article by Alan Stevens and Fiona Moore argues that Nation's original concept owed more to the Cuban missile crisis, with Chen cast in the role of J.F. Kennedy. See http://www.kaldorcity.com/features/articles/masterplan.html

p. 144 **very superior** – Pixley, 'The Daleks Master Plan'

p. 145 **I've already told** – BBC WAC T5/1246/1

p. 145 **good clean fun** – *Daily Express*, 22 December 1965

p. 145 **strangely reminiscent** – *Times*, 22 December 1965

p. 146 **There was a terrible fight** – Paul Fishman, PC

p. 146 **The Daleks were** – drwhointerviews.wordpress.com/2009/10/23/david-whitaker-1970s, retrieved 1 December 2010

p. 146 **I got along** – Peel, *Starburst*, 1995

p. 146 **I had a go** – Beryl Vertue, PC

p. 147 **very serious reservations** – Pixley, 'Daleks' Invasion USA 1967 A.D.'

p. 147 **I went to the United States** – Fleming, *Starburst*, 1979

p. 148 **I didn't like them** – Nazarro, *Doctor Who Magazine*, 1989

p. 148 **ludicrously small** – BBC WAC RCONT18

p. 149 **really ambitious** – Pixley, 'Daleks' Invasion USA 1967 A.D.'

p. 149 **children's science fiction** – ibid.

p. 150 **a sort of dynamic** – Goss, *Daleks! Conquer and Destroy*

p. 150 **no value** – Terrance Dicks, PC

9 Avenging and Persuading

p. 152 **Television is a monster** – Moseley, *Roger Moore*, pp. 147–8

p. 152 **I always saw the scripts** – ibid.

p. 153 **Action dramas** – Chapman, *Saints and Avengers*, p. 174

p. 154 **The enormous advantage** – *Daily Mail*, 27 November 1969

p. 155 **anything to declare** – *Dept S*: 'A Cellar Full of Silence'

p. 155 **the actual room** – *Dept S*: 'The Man in the Elegant Room'

p. 155 **I couldn't bear** – *Dept S*: 'A Cellar Full of Silence'

p. 156 **the *Marie Celeste*** – *Fantasy Empire* #4, 1982

p. 156 **adventure-thriller** - Macnee and Rogers, *The Avengers*, p. 15

p. 156 **He came in** – Brian Clemens, PC

p. 157 **Every time I got** – *SFX* #51, May 1999

p. 157 **It got wilder** – Peel, *Starburst*, 1995

p. 160 **He turned in** – Brian Clemens, PC

p. 160 **I am not** – Nazarro, *TV Zone* #35

p. 160 **He wasn't suited** – Brian Clemens, PC

p. 160 **I wouldn't have cast her** – Brian Clemens, PC

p. 160 **arguably the best** – *Times*, 10 October 1968

p. 161 **really weird** – *Fantasy Empire* #4, 1982

p. 161 **the best of all** – Cornell, Day and Topping, *The Avengers Dossier*, p. 228

p. 161 **They rate as** – Macnee and Rogers, *The Avengers*, p.15

p. 161 **The country needs the money** – Moore, *My Word Is My Bond*, p. 156

p. 162 **anti-smoking lobby** – ibid. p.157

p. 163 **I always try** – *Times*, 18 September 1971

p. 163 **every little fabric** – *Persuaders*: 'A Home of One's Own'

p. 164 **what was originally** – Chapman, *Saints and Avengers*, p. 241

p. 165 **had always wanted** – Roger Moore, PC

p. 165 **It was a great comfort** – Groves, *The Terry Nation Story*

p. 165 **drive me bananas** – Ophir, Gies and Best, *Horizon*, 1989

p. 166 **Making any long running** – Roger Moore, PC

p. 166 **making changes** – Roger Moore, PC

p. 166 **He was demanding** – Peel, *Starburst*, 1995

p. 166 **Tony on the screen** – La Rivière and Cock, *The Morning After: Remembering the Persuaders!*

p. 166 **reached new heights** – Chester, *All My Shows Are Great*, p. 184

p. 166 **Mostly it is lousy** – *Times*, 29 October 1971

p. 166 **Awful** – *Observer*, 10 October 1971

p. 166 **not a nude in sight** – *Observer*, 26 September 1971

p. 166 **Tooth rot** – *Guardian*, 16 October 1971

p. 167 **tongue-in-cheek** – Curtis, *The Autobiography* p. 238

p. 167 **I had to say** – *Times*, 25 June 1973

p. 167 **Get out your gat** – Kavanagh, *Tommy Handley*, p. 135

p. 167 **multiplied by three networks** – *Guardian*, 26 February 1971

p. 168 **why don't we quit** – La Rivière and Cock, *The Morning After: Remembering the Persuaders!*

10 Darkness Descends

p. 171 **That's not Mr Heath** – Dicks, *Terry Nation's Dalek Special*, p. 22

p. 171 **We sat down** – Brian Clemens, PC

p. 172 **I shall be charitable** – *Guardian*, 9 July 1970

p. 172 **a would-be thriller** – *Times*, 10 July 1970

p. 172 **all the surprise** – *Daily Express*, 10 July 1970

p. 173 **I promise you** – BBC WAC RCONT 20

p. 174 **is leaving things** – BBC WAC T65/85/1

p. 178 **the dark recesses** – 'Chase' ep. 4: 'Journey into Terror'

p. 178 **All your life** – DVD production text, 'Chase' ep. 4: 'Journey into Terror'

p. 179 **railway nuts** – *Observer*, 8 October 1972

p. 180 **This position** – BBC WAC T65/85/1

p. 181 **I stopped** – Beryl Vertue, PC

p. 181 **Roger was a legend** – Barry Cryer, PC

p. 181 **good guy, bad guy** – DVD commentary, 'Planet' ep. 6

p. 181 **a rottweiler** – ibid.

p. 181 **I think Terry** – Terrance Dicks, PC

p. 183 **It was very much** – Owen and Burford, *The Pinewood Story*, p. 137

p. 183 **I was grateful** – Howerd, *On the Way I Lost It*, p. 279

p. 183 **As good an attempt** – *Times*, 19 April 1973

p. 183 **his funniest film role** – *Daily Mirror*, 30 March 1973

p. 183 **for much of the time** – *Daily Express*, 30 March 1973

p. 183 **obviously tried** – *Guardian*, 29 March 1973

p. 183 **nailing a kipper** – *Observer*, 1 April 1973

11 Dalek Renaissance

p. 184 **We had a story** – Terrance Dicks, PC

p. 184 **bottle of champagne** – DVD commentary, 'Planet' ep. 6

p. 185 **Peter Vincent** – Barry Cryer, PC

p. 186 **You can't solve** – Carpenter, *Spike Milligan*, p. 277

p. 186 **Spike's racist humour** – Carpenter, *Spike Milligan*, p. 280

p. 186 **Dalek Hugless-Doom** – *Guardian*, 23 October 1973

p. 186 **the second coming** – Howe, Stammers and Walker, *Doctor Who: The Seventies*, p. 44

p. 186 **I must have visited** – Charles Braham, PC

p. 187 **part of the rock and roll generation** – Hernon, *The Blair Decade*, p. 17

p. 187 **In the present climate** – DVD production texts, 'Planet' ep. 4

p. 188 **I had known Jon** – Nazarro, *Doctor Who Magazine*, 1989

p. 188 **flamboyant dandy** – *Fantasy Empire* #3, 1982

p. 189 **One of the reasons** – Terrance Dicks, PC

p. 189 **vegetation that's more** – 'Planet' ep. 1

p. 190 **She turned up late** – DVD commentary, 'Planet' ep. 3

p. 190 **cryovolcanoes** – I'm indebted here, as elsewhere, to comments from Lance Perkins

p. 191 **Even though the Doctor** – *Times*, 9 April 1973

p. 191 **I cannot** – BBC WAC T5/1247/1

p. 191 **harmless things** – *Radio Times*, 13 December 1973

p. 191 ***Quatermass, Maigret*** – DVD production text, 'Daleks' ep. 7: 'The Rescue'

p. 192 **beyond dispute** – *Observer*, 26 May 1974

p. 192 **My father was killed** – 'Death' ep. 2

p. 192 **SELL-OUT** – Hill, *Tribune 40*, p. 182

p. 193 **the curse of** – DVD commentary, 'Planet' ep. 5

p. 193 **The main necessity** – BBC WAC T65/29/1

p. 193 **The idea of a city** – ibid.

p. 194 **a very good story** – Molesworth, *Terror Nation*

p. 194 **a smashing set** – DVD production text, 'Genesis' ep. 6

p. 196 **I think the imagery** – DVD production text, 'Genesis' ep. 2

p. 196 **our final mutational form** – 'Genesis' ep. 2

p. 197 **mad professor** – Nazarro, *Doctor Who Magazine*, 1989

p. 197 **on all-fours** – Wells, *The Island of Doctor Moreau*, ch. 12

p. 197 **early experiments** – 'Genesis' ep. 2

p. 197 **This thing** – Nazarro, *Doctor Who Magazine*, 1989

p. 197 **Davros is contained** – DVD production text, 'Genesis' ep. 2

p. 198 **So I thought** – DVD production text, 'Genesis' ep. 4

p. 198 **The courage and resourcefulness** – Nation, 'Blake's 7: Series Two'

p. 198 **If you had created** – 'Genesis' ep. 5

p. 199 **Today the Kaled race** – 'Genesis' ep. 4

p. 200 **It's the villains** – *Fantasy Empire* #2, 1981

p. 200 **Such was the level** – Caulfield, *Mary Whitehouse*, pp. 152–3

p. 201 **Continuity on *Doctor Who*** – Terrance Dicks, PC

p. 201 **I see no limit** – *South Wales Echo*, 2 March 1974

12 Journal of a Plague Year

p. 203 **The critics** – *Sunday Telegraph Seven* magazine, 31 May 2009

p. 203 **Problems of overpopulation** – Foreword to Loraine, *The Death of Tomorrow*

p. 204 **Bubonic plague** – BBC WAC RCONT 20

p. 204 **In those days** – Cross and Priestner, *The End of the World*, p. 16

p. 205 **Incredible, isn't it?** – *Radio Times*, 12–18 April 1975

p. 205 **We are at the end** – *Daily Mirror*, 11 December 1964

p. 205 **We had a big house** – Nazarro, *TV Zone* #31

p. 205 **We had geese** – ibid.

p. 205 **My wife was exhausted** – Macomber, *Liberator's Log*, vol. 5 no. 7

p. 205 **She slaved through** – *Horizon*, June 1989

p. 205 **It is only since** – *Radio Times*, 12–18 April 1975

p. 206 **I've been thinking** – *Daily Express*, 12 April 1975

p. 206 **The Earth can start** – http://www.kaldorcity.com/people/dtinterview.html

p. 206 **It's the land** – DVD production text, 'Invasion' ep. 4: 'The End of Tomorrow'

p. 206 **The most valuable** – DVD production text, 'Invasion' ep. 5: 'The Waking Ally'

p. 207 **Survival at all costs** – 'Invasion' ep. 4: 'The End of Tomorrow'

p. 207 **The thing about Terry Nation** – DVD commentary, 'Planet' ep. 3

p. 208 **New York must spend** – Asimov, *The Caves of Steel*, pp. 95–7

p. 211 **He wants a coalition** – McIntosh, *Challenge to Democracy*, p. 184

p. 211 **Different people** – *Times*, 1 January 2004

p. 212 **volunteers on call** – *Times*, 7 April 1975

p. 212 **Two years ago** – *Sun*, 22 January 1977

p. 212 **Just as Doctor Who** – *Observer*, 4 May 1975

p. 213 **Cartridges** – Jack Ronder, *Survivors*: 'Starvation'

p. 214 **A man of forty** – DVD production text, 'Invasion' ep. 2: 'The Daleks'

p. 214 **it's up to somebody** – *Survivors*: 'Genesis'

p. 214 **I couldn't be a leader** – *Survivors*: 'Gone Away'

p. 214 **Nobody doubted** – Nation, *Survivors*, p. 128

p. 217 **At times** – *Daily Mail*, 17 April 1975

p. 217 **impressive, creepy** – *Guardian*, 30 April 1975

p. 217 **perfectly passable** – *Guardian*, 17 April 1975

p. 217 **It has slowed down** – *Times*, 15 May 1975

p. 218 **written by** – *Guardian*, 25 June 1975

p. 219 **One night** – Nazarro, *TV Zone* #31

p. 219 **I'd like to be able** – Groves, *The Terry Nation Story*

p. 220 **didn't suit their image** – Murray, *Into the Unknown*, p. 120

p. 220 **This one was** – Macomber, *Liberator's Log*, vol. 5 no. 7

p. 220 **thick as a board** – Nazarro, *TV Zone* #31

13 Surviving

p. 221 **I fell out instantly** – Peel, *Starburst*, 1995

p. 221 **Wartime Broadcasting** – *Daily Telegraph*, 3 October 2008

p. 222 **a tortuous affair** – interview included in *Survivors* DVD box set and DVD commentary, ep. 1: 'The Fourth Horseman'

p. 222 **He wanted to get** – Nazarro, *TV Zone* #31

p. 222 **He was basically** – Cross and Priestner, *The End of the World*, p. 35

p. 223 **I came up with this idea** – Brian Clemens, PC

p. 223 **ever so badly** – *SFX* #51, May 1999

p. 223 **After I spent** – Brian Clemens, PC

p. 223 **Micawber fixation** – Wyndham, *The Day of the Triffids*, p. 202

p. 223 **There won't always** – ibid., p. 203

p. 224 **The church was crammed** – Doyle, *The Poison Belt*, ch. 5

p. 224 **I didn't think** – *SFX* #51, May 1999

p. 224 **I wrote to Terry** – Brian Clemens, PC

p. 224 **all the regulars** – BBC WAC RCONT 21

p. 224 **It was a shock** – interview included in *Survivors* DVD box set

p. 224 **Thinking hard** – BBC WAC RCONT 21

p. 225 **In my judgement** – ibid.

p. 225 **I was happier** – interview included in *Survivors* DVD box set

p. 227 **They seemed to think** – Ophir, Gies and Best, *Horizon*, 1989

p. 227 **I'm one of the few** – ibid.

p. 227 **Women are better** – *Daily Express*, 12 April 1975

p. 228 **I become a matriarch** – *Daily Mirror*, 16 April 1975

p. 228 **I was wrong** – Nation, *Survivors*, p. 64

p. 228 **I don't come easily** – Ophir, Gies and Best, *Horizon*, 1989

* **You may be queen** – *Survivors*: 'A Beginning'

p. 228 **Some roads** – Nation, *Survivors*, p. 198

p. 229 **When there was nothing left** – ibid., p. 108

p. 229 **It goes down** – *Guardian*, 17 April 1975

p. 230 **a man to whom** – Nation, *Survivors*, p. 119

p. 230 **his past campaigns** – ibid., p. 188

p. 230 **this guy had scrounged** – Macomber, *Liberator's Log* vol. 5 no. 7

p. 230 **Damn!** – Nation, *Survivors*, p. 74

p. 230 **I want to cross** – ibid., p. 206

p. 230 **In this country** – ibid., p. 117

p. 232 **Really what I wanted** – Nazarro, *TV Zone* #31

p. 232 **the novel of the length** – Ophir, Gies and Best, *Horizon*, 1989

p. 233 **the sorest pair** – Nation, *Rebecca's World*, p. 17

p. 233 **Nature has endowed me** – ibid., p. 105

p. 234 **We are the victors** – ibid., p. 119

p. 234 **Call me silly** – ibid., p. 43

p. 234 **a pleasant, entertaining** – *Daily Express*, 5 December 1975

p. 234 **I'd been reading** – Groves, *The Terry Nation Story*

p. 236 **more and more silly** – Williams, *Diaries*, p. 503

14 Fighting the Federation

p. 237 **I said to my wife** – Ophir, Gies and Best, *Horizon*, 1989

p. 237 **was so hot** – Croft, *You Have Been Watching*, p. 208

p. 237 **I don't understand** – Chester, *All My Shows Are Great*, pp. 136–7

p. 238 **A group of criminals** – Attwood, *Blake's 7: The Programme Guide*, p. 7

p. 238 **witty, glossy** – BBC WAC T65/90/1

p. 238 **cracking Boy's Own** – ibid.

p. 239 **it is our intention** – ibid.

p. 240 **Virtually all revolutionary** – Nation, 'Blake's 7: Series Two'

p. 241 **If you grew up** – Nazarro, *TV Zone* #34

p. 241 **Terry Nation** – Darrow, *You're Him, Aren't You?*, p. 71

p. 241 **his reckless daring** – Orczy, *The Scarlet Pimpernel*, ch. 23

p. 241 **Sport, Madame la Comtesse** – ibid., ch. 4

p. 241 **the Scarlet Pumpernickel** – *Persuaders*: 'Five Miles to Midnight'

p. 242 **He was supposed** – Ophir, Gies and Best, *Horizon*, 1989

p. 242 **To a man of my spirit** – Hope, *The Prisoner of Zenda*, ch. 1

p. 242 **a thoroughly decent** – *Daily Mail*, 10 January 1978

p. 242 **One of the many** – *Horizon*, December 1988

p. 244 **the philosophy of an assassin** – *B7*: 'Seek – Locate – Destroy'

p. 244 **The Federation is degenerate** – *B7*: 'Pressure Point'

p. 246 **Authors, unless they are careful** – Usborne, *Clubland Heroes*, p. 182

p. 246 **Stories of his exploits** – *B7*: 'Project Avalon'

p. 246 **Any damage** – B7: 'Seek – Locate – Destroy'

p. 248 **It was a hell** – Stevens and Brown, 'Chris Boucher', *DWB 108*

p. 248 **During those thirteen weeks** – Nazarro, *TV Zone* #33

p. 249 **99.9 per cent** – Fleming, *Starburst*, 1979

p. 250 **We wanted to show** – Nazarro, *TV Zone* #33

p. 251 **This wasn't a polite computer** – ibid.

p. 251 **I plan to live** – B7: 'Time Squad' **Blake's 7 has turned out** – *Daily Express*, 24 January 1978

p. 251 **a mix of olde-world** – *Guardian*, 10 January 1978

p. 252 **Terry Nation's new series** – *Times*, 24 January 1978

p. 252 **the *Star Wars* boom** – *Observer*, 29 January 1978

p. 252 **For all those adults** – *Daily Mail*, 10 January 1978

p. 252 **I enjoyed and admired** – Rigelsford, *The Making of Terry Nation's Blake's 7*, p. 7

p. 252 **When we did** – *Guardian*, 15 July 1989

p. 252 **Well that's us finished** – Stevens and Brown, 'Chris Boucher', *DWB 108*

p. 252 **I do not accept** – BBC WAC T65/90/1

p. 253 **strange, bastard medium** – DVD commentary, B7: 'Shadow'

p. 253 **its drugged, dejected masses** – *Daily Mail*, 10 January 1978

15 The Story Continues

p. 255 **approaches were made** – see also Oliver, *The Blake's 7 Merchandise Guide*

p. 255 **I knew I wanted** – Nikkel and Dougherty, *Information*

p. 255 **Basically you get** – Stevens and Brown, 'Chris Boucher', *DWB 107*

p. 256 **Terry was happy** – Trevor Hoyle, PC

p. 256 **People knew about** – Terrance Dicks, PC

p. 256 **I had a very good agent** – Peel, *Starburst*, 1995

p. 257 **I wanted the weight** – Nazarro, *TV Zone* #33

p. 257 **Terry said that he had** – BBC WAC RCONT 21

p. 257 **He didn't seem** – Stevens and Brown, 'Chris Boucher', *DWB* 108

p. 257 **Chris Boucher** – Nazarro, *TV Zone* #33

p. 258 **Blake's 7 is a space adventure** – Nation, 'Blake's 7: Series Two'

p. 258 **We stamped on that idea** – Chris Boucher interview, 'The Anorak Zone', 2003

p. 258 **I kept piling it on** – Nazarro, *TV Zone* #33

p. 258 **unenviable task** – Darrow, *You're Him, Aren't You?*, p. 85

p. 259 **Servalan hit on** – ibid., p. 144

p. 259 **dominant, arrogant anti-hero** – Elizabeth Coldwell, 'Science Frictions' in *Forum* vol. 31, no. 3 (1997)

p. 259 **I never really saw her** – Stevens and Brown, 'Chris Boucher', *DWB* 108

p. 262 **It was Terry's instinct** – Stevens and Moore, *Liberation*, p. 64

p. 262 **We made the decision** – Nazarro, *TV Zone* #33

p. 263 **From that time on** – Nazarro, *TV Zone* #35

p. 263 **There is a legend** – DVD production text, 'Destiny' ep. 4

p. 263 **Two vast computers** – 'Destiny' ep. 4

p. 264 **So, the long darkness** – 'Destiny' ep. 3

p. 264 **'Destiny of the Daleks'** – DVD production text, 'Destiny' ep. 1

p. 264 **To be honest** – DVD commentary, 'Destiny' ep. 2

p. 265 **Oh, I'm sure** – 'Destiny' ep. 4

p. 265 **If you're supposed** – 'Destiny' ep. 2

p. 266 **I upset Terry** – Groves, *The Terry Nation Story*

p. 266 **the copyright in** – BBC WAC RCONT 21

p. 267 **nicknames for Thatcher** – *Guardian*, 21 March 1980

p. 269 **I was fascinated** – Nazarro, *TV Zone* #34

p. 269 **You'll notice that** – BBC WAC T65/72/1

p. 270 **I actually missed** – Nazarro, *TV Zone* #35

16 To America and Beyond

p. 271 **It's a marvellous** – Fleming, *Starburst*, 1979

p. 272 **I didn't have** – Peel, *Starburst*, 1995

p. 272 **I believe that I wrote** – Ophir, Gies and Best, *Horizon*, 1989

p. 273 **I did admire** – Nazarro, *TV Zone* #34

p. 273 **purposely did not let** – interview c.1995, included on DVD issue of *Blake's 7*, season four

p. 273 **It was an ending** – Stevens and Brown, 'Chris Boucher', *DWB* 108

p. 274 **They paid me** – Peel, *Starburst*, 1995

p. 274 **What is difficult** – Ophir, Gies and Best, *Horizon*, 1989

p. 274 **Typical!** – Terry Nation and Stephen Downing, *MacGyver*, 'Thief of Budapest'

p. 275 **a kamikaze episode** – Ophir, Gies and Best, *Horizon*, 1989

p. 275 **He absolutely loved** – Groves, *The Terry Nation Story*

p. 275 **Hope is game** – Faye-Saunders, *Radio Times Guide to Films*, p. 911

p. 276 **strange vehicles** – Macomber, *The Liberator's Log*, vol. 5 no. 6

p. 276 **We were so close** – Ophir, Gies and Best, *Horizon*, 1989

p. 276 **plenty of other factors** – for further discussion of this, see Cross, *Worlds Apart*, pp. 10–11

p. 276 **next year** – Ophir, Gies and Best, *Horizon*, 1989

p. 277 **That's the kind of thing** – Darrow, *You're Him, Aren't You?*, p. 125

p. 277 **Nothing has been happening** – Nazarro, *TV Zone* #34

p. 277 **part of an organized lobby** – *Times*, 14 November 1983

p. 277 **When the *Blake's 7 Magazine*** – Darrow, *You're Him, Aren't You?*, p. 144

p. 278 **the British public** – Gittins, *Top of the Pops*, p. 53

p. 278 **because they thought** – Cross and Priestner, *The End of the World*, p. 231

p. 278 **I retain an enormous** – Foreword to Peel and Nation, *The Official Doctor Who & the Daleks Book*

p. 279 **American aficionados** – *Times*, 13 March 1997

p. 279 **He loved it** – Groves, *The Terry Nation Story*

p. 279 **was rubbish** – appearance on *Room 101* (BBC TV), 15 April 2002

p. 280 **We were told** – Howe, Stammers and Walker, *Doctor Who: The Eighties*, p. 171

p. 281 **Your day's gone** – Sykes, *If I Don't Write It, Nobody Else Will*, p. 453

p. 282 **My agent and I** – Davies, *Dalekmania*

p. 282 **We were forced** – Segal and Russell, *Doctor Who: Regeneration*, p. 82

p. 283 **Mr Hancock had demanded** – *Daily Telegraph*, 5 August 2004

p. 283 **We want to protect** – *Guardian*, 5 August 2004

p. 283 **too evil** – *News of the World*, 4 July 2004

p. 283 ***Doctor Who* without Daleks** – *Sun*, 2 July 2004

p. 284 **thanks to the *Sun*'s campaign** – *Sun*, 7 August 2004

p. 284 **Whoever's in charge** – *Daily Telegraph*, 10 August 2004

p. 284 **This was the one** – *Daily Express*, 2 May 2005

p. 284 **For thirty** – *Sunday Mirror*, 1 May 2005

p. 284 **It's a bit like** – interviewed on *Doctor Who Confidential* (BBC TV), 30 April 2005

p. 285 **a raving, grinning maniac** – *Times*, 10 December 2008

p. 285 **croak-voiced Daleks** – James MacTaggart Memorial Lecture, 1993

p. 286 **I'm not sure I want** – Ophir, Gies and Best, *Horizon*, 1989

p. 286 **I don't know** – Peel, *Starburst*, 1995

OUTRO: Closing Credits

p. 288 **My intention is always** – Fleming, *Starburst*, 1979

p. 289 **Let every part** – Hewison, *Culture and Consensus*, p. 44

p. 290 **right to triviality** – Thompson, *Discrimination and Popular Culture* p.61

p. 290 **The disquiet about television** – Hewison, *Culture and Consensus*, p. 118

p. 290 **I was determined** – Tinker, *The Television Barons*, pp. 47–8

p. 292 **a follow-up** – Kibble-White and Williams, *The Encyclopaedia of Classic Saturday Night Telly*, p. 14

p. 292 **the function of people** – BFI Screen Online

p. 292 **I'd get very uneasy** – Ophir, Gies and Best, *Horizon*, 1989

p. 292 **If Terry sent you** – *Fantasy Empire* #4, 1982

p. 293 **It was not difficult** – Groves, *The Terry Nation Story*

p. 293 **I didn't want** – Ophir, Gies and Best, *Horizon*, 1989

p. 293 **written at white heat** – Haggard, *She*, p. xv

p. 293 **lapped up** – *Daily Mirror*, 11 December 1964

p. 294 **I delivered something** – Nazarro, *TV Zone* #33

p. 294 **If I had my way** – Nikkel and Dougherty, *Information*

p. 294 **Terry Nation had a thing** – DVD commentary, 'Planet' ep. 3

p. 296 **As a wartime child** – Fleming, *Starburst*, 1979

p. 296 **Much of sci-fi** – *Guardian*, 15 July 1989

p. 297 **Whilst we remain** – Nation, 'Blake's 7: Series Two'

p. 298 **They'd watch from** – Davies, *Dalekmania*

p. 299 **To have written** – Ophir, Gies and Best, *Horizon*, 1989

p. 299 **I suppose that** – *South Wales Echo*, 2 March 1974

p. 299 **A type of robot** – Oxford English Dictionary (oed.com – retrieved 28 November 2010)

p. 299 **A good story** – Nazarro, *TV Zone* #33

Bibliography

A. Interviews with Terry Nation

In the last few years of his life, Nation gave several interviews to fan and genre magazines which remain the best record of his opinions on his work. Other newspaper articles are cited in the References.

Howard Loxton, *Guardian* (31 January 1966)

Brian Hoey, *Sunday Best* (BBC Radio 4, 6 February 1972), available on *Doctor Who at the BBC* (BBC CD)

Denis Frost, *Today* (BBC Radio 4, 8 January 1973), available on *Doctor Who at the BBC* (BBC CD)

John Stead, *South Wales Echo* (2 March 1974)

John Fleming, *Starburst*, volume 1, number 6 (January 1979)

Chris Stuart, BBC Radio Wales (unknown date, c.1985)

Jamie Nikkel and Diana Dougherty, *Information: The Newsletter of Star One, the Bay Area Blake's 7 & British Media Club*, volume 3, issue 5 (July 1988)

Joe Nazarro, *Doctor Who Magazine*, issue 145 (February 1989)

Jackie Ophir, Diane Gies and Nicola Best, *Horizon: The Blake's 7 Appreciation Society*, issue 22 (June 1989)

Michael Macomber, *The Liberator's Log: Newsletter of the Cygnus Alphans, a Delaware Valley Blake's 7 Fan Club*, volume 5, issues 6 and 7 (February–March 1992)

Joe Nazarro, *TV Zone*, issues 31, 33, 34 and 35 (June–October 1992)

John Peel, *Starburst*, issue 200 (April 1995)

B. Archives

I am extremely grateful to Deb Boultwood for allowing me access to documents from the archives of her father, Dave Freeman; to Paul Fishman, who similarly allowed me access to his archive of Daleks material; and to Anthony Brockway for sharing items from his own collection.

The following files at the BBC Written Archives Centre (WAC) in Reading have been consulted and quoted from:

RCONT1 Terry Nation; RCONT18 Terry Nation; RCONT20 Terry Nation; RCONT21 Terry Nation; T5/1241/1 *Doctor Who*: 'The Chase'; T5/1246/1 *Doctor Who*: 'The Daleks' Master Plan'; T5/1247/1 *Doctor Who*: 'The Daleks' Master Plan'; T12/391/5 *The Ted Ray Show*; T65/29/1 *Doctor Who*: 'Death to the Daleks'; T65/72/1 *Blake's 7* series one, two and three copyright billing; T65/85/1 *The Incredible Robert Baldick*; T75/90/1 *Blake's 7* General; Teli/c/781/5948

Also quoted from is 'Blake's 7: Series Two', a paper written by Terry Nation in 1978.

C. Documentaries and DVDs

Many of the following were made for inclusion as special features or extras on DVD releases of various television shows. The Doctor Who *DVDs are included since the commentaries and the subtitled production notes are an invaluable source of information; similarly the* Blake's 7 *DVDs and the 2003 edition of the* Survivors *DVDs contain commentaries and — in the latter case — interviews.*

Blake's 7 (BBC DVD, 2003–6) – commentary: Chris Boucher, Jan Chappell, Brian Croucher, Paul Darrow, Stephen Greif, Michael Keating, Sally Knyvette, David Maloney, Jacqueline Pearce, Gareth Thomas

Steve Broster, *The Rumble in the Jungle: Remembering 'Planet of the Daleks'* (2 Entertain, 2009)

Phil Clarke, *30 Years* (BBC Radio 2, 20 November 1993), available on *Doctor Who at the BBC* (BBC CD)

Kevin Davies, *Dalekmania* (Amity, 1995)

Doctor Who: 'The Daleks' (BBC DVD, 2006) – production text: Martin Wiggins; commentary: Carole Ann Ford, Christopher Barry, Verity Lambert, Richard Martin, Gary Russell, William Russell

Doctor Who: 'The Keys of Marinus' (BBC DVD, 2009) – production text: Richard Molesworth; commentary: Raymond Cusick, Carole Ann Ford, John Gorrie, William Russell

Doctor Who: 'The Dalek Invasion of Earth' (BBC DVD, 2003) – production text: Martin Wiggins; commentary: Carole Ann Ford, Verity Lambert, Richard Martin, Gary Russell, William Russell

Doctor Who: 'The Chase' (BBC DVD, 2010) – production text: Richard Bignell; commentary: Richard Martin, Maureen O'Brien, Peter Purves, William Russell

Doctor Who: 'Planet of the Daleks' (BBC DVD, 2009) – production text: Martin Wiggins; commentary: Terrance Dicks, Prentis Hancock, Barry Letts, Katy Manning, Tim Preece

Doctor Who: 'Genesis of the Daleks' (BBC DVD, 2006) – production text: Richard Molesworth; commentary: Tom Baker, David Maloney, Peter Miles, Elizabeth Sladen

Doctor Who: 'Destiny of the Daleks' (BBC DVD, 2007) – production text: Richard Molesworth; commentary: David Gooderson, Ken Grieve, Lalla Ward

Paul Giddings, *Cusick in Cardiff* (2 Entertain, 2009)

James Goss, *Daleks Beyond the Screen* (2 Entertain, 2009)

James Goss, *Daleks! Conquer and Destroy* (2 Entertain, 2009)

James Goss, *The Thrill of the Chase* (2 Entertain, 2009)

Steve Groves, *The Terry Nation Story: A Radio Wales Arts Show Special* (Parrog Productions for BBC Radio Wales)

Marcus Hearn, *Stripped for Action: The Story of Doctor Who Comics* (2 Entertain, 2009)

Richard Molesworth, *Terror Nation: Terry Nation and Doctor Who* (2 Entertain, 2007)

Stewart La Rivière and Thomas Cock, *The Morning After: Remembering the Persuaders!* (Swinging Star, 2006)

Stewart La Rivière and Thomas Cock, *The Saint Steps in to Television* (Swinging Star, 2006)

Survivors: Series One (BBC DVD, 2003) – commentary: Lucy Fleming, Ian McCulloch, Andy Priestner, Pennant Roberts, Carolyn Seymour; plus interviews with: Lucy Fleming, Ian McCulloch, Pennant Roberts, Tanya Ronder, Carolyn Seymour

D. Non-fiction books and articles

Some of the material quoted, as will be apparent from the References, comes from newspapers and magazines, but the following books have also been consulted. Where a paperback or revised edition is shown, it indicates that any page references cited are to that edition.

Kingsley Amis, *New Maps of Hell* (Victor Gollancz, 1960; pbk edn: New English Library, 1969)

Arthur Askey, *Before Your Very Eyes* (Woburn Press, 1975; pbk edn: Coronet, 1977)

Tony Attwood (ed.), *Blake's 7: The Programme Guide* (W.H. Allen, 1982; rev pbk edn: Virgin Books, 1994)

Robert Baden-Powell, *Scouting for Boys: A Handbook for Instruction in Good Citizenship* (Scout Association, 1908; pbk edn: 1994)

J.G. Ballard, *Miracles of Life: An Autobiography* (Fourth Estate, 2008; pbk edn: HarperCollins, 2008)

Martin Barker, *A Haunt of Fears: The Strange History of the British Horror Comics Campaign* (Pluto, 1984)

Tony Benn (ed. Ruth Winstone), *Against the Tide: Diaries 1973-76* (Hutchinson, 1989; pbk edn: Arrow, 1990)

Bernard Bergonzi, *The Early H.G. Wells: A Study of the Scientific Romances* (Manchester University Press, 1961)

Jonathan Bignell and Andrew O'Day, *Terry Nation* (Manchester University Press, 2004)

Ronald Blythe, *The Age of Illusion: Some Glimpses of Britain between the Wars 1919–1940* (Hamish Hamilton, 1963; pbk edn: Oxford University Press, 1983)

Christopher Booker, *The Neophiliacs: A Study of the Revolution in English Life in the Fifties and Sixties* (Collins, 1969; pbk edn: Fontana, 1970)

Julia Briggs, *Night Visitors: The Rise and Fall of the English Ghost Story* (Faber and Faber, 1977)

David Butler and Anne Sloman, *British Political Facts 1900–1979* (Macmillan, 1980, 5th edition)

David Butler (ed.), *Time and Relative Dissertations in Space: Critical Perspectives on Doctor Who* (Manchester University Press, 2007)

William Vivian Butler, *The Durable Desperadoes* (Macmillan, 1973)

Humphrey Carpenter, *Spike Milligan: The Biography* (Hodder & Stoughton, 2003; rev pbk edn: 2004)

Andrew Cartmel, *Through Time: An Unauthorised and Unofficial History of Doctor Who* (Continuum, 2005)

Max Caulfield, *Mary Whitehouse* (Mowbrays, 1975)

James Chapman, *Saints and Avengers: British Adventure Series of the 1960s* (I.B. Tauris, 2002)

Lewis Chester, *All My Shows Are Great: The Life of Lew Grade* (Aurum, 2010)

John R. Cook and Peter Wright (eds), *British Science Fiction Television: A Hitchhiker's Guide* (I.B. Tauris, 2006)

Paul Cornell, Martin Day and Keith Topping, *The Avengers Dossier: The Definitive Unauthorised Guide* (Virgin Books, 1998)

David Croft, *You Have Been Watching . . .* (BBC Books, 2004)

Rich Cross, *Worlds Apart: The Unofficial and Unauthorised Guide to the BBC's Remake of Survivors* (Classic TV Press, 2010)

Rich Cross and Andy Priestner, *The End of the World: The Unofficial and Unauthorised Guide to Survivors* (Telos Publishing, 2005)

Tony Curtis and Barry Paris, *The Autobiography* (William Heinemann, 1994)

Paul Darrow, *You're Him, Aren't You? An Autobiography* (Big Finish, 2006)

Terrance Dicks (ed.), *Terry Nation's Dalek Special* (Target, 1979)

Jeff Evans, *The Penguin TV Companion* (Penguin, 2001)

Kilmeny Faye-Saunders (ed.), *Radio Times Guide to Films* (BBC Worldwide, 2000)

Paul Ferris, *Sir Huge: The Life of Huw Wheldon* (Michael Joseph, 1990)

John Fisher, *Tony Hancock: The Definitive Biography* (HarperCollins, 2008)

Paul Gambaccini and Rod Taylor, *Television's Greatest Hits: Every Hit Television Programme since 1960* (Network Books, 1993)

Denis Gifford, *The Golden Age of Radio* (B.T. Batsford, 1985)

Ian Gittins, *Top of the Pops: Mishaps, Miming and Music – The Adventures of TV's No. 1 Pop Show* (BBC, 2007)

Cliff Goodwin, *When the Wind Changed: The Life and Death of Tony Hancock* (Century, 1999)

Freddie Hancock and David Nathan, *Hancock* (William Kimber, 1969; pbk edn: BBC Publications, 1986)

Ian Hernon, *The Blair Decade* (Politico's, 2007)

Robert Hewison, *Culture and Consensus: England, Art and Politics since 1940* (Methuen, 1995; rev edn: 1997)

Douglas Hill (ed.), *Tribune 40: The First Forty Years of a Socialist Newspaper* (Quartet, 1977)

David J. Howe, Mark Stammers and Stephen James Walker, *Doctor Who: The Sixties* (Doctor Who Books, 1992; pbk edn: 1993)

David J. Howe, Mark Stammers and Stephen James Walker, *Doctor Who: The Seventies* (Doctor Who Books, 1994; pbk edn: 1995)

David J. Howe, Mark Stammers and Stephen James Walker, *Doctor Who: The Eighties* (Doctor Who Books, 1996; pbk edn: 1997)

Frankie Howerd, *On the Way I Lost It: An Autobiography* (W.H. Allen, 1976)

Clive James, *Visions Before Midnight: Television Criticism from the Observer 1972–76* (Jonathan Cape, 1977; pbk edn: Picador, 1981)

Paul Jennings, *The Paul Jennings Reader: Collected Pieces 1943–89* (Bloomsbury, 1990)

Ted Kavanagh, *Tommy Handley* (Hodder and Stoughton, 1949)

Jack Kibble-White and Steve Williams, *The Encyclopaedia of Classic Saturday Night Telly* (Allison & Busby, 2007; pbk edn: 2008)

Joan Le Mesurier, *Lady Don't Fall Backwards: A Memoir* (Sidgwick & Jackson, 1988)

Eiluned and Peter Lewis, *The Land of Wales* (B.T. Batsford, 1937)

Peter Lewis, *The Fifties* (Heinemann, 1978)

Mark Lewisohn, *Radio Times Guide to TV Comedy* (BBC Worldwide, 1998)

Jimmy Logan and Billy Adams, *It's a Funny Life* (B&W Publishing, 1998)

John A. Loraine, *The Death of Tomorrow* (Heinemann, 1972)

Robert Lynd, *Life's Little Oddities* (J.M. Dent, 1941)

Graham McCann, *Spike & Co: Inside the House of Fun with Milligan, Sykes, Galton & Simpson* (Hodder & Stoughton, 2006)

Ronald McIntosh, *Challenge to Democracy: Politics, Trade Union Power and Economic Failure in the 1970s* (Politico's, 2006)

Patrick Macnee and Marie Cameron, *Blind in One Ear* (Harrap, 1988)

Patrick Macnee and Dave Rogers, *The Avengers: The Inside Story* (Titan Books, 2008)

George Melly, *Revolt into Style: The Pop Arts in Britain* (Allen Lane, 1970)

Bob Monkhouse, *Crying With Laughter: My Life Story* (Century, 1993)

Roger Moore, *My Word Is My Bond: The Autobiography* (Michael O'Mara Books, 2008)

Roy Moseley with Philip and Martin Masheter, *Roger Moore: A Biography* (New English Library, 1985)

Frank Muir, *A Kentish Lad: The Autobiography of Frank Muir* (Bantam, 1997; pbk edn: Corgi, 1998)

Andy Murray, *Into the Unknown: The Fantastic Life of Nigel Kneale* (Headpress, 2006)

Richard Nichols, *Radio Luxembourg: The Station of the Stars* (Comet, 1983)

Denis Norden, Sybil Harper and Norma Gilbert, *Coming to You Live! Behind-the-Screen Memories of Forties and Fifties Television* (Methuen, 1985)

Philip Oakes, *Tony Hancock* (Woburn-Futura, 1975)

Mark Oliver, *The Blake's 7 Merchandise Guide* (Telos, forthcoming)

George Orwell, *The Road to Wigan Pier* (Victor Gollancz, 1937)

George Orwell, 'Boys Weeklies' (1939) in *Inside the Whale and Other Essays* (Victor Gollancz, 1940)

Bill Osgerby and Anna Gough-Yates (eds), *Action TV: Tough Guys, Smooth Operators and Foxy Chicks* (Routledge, 2001)

Gareth Owen and Brian Burford, *The Pinewood Story: The Authorised History of the World's Most Famous Film Studio* (Reynolds & Hearn, 2000)

John Peel, 'I Can Take Comedy Very Seriously', interview with Dennis Spooner in *Fantasy Empire* issue 4, 1982

John Peel and Terry Nation, *The Official Doctor Who and the Daleks Book* (St Martin's Press, 1988)

P.M. Pickard, *I Could a Tale Unfold: Violence, Horror and Sensationalism in Stories for Children* (Tavistock Publications, 1961)

Malcolm Pill, *A Cardiff Family in the Forties* (Merton Priory Press, 1999)

David Pirie, *A New Heritage of Horror: The English Gothic Cinema* (I.B. Tauris, 2008)

Andrew Pixley, 'The Daleks Master Plan', *Doctor Who Magazine* issue 272, 16 December 1998

Andrew Pixley, 'Daleks' Invasion USA 1967 A.D.', *Doctor Who Magazine* issue 406, 1 April 2009

Andrew Quicke, *Tomorrow's Television: An Examination of British Broadcasting Past, Present and Future* (London, 1976)

Ted Ray, *My Turn Next: A Book for Happy Tipplers* (Museum Press, 1963)

Adrian Rigelsford, *The Making of Terry Nation's Blake's 7* (Boxtree, 1995)

Robert Ross, *Sid James: Cockney Rebel* (JR Books, 2009)

Paul Scoones, 'Terry Nation: Writing for the Screen', *TSV #51* (June, 1997)

Philip Segal and Gary Russell, *Doctor Who: Regeneration* (HarperCollins, 2000)

Dominic Shellard (ed.), *The Golden Generation: New Light on Post-War British Theatre* (British Library, 2008)

Irene Shubik, *Play for Today: The Evolution of British Drama* (Davis-Poynter, 1975)

Joan Sims, *High Spirits* (Partridge, 2000)

Alan Stevens and Anthony Brown, 'Chris Boucher', interview in *Dr Who Bulletin* issue 107 November 1992 to issue 109 January 1993

Alan Stevens and Fiona Moore, *Liberation: The Unofficial and Unauthorised Guide to Blake's 7* (Telos Publishing, 2003)

Paul Matthew St Pierre, *Song and Sketch Transcripts of British Music Hall Performers Elsie and Doris Waters* (Edwin Mellen Press, 2003)

Eric Sykes, *If I Don't Write It, Nobody Else Will* (Fourth Estate, 2005; pbk edn: Harper Perennial 2006)

Julian Symons, *Bloody Murder: From the Detective Story to the Crime Novel – a History* (Faber & Faber, 1972; rev pbk edn: Penguin, 1974)

Ben Thompson, *Sunshine on Putty: The Golden Age of British Comedy from Vic Reeves to The Office* (Fourth Estate, 2004; rev pbk edn: Harper Perennial, 2004)

Denys Thompson (ed.), *Discrimination and Popular Culture* (Pelican, 1964)

Jack Tinker, *The Television Barons* (Quartet, 1980)

Martin Tropp, *Mary Shelley's Monster: The Story of Frankenstein* (Houghton Mifflin, 1977)

Alwyn W. Turner, *Crisis? What Crisis? Britain in the 1970s* (Aurum, 2008)

Alwyn W. Turner, *Halfway to Paradise: The Birth of British Rock* (V&A Publishing, 2008)

Alwyn W. Turner, *My Generation: The Glory Years of British Rock* (V&A Publishing, 2010)

Richard Usborne, *Clubland Heroes: A Nostalgic Study of Some Recurrent Characters in the Romantic Fiction of Dornford Yates, John Buchan and Sapper* (Constable, 1953)

Mark Ward, *Out of the Unknown: A Guide to the Legendary BBC Series* (Kaleidoscope, 2004)

Colin Watson, *Snobbery with Violence: English Crime Stories and Their Antecedents* (Eyre & Spottiswoode, 1971; rev edn: Eyre Methuen, 1979)

Leonard White, *Armchair Theatre: The Lost Years* (Kelly Publications, 2003)

Kenneth Williams (ed. Russell Davies), *The Kenneth Williams Diaries* (HarperCollins, 1993)

Roger Wilmut, *Tony Hancock – 'Artiste'* (Eyre Methuen, 1978)

Roger Wilmut, *Kindly Leave the Stage! The Story of Variety 1919–1960* (Methuen London, 1985; pbk edn: 1989)

E. Fiction

This is, necessarily, only the briefest of guides to the fiction consulted during the writing of this book, covering those works that are quoted. Where a paperback or revised edition is shown, it indicates that any page references cited are to that edition.

Isaac Asimov, *The Caves of Steel* (TV Boardman, 1954; pbk edn: HarperCollins, 1993)

Ray Bradbury, 'The Fox and the Forest' in *The Illustrated Man* (Doubleday, 1951; pbk edn: Corgi, 1955)

John Buchan, *Huntingtower* (Hodder & Stoughton, 1922)

John Buchan, *The Island of Sheep* (Hodder & Stoughton, 1936)

Leslie Charteris, *The Happy Highwayman* (Hodder & Stoughton, 1933; pbk edn: 1953)

Leslie Charteris, *The Saint Goes On* (Hodder & Stoughton, 1934; pbk edn: 1955)

Leslie Charteris, *Saint Errant* (Hodder & Stoughton, 1949; pbk edn: Coronet, 1972)

Brian Clemens, adapted by Ted Hart, *More Stories from Thriller* (Fontana, 1975)

John Creasey, *The Baron Returns* (George H. Harrap, 1937, published under pseudonym Anthony Morton; pbk edn: Corgi, 1965)

John Creasey, *Red Eye for the Baron* (Hodder & Stoughton, 1958, published under pseudonym Anthony Morton; pbk edn: Pan, 1962)

Philip K. Dick, 'Imposter' (1953), reprinted in *Minority Report* (Gollancz, 2002)

Arthur Conan Doyle, *The Complete Professor Challenger Stories* (John Murray, 1952)

John Eyers, *Survivors: Genesis of a Hero* (Weidenfeld & Nicolson, 1977; pbk edn: Futura, 1977)

Gillian Freeman, *The Leader* (Anthony Blond, 1965)

Ray Galton and Alan Simpson, *Hancock's Half Hour* (Woburn Press, 1974)

H. Rider Haggard, *She* (Longmans Green, 1887; pbk edn: Oxford University Press, 1991)

Robert A. Heinlein, *Starship Troopers* (Putnam, 1959; pbk edn: Ace, 1987)

William Hope Hodgson, *Carnacki the Ghost-Finder* (Nash, 1913)

Anthony Hope, *The Prisoner of Zenda* (Macmillan, 1894)

Trevor Hoyle, *Blake's 7* (Sphere Books, 1977)

Trevor Hoyle, *Blake's 7: Project Avalon* (Arrow Books, 1979)

Trevor Hoyle, *Blake's 7: Scorpio Attack* (BBC, 1981)

John Mortimer, *Paradise Postponed* (Viking, 1985; pbk edn: Penguin, 1986)

Robert Muller, *The Lost Diaries of Albert Smith* (Jonathan Cape, 1965; pbk edn: *After All, This Is England*, Penguin, 1967)

Bernard Newman, *The Blue Ants* (Digit, 1963)

Baroness Orczy, *The Scarlet Pimpernel* (Hutchinson, 1905)

Clifford D. Simak, 'Immigrant' (1954), in Brian Aldiss (ed.), *Galactic Empires* (St Martin's Press, 1976; pbk edn: Legend, 1988)

Frederick E. Smith, based on screenplays by Terry Nation, *The Persuaders! Book Two* (Pan, 1972)

John Summers, *Edge of Violence* (Leslie Frewin, 1969)

John Summers, *The Raging Summer* (Michael Joseph, 1972)

Horace Walpole, *The Castle of Otranto* (1764; pbk edn: Oxford University Press, 1996)

H.G. Wells, *The Time Machine* (William Heinemann, 1895)

H.G. Wells, *The Island of Dr Moreau* (William Heinemann, 1896)

H.G. Wells, *The War of the Worlds* (William Heinemann, 1898)

H.G. Wells, *The First Men in the Moon* (George Newnes, 1901)

John Wyndham, *The Day of the Triffids* (Michael Joseph, 1951; pbk edn: Penguin, 1954)

F. Websites

625 Online (625.org.uk)

The Anorak Zone (anorakzone.com)

BBC (bbc.co.uk)

BFI Screen Online (screenonline.org.uk)

British Television Drama (britishtelevisiondrama.org.uk)
Dalek 6388 (dalek6388.co.uk)
Dave Freeman (davefreeman.co.uk)
Doctor Who Interviews (drwhointerviews.wordpress.com)
Harry Worth (harryworth.co.uk)
Internet Movie Database (IMDb.com)
Magic Bullet (kaldorcity.com)
Memorable TV (memorabletv.com)
The Morning After (itc-classics.com)
The Saint (saint.org)
Survivors: A World Away (survivors-mad-dog.org.uk)
Television Heaven (televisionheaven.co.uk)
Wikipedia (en.wikipedia.org)

Further Reading

The only existing book on Terry Nation is Jonathan Bignell and Andrew O'Day's *Terry Nation* (Manchester University Press, 2004), an academic study which focuses on his science fiction work. For Nation's own accounts of his career, see in particular the interviews with Jackie Ophir, Diane Gies and Nicola Best in the magazine of the Blake's 7 Appreciation Society, *Horizon*, issue 22 (June 1989), and with Joe Nazarro in *TV Zone* issues 31, 33, 34 and 35 (June–October 1992).

Graham McCann's *Spike & Co: Inside the House of Fun with Milligan, Sykes, Galton & Simpson* (Hodder & Stoughton, 2006) is the definitive account of Associated London Scripts. Long out of print, Denis Gifford's *The Golden Age of Radio* (B.T. Batsford, 1985) remains an essential reference work, even in the age of the internet.

Of the many books on *Doctor Who*, David J. Howe, Mark Stammers and Stephen James Walker's series *Doctor Who: The Sixties*, *Doctor Who: The Seventies* and *Doctor Who: The Eighties* (Doctor Who Books, 1992–7) are recommended, as is *Time and Relative Dissertations in Space* (Manchester University Press, 2007), edited by David Butler.

James Chapman's *Saints and Avengers: British Adventure Series of the 1960s* (I.B. Tauris, 2002) is an entertaining take on some of the key ITC shows.

For *Survivors* and *Blake's 7*, see respectively Rich Cross and Andy Priestner's *The End of the World: The Unofficial and Unauthorised Guide to Survivors* (Telos Publishing, 2005), and Alan Stevens and Fiona Moore's *Liberation: The Unofficial and Unauthorised Guide to Blake's 7* (Telos Publishing, 2003). Both are excellent.

And finally, the best books on the fiction of Nation's youth are still Richard Usborne's *Clubland Heroes* (Constable, 1953) and William Vivian Butler's *The Durable Desperadoes* (Macmillan, 1973). They're even more fun than the novels they chronicle.

Acknowledgements

Primarily I must thank those who were kind enough to share their memories of Terry Nation, to supply additional information, to put me in touch with others or simply to point me in the right direction when I might otherwise have got lost:

Alan Simpson, Anthony Brockway, Barry Cryer, Beryl Vertue, Brian Clemens, Carey Clifford, Charles Braham, Cy Town, David Gooderson, David Foster-Smith, David Howe, David Richardson, Deb Boultwood, Dudley Sutton, Gareth Owen, Harry Greene, Ian Dickerson, Jaz Wiseman, Jonathan Bignell, John Flaxman, Mat Irvine, Michelle Coomber, Paul Fishman, Peter Purves, Ray Galton, Sir Roger Moore, Roy Baines, Stan Stennett, Tanya Howarth, Terrance Dicks, Tessa Le Bars, Tony Tanner, Trevor Hoyle and Wyn Calvin.

I'm grateful to all of them and to those who wished not to be named (or whom I inadvertently forgot to mention).

In particular, my thanks to Alan Stevens, Mark Oliver, Steve Groves and Stuart Cooper, who allowed me advance access to material in order that I could meet my deadlines, and to Richard Cross for being helpful beyond the call of duty.

Lance Parkin and Paul Magrs were kind enough to read this in its unpolished first draft and make extremely helpful comments, suggestions and corrections.

Obviously none of the above should be considered to condone the contents of this book. Apologies too to everyone whose work and words I've quoted in such a cavalier fashion, probably missing all the important points.

As ever, there's a whole heap of people at Aurum without whose contributions this book would never have made it to the shelves, including: Barbara Phelan, Bill McCreadie, Graham Coster, Graham Eames, Jodie

Mullish, Liz Somers and Natalie Ridgway. Mark Swan designed the jacket and Steve Gove was a superb text editor.

I continue to be grateful for the support and advice of Thamasin Marsh, who lived with this project for its entire duration.

Finally, and especially, my thanks to my editor, Sam Harrison, whose suggestion this book was, and who has been hugely helpful throughout. It's been a pleasure working with him, and any complaints about anything you have read should be addressed directly to him.

This book is dedicated to Harry Greene and John Summers, two men I've been privileged to know and who also happened to know Terry Nation.

Index